# Instructor's Manual to Accompany

# THE ART OF
# PUBLIC SPEAKING

## FIFTH EDITION

## STEPHEN E. LUCAS
University of Wisconsin · Madison

**McGraw-Hill, Inc.**
New York  St.Louis  San Francisco  Auckland  Bogotá
Caracas  Lisbon  London  Madrid  Mexico City  Milan  Montreal
New Delhi  San Juan  Singapore  Tokyo  Toronto

**Instructor's Manual to Accompany  Lucas**
**THE ART OF PUBLIC SPEAKING**
**Fifth Edition**

ISBN 0-07-039016-9

1234567890 BKM BKM 90987654

# Contents

## Evaluation and Instructional Forms

## Analyses of Speeches from *The Art of Public Speaking*

# Preface

This manual is a guide to teaching from *The Art of Public Speaking*. It is intended primarily for the benefit of new and less experienced instructors, but I hope you will find it valuable even if you have been teaching public speaking for many years.

The first part of the manual presents course outlines based on *The Art of Public Speaking* for both the semester and quarter systems. Part II explains the speech assignments included in the course outlines and offers alternative assignments as well. Part III discusses evaluation and grading and includes several forms for evaluating student speeches.

Part IV is a chapter-by-chapter guide to *The Art of Public Speaking*. For each chapter of the book it provides a statement of objectives, a chapter outline, discussions of the application exercises presented in the book, additional suggestions for exercises and classroom activities, and a bibliography of supplementary learning and teaching resources.

In addition to the exercises in the book and in this manual, instructors will find more than 150 speech assignments and classroom activities in the two anthologies of selections from *The Speech Communication Teacher* that accompany this edition of *The Art of Public Speaking*. Written by teachers for teachers, these articles offer a wealth of practical ideas for classroom use.

Part V of this manual contains speeches for analysis and evaluation. All of these speeches were in previous editions of the book and are included here for the convenience of instructors who wish to continue using them. They supplement the speeches in the Appendix of the book, and each is followed by a brief guide for classroom discussion.

Instructors who have used this manual in conjunction with previous editions of *The Art of Public Speaking* will notice three major changes. First, in response to many requests, I have added a full-sentence outline of each chapter in the book. Second, I have updated, reorganized, and significantly expanded the bibliography of extra teaching and learning resources for each chapter. In doing so, my aim has been to provide instructors the most current guide to additional resources available with any public speaking textbook.

Third, unlike previous editions, this manual no longer contains examination questions. For the convenience of instructors, exam questions are now in a separate volume entitled *Test Bank to Accompany The Art of Public Speaking*. The *Test Bank* contains 1,363 true-false, multiple-choice, short-answer, and essay questions. It also provides three preconstructed quizzes for each chapter, as well as several sample final examinations. As a special feature, the *Test Bank* also includes a guest essay by Anita Vangelisti of the University of Texas on test construction and assessment.

This manual has once again been printed on 8 1/2 x 11 tear-out pages, so instructors can easily reproduce exercises, speeches, and evaluation forms for use in the classroom. Finally, to facilitate classroom discussion, many exercises from the manual are included in the package of more than 100 full-color overhead transparencies that accompanies this edition of *The Art of Public Speaking*.

# Part I

# SUGGESTED COURSE

# OUTLINES

## Introduction to Part I

*The Art of Public Speaking* is easily adapted to a wide variety of class schedules and teaching methods. The following class outlines reflect one approach to the course. They take students through a series of reading, application, and speaking assignments that build systematically upon one another. They are also designed to allow students to undertake their first graded speaking assignment without having to read practically the whole book. Reading assignments are structured to give students adequate preparation time for each speech.

The first part of the syllabus culminates in the informative speech and focuses on such basic matters as analyzing the audience, choosing a topic and specific purpose, and organizing the speech. The second part culminates in the persuasive speech and focuses on more complex matters such as the target audience, building credibility, and using evidence and reasoning. The third part culminates in the commemorative speech and focuses on the effective use of language. By the fourth part, which culminates in the final speech, students have been exposed to all the major skills of speechmaking discussed in the textbook. Now the instructor can concentrate on strengthening students' command of those skills.

The course outlines presented here are for a class of roughly twenty students. If you have an appreciably higher enrollment, you will probably have to reduce the length of the speeches or increase the number of class sessions devoted to the presentation of student speeches.

Finally, although these outlines include suggestions for classroom discussion based on selected application exercises in *The Art of Public Speaking*, there are many more exercises in the book, in this manual, and in the two anthologies of selections from *The Speech Communication Teacher* that accompany this edition of the book. You should have no trouble choosing exercises that best fit your teaching emphases and the needs of your students.

The speaking assignments indicated in the course outlines are explained in Part II of this manual.

# Outline For a 15-Week, 45-Hour Semester

| Class Meeting | Topic-Activity | Reading |
|---|---|---|
| 1 | **Course Overview**<br><br>Introduce yourself; hand out syllabi; explain grading and attendance policies. Assign introductory speeches. | |
| 2 | **Basic Principles of Speech Communication**<br><br>Focus class discussion on selected application exercises, text p. 25, or additional exercise 2 on p. 64 of this manual. | Chapter 1 |
| 3 | **Ethics and Public Speaking**<br><br>Focus class discussion on application exercises 1 and 3, text pp. 46-47. Have students develop a code of ethical speaking for their classroom as explained in additional exercise 2 on p. 82 of this manual. Hand out and discuss the Checklist for Ethical Public Speaking printed on p. 83 of this manual. | Chapter 2 |
| 4 | **Introductory Speeches** | |
| 5 | **Introductory Speeches** | |

| Class Meeting | Topic-Activity | Reading |
|---|---|---|
| 6 | **Speaking to Inform**<br><br>Assign informative speeches. Focus class discussion on kinds of informative speeches, guidelines for informative speaking, and the sample speech with commentary at the end of Chapter 14, text pp. 328-331. Show the videotape of "Dandelions: The Uncommon Weed." | Chapter 14 |
| 7 | **Choosing Topics and Purposes**<br><br>Focus class discussion on application exercises 2-5, text pp. 86-87. | Chapter 4 |
| 8 | **Analyzing the Audience**<br><br>Focus class discussion on application exercises 2 and either 1, 4, or 5, text pp. 112-113. Use additional exercise 1 on p. 132 of this manual as a classroom activity. | Chapter 5 |
| 9 | **Organizing the Body of the Speech**<br><br>Focus class discussion on application exercises 1-3, text pp. 192-193. Use additional exercises as needed from pp. 180-183 of this manual. | Chapter 8 |
| 10 | **Introductions and Conclusions**<br><br>Focus class discussion on application exercise 1, text p. 216. Use additional exercises 1 or 3 on pp. 192-194 of this manual as a classroom activity. Show appropriate portions of the "Introductions, Conclusions, and Visual Aids" videotape. | Chapter 9 |

| Class Meeting | Topic-Activity | Reading |
|:---:|---|---|
| 11 | **Outlining the Speech**<br><br>Focus class discussion on application exercises 1-3, text pp. 234-235. | Chapter 10 |
| 12 | **Delivering the Speech**<br><br>Focus class discussion on principles of effective delivery. Select from application exercises 1-4, text pp. 284-285, or the additional exercises on pp. 238-243 of this manual. | Chapter 12 |
| 13 | **Using Visual Aids**<br><br>Focus class discussion on exercise 2, text p. 307. Use additional exercises 1 and 2 on p. 254 of this manual as classroom activities. Show appropriate sections of the "Introductions, Conclusions, and Visual Aids" videotape. | Chapter 13 |
| 14 | **Informative Speeches** | |
| 15 | **Informative Speeches** | |
| 16 | **Informative Speeches** | |
| 17 | **Informative Speeches** | |
| 18 | **Introduction to Persuasive Speaking**<br><br>Assign persuasive speeches. Focus class discussion on application exercises 1, 2, and 4, text pp. 363-364. | Chapter 15 |

| Class Meeting | Topic-Activity | Reading |
|:---:|---|:---:|
| 19 | **Gathering Materials**<br><br>Take library tour—see additional exercise 1 on p. 148 of this manual. Assign selected application exercises, text pp. 140-141. | Chapter 6 |
| 20 | **Using Supporting Materials**<br><br>Focus class discussion on application exercises 1-2, text pp. 169-170. | Chapter 7 |
| 21 | **Methods of Persuasion**<br><br>Focus class discussion on selected application exercises, text pp. 395-397. Show the videotape of "The Dangers of Chewing Tobacco." | Chapter 16 |
| 22 | **Analysis of Persuasive Speeches**<br><br>Have students prepare brief analyses of the assigned speech or speeches. Good candidates for analysis include Steven Harris, "Family Medical Histories: A Proven Lifesaver," and Sandy Hefty, "A Friend in Need." | Selections from Appendix speeches |
| 23 | **Listening to Speeches**<br><br>Focus class discussion on exercise 2, text p. 64. As part of this exercise, have students complete the Listening Self-Evaluation Form on p. 102 of this manual. Choose from additional exercises on pp. 103-106 of this manual for classroom activities. | Chapter 3 |
| 24 | **Persuasive Speeches** | |

| Class Meeting | Topic-Activity | Reading |
|---|---|---|
| 25 | **Persuasive Speeches** | |
| 26 | **Persuasive Speeches** | |
| 27 | **Persuasive Speeches** | |
| 28 | **Midterm Examination** | |
| 29 | **Commemorative Speaking**<br><br>Assign commemorative speech. Focus class discussion on application exercise 3, text p. 415. Show the videotape of "James 'Cool Papa' Bell." | Chapter 17, especially pp. 407-410 |
| 30 | **Return and review midterm examinations.** | |
| 31 | **Using Language Effectively**<br><br>Focus class discussion on selections from application exercises 1-4, text pp. 261-262, and additional exercises on pp. 218-226 of this manual. | Chapter 11 |
| 32 | **Using Language Effectively**<br><br>Have students prepare a brief analysis of King's speech as directed in application exercise 5, text p. 262. Show the videotape of "I Have a Dream" in class and focus discussion on King's use of language. | Martin Luther King, "I Have a Dream," text pp. 450-454 |

| Class Meeting | Topic-Activity | Reading |
|:---:|---|:---:|
| 33 | **Commemorative Speeches** | |
| 34 | **Commemorative Speeches** | |
| 35 | **Commemorative Speeches** | |
| 36 | **The Final Speech**<br><br>Assign final speeches and begin review of elements students most need to concentrate on in preparing the final speech. Major items usually are use of supporting materials, organization and outlining, and delivery. | |
| 37 | **Preparing for the Final Speech: Supporting Materials**<br><br>Focus class discussion on application exercises from Chapter 7, or on analyzing speeches from the text Appendix or from Part V of this manual. | Review Chapter 7 |
| 38 | **Preparing for the Final Speech: Organization and Outlining**<br><br>Focus class discussion on selected application exercises from Chapters 8-10 and additional exercises from this manual. | Review Chapters 8-10 |

| Class Meeting | Topic-Activity | Reading |
|---|---|---|
| 39 | **Preparing for the Final Speech: Delivery**<br><br>By this point in the course, many students are ready to work on polishing their delivery skills. Choose from among the application exercises in Chapter 12 of the text and the additional exercises in this manual. | Review Chapter 12 |
| 40 | **Final Speeches** | |
| 41 | **Final Speeches** | |
| 42 | **Final Speeches** | |
| 43 | **Final Speeches** | |
| 44 | **Final Speeches** | |
| 45 | **Summary and Review for Final Examination** | |

# Outline For a One-Semester Course
# With a Unit on Group Discussion

| Class Meeting | Topic-Activity | Reading |
|---|---|---|
| 1 | **Course Overview**<br><br>Introduce yourself; hand out syllabi; explain grading and attendance policies. Assign introductory speeches. | |
| 2 | **Basic Principles of Speech Communication**<br><br>Focus class discussion on selected application exercises, text p. 25, or additional exercise 2 on p. 64 of this manual. | Chapter 1 |
| 3 | **Ethics and Public Speaking**<br><br>Focus class discussion on application exercises 1 and 3, text pp. 46-47. Have students develop a code of ethical speaking for their classroom as explained in additional exercise 2 on p. 82 of this manual. Hand out and discuss the Checklist for Ethical Public Speaking printed on p. 83 of this manual. | Chapter 2 |
| 4 | **Introductory Speeches** | |
| 5 | **Introductory Speeches** | |

| Class Meeting | Topic-Activity | Reading |
|---|---|---|
| 6 | **Speaking to Inform**<br><br>Assign informative speeches. Focus class discussion on kinds of informative speeches, guidelines for informative speaking, and the sample speech with commentary at the end of Chapter 14, text pp. 328-331. Show the videotape of "Dandelions: The Uncommon Weed." | Chapter 14 |
| 7 | **Choosing Topics and Purposes**<br><br>Focus class discussion on application exercises 2-5, text pp. 86-87. | Chapter 4 |
| 8 | **Analyzing the Audience**<br><br>Focus class discussion on application exercises 2 and either 1, 4, or 5, text pp. 112-113. Use additional exercise 1 on p. 132 of this manual as a classroom activity. | Chapter 5 |
| 9 | **Organizing the Body of the Speech**<br><br>Focus class discussion on application exercises 1-3, text pp. 192-193. Use additional exercises as needed from pp. 180-183 of this manual. | Chapter 8 |
| 10 | **Introductions and Conclusions**<br><br>Focus class discussion on application exercise 1, text p. 216. Use additional exercises 1 or 3 on pp. 192-194 of this manual as a classroom activity. Show appropriate portions of the "Introductions, Conclusions, and Visual Aids" videotape. | Chapter 9 |

| Class Meeting | Topic-Activity | Reading |
|---|---|---|
| 11 | **Outlining the Speech**<br><br>Focus class discussion on application exercises 1-3, text pp. 234-235. | Chapter 10 |
| 12 | **Delivering the Speech**<br><br>Focus class discussion on principles of effective delivery. Select from application exercises 1-4, text pp. 284-285, or the additional exercises on pp. 238-243 of this manual. | Chapter 12 |
| 13 | **Using Visual Aids**<br><br>Focus class discussion on exercise 2, text p. 307. Use additional exercises 1 and 2 on p. 254 of this manual as classroom activities. Show appropriate sections of the "Introductions, Conclusions, and Visual Aids" videotape. | Chapter 13 |
| 14 | **Informative Speeches** | |
| 15 | **Informative Speeches** | |
| 16 | **Informative Speeches** | |
| 17 | **Informative Speeches** | |
| 18 | **Introduction to Persuasive Speaking**<br><br>Assign persuasive speeches. Focus class discussion on application exercises 1, 2, and 4, text pp. 363-364. | Chapter 15 |

| Class Meeting | Topic-Activity | Reading |
|---|---|---|
| 19 | **Gathering Materials**<br><br>Take library tour—see additional exercise 1 on p. 148 of this manual. Assign selected application exercises, text pp. 140-141. | Chapter 6 |
| 20 | **Using Supporting Materials**<br><br>Focus class discussion on application exercises 1-2, text pp. 169-170. | Chapter 7 |
| 21 | **Methods of Persuasion**<br><br>Focus class discussion on selected application exercises, text pp. 395-397. Show the videotape of "The Dangers of Chewing Tobacco." | Chapter 16 |
| 22 | **Analysis of Persuasive Speeches**<br><br>Have students prepare brief analyses of the assigned speech or speeches. Good candidates for analysis include Steven Harris, "Family Medical Histories: A Proven Lifesaver," and Sandy Hefty, "A Friend in Need." | Selections from Appendix speeches |
| 23 | **Listening to Speeches**<br><br>Focus class discussion on exercise 2, text p. 64. As part of this exercise, have students complete the Listening Self-Evaluation Form on p. 102 of this manual. Choose from additional exercises on pp. 103-106 of this manual for classroom activities. | Chapter 3 |
| 24 | **Persuasive Speeches** | |

| Class Meeting | Topic-Activity | Reading |
|---|---|---|
| 25 | **Persuasive Speeches** | |
| 26 | **Persuasive Speeches** | |
| 27 | **Persuasive Speeches** | |
| 28 | **Midterm Examination** | |
| 29 | **Commemorative Speaking**<br><br>Assign commemorative speech. Focus class discussion on application exercise 3, text p. 415. Show the videotape of "James 'Cool Papa' Bell." | Chapter 17, especially pp. 407-410 |
| 30 | **Return and review midterm examinations.** | |
| 31 | **Using Language Effectively**<br><br>Focus class discussion on selections from application exercises 1-4, text pp. 261-262, and additional exercises on pp. 218-226 of this manual. | Chapter 11 |
| 32 | **Using Language Effectively**<br><br>Have students prepare a brief analysis of King's speech as directed in application exercise 5, text p. 262. Show the videotape of "I Have a Dream" in class and focus discussion on King's use of language. | Martin Luther King, "I Have a Dream," text pp. 450-454 |

| Class Meeting | Topic-Activity | Reading |
|---|---|---|
| 33 | **Commemorative Speeches** | |
| 34 | **Commemorative Speeches** | |
| 35 | **Commemorative Speeches** | |
| 36 | **Introduction to Small-Group Discussion**<br><br>Assign group discussion projects. Discuss Chapter 18, with special emphasis on pp. 418-427. | Chapter 18, especially pp. 418-427 |
| 37 | **Problem-Solving in Small Groups**<br><br>Focus class discussion on the reflective-thinking method; use application exercises 1 and 3, text pp. 436-437. | Chapter 18 especially pp. 427-438 |
| 38 | **Decision-Making Processes in Small Groups**<br><br>Do "Lost on the Moon" or "Hostages" activity from pp. 332-340 of this manual. | |
| 39 | **Group Project Work**<br><br>Have the groups work on their projects in class. This will give you a chance to meet briefly with each group to assess its progress and to offer guidance. | |
| 40 | **Group Presentations** | |

| Class Meeting | Topic-Activity | Reading |
|:---:|:---|:---:|
| 41 | **Group Presentations** | |
| 42 | **Group Presentations** | |
| 43 | **Group Presentations** | |
| 44 | **Group Presentations** | |
| 45 | **Summary and Review for Final Examination** | |

# Outline For a 10-Week, 30-Hour Quarter
## OR
## A 15-Week, 30-Hour Semester

| Class Meeting | Topic-Activity | Reading |
|:---:|---|:---:|
| 1 | **Course Overview**<br><br>Introduce yourself; hand out syllabi; explain grading and attendance policies. Assign introductory speeches. | |
| 2 | **Basic Principles of Speech Communication**<br><br>Focus class discussion on selected application exercises, text p. 25, or additional exercise 2 on p. 64 of this manual. | Chapter 1 |
| 3 | **Ethics and Public Speaking**<br><br>Focus class discussion on application exercises 1 and 3, text pp. 46-47. Have students develop a code of ethical speaking for their classroom as explained in additional exercise 2 on p. 82 of this manual. Hand out and discuss the Checklist for Ethical Public Speaking printed on p. 83 of this manual. | Chapter 2 |
| 4 | **Introductory Speeches** | |
| 5 | **Introductory Speeches** | |

| Class Meeting | Topic-Activity | Reading |
|---|---|---|
| 6 | **Speaking to Inform**<br><br>Assign informative speeches. Focus class discussion on kinds of informative speeches, guidelines for informative speaking, and the sample speech with commentary at the end of Chapter 14, text pp. 328-331. Show the videotape of "Dandelions: The Uncommon Weed." | Chapter 14 |
| 7 | **Choosing Topics and Purposes**<br><br>Focus class discussion on application exercises 2-5, text pp. 86-87. | Chapter 4 |
| 8 | **Analyzing the Audience**<br><br>Focus class discussion on application exercises 2 and either 1, 4, or 5, text pp. 112-113. Use additional exercise 1 on p. 132 of this manual as a classroom activity. | Chapter 5 |
| 9 | **Organizing the Body of the Speech**<br><br>Focus class discussion on application exercises 1-3, text pp. 192-193; application exercise 1, text p. 216; and additional exercise 1, p. 192 of this manual. Show appropriate portions of the "Introductions, Conclusions, and Visual Aids" videotape. | Chapters 8-9 |
| 10 | **Outlining the Speech**<br><br>Focus class discussion on application exercises 1-3, text pp. 234-235. | Chapter 10 |

| Class Meeting | Topic-Activity | Reading |
|---|---|---|
| 11 | **Delivering the Speech and Using Visual Aids**<br><br>Focus class discussion on principles of effective delivery. Select from application exercises 1-4, text pp. 284-285, or the additional exercises on pp. 238-243 of this manual. If visual aids are required for the informative speech, discuss application exercise 2, text p. 307. Use additional exercises 1 and 2 on p. 254 of this manual as a classroom activity. Show appropriate portions of the "Introductions, Conclusions, and Visual Aids" videotape. | Chapters 12-13 |
| 12 | **Informative Speeches** | |
| 13 | **Informative Speeches** | |
| 14 | **Informative Speeches** | |
| 15 | **Introduction to Persuasive Speaking**<br><br>Assign persuasive speeches. Focus class discussion on application exercises 1, 2, and 4, text pp. 363-364. | Chapter 15 |
| 16 | **Gathering Materials**<br><br>Take library tour—see additional exercise 1 on p. 148 of this manual. Assign selected application exercises, text pp. 140-141. | Chapter 6 |
| 17 | **Using Supporting Materials**<br><br>Focus class discussion on application exercises 1-2, text pp. 169-170. | Chapter 7 |

| Class Meeting | Topic-Activity | Reading |
|---|---|---|
| 18 | **Methods of Persuasion**<br><br>Focus class discussion on selected application exercises, text pp. 395-397. Show the videotape of "The Dangers of Chewing Tobacco." | Chapter 16 |
| 19 | **Listening to Speeches**<br><br>Focus class discussion on exercise 2, text p. 64. As part of this exercise, have students complete the Listening Self-Evaluation Form on p. 102 of this manual. Choose from additional exercises on pp. 103-106 of this manual for classroom activities. | Chapter 3 |
| 20 | **Persuasive Speeches** | |
| 21 | **Persuasive Speeches** | |
| 22 | **Persuasive Speeches** | |
| 23 | **Persuasive Speeches** | |
| 24 | **Commemorative Speaking**<br><br>Assign commemorative speech. Focus class discussion on application exercise 3, text p. 415. Show the videotape of "James 'Cool Papa' Bell." | Chapter 17, especially pp. 407-410 |

| Class Meeting | Topic-Activity | Reading |
|---|---|---|
| 25 | **Using Language Effectively**<br><br>Focus class discussion on selections from application exercises 1-4, text pp. 261-262, and additional exercises on pp. 218-226 of this manual. | Chapter 11 |
| 26 | **Using Language Effectively**<br><br>Have students prepare a brief analysis of King's speech as directed in application exercise 5, text p. 262. Show the videotape of "I Have a Dream" in class and focus discussion on King's use of language. | Martin Luther King, "I Have a Dream," text pp. 450-454 |
| 27 | **Commemorative Speeches** | |
| 28 | **Commemorative Speeches** | |
| 29 | **Commemorative Speeches** | |
| 30 | **Summary and Review for Final Examination** | |

# Outline For a 10-Week, 40-Hour Quarter

| Class Meeting | Topic-Activity | Reading |
|---|---|---|
| 1 | **Course Overview**<br><br>Introduce yourself; hand out syllabi; explain grading and attendance policies. Assign introductory speeches. | |
| 2 | **Basic Principles of Speech Communication**<br><br>Focus class discussion on selected application exercises, text p. 25, or additional exercise 2 on p. 64 of this manual. | Chapter 1 |
| 3 | **Ethics and Public Speaking**<br><br>Focus class discussion on application exercises 1 and 3, text pp. 46-47. Have students develop a code of ethical speaking for their classroom as explained in additional exercise 2 on p. 82 of this manual. Hand out and discuss the Checklist for Ethical Public Speaking printed on p. 83 of this manual. | Chapter 2 |
| 4 | **Introductory Speeches** | |
| 5 | **Introductory Speeches** | |

| Class Meeting | Topic-Activity | Reading |
|---|---|---|
| 6 | **Speaking to Inform**<br><br>Assign informative speeches. Focus class discussion on kinds of informative speeches, guidelines for informative speaking, and the sample speech with commentary at the end of Chapter 14, text pp. 328-331. Show the videotape of "Dandelions: The Uncommon Weed." | Chapter 14 |
| 7 | **Choosing Topics and Purposes**<br><br>Focus class discussion on application exercises 2-5, text pp. 86-87. | Chapter 4 |
| 8 | **Analyzing the Audience**<br><br>Focus class discussion on application exercises 2 and either 1, 4, or 5, text pp. 112-113. Use additional exercise 1 on p. 132 of this manual as a classroom activity. | Chapter 5 |
| 9 | **Organizing the Speech**<br><br>Focus class discussion on application exercises 1-3, text pp. 192-193; application exercise 1, text p. 216; and additional exercise 1, p. 192 of this manual. Show appropriate sections of the "Introductions, Conclusions, and Visual Aids" videotape. | Chapters 8-9 |
| 10 | **Outlining the Speech**<br><br>Focus class discussion on application exercises 1-3, text pp. 234-235. | Chapter 10 |

| Class Meeting | Topic-Activity | Reading |
|---|---|---|
| 11 | **Delivering the Speech and Using Visual Aids**<br><br>Focus class discussion on principles of effective delivery. Select from application exercises 1-4, text pp. 284-285, or the additional exercises on pp. 238-243 of this manual. If visual aids are required for the informative speech, discuss application exercise 2 on text p. 307. Use additional exercises 1 and 2 on p. 254 of this manual as a classroom activity. Show appropriate sections of the "Introductions, Conclusions, and Visual Aids" videotape. | Chapters 12-13 |
| 12 | **Informative Speeches** | |
| 13 | **Informative Speeches** | |
| 14 | **Informative Speeches** | |
| 15 | **Informative Speeches** | |
| 16 | **Introduction to Persuasive Speaking**<br><br>Assign persuasive speeches. Focus class discussion on application exercises 1, 2, and 4, text pp. 363-364. | Chapter 15 |
| 17 | **Gathering Materials**<br><br>Take library tour—see additional exercise 1 on p. 148 of this manual. Assign selected application exercises, text pp. 140-141. | Chapter 6 |

| Class Meeting | Topic-Activity | Reading |
|---|---|---|
| 18 | **Using Supporting Materials**<br><br>Focus class discussion on application exercises 1-2, text pp. 169-170. | Chapter 7 |
| 19 | **Methods of Persuasion**<br><br>Focus class discussion on selected application exercises, text pp. 395-397. Show the videotape of "The Dangers of Chewing Tobacco." | Chapter 16 |
| 20 | **Listening to Speeches**<br><br>Focus class discussion on exercise 2, text p. 64. As part of this exercise, have students complete the Listening Self-Evaluation Form on p. 102 of this manual. Choose from additional exercises on pp. 103-106 of this manual for classroom activities. | Chapter 3 |
| 21 | **Persuasive Speeches** | |
| 22 | **Persuasive Speeches** | |
| 23 | **Persuasive Speeches** | |
| 24 | **Persuasive Speeches** | |
| 25 | **Midterm Examination** | |

| Class Meeting | Topic-Activity | Reading |
|---|---|---|
| 26 | **Commemorative Speaking**<br><br>Assign commemorative speech. Focus class discussion on application exercise 3, text p. 415. Show the videotape of "James 'Cool Papa' Bell." | Chapter 17, especially pp. 407-410 |
| 27 | **Using Language Effectively**<br><br>Focus class discussion on selections from application exercises 1-4, text pp. 261-262, and additional exercises on pp. 218-226 of this manual. | Chapter 11 |
| 28 | **Using Language Effectively**<br><br>Have students prepare a brief analysis of King's speech as directed in application exercise 5, text p. 262. Show the videotape of "I Have a Dream" in class and focus discussion on King's use of language. | Martin Luther King, "I Have a Dream," text pp. 450-454 |
| 29 | **Commemorative Speeches** | |
| 30 | **Commemorative Speeches** | |
| 31 | **Commemorative Speeches** | |
| 32 | **The Final Speech**<br><br>Assign final speeches and begin review of elements students most need to concentrate on in preparing the final speech. Major items usually are use of supporting materials, organization and outlining, and delivery. | |

| Class Meeting | Topic-Activity | Reading |
|---|---|---|
| 33 | **Preparing for the Final Speech: Supporting Materials**<br><br>Focus class discussion on application exercises from Chapter 7, or on analyzing speeches from the text Appendix or from Part V of this manual. | Review Chapter 7 |
| 34 | **Preparing for the Final Speech: Organization and Outlining**<br><br>Focus class discussion on selected application exercises from Chapters 8-10 and additional exercises from this manual. | Review Chapters 8-10 |
| 35 | **Preparing for the Final Speech: Delivery**<br><br>By this point in the course, many students are ready to work on polishing their delivery skills. Choose from among the application exercises in Chapter 12 of the text and the additional exercises in this manual. | Review Chapter 12 |
| 36 | **Final Speeches** | |
| 37 | **Final Speeches** | |
| 38 | **Final Speeches** | |
| 39 | **Final Speeches** | |
| 40 | **Summary and Review for Final Examination** | |

# Part II

# SPEAKING ASSIGNMENTS

# Introduction to Part II

There are many kinds of speaking assignments that can be used in conjunction with *The Art of Public Speaking*. Most of those described below are keyed to the course outlines presented in Part I of this manual. When there are two or more options offered for a round of speeches (Option A, Option B, etc.), you should select one option, so the entire class is performing the same assignment during that round of speeches.

In addition to the formal speaking assignments presented here, the application exercises in the text and the additional exercises in Part IV of this manual contain a number of suggestions for speaking activities. So also do the two volumes of selections from *The Speech Communication Teacher* that are part of the *Instructional Resource Package* for this edition of *The Art of Public Speaking*. A listing of the speech assignments in these volumes is presented on pages 41-42 below.

## Introductory Speech, Option A

A two-minute speech introducing a classmate. The speech should be delivered extemporaneously from brief notes that occupy no more than one side of a single 4 x 6 index card. Stress that students are not to read their speeches and should use as much eye contact as possible.

In preparation for the speech, have students pair off and interview one another. The interviewing can be done in the last 15 to 20 minutes of the first class meeting. The assignment usually works better, however, if students conduct their interviews out of class. This gives them time to prepare questions for the interviews and allows for longer, more flexible interviews.

In their speeches, students will need to provide basic information such as the name of the person they are introducing, his or her home town, academic major, personal interests, hobbies, aspirations, and the like. But the speech need not be a routine recitation of biographical data. Encourage students to be creative in their interview questions and in their speeches.

This speech should not be graded. It is designed to give students a brief, initial exposure to speaking in front of an audience in a low-risk situation. It is also an excellent ice-breaking assignment that gives students a chance to learn about their classmates.

## Introductory Speech, Option B

A two-minute speech introducing a classmate. The speech should be delivered extemporaneously from brief notes that occupy no more than one side of a single

4 x 6 index card. Stress that students are not to read their speeches and should use as much eye contact as possible.

Unlike Option A above, this speech focuses specifically on the cultural background of the student being introduced to the class. Possible topics might include social customs, family traditions, holidays, clothing, food, religious traditions, sporting activities, and the like.

As in Option A, have students pair off and interview one another. The interviewing can be done in the last 15 to 20 minutes of the first class meeting. The assignment usually works better, however, if students conduct their interviews out of class. This gives them time to prepare questions for the interviews and allows for longer, more flexible interviews. If there is significant cultural diversity in your class, arrange the interview pairs so students interview someone whose cultural background is markedly different from their own.

Like Option A, this speech should not be graded. It is designed to give students a brief, initial exposure to speaking in front of an audience in a low-risk situation. Also like Option A, it is a fine ice-breaking assignment that gives students a chance to learn about their classmates.

## Introductory Speech, Option C

A two-minute speech of self-introduction. The speech should be delivered extemporaneously from brief notes that occupy no more than one side of a single 4 x 6 index card. Stress that students are not to read their speeches and should use as much eye contact as possible.

In their speeches, students begin by telling their name, home town, year in school, and academic major. They may focus the remainder of the speech however they wish—on describing an unusual or significant personal experience, on expressing an important personal belief or pet peeve, on explaining a favorite hobby or interest, on discussing someone who has been particularly influential in the speaker's life, etc. The purpose of the speech is not to persuade the audience to share the speaker's views, but to give the audience insight into the speaker's background, personality, attitudes, or aspirations.

This speech should not be graded. It is designed to give students a brief, initial exposure to speaking in front of an audience in a low-risk situation. A good ice-breaking assignment, it also gives students a chance to learn about their classmates.

## Introductory Speech, Option D

A two-minute speech of self-introduction. The speech should be delivered extemporaneously from brief notes that occupy no more than one side of a single 4 x 6 index card. Stress that students are not to read their speeches and should use as much eye contact as possible.

In their speeches, students explain a significant aspect of their cultural background and how it has made a difference in their lives. Possible topics might include social customs, family traditions, holidays, clothing, food, religious traditions, sporting activities, etc. Encourage students to be creative in preparing their speeches and in finding ways to illustrate how the aspect of their culture they choose to explain relates to their personal lives.

Like the other options for introductory speeches, this assignment should not be graded. It is designed to give students a brief, initial exposure to speaking in front of an audience in a low-risk situation. This speech works especially well as an ice-breaker in classes with substantial cultural diversity.

## Introductory Speech, Option E

A two-minute speech of self-introduction based on a newspaper or magazine article. The speech should be delivered extemporaneously from brief notes that occupy no more than one side of a single 4 x 6 index card. Stress that students are not to read their speeches and should use as much eye contact as possible.

To prepare for the speech, each student should go to the library and read through a newspaper from the day they were born or a magazine such as *Time* or *Newsweek* from the week they were born. They should then select an item—article, advertisement, photograph, editorial, etc.—from the newspaper or magazine that relates to the speaker's life in some meaningful way. Using that item as a point of departure, the student should construct a speech that explains some aspect of her or his personality, background, beliefs, or aspirations.

This assignment usually produces fairly interesting and creative speeches of self-introduction. It also gets students into the library right at the start of the course and provides them some insight into the state of the world when they were born. Indeed, many students find this aspect of the assignment so interesting that they spend a fair amount of time just reading through the magazine or newspaper they have chosen.

A good ice-breaking assignment, this speech should not be graded. Like the previous options, it is designed to give students a brief, initial exposure to speaking before an audience in a situation of minimal risk.

## Introductory Speech, Option F

A two-minute speech of self-introduction based on a personal object. The speech should be delivered extemporaneously from brief notes that occupy no more than one side of a single 4 x 6 index card. Stress that students are not to read their speeches and should use as much eye contact as possible.

In preparation for this speech, have students select an object that represents a significant aspect of their background, personality, values, ambitions, etc. Using the chosen object as a point of departure, each student should develop a speech that explains how it relates to her or his life. For example, a journalism major might select a newspaper as a way to explain her or his professional goals. A new father might select a diaper as a vehicle for discussing his experiences as a parent. An avid tennis player might settle on a tennis racket to illustrate her passion about the sport.

If possible, students should bring the object of their speech to class on the day of their presentation. If this is not possible because the object is too large, too rare, or too valuable, the student should bring in a model, drawing, or photograph of the object. The purpose of this speech is not to explain the object in detail, but to use it as a vehicle for the speaker to introduce herself or himself to the class.

Like Option E above, this assignment usually produces interesting and creative speeches of self-introduction. It is designed to help create a cohesive, supportive classroom atmosphere and to give students a brief, initial speaking experience in a low-risk situation. Like the other introductory speeches described above, it should not be graded.

## Informative Speech, Option A

A speech of 5 to 6 minutes informing the audience about some object, process, concept, or event. If desired, the assignment can be narrowed to concentrate specifically on a particular aspect of information giving, such as definition, demonstration, or explanation. Encourage students to select topics that are useful and interesting. Students should turn in a complete preparation outline, but the speech itself should be delivered extemporaneously from a brief speaking outline.

Because this is the first graded speech, evaluation should focus on such basic matters as establishing eye contact, avoiding distracting mannerisms, formulating a sharp specific purpose statement, fulfilling the functions of an introduction and conclusion, limiting main points and arranging them properly, and employing connectives effectively.

## Informative Speech, Option B

A speech of 5 to 6 minutes informing the audience about some object, process, concept, or event. Use of a visual aid is required. Students should turn in a complete preparation outline, but the speech itself should be delivered extemporaneously from a brief speaking outline.

This assignment is the same as Option A above, except for the stipulation that the speaker use a visual aid. Requiring a speech with visual aids gives students experience in a kind of speaking that is common in business and professional situations. Requiring such a speech early in the course usually increases student interest in the speeches, reduces the speakers' nervousness, and encourages them to rely less on their notes.

Urge students to be creative in selecting their visual aids and conscientious in following the guidelines for using them presented in Chapter 13. Decide whether you will impose any restrictions on the kinds of visual aids students can use and, if possible, provide an easel on which speakers can display their graphs, charts, and drawings.

## Informative Speech, Option C

A speech of 5 to 6 minutes demonstrating the steps of a process or how to perform the steps of a process. As in Option B above, use of a visual aid is required. Students should turn in a complete preparation outline, but the speech itself should be delivered extemporaneously from a brief speaking outline.

Students should make sure they present the steps of their process clearly and systematically, leaving out none of the essential steps along the way. In all but a few cases, these speeches will fall naturally into chronological order. Be sure to have students follow the guidelines for visual aids discussed in Chapter 13, and have them pay special attention to the section on speeches about processes in Chapter 14.

## Informative Speech, Option D

A speech of 5 to 6 minutes in which students explain a significant aspect of a culture different from their own. Possible topics include social customs, family traditions, holidays, clothing, food, religious traditions, sporting activities, and the like. Students should turn in a preparation outline, but the speech itself should be delivered extemporaneously from a brief speaking outline.

Library research is required for this speech. If students have had direct contact with a different culture, they should be encouraged to supplement their library research with their personal experience, but the speech is not to be a travelogue or a presentation on "My Summer in Europe" or "My Year as an Exchange Student in Brazil." On the other hand, a speech on how Europeans spend their summer vacations or on the educational system of Brazil would be fine.

Because students are sometimes resistant when they are required to speak about a different culture, it can be helpful to present this as the "World Travel Agency" speech. If you take this approach, tell students that the class is going to travel around the world via their speeches. They will "visit" as many different countries as there are students in the class.

To help students choose topics as quickly as possible, prepare two sets of 3 x 5 index cards. Write the name of a different country on each card in the first set. Then write two or three cultural features on each card in the second set. Put each set of cards in a separate bag and have students randomly pick a card from each bag. When they are finished, they will have a country card (for instance, Italy) and a topic card (including, for example, sports, family traditions, and politics). The student will then speak on one of those three aspects of Italian life.

However students choose their topics, they should be encouraged to be imaginative in composing their speeches. It is not enough to summarize encyclopedia information about the country on which they are speaking. As in any informative speech, students need to explain ideas clearly and to think about ways to relate the topic to the audience.

Some instructors require a visual aid for this speech. Others encourage the use of a visual aid but do not require it.

## Persuasive Speech, Option A

A speech of 7 to 8 minutes designed to persuade the audience for or against a question of policy. Speakers may seek either passive agreement or immediate action from the audience, though they should be encouraged to seek the latter if there is appropriate action for the audience to take. In either case, students should be sure to deal with all three basic issues of policy speeches—need, plan, and practicality. A complete preparation outline should be submitted. Delivery of the speech is to be extemporaneous.

This speech will require considerable research and skillful use of the methods of persuasion. Special emphasis should be given to evidence and reasoning. This is also an excellent assignment for stressing audience analysis and adaptation. You may wish to have students prepare an audience analysis questionnaire similar to that discussed in Chapter 5 to help them identify and adapt to their target audience.

## Persuasive Speech, Option B

A speech of 7 to 8 minutes designed to persuade the audience on either a question of fact or a question of value. A complete preparation outline should be submitted. Delivery of the speech is to be extemporaneous.

As with Option A above, this speech will require considerable research and skillful handling of the methods of persuasion. Also as with Option A, this is an excellent assignment for stressing audience analysis and adaptation. Students who speak on a question of fact will need to give special attention to evidence and reasoning. Students who speak on a question of value must be sure to identify their standards for judgment and to justify their value judgment in light of those standards.

## Commemorative Speech

A speech of 4 to 5 minutes paying tribute to a person, a group of people, an institution, or an idea. The subject may be historical or contemporary, famous or obscure. A preparation outline is not required. This speech should be written out and delivered from manuscript. Students should hand in their manuscripts after their speeches.

This assignment calls for a less didactic speech than the informative and persuasive speeches. It focuses particularly on the use of language, and it gives students experience in speaking from a manuscript. Encourage students to use language imaginatively and to experiment with the devices for enhancing clarity and vividness discussed in Chapter 11. Also stress that students must rehearse their speeches thoroughly, so as to present them with strong eye contact and dynamic vocal variety.

## After-Dinner Speech

A speech of 4 to 5 minutes designed to entertain. A preparation outline is not required. This speech should be written out and delivered from manuscript, and it should be thoroughly rehearsed so it can be presented with maximum eye contact and strong vocal variety. Students should hand in their manuscripts after their speeches.

This assignment demands considerable creativity on the part of students. It calls for a clever speech that makes a thoughtful point even as it approaches the topic in a light-hearted, diverting manner. Encourage students to choose topics based on their own experience and with which most members of the audience can easily identify—family interactions, job matters, school activities, travel adventures, and the like. Stress that the speech is not to be simply a string of jokes and that any humor must be in good taste.

Like the commemorative speech, this assignment also offers a special opportunity to focus on the use of language. Encourage students to use language imaginatively and to experiment with the stylistic devices discussed in Chapter 11.

## Final Speech, Option A

A speech of 8 to 10 minutes that may be either informative or persuasive. A complete preparation outline should be required. Delivery of the speech is to be extemporaneous.

You can allow students to choose individually whether to give an informative speech or a persuasive speech. Usually, however, it is best to assign the entire class one or the other kind of speech. Whichever kind you assign, let students know that this speech is particularly important. Criteria for evaluation include all major aspects of speech preparation and delivery covered since the first day of class.

## Final Speech, Option B

A speech of 8 to 10 minutes that is to be a major revision of an informative or persuasive speech given earlier in the term. A complete preparation outline should be required. Delivery of the speech is to be extemporaneous.

Because time is often cramped at the end of the term, this assignment provides for a full-length speech without requiring that students start from scratch in choosing and researching an entirely new topic. It also gives students an opportunity to learn more about the revision process, which is essential to speeches outside the classroom.

If this assignment is to succeed, you must tell each student which previous speech he or she is to revise, must be quite specific in identifying for each student the kinds of revisions that are necessary, and must make clear that major revisions— including additional research—are required if the speech is to receive a grade of B or better. Otherwise, you are likely to get little more than warmed-over rehashes of speeches you have already heard. Criteria for evaluation include all major aspects of speech preparation and delivery covered since the first day of class.

## Final Speech, Option C

A speech of 8 to 10 minutes informing the audience about a prominent public speaker. A complete preparation outline should be required. Delivery of the speech is to be extemporaneous.

Students can choose either a historical figure or a contemporary speaker for this assignment. In either case, students should deal with the following points in their speeches, though not necessarily in this order: (a) biographical background about the speaker; (b) the importance of public speaking in her or his career; (c) major ideas of her or his speeches; (d) analysis of the speaker's techniques, including organization, language, and delivery.

Complex and challenging, this speech requires substantial library research and allows students to apply the principles learned in class to established public speakers. Although it usually works best in more advanced classes, it can succeed in the introductory course as well. Make the assignment early in the course, so students can work on it throughout the term. In addition, give students a list of speakers from which they can choose. Helpful sources in this regard are *American Orators before 1900* and *American Orators of the Twentieth Century*, both edited by Bernard K. Duffy and Halford R. Ryan.

Encourage students to do all they can to make the speeches creative and interesting by following the guidelines for informative speaking discussed in Chapter 14. Students who choose historical speakers may be able to use photographs or slides as visual aids; those who speak on current figures might consider showing videotapes of their subject in action. In either case, students should review Chapter 13 to make sure they use their visual aids properly and integrate them smoothly into the speech.

## Impromptu Speech

A 2-minute speech to be delivered impromptu. The focus of the speech may be informative, persuasive, or entertaining.

Create a list of topics such as my family, my home town, my best friend, my favorite sport, my most embarrassing moment, my worst class, my biggest thrill, my biggest complaint, etc. Have students draw three topics and choose one to speak about. Give each speaker a few minutes to gather his or her thoughts before beginning to speak. You can do this by having the first three or four speakers choose their topics at the beginning of class. Then, as each speaker finishes, have a new student select his or her topic. Give the speakers time signals when they have one minute to go and then again when they have 30 seconds left.

This can be used as a regular, graded assignment or as an informal, non-graded speaking experience. In either case, try to keep the atmosphere low-key, since students are often particularly apprehensive about speaking impromptu.

For further discussion of approaches to impromptu speaking, see Additional Exercise/Activity 4 on pages 240-242 of this manual.

## Problem-Solving Group Discussion with Symposium

Divide the class into small groups of four to six members. First, each group will be responsible for a problem-solving project in which they investigate a question of policy and recommend solutions to it. In their deliberations, the group should follow the reflective-thinking method of decision-making explained in Chapter 18. Members of the group should understand that this project will require research and group meetings outside of class.

Second, the group will be responsible for organizing and conducting a symposium in which the group presents its report to the class. One way to structure the symposium is to allow each speaker 4 to 5 minutes to explain the work of the group at each stage of the reflective-thinking process. Another approach is to have each speaker spend 4 to 5 minutes detailing some aspect of the group's recommended solutions. If time allows, follow the symposium with a question-and-answer session or general class discussion.

You can either assign topics to the groups or allow each group to choose its own topic. Students should be graded both on the quality of the group's presentation and on their individual contributions to the group.

For other approaches to this assignment, see Additional Exercises 3 and 4 on pages 340-343 of this manual.

## Additional Speech Assignments

When preparing the instructional supplements to the fourth edition of *The Art of Public Speaking*, I compiled an anthology of 92 articles related to the public speaking course from *The Speech Communication Teacher*. Entitled *Selections from the Speech Communication Teacher, 1986-1991*, the anthology was so well received that I have put together a second collection, *Selections from the Speech Communication Teacher, 1991-1994*. Both volumes are available to instructors as part of the *Instructional Resource Package* that accompanies the current edition of *The Art of Public Speaking*.

Included in these two volumes are a number of articles describing speech assignments, many of which are highly creative and offer excellent alternatives to the assignments described earlier in this section of the *Instructor's Manual*. To give you a sense of the variety of assignments presented, the relevant articles are listed below. Articles marked with an asterisk are in *Selections from the Speech Communication Teacher, 1991-1994*. All others are in *Selections from the Speech Communication Teacher, 1986-1991*. Individual articles can be located by consulting the table of contents in the appropriate volume.

## Introductory Speeches

Helen Meldrum, "Using *Vital Speeches of the Day* in the Introductory Speech Classroom"

Sean Raftis, "Brush with Greatness"

Valerie L. Schneider, "The Personal Experience Speech in Public Speaking"

Scott Smithson, "Interviewing: A Triadic Exercise"

*Willard A. Underwood, "Using Condensed Interviews to Improve Classroom Interaction"

Lynne Webb, "The Analogy Speech"

## Informative Speeches

Barbara Adler, "A Speech About a Great American Speech"

J. Jeffrey Auer, "Creating an Extra and 'Real Life' Public Speaking Assignment"

*A. Anne Bowers, Jr., "The Telephone Interview"

James Corey, "International Bazaar"

Katherine Rowan, "The Speech to Explain Difficult Ideas"

## Persuasive Speeches

C. Darrell Langley, "The Heckling Speech"

*Raed A. Mohsen, "Out on Campus: A Challenging Public Speaking Experience"

Charlynn Ross, "The Challenging Audience Exercise"

## Impromptu Speeches

Kathleen Beauchene, "Using Quotations as Impromptu Speech Topics"

Randall Bytwerk, "The 'Just a Minute' Impromptu Exercise"

Diane Grainer, "Creativity vs. 'My Speech Is About Avocados'"

Reed Markham, "Power Minutes"

Wilma McClarty, "Nomination Speech: The Ideal Date"

Bruce C. McKinney, "The 'Jeopardy' of Impromptu Speaking"

Ed Purdy, "Painless Impromptu Speaking"

*Michael G. Stahl and Lori Adams, "Two Takes on Impromptu Speaking Topics: Retiring the Hat"

*Naomi Sugimoto, "Impromptu Fortune-Telling Exercise"

Jeanette Wall, "Me? Give an Impromptu Speech? No Way!"

Dorothy Wilks, "Two Birds with One Stone"

## Speeches for Special Occasions

Randall E. Majors, "Practical Ceremonial Speaking: Three Speech Activities"

*Martin Lamansky, "Getting to Know My Hero: The Speech of Tribute"

*Barry Cole Poyner, "Adding a Ceremonial Touch"

*Shirley Sikes, "Introducing the Speaker"

*Suzanne Walter, "Introduction of a Speaker: Multipurpose and Multicultural"

## General

Rhonda Ehrler, "Extemporizing Through Humor and Repetition"

*Kathy Norris, "The Speech Shopping Channel"

*Lawrence Rifkind, "The Outstanding Speaker Contest"

# Part III

# EVALUATION AND GRADING

# Introduction to Part III

Evaluating student work and assigning grades are among the most difficult tasks facing any teacher. Students take their grades very seriously, and if they believe they are being assessed unfairly, they will quickly develop a negative view of the teacher and, perhaps, of the course in general. Moreover, the self-confidence that is essential for beginning speakers can be seriously damaged if the teacher is insensitive to their need for encouragement and positive reinforcement.

Yet instructors also have an obligation to assess students objectively on the quality of the work they produce. You cannot give students higher grades than they deserve just to maintain good feelings in the class. Striking a balance between the psychological needs of the students and the integrity of the grading system is one of the most difficult challenges facing a teacher of public speaking.

There are two major considerations in meeting this challenge. The first is assessing student work fairly, objectively, and consistently. The second is explaining your assessment to students so they accept it as fair, objective, and consistent. The former revolves around your grading criteria and how you apply them. The latter depends on your ability to communicate effectively with students about your assessment of their work, and is every bit as important as the assessment itself. As this section of the manual proceeds, we shall address both of these aspects of grading and evaluation.

## Criteria, Exams, and Grading Scales

When grading speeches, do all you can to let students know when and how they will be evaluated. Explain speech assignments clearly and notify students of their speaking dates well in advance. Tell students the objectives of each assignment so they will know what to concentrate on in preparing their speeches. Also, be as specific as possible about your criteria for grading speeches. You may find it helpful to give students, on the first day of class, a sheet similar to the one on page 48, listing your basic criteria for grading speeches.

Although there is no substitute for experience when it comes to grading speeches, there are some steps you can take, if you are a new instructor, to sharpen your evaluative skills. One is to talk about grading with experienced instructors who are willing to share their philosophy, methods, and criteria. Another is to view a number of student speeches—either on videotape or in other sections—and see how your assessments of them stack up against those of veteran teachers. Yet another is to have a more seasoned instructor visit your class on a day when students are giving speeches. By comparing the grades you assigned with those the other instructor would have assigned had it been his or her class, you can get a good sense of whether you need to make any adjustments in either your criteria or your methods of evaluation.

Whereas the speeches indicate how well students have mastered the skills of speechmaking, written examinations gauge how well students understand the principles underlying those skills. There are many approaches to written examinations in public speaking classes. Some instructors give one or two major examinations. Others supplement major examinations with periodic brief quizzes. Still others rely solely on a series of quizzes. Some instructors prefer objective questions; others essay questions; others a mixture of question types. To help you construct examinations, the *Test Bank* that accompanies *The Art of Public Speaking* contains 1,363 true-false, multiple-choice, short-answer, and essay questions. In addition, it offers three preconstructed quizzes for each chapter of the book, as well as several complete sample final examinations that illustrate different approaches to testing and evaluation. Finally, the *Test Bank* includes a guest essay by Anita Vangelisti of the University of Texas on test construction and assessment.

There are a number of ways to weight individual assignments and determine final grades. Below is one system based on the assignments in the course outlines presented in Part I of this manual. It can be adjusted easily to reflect your assignments and your approach to determining final grades.

| Assignment | Proportion of Final Grade |
| --- | --- |
| informative speech | 10 percent |
| persuasive speech | 20 percent |
| commemorative speech or after-dinner speech | 15 percent |
| final speech | 20 percent |
| examinations | 25 percent |
| class participation and miscellaneous assignments | 10 percent |

To maintain the integrity of your grading system, you will need a firm attendance policy. Public speaking is a participation course. It also runs on a very tight schedule. If students habitually skip class when they are assigned to speak, the syllabus will be thrown off very quickly. Many instructors assign an automatic grade penalty to any student who fails to deliver a speech on the specified day because of an unexcused absence. Many also limit students to a maximum of two or three unexcused absences for the entire course. Excessive absences result in a reduction of the student's final grade. Whatever policy you adopt, be sure to write it on your syllabus so students will be aware of it from the very beginning of the course.

# Evaluation Forms

No matter how grades are assigned, it is important that students receive written evaluations of their speeches. Because such evaluations are usually the major channel of feedback from the instructor about the speeches, they need to be handled with great care. Evaluation forms should indicate clearly the elements of the speech on which the student is being assessed. They should also allow room for written comments.

Pages 48 to 55 of this manual contain seven speech evaluation forms. The first three are suitable for almost any kind of speech. The fourth is designed specifically for persuasive speeches on questions of policy, the fifth for commemorative speeches, the sixth for after-dinner speeches, and the seventh for speeches using Monroe's motivated sequence. The last four are included to suggest how evaluation forms can be adapted to the specific requirements of particular speech assignments.

In addition to varying slightly in content, each form has a somewhat different format. You may wish to use these forms as they are, or you may prefer to create your own by experimenting with formats and evaluation items. Regardless of which form you use, if you give your students a copy at the beginning of each speech assignment, they can use it as a checklist when preparing their speeches.

# Strategies of Evaluation

The most difficult task when evaluating speeches is to maintain a positive, encouraging tone while at the same time being candid with students about the shortcomings of their speeches. Evaluations should be realistic in appraising the speech, but they should be offered in a kind, optimistic tone that provides hope and encouragement for future speeches.

Whether you are preparing a written evaluation, discussing speeches in class, or meeting individually with students in a post-speech conference, it is usually a good idea to adopt the "good news/bad news" strategy of evaluation. That is, focus first on what the student did well in her or his speech. Be sure to find some positive comments, even if nothing more than "Excellent choice of topic," "Nice job of meeting the time limits," or "You certainly have a strong speaking voice." In most cases, you will have a fair number of substantive positive comments to make.

Once you have provided the "good news," you can turn to the "bad news"—that is, comments about the weaknesses of the speech. There is no need, in composing these comments, to construct a high-powered rhetorical analysis. Your objective is to help students grow as speakers by letting them know exactly what they need to correct and what steps they can take to improve. Try to give each speaker a few specific items to work on in the next speech. This will focus your students' energy and give them a concrete sense of your expectations.

# Evaluations by Students

It is also useful to have students fill out evaluation forms on their peers' speeches. One way to do this is to assign each student a partner who is responsible for providing a detailed, constructive evaluation of their partner's speech. Another approach is to assign a group of students as critics for each day's speeches. These students should fill out an evaluation form for each speech delivered that day. By the end of the unit, each student will have served as a critic for one day.

There are several schools of thought about dealing with student evaluations. Some instructors read the evaluations and grade them to encourage thorough, helpful, encouraging critiques. Whether or not you assign a grade to the evaluations, you should always look them over before giving them to the speaker to make sure they are sufficiently detailed and do not contain any destructive comments.

How much weight should be put on student evaluations in determining the speaker's grade? There are obvious dangers in having a student's grade hinge in any formal way on the responses of his or her classmates. In my own experience, student evaluations are most helpful as a way to encourage students to listen carefully to their classmates' speeches and to provide additional feedback to speakers.

In most cases, the students' judgments on such basic matters as organization and delivery will reflect fairly closely those of the instructor. There is always the possibility, however, that you will rate highly a speech to which students give low ratings, or vice versa. In such circumstances, you should double check your evaluation to make sure you are satisfied with it. If, after doing so, you are convinced that your original assessment is correct, you should write a note to the speaker on your evaluation form noting that her or his classmates appear to have overestimated (or underestimated) the speech and that the grade reflects your judgment rather than that of the student evaluators.

If your evaluation of the speech is higher than that of the speaker's classmates, the speaker will gladly defer to your wisdom and insight. If your evaluation is lower than that of the speaker's classmates, the speaker may challenge your wisdom and insight. In such circumstances, you should explain exactly what was wrong with the speech and how the speaker can improve next time. You should not allow students to browbeat you into changing your evaluation.

Finally, it is important to recognize that, no matter what you do, you cannot please all students when it comes to evaluation and grading. Even the most experienced, most effective teachers have students who are disgruntled over their grades. All you can do is assess your students fairly and seek to communicate that assessment clearly, concisely, and constructively. The rest is up to your students.

# CRITERIA USED FOR EVALUATING SPEECHES

The *average speech* (grade C) should meet the following criteria:

1.  Conform to the kind of speech assigned (informative, persuasive, etc.)
2.  Be ready for presentation on the assigned date
3.  Conform to the time limit
4.  Fulfill any special requirements of the assignment—such as preparing an outline, using visual aids, conducting an interview, etc.
5.  Have a clear specific purpose and central idea
6.  Have an identifiable introduction, body, and conclusion
7.  Show reasonable directness and competence in delivery
8.  Be free of serious errors in grammar, pronunciation, and word usage

The *above average speech* (grade B) should meet the preceding criteria and also:

1.  Deal with a challenging topic
2.  Fulfill all major functions of a speech introduction and conclusion
3.  Display clear organization of main points and supporting materials
4.  Support main points with evidence that meets the tests of accuracy, relevance, objectivity, and sufficiency
5.  Exhibit proficient use of connectives—transitions, internal previews, internal summaries, and signposts
6.  Be delivered skillfully enough so as not to distract attention from the speaker's message

The *superior speech* (grade A) should meet all the preceding criteria and also:

1.  Constitute a genuine contribution by the speaker to the knowledge or beliefs of the audience
2.  Sustain positive interest, feeling, and/or commitment among the audience
3.  Contain elements of vividness and special interest in the use of language
4.  Be delivered in a fluent, polished manner that strengthens the impact of the speaker's message

The *below average speech* (grade D or F) is seriously deficient in the criteria required for the C speech.

# Speech Evaluation Form

Speaker _____

Topic _____

*Rate the speaker on each point:*     E-*excellent*     G-*good*     A-*average*     F-*fair*     P-*poor*

---

**Comments**

**INTRODUCTION**

Gained attention and interest     E     G     A     F     P

Introduced topic clearly          E     G     A     F     P

Established credibility           E     G     A     F     P

Previewed body of speech          E     G     A     F     P

Related to audience               E     G     A     F     P

---

**BODY**

Main points clear                 E     G     A     F     P

Main points fully supported       E     G     A     F     P

Organization well planned         E     G     A     F     P

Language accurate                 E     G     A     F     P

Language clear, concise           E     G     A     F     P

Language appropriate              E     G     A     F     P

Connectives effective             E     G     A     F     P

---

**CONCLUSION**

Prepared audience for ending      E     G     A     F     P

Reinforced central idea           E     G     A     F     P

---

**DELIVERY**

Maintained eye contact            E     G     A     F     P

Used voice effectively            E     G     A     F     P

Presented visual aids well        E     G     A     F     P

Used nonverbal communication      E     G     A     F     P
   effectively

---

**OVERALL EVALUATION**

Topic challenging                 E     G     A     F     P

Specific purpose well chosen      E     G     A     F     P

Speech adapted to audience        E     G     A     F     P

Speech completed in time limit    E     G     A     F     P

---

# Speech Evaluation Form

Speaker _____

Topic _____

*Rate the speaker on each point:*   *E-excellent*   *G-good*   *A-average*   *F-fair*   *P-poor*

**INTRODUCTION**

| | |
|---|---|
| Gained attention and interest | E  G  A  F  P |
| Introduced topic clearly | E  G  A  F  P |
| Related topic to audience | E  G  A  F  P |
| Established credibility | E  G  A  F  P |
| Previewed body of speech | E  G  A  F  P |

**BODY**

| | |
|---|---|
| Main points clear | E  G  A  F  P |
| Main points fully supported | E  G  A  F  P |
| Organization well planned | E  G  A  F  P |
| Language accurate | E  G  A  F  P |
| Language clear | E  G  A  F  P |
| Language appropriate | E  G  A  F  P |
| Connectives effective | E  G  A  F  P |

**CONCLUSION**

| | |
|---|---|
| Prepared audience for ending | E  G  A  F  P |
| Reinforced central idea | E  G  A  F  P |
| Vivid ending | E  G  A  F  P |

**DELIVERY**

| | |
|---|---|
| Began speech without rushing | E  G  A  F  P |
| Maintained strong eye contact | E  G  A  F  P |
| Avoided distracting mannerisms | E  G  A  F  P |
| Articulated words clearly | E  G  A  F  P |
| Used pauses effectively | E  G  A  F  P |
| Used vocal variety to add impact | E  G  A  F  P |
| Presented visual aids well | E  G  A  F  P |
| Communicated enthusiasm for topic | E  G  A  F  P |
| Departed from lectern without rushing | E  G  A  F  P |

**OVERALL EVALUATION**

| | |
|---|---|
| Met assignment | E  G  A  F  P |
| Topic challenging | E  G  A  F  P |
| Specific purpose well chosen | E  G  A  F  P |
| Message adapted to audience | E  G  A  F  P |
| Speech completed within time limit | E  G  A  F  P |
| Held interest of audience | E  G  A  F  P |

What did the speaker do most effectively? _____

_____

What should the speaker pay special attention to next time? _____

_____

General Comments: _____

_____

_____

_____

# Speech Evaluation Form

**Speaker** _____

**Topic** _____

*Rate the speaker on each point:*    *E-excellent*    *G-good*    *A-average*    *F-fair*    *P-poor*

What was the speaker's specific purpose? _____

_____

| | | | | | |
|---|---|---|---|---|---|
| Introduction gain attention? | E | G | A | F | P |
| Introduction reveal the topic clearly? | E | G | A | F | P |
| Introduction relate topic to the audience? | E | G | A | F | P |
| Introduction establish credibility? | E | G | A | F | P |
| Introduction preview the body of the speech? | E | G | A | F | P |

List the main points of the speech. On the line at right note the kinds of supporting materials used for each:    *S-statistics*    *E-examples*    *T-testimony*

I. _____    _____

II. _____    _____

III. _____    _____

IV. _____    _____

V. _____    _____

What pattern of organization did the speaker use? _____

_____

| | | | | | |
|---|---|---|---|---|---|
| Conclusion reinforce the central idea? | E | G | A | F | P |
| Conclusion end on a strong note? | E | G | A | F | P |
| Speaker's language clear? | E | G | A | F | P |
| Speaker's language vivid? | E | G | A | F | P |
| Speaker's language appropriate? | E | G | A | F | P |
| Speaker maintain strong eye contact? | E | G | A | F | P |
| Speaker have sufficient vocal variety? | E | G | A | F | P |
| Speaker articulate words clearly? | E | G | A | F | P |
| Speaker seem poised and confident? | E | G | A | F | P |
| Speaker communicate enthusiasm for the topic? | E | G | A | F | P |
| Overall evaluation of the speech | E | G | A | F | P |

# Policy Speech Evaluation Form

**Speaker** _____

**Topic** _____

*Rate the speaker on each point:*    *E-excellent*    *G-good*    *A-average*    *F-fair*    *P-poor*

| | | E | G | A | F | P |
|---|---|---|---|---|---|---|
| 1. | Introduction gained attention and interest? | E | G | A | F | P |
| 2. | Main points clearly organized and easy to follow? | E | G | A | F | P |
| 3. | Main points supported with sufficient evidence? | E | G | A | F | P |
| 4. | Evidence from qualified sources? | E | G | A | F | P |
| 5. | Reasoning clear and sound? | E | G | A | F | P |
| 6. | Need issue dealt with convincingly? | E | G | A | F | P |
| 7. | Speaker's plan clearly explained? | E | G | A | F | P |
| 8. | Practicality of plan demonstrated? | E | G | A | F | P |
| 9. | Connectives used effectively? | E | G | A | F | P |
| 10. | Language clear and concise? | E | G | A | F | P |
| 11. | Conclusion reinforced the central idea? | E | G | A | F | P |
| 12. | Sufficient eye contact? | E | G | A | F | P |
| 13. | Voice used to add impact? | E | G | A | F | P |
| 14. | Nonverbal communication effective? | E | G | A | F | P |
| 15. | Speech well adapted to the audience? | E | G | A | F | P |
| 16. | Overall evaluation of the speech | E | G | A | F | P |

Comments: _____

_____

_____

_____

_____

# Commemorative Speech Evaluation Form

**Speaker** _____

**Topic** _____

*Rate the speaker on each point:*    *E-excellent*    *G-good*    *A-average*    *F-fair*    *P-poor*

| | | | | |
|---|---|---|---|---|
| Introduction gained attention | E | G | A | F | P |
| Subject introduced clearly | E | G | A | F | P |
| Main ideas easily followed | E | G | A | F | P |
| Language clear | E | G | A | F | P |
| Language vivid | E | G | A | F | P |
| Topic dealt with creatively | E | G | A | F | P |
| Speech adapted to audience | E | G | A | F | P |
| Sufficient eye contact | E | G | A | F | P |
| Voice used effectively | E | G | A | F | P |
| Nonverbal communication effective | E | G | A | F | P |
| General evaluation of the speech | E | G | A | F | P |

## Comments

# After-Dinner Speech Evaluation Form

**Speaker** _____

**Topic** _____

*Rate the speaker on each point:*    *E-excellent*    *G-good*    *A-average*    *F-fair*    *P-poor*

| | | | | |
|---|---|---|---|---|
| Topic appropriate | E | G | A | F | P |
| Introduction gained attention | E | G | A | F | P |
| Subject introduced clearly | E | G | A | F | P |
| Main ideas easily followed | E | G | A | F | P |
| Topic dealt with creatively | E | G | A | F | P |
| Language clear, concrete | E | G | A | F | P |
| Language vivid, colorful | E | G | A | F | P |
| Supporting materials entertaining | E | G | A | F | P |
| Humor tasteful | E | G | A | F | P |
| Strong eye contact | E | G | A | F | P |
| Voice used expressively | E | G | A | F | P |
| Speech adapted to audience | E | G | A | F | P |
| Overall evaluation of speech | E | G | A | F | P |

**Comments**

# Monroe's Motivated Sequence Evaluation Form

**Speaker** _____

**Topic** _____

*Rate the speaker on each point:*    *E-excellent*    *G-good*    *A-average*    *F-fair*    *P-poor*

---

**ATTENTION STEP**                                                                   Comments
Gained attention of listeners        E   G   A   F   P
Introduced topic clearly             E   G   A   F   P
Showed importance of topic           E   G   A   F   P
  to this audience

---

**NEED STEP**
Need clearly explained               E   G   A   F   P
Need demonstrated with               E   G   A   F   P
  evidence
Need related to audience             E   G   A   F   P

---

**SATISFACTION STEP**
Plan clearly explained               E   G   A   F   P
Plan well thought out                E   G   A   F   P

---

**VISUALIZATION STEP**
Practicality of plan shown           E   G   A   F   P
Benefits of plan related to          E   G   A   F   P
  audience

---

**ACTION STEP**
Call for specific action             E   G   A   F   P
  by audience
Vivid concluding appeal              E   G   A   F   P

---

**DELIVERY**
Maintained eye contact               E   G   A   F   P
Extemporaneous and                   E   G   A   F   P
  conversational
Poised, confident presentation       E   G   A   F   P
Words articulated clearly            E   G   A   F   P
Nonverbal communication              E   G   A   F   P
  effective
Communicated enthusiasm              E   G   A   F   P
  for topic

---

**OVERALL EVALUATION**
Language clear, concise              E   G   A   F   P
Connectives effective                E   G   A   F   P
Completed in time limit              E   G   A   F   P
Speaker's purpose achieved           E   G   A   F   P

---

# Part IV

# CHAPTER-BY-CHAPTER

# GUIDE TO

# *THE ART OF PUBLIC SPEAKING*

# Chapter 1 Speaking in Public

## Chapter Objectives

*After reading this chapter, students should be able to:*

1. Explain the value of a course in public speaking.

2. Identify the major similarities and differences between public speaking and everyday conversation.

3. Explain why a certain amount of nervousness is normal—even desirable—for a public speaker.

4. Discuss methods of controlling nervousness and of making it work for, rather than against, a speaker.

5. Identify the basic elements of the speech communication process.

6. Explain how the cultural diversity of today's world can influence public speaking situations.

7. Define ethnocentrism and explain why public speakers need to avoid it when addressing audiences of diverse racial, ethnic, or cultural background.

## Chapter Outline

I. Public speaking is a vital means of communication (*text pages 2-3*).
   A. Throughout history people have used the art of public speaking to spread their ideas and influence.
   B. The need for public speaking will touch almost every person at some time in her or his life.
      1. Public speaking helps people succeed in nearly all professions.
      2. Public speaking is valuable in numerous facets of community life.

II.   There are a number of similarities between public speaking and everyday conversation (*text pages 3-6*).
      A.   Public speaking and conversation share three major goals.
           1.   The first goal is to inform people about things they do not know.
           2.   The second goal is to persuade people to believe something or to take a certain course of action.
           3.   The third goal is to entertain people and make them feel happy and good about themselves.
      B.   Public speaking and conversation require similar skills.
           1.   In both, people organize their thoughts logically.
           2.   In both, people tailor their message to an audience.
           3.   In both, people tell a story for maximum impact.
           4.   In both, people adapt to feedback from listeners.

III.  There are four key differences between public speaking and everyday conversation (*text pages 6-7*).
      A.   Public speaking is more highly structured than ordinary conversation.
           1.   There are usually time limits on the length of a speech.
           2.   In most situations listeners do not interrupt a public speaker to voice questions or comments.
      B.   Public speaking requires more formal language than ordinary conversation.
           1.   Listeners usually react negatively to slang, jargon, and bad grammar in public speeches.
           2.   Because a public speech is supposed to be "special," most successful speakers elevate and polish their language when addressing an audience.
      C.   Public speaking requires a different method of delivery from ordinary conversation.
           1.   When conversing informally, most people talk quietly, interject stock phrases such "you know," "like," and "really," adopt a casual posture, and the like.
           2.   Effective public speakers adopt a more formal manner of delivery and avoid distracting mannerisms and verbal habits.
      D.   With study and practice, most people are able to master these differences and expand their conversational skills into speechmaking.

IV.   One of the major concerns of students in any speech class is stage fright (*text pages 8-11*).
      A.   It is entirely normal to feel nervous about the prospect of giving a public speech.
      B.   Even experienced public speakers have stage fright before their presentations.

C. There are two major ways students can develop confidence in their speechmaking abilities.
    1. One is to take a speech class in which they will learn about speechmaking and gain speaking experience.
    2. Another is to be thoroughly prepared for every speech they present.
        a. It is difficult to be confident of success when one stands up to speak without knowing what to say or how to say it.
        b. Most people find that their confidence increases dramatically when they practice a speech until they have full command of the ideas and the delivery.

D. In addition, there are a number of specific tips that successful speakers follow to help control stage fright.
    1. Successful speakers think positively.
    2. Successful speakers are at their physical and mental best when they speak.
    3. Successful speakers concentrate on communicating with their audience rather than on their nervousness.
    4. Successful speakers take a few deep breaths before starting to speak.
    5. Successful speakers work particularly hard on their introductions.
    6. Successful speakers make eye contact with people in the audience.
    7. Successful speakers use visual aids to help occupy the attention of the audience.

E. Finally, it is helpful for a speaker to know two very important facts.
    1. Listeners usually cannot tell how tense a speaker is—especially if the speaker works to act confident on the outside.
    2. Making a mistake in a speech is no catastrophe.
        a. Even accomplished speakers make mistakes.
        b. Most of the time no one besides the speaker notices the mistake.

V. Public speaking helps people develop critical thinking skills (*text pages 12-13*).
A. Critical thinking involves a number of skills.
    1. Critical thinking involves being able to assess the strengths and weaknesses of an argument.
    2. Critical thinking involves distinguishing fact from opinion.
    3. Critical thinking involves judging the credibility of sources.
    4. Critical thinking involves assessing the quality of evidence.
    5. Critical thinking involves discerning the relationships among ideas.

B.    These—and other—critical thinking skills are enriched by a public speaking class.
1.    As students organize their speeches, their ideas will become more clear and cohesive.
2.    As students work on expressing their ideas accurately, their thinking will become more precise.
3.    As students learn about the role of reasoning and evidence in speeches, they will become better able to assess reasoning and evidence in all types of situations.

VI.    There are seven elements of the speech communication process (*text pages 13-18*).
A.    Speech communication begins with a speaker.
1.    The speaker is the person who presents the message.
2.    Successful speakers combine technical skill with personal enthusiasm.
B.    The message is whatever a speaker communicates to someone else.
1.    The goal of a speaker is to have the intended message be the message that is actually communicated.
2.    Achieving this depends both on what the speaker says (the verbal message) and how the speaker says it (the nonverbal message).
C.    The channel is the means by which a message is communicated.
1.    Public speakers may use one or more of several channels— microphone, radio, television, etc.
2.    In speech class, the channel is the most direct because listeners see and hear the speaker without any media or electronic intervention.
D.    The listener is the person who receives the communicated message.
1.    Everything a speaker says is filtered through a listener's frame of reference.
a.    A listener's frame of reference is the sum total of his or her knowledge, experience, goals, values, and attitudes.
b.    Because a speaker and listener are different people, they can never have exactly the same frame of reference.
2.    Because people have different frames of reference, a public speaker must take care to adapt the message to the particular audience being addressed.
E.    Feedback consists of messages sent from the listener to the speaker.
1.    Most communication situations involve two-way communication, in which the speaker can see how the audience is responding.
2.    Successful public speakers learn to interpret the feedback sent by listeners and to adjust their messages in response to the feedback.

F. Interference is anything that impedes the communication of a message.
   1. Interference can be either external or internal.
      a. External interference comes from outside the audience—such as a ringing telephone, the noise of traffic, or static in a microphone.
      b. Internal interference comes from within the audience—such as poor listening skills or lack of concentration.
   2. Successful public speakers work to hold their listeners' attention despite interference.
G. The situation is the time and place in which speech communication occurs.
   1. Speech communication always takes place in a particular situation.
      a. A conversation might occur over a candlelight dinner or in a noisy tavern.
      b. A public speech might be presented in a small classroom, in a large auditorium, or at outdoor graduation ceremonies.
   2. Successful public speakers are alert to the situation and adjust their remarks to it.

VII. Public speakers need to be aware of and responsive to the growing multiculturalism of today's world (*text pages 18-23*).
   A. The United States has become the most diverse society on the face of the earth.
      1. For more than a century European immigrants and African Americans made the U.S. the "melting pot" of the world.
      2. Today another great wave of immigration—mostly from Asia and Latin America—is making the U.S. a multicultural society of unparalleled diversity.
   B. Cultural diversity is more than a U.S. phenomenon.
      1. We are living in an age of international multiculturalism.
      2. Air travel, immigration, and electronic communication are making all nations and cultures part of a vast "global village."
   C. Diversity and multiculturalism are such basic facts of life in today's world that they affect many public speaking situations.
      1. Because of the growing diversity of modern life, audiences often include people of different cultural, racial, and ethnic backgrounds.
      2. Speechmaking becomes more complex as cultural diversity increases.
      3. To be successful, public speakers need to take account of cultural differences between themselves and their listeners.

D.  It is especially important for public speakers to avoid ethnocentrism.
  1.  Ethnocentrism is the belief that one's own culture or group is superior to all others.
    a.  Ethnocentrism can play a positive role in creating group pride and loyalty.
    b.  Ethnocentrism can be destructive when it leads to prejudice and hostility.
  2.  Speakers can avoid ethnocentrism by respecting diverse cultural values.
    a.  They should remember that all societies have special beliefs and customs.
    b.  Although speakers do not have to agree with the beliefs and customs of all people, they will not be successful unless they show respect for the cultures of the people they address.
  3.  Speakers can also take specific steps to adapt to listeners of diverse cultural, racial, and ethnic backgrounds.
    a.  When preparing the speech, they should put themselves in the place of listeners from different backgrounds to make sure the speech is clear and appropriate.
    b.  They should use examples, comparisons and other supporting materials that can clarify ideas for a wide range of listeners.
    c.  They should consider using visual aids to bridge gaps in language or cultural background.
    d.  When presenting the speech, they should be alert to feedback that might indicate the audience is having difficulty understanding.
E.  Listeners also need to avoid ethnocentrism.
  1.  Audiences have a responsibility to listen courteously and attentively to speakers of all cultural backgrounds.
  2.  They need to be on guard against the temptation to reject speakers from different backgrounds on the basis of accent, personal appearance, or manner of delivery.

## Application Exercises *(from text page 25)*

1.  Think back on an important conversation you had recently in which you wanted to achieve a particular result. (*Examples*: Trying to convince your parents you should live in off-campus housing rather than in a dormitory; asking your employer to change your work schedule; explaining to a friend how to change the oil and filter in a car; trying to persuade a professor to accept your term paper a week late; attempting to talk your spouse into buying the VCR you like rather than the one he or she prefers.) Work up a brief analysis of the conversation.

In your analysis, explain the following: (1) your purpose in the conversation and the message strategy you chose to achieve your purpose; (2) the communication channels used during the conversation and how they affected the outcome; (3) the interference—internal or external—you encountered during the conversation; (4) the steps you took to adjust to feedback; (5) the strategic changes you would make in preparing for and carrying out the conversation if you had it to do over again.

> **Discussion:** *This exercise can be a very effective vehicle for class discussion about the basic elements of the speech communication process and how they interact. By stressing the strategic aspects of everyday conversation, this exercise also points to the similarities between conversation and public speaking. Students should find that much of the strategic thinking that goes into preparing a speech is quite similar to the strategic thinking they often put into ordinary conversation.*

2.    Divide a sheet of paper into two columns. Label one column "Characteristics of an Effective Public Speaker." Label the other column "Characteristics of an Ineffective Public Speaker." In the columns, list and briefly explain what you believe to be the five most important characteristics of effective and ineffective speakers. Be prepared to discuss your ideas in class.

> **Discussion:** *When this exercise is discussed in class, it provides the basis for generating a set of criteria for effective speechmaking that is agreed upon by the entire class. You, of course, should know ahead of time the criteria you want to stress, so you can direct the class discussion in that direction.*

3.    On the basis of the lists you developed for Exercise 2, candidly evaluate your own strengths and weaknesses as a speaker. Identify the three primary aspects of speechmaking you most want to improve.

> **Discussion:** *This exercise encourages students to set specific goals for improving their public speaking. At various times in the term, you and the student can weigh her or his progress against the goals. Some teachers have students reassess their goals every few weeks. At the end of the course, you may want students to judge how well they have met their goals and to reassess their strengths and weaknesses as speakers in light of what they have learned in the course.*

## Additional Exercises and Activities

1.    On the first day of class have students fill out and return the questionnaire on the next page of this manual. This will give you a pretty clear early picture of the background and needs of the students enrolled in your class.

2.    Show students the videotape "Be Prepared to Speak," which is part of the videotape supplement to *The Art of Public Speaking*. Afterward, discuss the tape and highlight its main points about speech preparation and presentation.

> **Discussion:**    *"Be Prepared to Speak" is a 27-minute color videotape that presents a dramatized overview of the entire public speaking process from choosing a topic to delivering the final presentation. Entertaining as well as informative, it shows students how to organize their ideas, develop an introduction and conclusion, rehearse the speech, overcome nervousness, and adapt to the audience and speaking occasion. The tape works especially well if shown early in the term—before the introductory speeches are presented. By giving students a concise introduction to all the steps of speech development and delivery, it prepares students for their initial speech without first having to read several chapters in the book.*

3.    Give students the following assignment: Think of a situation in which you sought to understand the message of, or to convey your own message to, someone from a different culture. The situation might have involved interpersonal communication, public speaking, or a mass media message such as a film or a television program. Write a brief analysis in which you explain (a) the participants in the communication situation, (b) the message that was meant to be communicated, (c) the difficulty you had communicating—or understanding—the message, (d) the outcome of the situation, and (e) what the situation reveals about the complexity of communicating with people of different cultural backgrounds. Be prepared to present your analysis in class.

> **Discussion:**   *This exercise works best in classes in which a fair proportion of students have had personal communication with people from different cultures. It can provide an excellent vehicle for discussing ethnocentrism and the barriers it poses to intercultural communication. Because students are dealing with their own experiences, the exercise helps make the abstract concept of ethnocentrism more immediate and personal.*

# STUDENT INTRODUCTION QUESTIONNAIRE

*Name* _____  *Year* _____

*Major* _____

What reason(s) do you have for taking this class?

Do you have any specific goals for improving your speaking? What are they? (What would you like to learn how to do? What particular problems would you like to overcome?)

What classes in speech and related fields (such as journalism or English composition) have you had here or at other schools?

What kinds of speaking experiences have you had in your classes, jobs, church, extracurricular activities, organizations, etc.?

When did you give your last speech? What was the topic?

What are your career plans? Will public speaking be important to your career? How so?

4.   Over the years a number of metaphors have been used to describe the mix of cultures in the United States. Best known is the melting pot metaphor, which originated in 1908 with *The Melting-Pot*, a play by Israel Zangwill, an English writer of Russian-Jewish heritage. According to this metaphor, the United States is like the kind of huge container used to melt and mix steel and other metals. As immigrants come to the United States, they blend together into one assimilated culture that is stronger than the individual cultures of which it is composed.

A second metaphor compares the U.S. to a set of streams or rivers each of which is composed of many people from different cultures. The streams or rivers flow separately, maintaining their unique identity until at some point they come together to form a mighty watershed in which the individual streams and rivers are combined into one.

In a third metaphor the U.S. is compared to a garden salad in which different cultures, like the different ingredients in a salad, are combined and tossed to create the final product without losing their individual texture and flavor.

A fourth metaphor likens the U.S. to a giant quilt or tapestry in which people of different cultural backgrounds, like the individual threads and patterns of a tapestry, are woven together to produce the overall design. Like the salad metaphor, in which the various ingredients retain their own texture and flavor, the tapestry metaphor stresses the uniqueness and importance of the individual threads, patterns, and colors out of which the whole fabric is constructed.

After presenting these metaphors to the class, conduct a class discussion in which students consider the strengths and weaknesses of each metaphor for describing the cultural diversity of life in the United States.

**Discussion:** *This exercise can be conducted in small groups or with the class as a whole. In either case, it is an excellent vehicle for prompting reflection about cultural diversity in the U.S. Here are some issues to consider:*

*First, although the melting pot metaphor was widely employed through most of this century, it has fallen into some disfavor in recent years because it does not stress the capacity of cultural groups to maintain their individual identities as they "melt" into a single American culture. Second, the comparison of the U.S. to a set of streams or rivers that combine to form a single body of water allows for the uniqueness of individual cultures until the point at which they merge into a common current. But this metaphor also implies that the streams and rivers are inferior to or less consequential than the great body of water they form when brought together.*

*Third, in both the salad and tapestry metaphors, individual elements of the whole retain their identity and uniqueness even as they are combined to create a larger entity. Comparing the U.S. to a tapestry, however, suggests that at some point U.S. culture as a whole is an inert, finished product, when in fact it is constantly changing and evolving. The salad metaphor, on the other hand, captures both the dynamic quality of cultural diversity in the U.S. and the distinctiveness of individual cultural groups. For fuller analysis of these metaphors, see Myron W. Lustig and Jolene Koester,* Intercultural Competence: Communication Across Cultures *(New York: HarperCollins, 1993), pp. 14-15, from which this discussion is adapted.*

5. If your class has a fair number of international students, conduct a class discussion in which the international students compare and contrast common nonverbal signals in their countries with those in the United States.

   **Discussion:** *Depending on the composition of your class, this can be an excellent way to generate discussion of the nonverbal dimension of intercultural communication. The exercise also sensitizes U.S. students to the communication customs of students from abroad and to the adaptations international students have to make to communicate effectively in the U.S. If you begin the discussion with such basic signals as those for "hello," "goodbye," "come here," "okay," and the like, it will usually move naturally to more complex signals. Given the nature of college students, the discussion will also probably turn at some point to obscene gestures unless you declare that subject off limits.*

   *For instructors who wish to know more about nonverbal communication among different cultures prior to discussion, Roger Axtell's* Gestures: The Do's and Taboos of Body Language Around the World *(New York: Wiley, 1991), provides a highly readable, illustrated treatment. An excellent set of general tips on teaching international students is presented by Charlynn Ross, "Suggestions for Teaching International Students," in Stephen E. Lucas (ed.),* Selections from The Speech Communication Teacher, 1986-1991 *(New York: McGraw-Hill, 1992), pp. 28-29, which is available as an instructional supplement to* The Art of Public Speaking.

6. Assign a two-minute speech of self-introduction in which students explain a significant aspect of their cultural background and how it has made a difference in their lives. Possible topics might include social customs, family traditions, holidays, clothing, food, religious traditions, sporting activities, and the like. Encourage students to be creative in preparing their speeches and in finding ways to illustrate how the aspect of their culture they choose to explain relates to their personal lives.

**Discussion:** *This assignment accomplishes three goals at once. First, it fulfills the need for an introductory, ungraded speech in which students can begin the process of feeling comfortable in front of an audience. Second, it allows everyone in the class to learn something about their fellow students, which is an important step in creating a supportive, cooperative classroom atmosphere. Third, by focusing on the different cultural backgrounds of people in the class, it creates opportunities to discuss cultural diversity and its impact on public speaking in general. For more details on this assignment, see Introductory Speech, Option D, on page 33 of this manual.*

7.    Assign a two-minute speech in which students introduce one of their classmates to the rest of the class. The speech should focus on some aspect of the cultural background of the person being introduced—social customs, family traditions, holidays, clothing, food, religious traditions, sporting activities, and the like. Encourage students to be creative in preparing their speeches and in talking about their classmates.

**Discussion:** *This assignment offers an alternative to Additional Exercise 6 above and accomplishes the same objectives. In preparation for the speech have students pair off and interview one another. If there is great cultural diversity in your class, arrange the interview pairs so that students interview someone with a substantially different cultural background from their own. Although the interviewing can be done in the last 15 to 20 minutes of the first class meeting, the assignment usually works better if students conduct their interviews out of class. This provides time for longer interviews and gives students a better chance to get to know one another. If this assignment is used for the introductory ice-breaker speech, it should not be graded. For more details, see Introductory Speech, Option B, on page 32 of this manual.*

8.    Assign an informative speech of five to six minutes in which students explain a significant aspect of a culture different from their own—social customs, family traditions, holidays, clothing, religious traditions, music, sporting activities, educational systems, etc. Library research is required for this speech. If students have had direct contact with a foreign culture, they should be encouraged to supplement their library research with their personal experience, but the speech is not to be a travelogue or a presentation on "My Summer in Europe" or "My Year as an Exchange Student in Brazil." However, a speech on how Europeans spend their summer vacations, or on the educational system of Brazil, would be fine.

**Discussion:** *Unlike Additional Exercises 6 and 7, this assignment involves a full-length, graded speech. The objectives with respect to cultural diversity, however, are much the same. Because students are sometimes resistant when they are required to speak on a different culture, it can be helpful to present this as the "World Travel Agency" speech. If you take this approach, tell students that the class is going to travel around the world via their speeches. They will "visit" as many different countries as there are students in the class.*

*To help students choose topics as quickly as possible, prepare two sets of 3 x 5 index cards. Write the name of a different country on each card in the first set. Then write two or three cultural features on each card in the second set (choose from the features listed at the start of this exercise, or, better yet, add some of your own devising). Put each set of cards in a separate bag and have students randomly pick a card from each bag. When they are finished, they will have a country card (for instance, Italy) and a topic card (including, for example, sports, family traditions, and politics). The student will then speak on one of those three aspects of Italian life.*

*However students choose their topics, they should be encouraged to be imaginative in composing their speeches. It is not enough to summarize encyclopedia information about their country. As in any informative speech, students need to explain ideas clearly and to think about ways to relate the topic to the audience. They also need to consider using visual aids. Indeed, many teachers require a visual aid for this speech. For further details on this assignment, see Informative Speech, Option D, on pages 35-36 of this manual.*

# Extra Teaching and Learning Resources

## General

Cohen, Jodi R. "The Relevance of a Course in Public Speaking." In Stephen E. Lucas (ed.), *Selections from the Speech Communication Teacher, 1986-1991*. New York: McGraw-Hill, 1992, pp. 2-3.

Curtis, Dan B., Winsor, Jerry L., and Stephens, Ronald D. "National Preferences in Business and Communication Education." *Communication Education*, 38 (1989), 6-14.

Ford, Wendy S. Zabava, and Wolvin, Andrew D. "The Differential Impact of a Basic Communication Course on Perceived Competencies in Class, Work, and Social Contexts." *Communication Education*, 42 (1993), 215-223.

Hart, Roderick P. "Why Communication? Why Education? Toward a Politics of Teaching." *Communication Education*, 42 (1993), 97-105.

Haynes, Lance W. "Public Speaking Pedagogy in the Media Age." *Communication Education*, 39 (1990), 89-102.

Modaff, John, and Hopper, Robert. "Why Speech is Basic." *Communication Education*, 33 (1984), 37-42.

Rubin, Rebecca B, and Graham, Elizabeth E. "Communication Correlates of College Success: An Exploratory Investigation." *Communication Education*, 37 (1988), 14-27.

Vangelisti, Anita L., and Daly, John A. "Correlates of Speaking Skills in the United States: A National Assessment." *Communication Education*, 38 (1989), 132-143.

## Speech Anxiety

Adams, Lori. "Speech Anxiety Simulation." *Speech Communication Teacher*, 7 (Fall 1992), 13.

Allen, Mike, Hunter, John E., and Donohue, William A. "Meta-Analysis of Self-Report Data on the Effectiveness of Public Speaking Anxiety Treatment Techniques." *Communication Education*, 38 (1989), 54-76.

Ayres, Joe, and Hopf, Tim. *Coping with Speech Anxiety*. Norwood, N.J.: Ablex, 1993.

Booth-Butterfield, Steven, and Cottone, R. Rocco. "Ethical Issues in the Treatment of Communication Apprehension and Avoidance." *Communication Education*, 40 (1991), 172-179.

Bourhis, John, and Allen, Mike. "The Needs of the Apprehensive Student." In Lawrence J. Hugenberg, Pamela L. Gray, and Douglas M. Trank (eds.), *Teaching and Directing the Basic Communications Course*. Dubuque, Iowa: Kendall/Hunt, 1993, pp. 271-276.

Cronin, Michael W., Grice, George L., and Olsen, Richard K., Jr. "The Effects of Interactive Video Instruction in Coping with Speech Fright." *Communication Education*, 43 (1994), 42-53.

Daly, John A., and McCroskey, James C. (eds.). *Avoiding Communication: Shyness, Reticence, and Communication Apprehension*. Beverly Hills, Calif.: Sage, 1984.

Desberg, Peter, and Marsh, George D. *Controlling Stagefright: Presenting Yourself to Audiences from One to One Thousand*. Oakland, Calif.: New Harbinger Publications, 1988.

Isaacson, Zelda. "Paradoxical Intention: A Strategy to Alleviate the Anxiety Associated with Public Speaking." *Speech Communication Teacher*, 8 (Summer 1993), 13-14.

Kelly, Lynne. "Implementing a Skills Training Program for Reticent Communicators." *Communication Education*, 38 (1989), 85-101.

Kelly, Lynne, and Keaten, James. "A Test of the Effectiveness of the Reticence Program at the Pennsylvania State University." *Communication Education*, 41 (1992), 361-374.

Langdon, Harry. "A Course on Stage Fright." In Stephen E. Lucas (ed.), *Selections from the Speech Communication Teacher, 1986-1991*. New York: McGraw-Hill, 1992, pp. 63-64.

Mino, Mary. "Building Confidence Through Oral Interpretation." *Speech Communication Teacher*, 9 (Winter 1994), 10-11.

Motley, Michael T., and Molloy, Jennifer L. "An Efficacy Test of a New Therapy (Communication-Orientation Motivation) for Public Speaking Anxiety." *Journal of Applied Communication Research*, 22 (1994), 48-58.

Rose, Heidi M., Rancer, Andrew S., and Crannell, Kenneth C. "The Impact of a Basic Course in Oral Interpretation and Public Speaking on Communication Apprehension." *Communication Reports*, 6 (1993), 54-60.

Stowell, Jessica. "Free Writing to Deal with Speech Anxiety." *Speech Communication Teacher*, 6 (Spring 1992), 15.

## Critical Thinking

Beall, Melissa L. "Thinking about Thinking." In Stephen E. Lucas (ed.), *Selections from the Speech Communication Teacher, 1986-1991*. New York: McGraw-Hill, 1992, pp. 19-20.

Fritz, Paul A., and Weaver, Richard L., II. "Teaching Critical Thinking in the Basic Speaking Course: A Liberal Arts Perspective." *Communication Education*, 35 (1986), 174-182.

Greg, John, and Renz, Mary Ann. "Critical Thinking." In Lawrence J. Hugenberg, Pamela L. Gray, and Douglas M. Trank (eds.), *Teaching and Directing the Basic Communications Course*. Dubuque, Iowa: Kendall/Hunt, 1993, pp. 9-22

Kurfis, Joanne Gainen. *Critical Thinking: Theory, Research, Practice, and Possibilities*. Washington, D.C.: Association for Study of Higher Education, 1988.

Newburger, Craig. "Testing Students' Ability to Distinguish Facts from Inferences." *Speech Communication Teacher*, 8 (Winter 1994), 13-14.

Proctor, Russell F., II. "Using Feature Films to Teach Critical Thinking." *Speech Communication Teacher*, 7 (Spring 1993), 11-12.

Schumer, Allison. "Speech Communication via Critical Thinking." In Stephen E. Lucas (ed.), *Selections from the Speech Communication Teacher, 1986-1991*. New York: McGraw-Hill, 1992, pp. 21-22.

Spicer, Karin-Leigh, and Hanks, William E. "Critical Thinking Activities for Public Speaking Textbooks." *Speech Communication Teacher*, 7 (Summer 1993), 6-7.

## The Speech Communication Process

Burgoon, Michael, Hunsaker, Frank G., and Dawson, Edwin J. *Human Communication*, 3rd ed. Thousand Oaks, Calif.: Sage, 1994.

Frandsen, Kenneth D., and Millis, Michael A. "On Conceptual, Theoretical, and Empirical Treatments of Feedback in Human Communication: Fifteen Years Later." *Communication Reports*, 6 (1993), 79-91.

Griffin, Em. *A First Look at Communication Theory*, 2nd ed. New York: McGraw-Hill, 1994.

Liska, Jo. "Bee Dances, Bird Songs, Monkey Calls, and Cetacean Sonar: Is Speech Unique?" *Western Journal of Communication*, 57 (1993), 1-26.

Littlejohn, Stephen W. *Theories of Human Communication*, 4th ed. Belmont, Calif.: Wadsworth, 1992.

Motley, Michael T. "On Whether One Can(not) Not Communicate: An Examination via Traditional Communication Postulates." *Western Journal of Speech Communication*, 54 (1990), 1-20.

Ruben, Brent D. *Communication and Human Behavior*, 3rd ed. Englewood Cliffs, N.J.: Prentice-Hall, 1992.

Trenholm, Sarah. *Human Communication Theory*, 2nd ed. Englewood Cliffs, N.J.: Prentice-Hall, 1991.

Tubbs, Stewart L., and Moss, Sylvia. *Human Communication*, 7th ed. New York: McGraw-Hill, 1994.

## Public Speaking in a Multicultural World

Axtell, Roger E. *Gestures: The Do's and Taboos of Body Language Around the World*. New York: Wiley, 1991.

Bowser, Benjamin P., Auletta, Gale S., and Jones, Terry. *Confronting Diversity Issues on Campus*. Newbury Park, Calif.: Sage, 1993.

Corey, James. "International Bazaar." In Stephen E. Lucas (ed.), *Selections from the Speech Communication Teacher, 1986-1991*. (New York: McGraw-Hill, 1992), p. 73.

Fuchs, Lawrence H. *The American Kaleidoscope: Race, Ethnicity, and the Civic Culture*. Hanover, N.H.: University Press of New England, 1990.

Garbowitz, Fred. "Changing Classroom Populations Call for Increased Diversity." In Stephen E. Lucas (ed.), *Selections from the Speech Communication Teacher, 1986-1991*. (New York: McGraw-Hill, 1992), pp. 26-27.

Gitterman, Martin R. "Improving Performance by Maximizing Feedback for Native and Non-Native Speakers of English." In Stephen E. Lucas (ed.), *Selections from the Speech Communication Teacher, 1986-1991*. (New York: McGraw-Hill, 1992), pp. 27-28.

Gleason, Philip. *Speaking of Diversity: Language and Ethnicity in Twentieth-Century America*. Baltimore: Johns Hopkins University Press, 1992

Gudykunst, William B., and Young, Yun Kim. *Communicating with Strangers: An Approach to Intercultural Communication*, 2nd ed. New York: McGraw-Hill, 1992.

Gudykunst, William B., and Young, Yun Kim (eds.). *Readings on Communicating with Strangers: An Approach to Intercultural Communication*. New York: McGraw-Hill, 1992.

Haleta, Laurie L., and Converse-Weber, Karyn. "The Needs of the Physically Handicapped Student." In Lawrence J. Hugenberg, Pamela L. Gray, and Douglas M. Trank (eds.), *Teaching and Directing the Basic Communications Course*. Dubuque, Iowa: Kendall/Hunt, 1993, pp. 277-282.

Hawkinson, Ken. "Two Exercises on Diversity and Gender." *Speech Communication Teacher*, 8 (Fall 1993), 2-4.

Hill, L. Brooks, and Javidi, Manoocher. "The Needs of the International Student." In Lawrence J. Hugenberg, Pamela L. Gray, and Douglas M. Trank (eds.), *Teaching and Directing the Basic Communications Course*. Dubuque, Iowa: Kendall/Hunt, 1993, pp. 263-270.

Klopf, Donald W. *Intercultural Encounters: The Fundamentals of Intercultural Communication*, 2nd ed. Englewood, Colo.: Morton Publishing, 1991.

Lustig, Myron W., and Koester, Jolene. *Intercultural Competence: Interpersonal Communication Across Cultures*. New York: HarperCollins, 1993.

Ross, Charlynn. "Suggestions for Teaching International Students." In Stephen E. Lucas (ed.), *Selections from the Speech Communication Teacher, 1986-1991.* New York: McGraw-Hill, 1992, pp. 28-29.

Samovar, Larry A., and Porter, Richard E. *Communication Between Cultures.* Belmont, Calif.: Wadsworth, 1991.

Samovar, Larry A., and Porter, Richard E. (eds.). *Intercultural Communication: A Reader,* 6th ed. Belmont, Calif.: Wadsworth, 1991.

Schlesinger, Arthur M. *The Disuniting of America: Reflections on a Multicultural Society.* New York: Norton, 1993.

Schumer, Allison. "Helping International Students Adapt to American Communication Norms." In Stephen E. Lucas (ed.), *Selections from the Speech Communication Teacher, 1986-1991.* New York: McGraw-Hill, 1992, p. 30.

Shankar, Archana Daya. "Issues of Ethnic Diversity in the Basic Course." In Lawrence J. Hugenberg, Pamela L. Gray, and Douglas M. Trank (eds.), *Teaching and Directing the Basic Communications Course.* Dubuque, Iowa: Kendall/Hunt, 1993, pp. 291-298.

Takaki, Ronald. *A Different Mirror: A History of Multicultural America.* Boston: Little, Brown, 1993.

*Time* (Fall 1993). Special issue devoted to "The New Face of America."

Walter, Suzanne. "Introduction of a Speaker: Multipurpose and Multicultural." *Speech Communication Teacher* (Spring 1993), 3.

Webster, Linda J. "The Needs of the Non-Traditional Student." In Lawrence J. Hugenberg, Pamela L. Gray, and Douglas M. Trank (eds.), *Teaching and Directing the Basic Communications Course.* Dubuque, Iowa: Kendall/Hunt, 1993, pp. 263-270.

Wood, Julia. "Diversity and Commonality: Sustaining Their Tension in Communication Courses." *Western Journal of Communication,* 57 (1993), 367-380.

## Films and Videos

"A Case Study for Critical Thinking: Vietnam." Insight Media (1987). 52 minutes.

"A World of Gestures." University of California Extension Center for Media and Independent Learning (1991). 28 minutes.

"American Tongues." Center for New American Media (1986). 40 minutes.

"Be Prepared to Speak." Kantola-Skeie Productions (1985). 27 minutes.

"Beyond Hate." Educational Video Group (1987). 60 minutes.

"Critical Thinking: How to Evaluate Information and Draw Conclusions." Insight Media (1986). 47 minutes.

"Cross-Cultural Communication in Diverse Settings." Insight Media (1992). 60 minutes.

"Diversity Series." Quality Media Resources (1993). Four-module set; 20 minutes per module.

"Doing Business Internationally." CRM Films (1992). 43 minutes.

"How to Get Your Point Across in 30 Seconds or Less." Coronet/MTI Film and Video (1986). 30 minutes.

"Managing Diversity." CRM Films (1991). 22 minutes.

Peters, Tom. "Ten Vital Rules for Giving Incredible Speeches and Why They're Irrelevant." Video Publishing House (1990). 32 minutes.

"Presentation Excellence." Video Publishing House (1984). 77 minutes.

"Stage Fright." Coronet/MTI Film and Video (1979). 13 minutes.

"Speaking Effectively to One or One Thousand," revised edition. CRM Films (1992). 21 minutes.

"The Communication Cycle." Insight Media (1989). 28 minutes.

"The Communication Process." RMI Media Productions (1986). 28 minutes.

"The Public Speaker and the Audience." RMI Media Productions (1986). 28 minutes.

"When You Have to Get Up and Talk—Starring George Plimpton." BBP (1985). 24 minutes.

# Chapter 2 Ethics and Public Speaking

## Chapter Objectives

*After reading this chapter, students should be able to:*

1.  Explain why a strong sense of ethical responsibility is vital for public speakers.

2.  Discuss the five guidelines for ethical speechmaking presented in the chapter.

3.  Define the differences among global plagiarism, patchwork plagiarism, and incremental plagiarism and explain why each type of plagiarism is unethical.

4.  Identify the three basic guidelines for ethical listening discussed in the chapter.

## Chapter Outline

I.   Questions of ethics are central to the art of public speaking (*text pages 30-32*).
     A.  Ethics is the branch of philosophy that deals with issues of right and wrong in human affairs.
     B.  Ethical issues arise when we ask whether a course of action is moral or immoral, fair or unfair, just or unjust, honest or dishonest.
     C.  Questions of ethics come into play whenever a public speaker faces an audience.
         1.  Because speechmaking is a form of power, it carries heavy ethical responsibilities.
         2.  Public speakers face ethical issues at every stage of the speechmaking process.

D.   As stated by the Roman rhetorician Quintilian, the ideal of commendable speechmaking is the good person speaking well.

II.   As there are guidelines for ethical behavior in other areas of life, so are there guidelines for ethical behavior in public speaking *(text pages 33-37)*.
A.   Public speakers should make sure their goals are ethically sound.
1.   As history demonstrates, public speaking can be used for either worthy or unworthy goals.
2.   Although there can be legitimate disagreements when it comes to assessing a speaker's goals, this is not a reason to avoid asking ethical questions.
3.   Responsible public speakers take care to assess the ethical soundness of their goals.
B.   Public speakers should be fully prepared for each speech.
1.   Being fully prepared is vital to delivering an effective speech, but it is also important ethically.
2.   Unprepared speakers waste the collective time of their listeners.
3.   Unprepared speakers may give the audience erroneous information or faulty advice that can lead to grievous consequences.
C.   Public speakers should be honest in what they say.
1.   Nothing is more important to ethical speechmaking than honesty.
2.   Ethical public speakers avoid blatant forms of dishonesty such as telling outright lies.
3.   They also avoid more subtle forms of dishonesty such as juggling statistics, quoting out of context, painting tentative findings as firm conclusions, citing unusual cases as typical examples, and the like.
D.   Public speakers should avoid name-calling and other forms of abusive language.
1.   Name-calling is the use of language to demean other individuals or groups.
2.   Whether based on race, religion, ethnicity, sexual orientation, or gender, name-calling degrades the personal dignity of the people being attacked.
a.   It conveys negative, stereotyped, and misleading information about those people.
b.   It implies that they are inferior and do not deserve to be treated with the same respect as other members of society.
3.   Name-calling also creates problems in public speaking when it is used to silence opposing voices.
a.   In the U.S. all citizens have the right to voice their ideas on issues of public consequence.
b.   Public speakers have an ethical obligation to help preserve that right by avoiding tactics such as name-calling that

automatically impugn the accuracy or respectability of statements made by groups or individuals who disagree with the speaker.

E. Public speakers should put ethical principles into practice.
1. Being ethical means behaving ethically all the time, not only when it is convenient.
2. Public speakers need to take their ethical responsibilities as seriously as their strategic objectives.
3. They should do their best to follow the guidelines for ethical speechmaking whenever they address an audience.

III. Plagiarism is one of the most serious ethical lapses a public speaker can commit *(text pages 37-42)*.
A. Plagiarism is presenting another person's language or ideas as one's own.
B. Plagiarism is a serious offense.
1. In the classroom, it can be punished with a failing grade or even expulsion from school.
2. Outside the classroom, it can damage a speaker's reputation or career.
C. There are three types of plagiarism.
1. Global plagiarism is taking an entire speech from a single source and passing it off as one's own.
2. Patchwork plagiarism occurs when a speaker patches a speech together by copying verbatim from two or three sources.
a. Copying word for word from a few sources is no less plagiarism than is copying from a single source.
b. Giving a speech is just like putting one's name on a paper in an English class.
c. The speaker warrants that the speech represents his or her own thinking, beliefs, and language.
3. Incremental plagiarism occurs when a speaker fails to give credit for specific parts—increments—of the speech that are borrowed from other people.
a. One form of incremental plagiarism is quoting someone verbatim without attributing the words to that person.
b. A second form of incremental plagiarism is paraphrasing an author without citing the author.
D. There are several ways to avoid falling into the trap of plagiarism.
1. Speakers should start work on their speeches as early as possible so they will have plenty of time to prepare a speech that is truly their own.
2. Speakers should consult a large number of sources in their research so they do not rely too heavily on one or two sources.

3.   Speakers should be careful when taking research notes to distinguish among direct quotations, paraphrases, and their own ideas so as to avoid accidental plagiarism.

IV.   Listeners, as well as speakers, have ethical obligations *(text pages 42-44)*.
   A.   Listeners should be courteous and attentive during the speech.
      1.   This responsibility is a matter of civility in any situation.
      2.   It is especially important in a speech classroom because novice speakers need encouraging and supportive audiences.
   B.   Listeners should avoid prejudging the speaker.
      1.   In addition to being a major cause of poor listening, jumping to conclusions about a speaker's ideas has serious ethical implications.
      2.   Just as speakers have an obligation to prepare fully and conscientiously, listeners have a responsibility to hear a speaker out before deciding to accept or reject the speaker's message.
   C.   Listeners should maintain the free and open expression of ideas.
      1.   A free society depends on the right of individual citizens to speak their minds on public issues.
      2.   Just as speakers need to avoid name-calling and other tactics that can undermine free speech, so listeners have an obligation to maintain the right of speakers to be heard.
      3.   Listeners can disagree entirely with a message but still support the speaker's right to express it.

# Application Exercises *(from text pages 46-47)*

1.   Look back at the story of Felicia Robinson on page 31. Evaluate her dilemma in light of the guidelines for ethical speechmaking presented in this chapter. Explain what you believe would be the most ethical course of action in her case.

   **Discussion:** *This exercise is designed to have students apply the guidelines for ethical public speaking discussed in the chapter. The best way to conduct the exercise is to discuss each guideline individually and then apply it to the case of Felicia Robinson. The case study approach used in this exercise is the preferred method of teaching ethics today, and it works exceedingly well in conveying the nature of ethical judgment and its application to public speakers. If students prepare this exercise before coming to class, it should generate a fruitful discussion.*

2.    The issue of insulting and abusive speech—especially slurs directed against people on the basis of race, religion, gender, or sexual orientation—is extremely controversial. Do you believe society should punish such speech with criminal penalties? To what degree are colleges and universities justified in trying to discipline students who engage in such speech? Do you feel it is proper to place any boundaries on free expression in order to prohibit insulting and abusive speech? Why or why not? Be prepared to explain your ideas in class.

> **Discussion:** *Few issues have generated more heat on college campuses—and in American society at large—in recent years than abusive language and how to deal with it. Most controversial is the question of whether schools can justifiably impose restrictions on "hate speech" against racial or religious minorities, women, gays, lesbians, and people with physical disabilities. Defensible arguments can be made on both sides of the question. The purpose of this exercise is not to have students reach the "right" answer, but to spark intelligent discussion. For an excellent overview of these issues, see Thomas L. Tedford,* Freedom of Speech in the United States, *2nd ed. (New York: McGraw-Hill, 1993) pp. 180-186, which is reprinted on pages 87-93 of this manual.*

3.    All the following situations could arise in your speech class. Identify the ethical issues in each and explain what, as a responsible speaker or listener, your course of action would be.

a.    You are speaking on the topic of prison reform. In your research, you run across two public opinion polls. One of them, an independent survey by the Gallup poll, shows that a majority of people in your state oppose your position. The other poll, suspect in its methods and conducted by a partisan organization, says a majority of people in your state support your position. Which poll do you cite in your speech? If you cite the second poll, do you point out its shortcomings?

> **Discussion:** *Like the other two scenarios in this exercise, this one is designed to relate ethical questions directly to situations students will face in their classroom speeches. In this scenario, of course, the most ethical decision would be to use the Gallup poll rather than the partisan poll, even though the latter supports the speaker's position. It would be especially unethical to use the partisan poll without indicating its weaknesses to the audience. This would clearly violate the speaker's obligation to be honest in presenting facts and figures.*

b.    When listening to an informative speech by one of your classmates, you realize that much of it is plagiarized from a magazine article you read a couple of weeks ago. What do you do? Do you say something when your instructor asks for comments about the speech? Do you mention your concern to the instructor after class? Do you talk with the speaker? Do you remain silent?

> **Discussion:**    *This case raises interesting questions about plagiarism and the ethical obligations of listeners. If faced with this situation in real life, most students would doubtless remain silent—not because they approved of the speaker's behavior, but because they would not want to "tell on" the speaker. Some might argue that even though plagiarism is wrong, students are under no ethical obligation to report someone who commits plagiarism in a speech. Because this is a complex issue, few classes are likely to reach agreement on it. They can, however, reach agreement on the fact that plagiarism is ethically wrong and that students who commit it should face stiff penalties if they are detected.*

c.    While researching your persuasive speech, you find a quotation from an article by a highly respected expert that will nail down one of your most important points. But as you read the rest of the article, you realize the author does not in fact support the policy you are advocating. Should you still include the quotation in your speech?

> **Discussion:** *This scenario gets at a fairly subtle point about ethics and public speaking. Yet it is a point worth discussing, for it shows that being an ethical speaker is not just a matter of "big" obligations such as having ethically sound goals and avoiding plagiarism. It also shows that one needs to consider the facts of a situation carefully in making ethical judgments.*
>
> *In the scenario at hand, at least three defensible ethical positions can be advanced: (1) That the speaker should not quote the expert in support of any point if the expert does not support the speaker's policy; (2) That the speaker can ethically quote the expert on one aspect of the topic (the existence of a problem, for example) as long as the speaker does not state or imply that the expert supports the speaker's position in general; (3) That the speaker cannot ethically quote the expert on any aspect of the topic unless the speaker states explicitly that the expert does not support the policy advocated by the speaker. The purpose of class discussion on this scenario is not to reach unanimous agreement on one of these three positions, but to make students aware of the ethical issues involved and, in the process, to heighten their sensitivity to the wide range of ethical issues faced by public speakers.*

## Additional Exercises and Class Activities

1.   Lead a class discussion in which students develop a code of ethical speaking for their classroom. The final product of the discussion will be a list titled "Ethical Speaking for Our Speech Class." By the end of the discussion, the entire class should not only agree on the content of the list, but should pledge themselves to follow it throughout the term.

> **Discussion:**   *This exercise works extremely well in promoting dialogue about the ethics of public speaking. It also relates abstract issues of ethics to the situation in which students will be giving speeches for the next several months. By developing their own rules for ethical speechmaking, students will be more committed to following those rules.*
>
> *Don't be surprised if much of the discussion turns on questions related to plagiarism. This is probably the most pressing ethical issue facing students in a speech classroom, and many do not have a clear understanding of what constitutes plagiarism and what does not.*
>
> *As students develop their code, encourage them to be specific in their criteria. For example, rather than saying "We will not plagiarize our speeches," they should try to develop more precise statements such as "We will not copy our speeches from the work of current or previous students," or "We will always cite the sources of ideas or supporting materials that we use in our speeches."*

2.   Hand out the checklist for ethical speaking printed on the next page of this manual. Have students keep the checklist with their course materials throughout the term.

> **Discussion:** *This checklist provides students a handy guide to the major ethical issues they are likely to confront when preparing their classroom speeches. Handing it out at the start of the term reinforces the message that students need to take their ethical responsibilities seriously. It also helps minimize the likelihood of students claiming, later in the term, that they were not properly informed about their ethical responsibilities. (With the exception of item 5 which deals with emotional appeal, all the items on the guidelines are mentioned in this chapter of the textbook. The ethics of emotional appeal is discussed in Chapter 16, pages 389-390).*

# CHECKLIST FOR ETHICAL PUBLIC SPEAKING

1. Have I examined my goals to make sure they are ethically sound?

   a. Can I defend my goals on ethical grounds if they are questioned or challenged?
   b. Would I want other people to know my true motives in presenting this speech?

2. Have I fulfilled my ethical obligation to prepare fully for the speech?

   a. Have I done a thorough job of studying and researching the topic?
   b. Have I prepared diligently so as not to communicate erroneous or misleading information to my listeners?

3. Is the speech free of plagiarism?

   a. Can I vouch that the speech represents my own work, my own thinking, my own language?
   b. Do I cite the sources of all quotations and paraphrases?

4. Am I honest in what I say in the speech?

   a. Is the speech free of any false or deliberately deceptive statements?
   b. Does the speech present statistics, testimony, and other kinds of evidence fairly and accurately?
   c. Does the speech contain valid reasoning?
   d. If the speech includes visual aids, do they present facts honestly and reliably?

5. Do I use emotional appeals ethically?

   a. Are emotional appeals appropriate to the speech topic?
   b. Is the speech built upon a firm foundation of facts and logic in addition to employing emotional appeal?

6. Do I use the power of language ethically?

   a. Do I avoid name-calling and other forms of abusive language?
   b. Does my language show respect for the right of free speech and expression?

7. All in all, have I made a conscious effort to put ethical principles into practice in preparing my speech?

3.    Lead a class discussion in which students develop a code of ethical listening for their speech classroom. The final product of the discussion will be a list titled "Ethical Listening for Our Speech Class." By the end of the discussion, the entire class should not only agree on the content of the list, but should pledge themselves to follow it throughout the term.

> **Discussion:** *A companion to Additional Exercise 1 above, this is an excellent way to get students thinking about the ethical obligations of listeners. Like Exercise 1, it relates ethical issues directly to the speech classroom and gives those issues more immediacy than might otherwise be the case. Also like Exercise 1, it allows students to formulate their own ethical criteria, thereby increasing the likelihood that they will feel committed to following those criteria.*
>
> *As with Exercise 1, encourage students to be specific as they develop their code. Rather than saying "We will listen courteously and attentively," for instance, they should work for statements such as "We will not do work for other classes while listening to our classmates' speeches," or "Even if we disagree with a speaker's position at the start of a speech, we will listen with an open mind to the entire speech before making a judgment about it." One way to generate criteria is to ask students what kinds of attitudes and behavior they would like to see in listeners to their own speeches.*

4.    Give each student the following assignment:  Identify a situation in your life in which an issue related to speech ethics was involved. The issue could have affected you either as a speaker or as a listener. Work up a brief analysis in which you explain the situation and the ethical issue (or issues) involved.

> **Discussion:** *This exercise can work very well to promote class discussion about ethical issues in public speaking. Because it deals with issues that are related to the experience of each student, the exercise often gives the discussion more immediacy than dealing with hypothetical ethical scenarios. It usually works best when given as a homework assignment so students have plenty of time to develop their analyses.*

5.    If your class meets during a presidential election year, ethical issues are bound to arise in relation to the candidates' campaign rhetoric. Such issues might include the use of negative campaigning, the distortion of evidence in campaign speeches and advertisements, the use of name-calling to denigrate the opposing candidate or party, and the tendency of candidates to say different things to different groups of voters. Set aside time periodically during the term to deal

with such issues—especially when they achieve prominence in press coverage of the campaign.

> **Discussion:** *Because presidential campaigns usually generate fairly intense reactions, they provide an excellent vehicle for getting students interested in questions of communication ethics. They also have a tendency to provoke heated discussion—especially among students who are fiercely partisan to one candidate or another. The challenge for instructors is to keep discussion focused on ethical issues rather than on the general merits and policies of each candidate. It is important that students learn to separate their feelings for and against the candidates from their reasoned judgments about the ethics of the candidates' rhetoric.*
>
> *The aims of this exercise can be achieved either through informal class discussion or through more formal assignments in which students—working individually or in groups—prepare systematic analyses for presentation in class. The same kind of exercise can also be used during local or state elections.*

6. Have students create "Speech Ethics" scrapbooks in which they keep magazine and newspaper articles that deal with ethical issues in public speaking. Articles can touch on any aspect of speech ethics, including consideration of a speaker's goals, preparation, truthfulness, evidence, reasoning, language, emotional appeal, or impact on audiences. Articles can also deal with the ethics of listening. Students should be sure to record the source and date of each article. Collect the scrapbooks near the end of the term.

> **Discussion:** *Once students start thinking about ethical issues and looking for articles that deal with them, it is astounding how many they can find. Although some instructors use this exercise as a required assignment, others use it as an extra-credit opportunity. In either case, if done properly it can be of considerable benefit for the students. Not only does it help sensitize them to the range, complexity, and importance of ethical issues in public speaking, but it often gets them to reading newspapers and magazines more regularly than they would otherwise.*

7. Students often ask about ghostwriting when dealing with the issue of plagiarism. Why, they ask, it is ethical for politicians, business leaders, and other public figures to have ghostwriters and unethical for students to have someone else write their speeches? If students raise this issue, be prepared to conduct a class discussion on the relationship between plagiarism and ghostwriting.

**Discussion:** *Scholars and popular commentators alike have spent a great deal of time on the subject of ghostwriting. Most regard it as ethically acceptable among politicians, business leaders, and other public figures as long as (1) the speaker does not deceive the audience by claiming to have written a speech when in fact it is ghostwritten, and (2) the speaker takes full responsibility for what he or she says regardless of who may have written the actual words of the speech.*

*Speeches given in the classroom, however, are quite different. Students are in a learning situation. They cannot learn the skills of speech preparation by having someone else compose their speeches for them. Nor can their performance in class be fairly evaluated if they do not do their own work. As noted in the chapter, when students stand up to deliver a speech, it is just like putting their name on a paper in their English class—they are declaring that the speech represents their own work, their own thinking, their own language.*

*For instructors who wish to assign students a brief reading on the ethical issues involved in ghostwriting, Richard L. Johannesen, Ethics in Human Communication, 3rd ed. (Prospect Heights, Ill: Waveland, 1990), pp. 133-135, provides an excellent overview. Ari Posner's "The Culture of Plagiarism," New Republic (April 18, 1988), pp. 19-24, is highly readable and takes a hard stand against the growing reliance on ghostwriters in a variety of professions.*

## Words that Wound: Abusive and Threatening Language*
### Thomas L. Tedford

Several years ago, a black architecture student returned some merchandise to a store and requested a refund. In order to get the refund, he was required to sign a form upon which an employee of the store had written, "Arrogant Nigger refuses exchange—says he doesn't like products." The student sued for damages but lost the case because the court found such language not "sufficiently severe" to merit damages. In the late 1980s, on the campus of the University of Wisconsin, minority students vigorously protested a mock slave auction. And at Tufts University in 1990, a male student was suspended for selling T-shirts stating "15 reasons why beer is better than women at Tufts." The fighting-words rule, with its focus on words spoken in a face-to-face confrontation between individuals, has little application to the types of nonconfrontational expression illustrated by these examples.

Society's concern with abusive speech and expressions of hatred is not new. In 1952 the U.S. Supreme Court upheld the constitutionality of the Illinois group libel law that made it a crime to portray persons of any "race, color, creed or religion" as depraved, criminal, or unchaste. Although Illinois later dropped the group libel law from its criminal code, the concept is still alive and is proposed from time to time in various legislative bodies as a way of dealing with hate messages. Other cases relating to the issue include the 1976-1977 controversy about permitting neo-Nazis to parade on the city streets of Skokie, Illinois, and the efforts by some feminists to permit suits against those who disseminate pornography perceived as demeaning to women. In order to analyze this issue in an organized way, we will first look at the problem as it concerns society at large. We will then examine what a number of institutions of higher education have done in recent years about "words that wound."

### Abusive Speech in Society at Large

The U.S. Supreme Court has so narrowed the fighting-words doctrine and the law of defamation that much insulting or threatening expression is not actionable under either criminal or tort law. This development has called forth arguments for change. Kent Greenawalt, for example, in *Speech, Crime, and the Uses of Language*, asserts four harms that result from abusive speech: (1) the threat of immediate violence, (2) offensiveness of the language to those who hear it, (3) psychological hurt to individuals, and (4) the long-term reinforcement of negative social attitudes (such as racism, sexism, and homophobia) that result from such expression. He

---

*From Thomas L. Tedford, *Freedom of Speech in the United States*, 2nd ed. (New York: McGraw-Hill, 1993), pp. 180-186. Reprinted with permission of Thomas L. Tedford and McGraw-Hill, Inc.

recommends that suits for damages be allowed in some instances and that criminal action be permitted in others. Let us look further at what proponents of civil and criminal action have to say about "words that wound."

*Civil Remedies for Abusive Speech*

One remedy for the victim of abusive speech is to sue for damages under the developing tort of intentional infliction of emotional distress. Although "emotional distress" is not as well established or as clearly defined as are defamation and invasion of privacy, some plaintiffs using the tort in racial harassment suits have won their cases. Delgado summarizes three such cases: one in which a black truck driver was called a "goddam nigger" and was fired from his job; a second in which a native of East India was called "a black nigger" and "member of an inferior race" by his job supervisor; and a third in which a waitress called a customer a "black son-of-a-bitch" and a "nigger."

Another proposal is to create a *new* tort which permits suits for class-based insults and epithets. Greenawalt proposes that when extreme emotional distress cannot be shown, that suits be allowed for speech that has the "intent to demean" or to inflict "grave humiliations" on persons. In his study of the harm caused by racist expression, Richard Delgado concludes that "not only those to whom racial insults are addressed but also the perpetrators and society as a whole are victimized." In response, Delgado recommends an independent tort for racial slurs. In order to prevail, he argues, the plaintiff should be required to prove that the language was "intended to demean through reference to race," that the person being sued knew the words were racially demeaning, and that the racial insult be recognized as such by a "reasonable person." He illustrates his proposal by saying that an epithet such as "You damn nigger" would be actionable, but that a phrase such as "you incompetent fool" would not be actionable because it lacks a racial component.

*Criminal Remedies for Abusive Speech*

A second approach to abusive and threatening speech is to make it a crime. Proponents of this approach argue that messages of hate should not be protected by the First Amendment, and that specific types of hate speech should be criminalized. One proposal for accomplishing this is to revive the concept of group libel. In her essay "Group Libel Revisited," Ruth McGaffey summarizes the arguments of those who favor group libel laws, and provides an example of such a law that was recommended to the city of Milwaukee in 1975. The proposed ordinance criminalized expression that portrayed "depravity, criminality, unchastity or lack of virtue of a class of citizens, or any race, color, creed or religion" or that exposed these groups to "contempt, derision or obloquy . . . which is productive of breach of the peace or riots." Although this proposal was not enacted into law, it does illustrate the group libel approach.

Another approach is to create a specific crime of racist speech. Greenawalt recommends this solution for the worst forms of hate messages, arguing that society should support narrowly drawn statutes criminalizing speech that humiliates and intimidates. The idea is more fully developed by Mari Matsuda, a Japanese-American professor of law at the University of Hawaii, who proposes that racist speech so devalues and degrades those toward whom it is addressed that it should be criminalized. Her real-life examples include a black worker who suffered direct racial epithets (complete with references to the Ku Klux Klan) and death threats on the job (including a noose placed near his work station) and the placing of swastikas near the desks of racial minorities employed in a fire department that was newly integrated.

Matsuda explains her "narrow definition" of the racist expression that she would criminalize, stating that such expression presents ideas that are "so historically untenable, so dangerous, and so tied to perpetuation of violence and degradation" of minorities that they are "outside the realm of protected discourse." Specifically, "racist hate messages" have three identifying characteristics, all three of which must be present for a criminal action to take place, namely: (1) the message must be one of "racial inferiority"; (2) it must be "directed against a historically oppressed group"; and (3) it must be "persecutorial, hateful, and degrading."

With proposals such as the above being argued in law schools and in legal journals, students of the First Amendment should be alert to developments in the legislatures and the courts. Meanwhile, on many college campuses in recent years, proponents of punishment for insulting and harassing expression have received a sympathetic ear. The result has been the development of new policies of "correct" campus speech. In response, there have been several legal challenges to the enforcement of those policies. Let us examine the issue in more detail.

## Abusive Speech on the Campus

In December of 1987, at the University of Connecticut, eight Asian-American students on their way to a dance were harassed for almost an hour by a group of football players who spat on them, called them "Oriental faggots," and challenged them to a fight. In the spring of 1989, at the University of Arizona in Tempe, a number of white fraternity members harassed a black student who was walking past some fraternity houses by chanting "Coon," "Nigger," and "Porchmonkey." A fight developed and police were required to restore order. In response to incidents of this type, a number of American colleges and universities have adopted codes of conduct prohibiting such harassment. Typically, the codes address insulting or threatening speech directed at racial or religious minorities, women, handicapped persons, and homosexuals. Punishment for violators ranges from a reprimand to expulsion from the institution. The discussion below first examines how the courts have responded to several controversies that have resulted from campus rules against abusive expression. This is followed by a summary of the position of a leading civil liberties organization—the American Civil Liberties Union—on the issue of abusive expression on the college campus.

## Campus-Speech Rules and the Courts

The initial response of a number of institutions of higher learning to abusive speech was to develop broad rules and regulations against abusive expression. These broad regulations covered a variety of forms of expression. For example, the University of Connecticut approved a rule that punished students for the use of "derogatory names, inappropriately directed laughter, inconsiderate jokes, and conspicuous exclusion [of another student] from conversation." The rule developed by the University of Pennsylvania prohibits language that "stigmatizes or victimizes individuals" as well as expression that "creates an intimidating or offensive environment." In 1991 a student who shouted racial epithets was permanently expelled from Brown University under school policy that prohibits "subjection of another person, group, or class of persons, to inappropriate, abusive, threatening, or demeaning actions, based on race, religion, gender, handicap, ethnicity, national origin, or sexual orientation."

One of the broadest regulations was developed at the University of Michigan. Entitled the "Policy on Discrimination and Discriminatory Harassment of Students in the University Environment," Michigan's rule was adopted by the board of regents in 1988. Although it excluded campus publications, such as the *Michigan Daily*—evidently on First Amendment grounds—it did cover university housing and "educational and academic centers, such as classroom buildings, libraries, research laboratories, recreation and study centers." Its provisions include punishment for:

> Any behavior, verbal or physical, that stigmatizes or victimizes an individual on the basis of race, ethnicity, religion, sex, sexual orientation, creed, national origin, ancestry, age, marital status, handicap or Vietnam-era veteran status. . .
> Sexual advances, requests for sexual favors, and verbal or physical conduct that stigmatizes or victimizes an individual on the basis of sex or sexual orientation where such behavior . . . [c]reates an intimidating, hostile, or demeaning environment for educational pursuits, employment or participation in University sponsored extra-curricular activities.

The policy was challenged in federal court by a University of Michigan graduate student in psychology who was concerned that the rule would prevent free academic discussion of a variety of controversial theories in his field, especially those claiming "biologically-based differences between sexes and races." The U.S. district court ruled for the student, declaring the policy unconstitutional both on First Amendment grounds and on the due process grounds of vagueness.

First, the court found the language of the policy so *overbroad* that it swept within its scope a significant amount of expression that was protected by the First Amendment. Second, the court found the policy *vague*—especially its use of terms such as "stigmatize" and "victimize." Such terms are not clear, as evidenced by the fact that even the counsel for the university could not explain what they meant when asked to do so by the judge during the hearings. Consequently, the court observed, students "of common understanding were necessarily forced to guess at whether a comment about a controversial issue would later be found to be sanctionable under the policy."

Two years after the Michigan decision, a U.S. district court in Wisconsin declared unconstitutional a similar hate-speech rule from the University of Wisconsin. The Wisconsin regulation, which was a part of the student conduct code, authorized disciplinary action against students in nonacademic situations for racist or discriminatory expression directed at an individual that demeaned "the race, sex, religion, color, creed, disability, sexual orientation, national origin, ancestry or age of the individual or individuals" or for expression that created a "hostile or demeaning environment" in educational activity. The district court rejected the university's *Chaplinsky*-based arguments in support of the regulation, announcing that the rule in question was unconstitutional for both overbreadth and vagueness. Concerning overbreadth, the Court noted that *Chaplinsky* was limited to words spoken in direct confrontation that were likely to cause an immediate breach of the peace. The university rule exceeded the scope of this requirement, for it is not limited to direct confrontation and imminent breach of the peace. Second, the Court said that the rule was vague "because it does not make clear whether the prohibited speech must actually create a hostile educational environment or whether the speaker must merely intend to create such an environment." For these reasons, said the district court, the Wisconsin regulation violates the Constitution.

Finally, in the late 1980s a tenured professor of philosophy at the City College of New York on several occasions published his view that "on average, blacks are significantly less intelligent than whites." For this he was threatened and his classes were disrupted by student protesters. Although the class disruptions violated school regulations, the college did not stop them. Also, the college appointed a faculty committee to investigate the controversy "to review the question of when speech both in and outside the classroom may go beyond the protection of academic freedom or become conduct unbecoming a member of the faculty." The committee, meeting in secret, did not announce the criteria for its deliberations and did not invite the teacher they were investigating to testify. Despite this, they concluded that the professor's comments on race were unprofessional and inappropriate, and they approved the creation of "shadow sections" (duplicate courses taught by other instructors) of the professor's courses so that students could avoid his classes.

Concerned about his freedom to speak, to teach, and to publish freely, the professor brought suit in federal court, alleging violations of his constitutional rights.

The U.S. District Court for the Southern District of New York ruled for the professor, announcing that the college had violated his First and Fourteenth Amendment rights. The Court observed that the professor had been "deprived of the freedom to which he is entitled to write and to speak in the areas of his scholarly interest." Also, because he had been deterred from seeking outside grants to fund his research, and because his classroom discussions had been "inhibited," he "was improperly deprived of his Fourteenth Amendment liberty and property interests."

As broadly worded regulations and *ad hoc* actions against "politically incorrect" campus speech are rejected as unconstitutional by the courts, some schools are turning to policies that are more narrowly drawn. In trying to develop rules which school officials hope will stand up in court, college and university attorneys often adapt principles of the fighting-words doctrine to the campus situation. This occurred in the late 1980s at the University of Connecticut after student Nina Wu hung a "humorous" poster on the door of her dormitory room that listed those who were "welcome," "tolerated," and to be "shot on sight." Those to be shot on sight included "bimbos, preppies, racists," and, according to testimony, "homos." Two students who did not think the poster was funny filed a complaint with the university under the antiharassment provisions of the student conduct code. According to these provisions, students were prohibited from communicating "slurs or epithets based on race, sex, ethnic origin, religion, or sexual orientation." University officials agreed with the complaint (with special focus on the "homos" epithet), and in April 1989, expelled Wu from university residential and dining halls. Wu sued the university in federal district court, charging a violation of her First Amendment rights. In a settlement approved by the court, the university restored her room-and-board privileges.

Furthermore, after losing the Wu case, the university agreed to change its antiharassment policy to a narrow one based on the fighting-words principle. The revised rule says "The face to face use of 'fighting words' by students to harass any person(s) on university property . . . is prohibited." The rule goes on to explain that the words must be used in a way that is "likely to provoke an immediate violent reaction," and words that include terms "widely recognized to be derogatory references to race, ethnicity, religion, sex, sexual orientation, disability and other personal characteristics." Time will tell whether or not this revised policy, and similar narrowly focused campus regulations aimed at "words that wound," will stand up under legal challenge.

*Campus-Speech Rules and Civil Liberties*

In 1990 the American Civil Liberties Union (ACLU), one of the nation's leading defenders of constitutional rights, formulated a position on the issue of abusive speech on the campus. Entitled "Free Speech and Bias on College Campuses," the ACLU policy statement begins by recognizing the problem of racist, sexist, and homophobic bias on the campus, and by proposing that, instead of restricting speech, colleges take constructive steps to combat the problem. The policy emphasizes the necessity for "freedom of thought and expression" in the field of education, and asserts that all members of "the academic community have the right to hold and to express views that others may find repugnant, offensive, or emotionally distressing." Consequently, the policy continues, the ACLU "opposes all campus regulations which interfere with the freedom of professors, students and administrators to teach, learn, discuss and debate or to express ideas, opinions or feelings" in the classroom and in public or private discourse.

After affirming its opposition to disciplinary codes that "reach beyond permissible boundaries into the realm of protected speech," the policy adds that the ACLU is not opposed to disciplinary codes "aimed at restricting acts of intimidation and invasion of privacy." The ACLU recognizes that the terms "harassment," "intimidation," and "invasion of privacy" are imprecise, and warns against applying them in an overbroad manner. The policy emphasizes that the terms are used here to describe *conduct* directed at a specific person or persons that is intended to "frighten, coerce, or unreasonably harry or intrude upon its target." A threatening phone call to a minority student's dormitory room is given as an example of such punishable conduct. The ACLU policy continues: "The fact that words may be used in connection with otherwise actionable conduct does not immunize such conduct from appropriate regulation." In addition to intimidating phone calls, examples of unprotected conduct that include elements of expression are threats of attack, extortion, and blackmail.

Finally, the ACLU policy lists a number of steps that colleges can take to address bigotry without offending First Amendment freedoms. These recommendations include the following: having the administration, faculty, and students undertake an organized effort to publicize the school's commitment to understanding and tolerance; conducting workshops, programs, and counseling on the subject of bias in its various forms; formulating a comprehensive plan for responding promptly to incidents of harassment and discrimination; working actively to attract more minorities to the administration, faculty, and the student body; and offering courses of study in various manifestations of prejudice.

# Extra Teaching and Learning Resources

## General

Arnett, Ronald C. "The Practical Philosophy of Communication Ethics and Free Speech as the Foundation for Speech Communication." *Communication Quarterly*, 38 (1990), 208-217.

Arnett, Ronald C. "The Status of Communication Ethics Scholarship in Speech Communication Journals from 1915 to 1985." *Central States Speech Journal*, 38 (1987), 44-61.

Blanchard, Kenneth, and Peale, Norman Vincent. *The Power of Ethical Management*. New York: Ballantine Books, 1988.

Bok, Sissila. *Lying: Moral Choice in Public and Private Life*. New York: Pantheon Books, 1978.

Bowie, Norman E. (ed.). *Making Moral Decisions*. New York: McGraw-Hill, 1985.

Day, Louis A. *Ethics in Media Communication: Cases and Controversies*. Belmont, Calif.: Wadsworth, 1991.

Denton, Robert E. (ed.). *Ethical Dimensions of Political Communication*. New York: Praeger, 1991.

Ekman, Paul. *Telling Lies: An Analysis of Lies, Liars, and Lie Catchers*. New York: Norton, 1985.

Greenawalt, Kent. *Speech, Crime, and the Uses of Language*. New York: Oxford University Press, 1989.

Greenberg, Karen Joy (ed.). *Conversations on Communication Ethics*. Norwood, N.J.: Ablex, 1991.

Haiman, Franklyn S. *Speech and Law in a Free Society*. Chicago: University of Chicago Press, 1981.

Haiman, Franklyn S. *"Speech Acts" and the First Amendment*. Carbondale, Ill.: Southern Illinois University Press, 1994.

Herrick, James A. "Rhetoric, Ethics, and Virtue." *Communication Studies*, 43 (1992), 133-149.

Jaska, James A., and Pritchard, Michael S. *Communication Ethics: Methods of Analysis*. Belmont, Calif.: Wadsworth, 1988.

Jensen, Vernon J. "Teaching Ethics in Speech Communication." *Communication Education*, 34 (1985), 324-330.

Johannesen, Richard L. *Ethics in Communication*, 3rd ed. Prospect Heights, Ill.: Waveland Press, 1990.

Katz, Stephen B. "The Ethics of Expediency: Classical Rhetoric, Technology, and the Holocaust." *College English*, 54 (1992), 255-275.

Mallon, Thomas. *Stolen Words: Forays into the Origins and Ravages of Plagiarism*. New York: Penguin Books, 1991.

Noddings, Nel. *Caring: A Feminine Approach to Ethics and Moral Education*. Berkeley, Calif.: University of California Press, 1984.

Nyberg, David. *The Varnished Truth: Truth Telling and Deceiving in Ordinary Life*. Chicago: University of Chicago Press, 1993.

O'Neil, Robert M. "An Inquiry into the Legal and Ethical Problems of Campus Hate Speech." In Raymond S. Rodgers (ed.), *Free Speech Yearbook: 1991*. Carbondale, Ill.: Southern Illinois University Press, 1991, pp. 26-30.

Posner, Ari. "The Culture of Plagiarism." *New Republic* (April 18, 1988), 19-20, 22, 24.

Tedford, Thomas L. *Freedom of Speech in the United States*, 2nd ed. New York: McGraw-Hill, 1993.

Rachels, James. *The Elements of Moral Philosophy*, 2nd ed. New York: McGraw-Hill, 1993.

Rachels, James. *The Right Thing To Do: Basic Readings in Moral Philosophy*. New York: Random House, 1989.

Smolla, Rodney M. *Free Speech in an Open Society*. New York: Random House, 1992.

Sunstein, Cass R. *Democracy and the Problem of Free Speech*. New York: Free Press, 1993.

Walker, Samuel. *Hate Speech: The History of an American Controversy*. Lincoln, Neb.: University of Nebraska Press, 1994.

Wellman, Carl. *Morals and Ethics*, 2nd ed. Englewood Cliffs, N.J.: Prentice-Hall, 1988.

Yoos, George E. "Rational Appeal and the Ethics of Advocacy." In Robert Connors, Lisa Ede, and Andrea Lunsford (eds.), *Essays in Classical Rhetoric and Modern Discourse*. Carbondale, Ill.: Southern Illinois University Press, 1984, pp. 82-97.

## Films and Videos

"Beyond Hate." Educational Video Group (1987). 60 minutes.

"Crediting Your Sources." RMI Media Productions (1991). 30 minutes.

"Diversity Series." Quality Media Resources (1993). Four-module set; 20 minutes per
module.

"First Amendment Freedoms." Insight Media (1989). 30 minutes.

"For Goodness Sake!" CRM Films (1993). 24 minutes.

# Chapter 3 Listening

## Chapter Objectives

*After reading this chapter, students should be able to:*

1. Explain the difference between hearing and listening.

2. Define the four different kinds of listening and explain their relationship to critical thinking.

3. Explain why good listening is important to effective speechmaking.

4. Identify the four major causes of poor listening.

5. Discuss the six ways to become a better listener presented in the text.

## Chapter Outline

I. Listening is an important skill to master *(text pages 50-51)*.
   A. Hearing and listening are different processes.
      1. Hearing is a physiological process that involves the vibration of sound waves on the eardrums and the firing of electrochemical impulses from the inner ear to the brain.
      2. Listening is a mental process that involves paying close attention to, and making sense of, what is heard.
   B. Most people are poor listeners.
      1. Researchers find that most people only understand about half of what they hear.
      2. After two days most people retain less than 25 percent of the original message.
   C. In our communication-oriented age, listening is more important than ever.

1. Listening is an important job skill.
   a. Effective listeners hold higher positions and are promoted more often than poor listeners.
   b. Business managers rank listening as the communication skill most crucial to their jobs.
   c. A survey of Fortune 500 companies showed that more than half provide listening training for their employees.
2. Effective listening is useful in all aspects of life, including academics.
   a. Close to 90 percent of class time in American colleges and universities is spent listening.
   b. Students with the highest grades are usually those with the strongest listening skills.

D. Listening is also an excellent way to improve one's speaking skills.
   1. Speakers get many of their ideas by listening to lectures, television, radio, etc.
   2. Listening attentively to good speeches is an excellent way to improve one's own speaking skills.

II. Listening skills are closely linked to critical thinking *(text pages 51-52)*.
   A. There are four types of listening.
      1. Appreciative listening is listening for pleasure or enjoyment.
         a. Listening to music is one example of appreciative listening.
         b. Listening to a comedy routine is another example of appreciative listening.
      2. Empathic listening is listening to provide emotional support for the speaker.
         a. A counselor practices empathic listening.
         b. Friends practice empathic listening when they discuss something with a person in distress.
      3. Comprehensive listening focuses on understanding the speaker's message.
         a. Listening to classroom lectures is one example of comprehensive listening.
         b. Getting directions to a friend's house is another instance of comprehensive listening.
      4. Critical listening involves evaluating a message either to accept it or reject it.
         a. Listening to a sales pitch is an opportunity for critical listening.
         b. Listening to a campaign speech is another opportunity to listen critically.
   B. Because comprehensive and critical listening are closely tied to critical thinking, they are most important for public speaking.

1. Several critical thinking skills are central to comprehensive listening.
   a. One such skill is the ability to summarize information.
   b. Another is the ability to recall facts.
   c. A third is the ability to distinguish main points from minor points.
2. Several critical thinking skills are important to critical listening.
   a. Separating fact from opinion is one.
   b. Spotting weaknesses in reasoning is another.
   c. Judging the quality of evidence is yet another.
3. Listening and critical thinking are so closely allied that training in listening is really training in thinking.

III. There are four main causes of poor listening *(text pages 52-57)*.
   A. Not concentrating is one cause of poor listening.
      1. Because the human brain processes information very efficiently, it is easy for listeners to become distracted.
         a. The human brain can process from 400 to 800 words a minute.
         b. This efficiency leaves people with a great deal of extra brain time to think about other things than what a speaker is saying.
      2. Because of this, listeners must force themselves to concentrate on a speaker's message.
   B. Listening too hard can also interfere with effective listening.
      1. Listening too hard involves trying to remember every detail of a message.
      2. When listeners focus on every detail, they often miss the speaker's main points.
   C. Jumping to conclusions also prevents listeners from hearing messages accurately.
      1. One way we jump to conclusions is by assuming we know what someone is going to say before that person actually speaks.
      2. Another way we jump to conclusions is by prematurely rejecting a speaker's ideas as boring or misguided without hearing the entire message.
   D. Focusing on delivery and personal appearance instead of listening to a speaker's message is another cause of poor listening.
      1. Some people are so put off by personal appearance, accents, or unusual vocal mannerisms that they do not bother to listen.
      2. This type of emotional censorship is deadly to communication.

IV. There are six ways to improve one's listening skills *(text pages 57-63)*.
   A. The first step in improving listening skills is to take listening seriously.
      1. Good listening is a skill that demands practice and self-discipline.

2.   One can become a better listener by working to improve listening skills.

B.   A second way to improve listening skills is to resist distractions.
   1.   Effective listeners make a conscious effort keep their minds on what the speaker is saying.
   2.   When they find their minds wandering, they force their attention back to the speech.

C.   A third way to improve listening skills is not to be diverted by appearance or delivery.
   1.   Effective listeners set aside preconceived negative judgments about a speaker's looks or manner of speech.
   2.   They also guard against being beguiled by a speaker's attractive appearance or hypnotic delivery skills.

D.   A fourth way to improve listening skills is to suspend judgment until hearing a speaker's full message.
   1.   Effective listeners realize they will hear things with which they disagree, but they make an effort not to reject a speaker out of hand.
   2.   They assess a speaker's evidence and reasoning before making a judgment.

E.   A fifth way to improve listening skills is to focus one's listening.
   1.   Effective listeners focus on a speaker's main points.
   2.   Effective listeners focus on the quality of a speaker's evidence.
      a.   They seek to assess whether the evidence is accurate.
      b.   They try to determine whether the evidence comes from objective sources.
      c.   They ask whether the evidence is relevant to the speaker's claims.
      d.   They gauge whether there is sufficient evidence to support the speaker's claims.
   3.   Effective listeners also focus on speaking techniques they can use in their own speeches.
      a.   They analyze the effectiveness of the introduction.
      b.   They assess the organization of the speech.
      c.   They study the speaker's use of language.
      d.   They diagnose the speaker's delivery.

F.   A sixth way to improve listening skills is to develop strong note-taking skills.
   1.   There is substantial research to show that note taking enhances listening.
   2.   Unfortunately, many people suffer from one or another of two weaknesses in note taking.
      a.   The first weakness is attempting to write down a speaker's every word.

b. The second weakness is concentrating only on fascinating tidbits of information.
3. Efficient note takers develop two good habits, both of which lead to stronger listening skills.
   a. They learn to concentrate on a speaker's main ideas and supporting materials.
   b. They use key-word outlines to summarize the speaker's message.

## Application Exercises *(from text page 64)*

1. Which of the four causes of poor listening do you consider the most important? Choose a specific case of poor listening in which you were involved. Explain what went wrong.

   **Discussion:** *This exercise is designed to have students think about the causes of poor listening in terms of their personal experience. If the students prepare this exercise before coming to class, it should generate a rich variety of examples for class discussion.*

2. Write a candid evaluation of your major strengths and weaknesses as a listener. Explain what steps you need to take to become a better listener. Be specific.

   **Discussion:** *This should be handled much like Exercise 2 in Chapter 1. At the end of the course, students can be asked to assess their progress both as speakers and as listeners. As part of this exercise, you may want to have students complete the Listening Self-Evaluation Form on the next page of this manual. The form is adapted from Lyman K. Steil, Larry L. Barker, and Kittie W. Watson,* Effective Listening *(New York: Random House, 1983).*

3. Watch the lead story on *60 Minutes* this week. Using the key-word method of note taking, record the main ideas of the story.

   **Discussion:** *This can be a good diagnostic tool to gauge which students take notes effectively and which do not. Because the lead story on 60 Minutes is usually somewhat controversial, this exercise can also illustrate how a person's listening is affected by his or her attitudes on the speaker's topic. For an alternative to this exercise, see items three and four under Additional Exercises and Activities for this chapter.*

# LISTENING SELF-EVALUATION

How often do you indulge in the following ten bad listening habits? Check yourself carefully on each one:

| HABIT | Almost always | Usually | Some-times | Seldom | Almost never | SCORE |
|---|---|---|---|---|---|---|
| 1. Giving in to mental distractions | ___ | ___ | ___ | ___ | ___ | |
| 2. Giving in to physical distractions | ___ | ___ | ___ | ___ | ___ | |
| 3. Trying to recall everything a speaker says | ___ | ___ | ___ | ___ | ___ | |
| 4. Rejecting a topic as uninteresting before hearing the speaker | ___ | ___ | ___ | ___ | ___ | |
| 5. Faking paying attention | ___ | ___ | ___ | ___ | ___ | |
| 6. Jumping to conclusions about a speaker's meaning | ___ | ___ | ___ | ___ | ___ | |
| 7. Deciding a speaker is wrong before hearing everything she or he has to say | ___ | ___ | ___ | ___ | ___ | |
| 8. Judging a speaker on personal appearance | ___ | ___ | ___ | ___ | ___ | |
| 9. Not paying attention to a speaker's evidence | ___ | ___ | ___ | ___ | ___ | |
| 10. Focusing on delivery rather than on what the speaker says | ___ | ___ | ___ | ___ | ___ | |
| | | | | | TOTAL | ___ |

**How to score:**
For every "almost always" checked, give yourself a score of　2
For every "usually" checked, give yourself a score of　4
For every "sometimes" checked, give yourself a score of　6
For every "seldom" checked, give yourself a score of　8
For every "almost never" checked, give yourself a score of　10

**Total score interpretation:**　Below 70 — You need lots of training in listening
From 71-90 — You listen well.
Above 90 — You listen exceptionally well.

4. Choose a lecture in one of your other classes. Analyze what the lecturer does most effectively. Identify three things the lecturer could do better to help students keep track of the lecture.

> **Discussion:** *The objective of this exercise is to focus attention on things a speaker can do to help listeners gain hold of the speaker's ideas. Usually students will produce a number of excellent suggestions—such as making sure the speech is well organized, previewing main points in the introduction, using internal summaries and transitions, employing visual aids, avoiding technical language, and the like. You can then urge that students be sure to follow these suggestions in their own speeches.*

## Additional Exercises and Activities

1. Lead a class discussion in which students develop a code of listening behavior for their speech classroom. The final product of this discussion will be a list entitled "Listening Behavior for Our Speech Class." By the end of the discussion, the entire class should not only agree on the content of the list, but should also pledge themselves to follow it throughout the term.

> **Discussion:** *This activity is especially helpful for relating general issues about listening directly to the classroom situation. As students create their listening code, encourage them to be specific in their criteria. For example, rather than saying "Pay attention to what the speaker is saying," they should try to develop more precise statements such as "Write down the speaker's main points," "Look attentive and interested while other students are speaking," and "Do not read the newspaper or work on other assignments during speeches."*
>
> *This exercise works well when the class is divided into groups of 4-5 students. Give each group 10-15 minutes to come up with a list of 8-10 items to guide listening behavior in the class. Then, working from the group lists, conduct a general discussion which eventuates in a listening code that is agreed upon by the entire class. Another approach is to have each student create her or his own list as part of a homework assignment. You can then move immediately to a general class discussion rather than first dividing the class into small groups.*

2. Have one student step outside of the classroom with you. Give her or him a written copy of the following message: "To get to Lou's place, turn left at the first traffic light and go two blocks until you see a yellow house." Leaving the written copy with you, the student should return to the classroom and whisper

the message to the person in the next seat. This person should then whisper the message to the person sitting next to him or her, and so on until the message has been relayed through the entire class. Have the last student to receive the message write it down on a sheet of paper and read it to the entire class. Then have the student to whom you gave the original message read that message to the class. There will almost always be an enormous variation between the original message and the message received by the last student.

> **Discussion:** *This exercise takes only a few minutes to complete. It illustrates dramatically—and often humorously—the great distortion that can take place between what a speaker says and what a listener hears. You can, of course, substitute any message you wish for that given in the exercise.*

3.  Bring two short editorials to class. Read one of the editorials to your students. Have them take notes and try to identify the main points and evidence of the editorial. Check the results in the class discussion, and give pointers for listening and taking notes more effectively. Then read the second editorial and give students a chance to apply those pointers. Again, check the results in a class discussion.

> **Discussion:** *Although this exercise takes much of a class session, it can be very helpful because it prepares students for listening to speeches. Because many students do poorly on the first editorial, the exercise also serves the useful function of illustrating to students how poorly they listen and how much they need to work to improve their note taking. For an alternative, see the next Additional Exercise/Activity.*

4.  Show your class one of the selections on the videotape of student speeches that accompanies *The Art of Public Speaking*. Have them take notes in which they try to demarcate where the introduction of the speech ends, to list the main points and subpoints in the body, and to identify where the conclusion begins. Check the results in a class discussion and give pointers for listening and taking notes more effectively. Then play another speech from the videotape and see if students do a better job of note taking. Again, check the results in a class discussion.

> **Discussion:** *Because the student speeches on the videotape are 6-8 minutes long, this activity takes a whole class session, but it is extremely helpful for students. It can be made even more helpful by selecting speeches for viewing that are connected with whatever speech assignment is coming up in class. That is, if you use this exercise as students are preparing the informative speech,*

*show two informative speeches. Not only will this help students with their listening skills, but it will give them additional exposure to the principles of informative speaking.*

5.  For each round of speeches, assign students specific listening tasks. For example, you might have a particular group of students (or all students) take notes on their classmates' speeches in an effort to identify the speakers' main points and evidence. After each speech, make a quick check of two or three listeners to see what they recorded.

    **Discussion:** *This is one way to help students improve their listening and note-taking skills throughout the course. An added benefit of the exercise is that as students try to take notes on their classmates' speeches, they discover how helpful it is when the speaker follows a clear method of organization, previews the main points at the end of the introduction, uses connectives to help listeners keep track of main points, recaps the speech in the conclusion, avoids distracting nonverbal mannerisms, and uses her or his voice to emphasize ideas. This helps students learn what they need to do as speakers to help listeners take good notes.*

6.  For at least one round of speeches, have students prepare evaluations of their peers' speeches using the evaluation form on page 51 of this manual.

    **Discussion:** *This is an excellent alternative to Additional Exercise/Activity 5 above. In addition to including the usual items for speech evaluation, the form on page 51 is designed to gauge students' listening skills by requiring them to state the speaker's specific purpose, main points, pattern of organization, and types of supporting materials. Some teachers use the form for every speech, and they report that it helps considerably to improve students' listening skills by the end of the quarter or semester.*

7.  Have students keep a personal journal of their listening activities for a full day. The journal should include brief descriptions of all the listening situations each student experienced during that day. It should also include the student's analysis of how well he or she listened in each situation and of why he or she did (or did not) listen effectively in each situation. At the end of the day, the student should fill out the Listening Self-Evaluation Form on page 102 of this manual. Finally, the journal should conclude with the student's honest assessment of her or his strengths and weaknesses as a listener and an explanation of what specific steps the student should take to become a better listener.

> **Discussion:** *This is a useful alternative to exercise 2 on page 64 of the textbook. Like that exercise, it is a way to get students to think about their personal listening habits and how to improve them. Some teachers have students complete a listening journal two or three times during the course, as a way for students to keep track of their progress (or lack of progress) in strengthening their listening skills.*

# Extra Teaching and Learning Resources

## General

Barker, Larry, Johnson, Patrice, and Watson, Kittie. "The Role of Listening in Managing Interpersonal and Group Conflict." In Deborah Borisoff and Michael Purdy (eds.), *Listening in Everyday Life: A Personal and Professional Approach*. Lanham, Md.: University Press of America, 1991, pp. 139-157.

Borisoff, Deborah, and Purdy, Michael (eds.). *Listening in Everyday Life: A Personal and Professional Approach*. Lanham, Md.: University Press of America, 1991.

Borisoff, Deborah, and Merrill, Lisa. "Gender Issues and Listening." In Deborah Borisoff and Michael Purdy (eds.), *Listening in Everyday Life: A Personal and Professional Approach*. Lanham, Md.: University Press of America, 1991, pp. 59-85.

Bostrom, Robert N. (ed.). *Listening Behavior: Measurement and Application*. New York: Guilford Press, 1990.

Coakley, Carolyn, and Wolvin, Andrew. "Listening in the Educational Environment." In Deborah Borisoff and Michael Purdy (eds.), *Listening in Everyday Life: A Personal and Professional Approach*. Lanham, Md.: University Press of America, 1991, pp. 163-164.

Coakley, Carolyn Gwynn, and Wolvin, Andrew D. (eds.). *Experiential Listening: Tools for Teachers and Trainers*. New Orleans, La.: Spectra, 1989.

Fiumara, Gemma C. *The Other Side of Language: A Philosophy of Listening*. London: Routledge, 1990.

Floyd, James J. *Listening: a Practical Approach*. Glenview, Ill.: Scott, Foresman, 1985.

Galvin, Kathleen. *Listening By Doing*. Lincolnwood, Ill.: National Textbook Company, 1985.

Handel, Stephen. *Listening*. Cambridge, Mass.: MIT Press, 1989.

Rhodes, Steven C. "What the Communication Journals Tell Us About Teaching Listening." *Central States Speech Journal*, 36 (1985), 24-32.

Steil, Lyman K. "Listening Training: The Key to Success in Today's Organizations." In Deborah Borisoff and Michael Purdy (eds.), *Listening in Everyday Life: A Personal and Professional Approach*. Lanham, Md.: University Press of America, 1991, pp. 201-227.

Sypher, Beverly Davenport, Bostrom, Robert N., and Seibert, Joy Hart. "Listening, Communication Abilities, and Success at Work." *Journal of Business Communication*, 26 (1989), 293-303.

Thomlison, Dean. "Intercultural Listening." In Deborah Borisoff and Michael Purdy (eds.), *Listening in Everyday Life: A Personal and Professional Approach*. Lanham, Md.: University Press of America, 1991, pp. 87-137.

Watson, Kittie W., and Barker, Larry L. "Listening Behavior: Definition and Measurement." In Robert N. Bostrom and Bruce Westley (eds.), *Communication Yearbook 8*. Beverly Hills, Calif.: Sage, 1984, pp. 178-197.

Wolff, Florence I., and Marsnik, Nadine C. *Perceptive Listening*, 2nd ed. Fort Worth, Texas: Harcourt Brace Jovanovich, 1992.

Wolvin, Andrew D., and Coakley, Carolyn Gwynn. *Listening*, 4th ed. Dubuque, Iowa: W.C. Brown, 1992.

Wolvin, Andrew D., and Coakley, Carolyn Gwynn. "A Survey of the Status of Listening Training in Some Fortune 500 Corporations." *Communication Education*, 40 (1991), 152-164.

Zimmerman, Jack, and Coyle, Virginia. "Council: Reviving the Art of Listening." *Utne Reader* (March/April 1991), pp. 79-85.

## Classroom Activities and Assignments

Bohlken, Bob. "Learning to Listen and You Listen to Learn." *Speech Communication Teacher*, 8 (Winter 1994), 8-9.

Forestieri, Mary C. "Listening Instruction." In Stephen E. Lucas (ed.), *Selections from the Speech Communication Teacher, 1986-1991*. New York: McGraw-Hill, 1992, pp. 44-45.

Hyde, Richard Bruce. "Council: Using a Talking Stick to Teach Listening." *Speech Communication Teacher*, 7 (Winter 1993), 1-2.

Portnoy, Enid. "Activities to Promote Students' Speaking and Listening Abilities." In Stephen E. Lucas (ed.), *Selections from the Speech Communication Teacher, 1986-1991*. New York: McGraw-Hill, 1992, pp. 45-46.

Ross, Roseanna. "What Is In the Shoe Box?" In Stephen E. Lucas (ed.), *Selections from the Speech Communication Teacher, 1986-1991*. New York: McGraw-Hill, 1992, pp. 46-47.

Schneider, Valerie L. "A Three-Step Process for Better Speaking and Listening." In Stephen E. Lucas (ed.), *Selections from the Speech Communication Teacher, 1986-1991*. New York: McGraw-Hill, 1992, pp. 47-48.

Schumer, Allison. "To Tell the Truth." *Speech Communication Teacher*, 7 (Fall 1992), 1-2.

## Films and Videos

"Effective Listening." RMI Media Productions (1986). 28 minutes.

"How to Listen Effectively." RMI Media Productions (1986). 28 minutes.

"Listening Assertively." RMI Media Productions (1986). 28 minutes.

"Many Hear—Some Listen." MTI Film and Video (1975). 12 minutes.

"The Art of Listening." Insight Media (1992). 27 minutes.

"The Listening Process." RMI Media Productions (1986). 28 minutes.

"The Power of Listening," revised version. CRM Films (1988). 22 minutes.

# Chapter 4 Selecting a Topic and a Purpose

## Chapter Objectives

*After reading this chapter, students should be able to:*

1. Explain three procedures they can use when having trouble choosing a speech topic.

2. Identify the difference between a general and a specific purpose.

3. Distinguish between the specific purpose and the central idea of a speech.

4. Formulate a specific purpose statement and a central idea in accordance with the guidelines presented in the text.

## Chapter Outline

I. The first step in speechmaking is choosing a topic *(text pages 68-73)*.
   A. Topics for classroom speeches can come from subjects about which students already know a great deal.
   B. Topics for classroom speeches can come from subjects about which a student is interested and wants to learn more.
   C. Topics for classroom speeches can come from issues about which students hold strong opinions and beliefs.
   D. There are three procedures to help students who experience trouble choosing a topic.
      1. The first is to make a quick inventory of interests, skills, experiences, or beliefs and use this list to generate subject areas.
      2. The second is to brainstorm by using categories such as people, places, events, processes, problems and policies, etc. to produce a list of ideas.

       3.    The third is to browse through encyclopedias, indexes, newspapers, or other reference materials in search of a topic.

    E.    Whatever method students use, they should settle on a topic as early as possible.

II.    After choosing a topic, speakers need to determine the general purpose of the speech *(text pages 73-74)*.

    A.    There are usually two general purposes for classroom speeches—to inform or to persuade.

    B.    When the general purpose is to inform, speakers act as teachers.

        1.    Their goal is to communicate information clearly, accurately, and interestingly.

        2.    They seek to enhance the knowledge and understanding of their listeners.

    C.    When the general purpose is to persuade, speakers act as advocates.

        1.    Their goal is to change the attitudes or actions of their audience.

        2.    They seek to get their listeners to believe something or to do something.

III.    Once the general purpose is clear, the next step is narrowing to the specific purpose *(text pages 74-80)*.

    A.    The specific purpose should indicate precisely what the speaker wants the audience to know or believe after the speech.

        1.    It should focus on a clearly defined aspect of the topic.

        2.    It should be expressed as a single infinitive phrase that includes the audience.

    B.    There are five tips for forming a good specific purpose statement.

        1.    It should be a full infinitive phrase, not a fragment.

        2.    It should be phrased as a statement, not a question.

        3.    It should avoid figurative language.

        4.    It should not contain two or more unrelated ideas.

        5.    It should not be too vague or general.

    C.    Once students have a specific purpose statement, they should ask themselves the following questions:

        1.    Does the specific purpose meet the assignment?

        2.    Can this specific purpose be accomplished effectively in the time allotted?

        3.    Is the specific purpose relevant to the audience?

        4.    Is the specific purpose too technical or trivial?

IV.    The central idea further refines and sharpens the specific purpose statement *(text pages 80-84)*.

    A.    The central idea is a concise statement of what the speaker expects to say in the speech.

      1.    It is more precise than the topic or the specific purpose statement.

      2.    It sums up the speech in a single statement.

  B.    Often called a thesis statement or subject sentence, the central idea encapsulates the main points to be developed in the body of the speech.

      1.    It is what the speaker wants the audience to remember when they have forgotten everything else about the speech.

      2.    It reveals more about the content of the speech than does the specific purpose statement.

  C.    Unlike the specific purpose statement, the central idea usually crystallizes late in the process of preparing a speech.

  D.    A well-worded central idea should meet four criteria.

      1.    It should be expressed in a full sentence.

      2.    It should not be in the form of a question.

      3.    It should avoid figurative language.

      4.    It should not be too vague or general.

## Application Exercises *(from text pages 85-87)*

1.    Using the method of brainstorming described in the chapter, come up with three topics you might like to deal with in your next classroom speech. For each topic, devise two possible specific purpose statements suitable for the speech assignment. Make sure the specific purpose statements fit the guidelines discussed in the chapter.

      **Discussion:**  *This exercise gives students an opportunity to practice brainstorming, to begin the process of selecting a topic for their next speech, and to work on framing specific purpose statements. In class discussion, you can assess not only the suitability of the students' topics but also how effectively the students have phrased their specific purposes.*

2.    Below are six topics. Choose three, and for each of the three compose two specific purpose statements—one suitable for an informative speech and one suitable for a persuasive speech.

| | |
|---|---|
| weight lifting | women's rights |
| electoral college | skin cancer |
| television | education |

**Discussion:** *This exercise works well to clarify the differences between specific purpose statements for informative speeches and specific purpose statements for persuasive speeches. Start with the first topic, and have one or two students share their specific purpose statements with the class. Discuss those statements briefly with the class, and then repeat the procedure with the next topic.*

3.    Here are several specific purpose statements for classroom speeches. Identify the problem with each, and rewrite the statement to correct the problem.

a.    To inform my audience about Thailand.

**Discussion:** *This specific purpose statement is too broad. A more effective statement would be "To inform my audience about the major customs of everyday life in Thailand."*

b.    To persuade my audience that something has to be done about the growing problem of tuberculosis in the United States.

**Discussion:** *This specific purpose statement is too broad; it does not specify what should be done about the growing problem of tuberculosis in the United States. A more effective specific purpose statement would be "To persuade my audience that the federal government should dramatically increase funding to deal with the growth of tuberculosis."*

c.    To inform my audience how to make perfect popcorn every time.

**Discussion:** *Although Orville Redenbacher would certainly find how to make perfect popcorn a consequential topic, this specific purpose statement is too trivial for most classroom speeches.*

d.    What is chronic fatigue syndrome?

**Discussion:** *This specific purpose statement is phrased as a question. A more effective statement would be "To inform my audience about the symptoms, causes, and treatment of chronic fatigue syndrome."*

e.    To inform my audience that being a Big Brother or a Big Sister is a cool experience.

**Discussion:** *This specific purpose statement is written in figurative language. A more effective statement would be "To persuade my audience to become a Big Brother or Big Sister."*

f.    Learn CPR.

**Discussion:** *This specific purpose statement is written as a fragment. A more effective statement would be "To persuade my audience to take a class at the Red Cross in which they learn CPR."*

g.  To inform my audience about the growth of credit-card fraud and the methods of sound financial planning.

> **Discussion:** *This specific purpose statement contains two separate ideas. A more effective statement would be "To inform my audience about the growth of credit card fraud." Or "To inform my audience about the methods of sound financial planning." Or even "To inform my audience how to manage their use of credit cards in a manner consistent with sound financial planning."*

h.  To inform my audience why square grooves are superior to U-shaped grooves on golf clubs.

> **Discussion:** *This specific purpose statement is too technical—and perhaps too trivial—for an audience not composed of golf enthusiasts. A more effective specific purpose statement for a classroom speech on golf might be "To inform my audience about the development of golf as a popular sport." Or "To inform my audience about the different kinds of clubs used in playing golf."*

4.  Below are four central ideas for speeches. Which two are from informative speeches and which two are from persuasive speeches?

The five major elements of art design are shape, space, color, line, and texture. *(informative)*

Our state should deal with the problem of incompetent lawyers by requiring all attorneys to pass recertification examinations every ten years. *(persuasive)*

A comprehensive program of parental leave should be instituted because it will benefit society as a whole as well as individual workers and families. *(persuasive)*

The three major types of sleep disorders are insomnia, narcolepsy, and apnea. *(informative)*

5.  Below are three sets of main points for speeches. For each set supply the general purpose, specific purpose, and central idea.

General Purpose:   *To inform*

Specific Purpose:   *To inform my audience about the three major races in downhill skiing.*

Central Idea:   *The three major races in downhill skiing are the downhill, the slalom, and the giant slalom.*

Main Points:

    I.   The first major race in alpine skiing is the downhill.

    II.   The second major race in alpine skiing is the slalom.

    III.  The third major race in alpine skiing is the giant slalom.

General Purpose: *To persuade*

Specific Purpose: *To persuade my audience to support the school-bond referendum.*

Central Idea: *The school-bond referendum should be supported because it will improve classroom facilities, increase the number of teachers, and upgrade instructional resources.*

Main Points:

    I.   You should support the school-bond referendum because it will improve classroom facilities.

    II.   You should support the school-bond referendum because it will increase the number of teachers.

    III.  You should support the school-bond referendum because it will upgrade instructional resources.

General Purpose: *To inform*

Specific Purpose: *To inform my audience about the major achievements of Jane Addams.*

Central Idea: *Jane Addams was a woman of many achievements as a social worker, a reformer, a suffragist, and a writer.*

Main Points:

    I.   As a social worker, Jane Addams founded the settlement house movement in Chicago.

    II.   As a reformer, Jane Addams campaigned for child-labor laws, unemployment compensation, and better public sanitation.

    III.  As a suffragist, Jane Addams fought to give women the vote.

    IV.  As a writer, Jane Addams is best known for her autobiographical *Twenty Years at Hull House.*

**Discussion:**   *The virtue of this exercise is that it clarifies the relationships among the specific purpose, the central idea, and the main points. It looks easy, but quite a few students have trouble with it. To facilitate class discussion, this exercise is also available as part of the transparency supplement that accompanies* The Art of Public Speaking. *(For a variation, see Additional Exercises/ Activities 1-2, pp. 115-118 below.)*

# Additional Exercises and Activities

1. Below are two central ideas for speeches. For each central idea provide the general purpose, specific purpose, and main points of the speech.

    General Purpose:

    Specific Purpose:

    Central Idea:      The four stages of alcoholism are the warning stage, the danger stage, the crucial stage, and the chronic stage.

    Main Points:      I.

                           II.

                           III.

                           IV.

    General Purpose:

    Specific Purpose:

    Central Idea:      You should join a sorority or fraternity because of the social, academic, and economic benefits.

    Main Points:      I.

                           II.

                           III.

**Discussion:** *This complements exercise 5 on page 87 of the text and gives students additional work in understanding the relationships among the general purpose, specific purpose, central idea, and main points of the speech. For another exercise along these lines see Additional Exercise/Activity 2 on pp. 117-118 of this manual. Here are the answers to the present exercise. To facilitate class discussion, the answers are also available as part of the transparency supplement that accompanies* The Art of Public Speaking.

General Purpose:    *To inform*

Specific Purpose:    *To inform my audience of the four stages of alcoholism.*

Central Idea:    The four stages of alcoholism are the warning stage, the danger stage, the crucial stage, and the chronic stage.

Main Points:    *I.    The first stage of alcoholism is the warning stage.*
*II.    The second stage of alcoholism is the danger stage.*
*III.    The third stage of alcoholism is the crucial stage.*
*IV.    The fourth stage of alcoholism is the chronic stage.*

General Purpose:    *To persuade*

Specific Purpose:    *To persuade my audience to join a sorority or a fraternity.*

Central Idea:    You should join a sorority or fraternity because of the social, academic, and economic benefits.

Main Points:    *I.    You should join a sorority or fraternity because of the social benefits.*
*II.    You should join a sorority or fraternity because of the academic benefits.*
*III.    You should join a sorority or fraternity because of the economic benefits.*

2.   Below are two central ideas for speeches. For each central idea provide the general purpose, specific purpose, and main points of the speech.


General Purpose:


Specific Purpose:


Central Idea:        The pyramids of ancient Egypt had three major uses—as tombs for the burial of monarchs, as temples for worshipping the gods, and as observatories for studying the stars.


Main Points:


General Purpose:


Specific Purpose:


Central Idea:        Handwriting analysts try to determine personality traits by examining the consistency, angularity, and size of a person's writing.


Main Points:

**Discussion:** *By not providing the number of main points, this exercise is somewhat more difficult than the previous one. It provides additional work for students who are having trouble with the relationships among the general purpose, specific purpose, central idea, and main points. Here is what the exercise should look like when all the blanks are filled in. To facilitate class discussion, the answers are also available as part of the transparency supplement that accompanies* The Art of Public Speaking.

General Purpose:   *To inform*

Specific Purpose:   *To inform my audience of the three major uses of the pyramids of ancient Egypt.*

Central Idea:   The pyramids of ancient Egypt had three major uses—as tombs for the burial of monarchs, as temples for worshipping the gods, and as observatories for studying the stars and the planets.

Main Points:
I.   *The first major use of the pyramids of ancient Egypt was as tombs for the burial of monarchs.*
II.   *The second major use of the pyramids of ancient Egypt was as temples for worshipping the gods.*
III.   *The third major use of the pyramids of ancient Egypt was as observatories for studying the stars and the planets.*

General Purpose:   *To inform*

Specific Purpose:   *To inform my audience how handwriting analysts try to determine personality traits by examining a person's handwriting.*

Central Idea:   Handwriting analysts try to determine personality traits by examining the consistency, angularity, and size of a person's handwriting.

Main Points:
I.   *Handwriting analysts try to determine personality traits by examining the consistency of a person's handwriting.*
II.   *Handwriting analysts try to determine personality traits by examining the angularity of a person's handwriting.*
III.   *Handwriting analysts try to determine personality traits by examining the size of a person's handwriting.*

3. Once students start to work on each speech assignment, set aside part of a class session to discuss the students' topics. Ask each student to reveal her or his topic and specific purpose. Ask other classmates to indicate whether they find the topic interesting and what suggestions they have for the speaker's approach to it.

> **Discussion:** *In some classes this works very well. In other classes—when the students are not well prepared or are reluctant to share their opinions—it is less effective. Some teachers use this activity quite successfully to help students focus their topics and adjust them to their classmates.*

4. Divide the class into groups of 5-6 students each. Assign each group one of the following resources to investigate for possible speech topics: (a) an issue of a magazine such as *Time, Newsweek,* or *U.S. News and World Report*; (b) the Sunday edition of the leading local newspaper; (c) any issue of a major national newspaper—*New York Times, Los Angeles Times, Washington Post, Christian Science Monitor*—that is available at the college library; (d) an hour of news broadcasting on CNN; (e) two nights of the evening news telecast on ABC, NBC, or CBS. On the basis of these resources, each group is responsible for bringing into class five speech topics and specific purpose statements for each of those topics. Conduct a class discussion on the kinds and quality of topics and specific purpose statements generated by each group.

> **Discussion:** *This exercise requires a fair amount of time outside of class and works especially well in courses that include a unit on group discussion. An added benefit of the exercise is that it often leads several students to topics that they eventually use in one or more of their speeches during the term.*

# Extra Teaching and Learning Resources

## General

Calano, Jimmy, and Salzman, Jeff. "Ten Ways to Fire Up Your Creativity." *Working Woman* (July 1989), pp. 94-95.

Dormen, Lesley, and Edidin, Peter. "Original Spin: Creativity Is Not Just for Geniuses and Artists." *Psychology Today* (July/August, 1989), pp. 46-52.

Hooper, Judith, and Teresi, Dick. "Brain Stretches: Exercises, Games, and Apparatus for Brain Training." *Health* (April 1989), 55-67.

Jablin, Frederic M. "Cultivating Imagination: Factors That Enhance and Inhibit Creativity in Brainstorming Groups." *Human Communication Research*, 7 (1981), 245-258.

Katula, Richard A., and Martin, Celest A. "Teaching Critical Thinking in the Speech Communication Classroom." *Communication Education*, 33 (1984), 160-167.

Kneupper, Charles W. "A Modern Theory of Invention." *Communication Education*, 32 (1983), 39-50.

## Classroom Activities and Assignments

Avadian, Brenda, and Thanos, Marilyn. "Speechmapping: The Road Through Speech Preparation and Delivery." In Stephen E. Lucas (ed.), *Selections from the Speech Communication Teacher, 1986-1991*. New York: McGraw-Hill, 1992, pp. 51-52.

Duffy, Susan. "Using Magazines to Stimulate Topic Choices for Speeches." In Stephen E. Lucas (ed.), *Selections from the Speech Communication Teacher, 1986-1991*. New York: McGraw-Hill, 1992, pp. 16-17.

Garrett, Roger L. "Helping Students Discover Interviewing Skills." In Stephen E. Lucas (ed.), *Selections from the Speech Communication Teacher, 1986-1991*. New York: McGraw-Hill, 1992, pp. 37-38.

Grainer, Diane. "Creativity vs. My Speech Is About Avocados." In Stephen E. Lucas (ed.), *Selections from the Speech Communication Teacher, 1986-1991*. New York: McGraw-Hill, 1992, p. 74.

Hugenberg, Lawrence W., and O'Neill, Daniel J. "Speaking on Critical Issue Topics in the Public Speaking Course." In Stephen E. Lucas (ed.), *Selections from the Speech Communication Teacher, 1986-1991*. New York: McGraw-Hill, 1992, pp. 17-18.

Smith, Robert E. "Clustering: A Way to Discover Speech Topics." *Speech Communication Teacher*, 7 (Winter 1993), 6-7.

Woodside, Daria. "Choosing Topics for Speeches: A Breath of Fresh Air (Earth, Water, and Fire)." *Speech Communication Teacher*, 7 (Fall 1992), 1-2.

## Films and Videos

"Be Prepared to Speak." Kantola-Skeie Productions (1985). 27 minutes.

"Choosing the Ideas and Words." RMI Media Productions (1986). 28 minutes.

"Ideas Into Action." CRM Films (1993). 10 minutes.

"Planning Your Speech." Coronet/MTI Film and Video (1976). 13 minutes.

"The Speaker's Purpose and Occasion." RMI Media Productions (1986). 30 minutes.

# Chapter 5 Analyzing the Audience

## Chapter Objectives

*After reading this chapter, students should be able to:*

1.  Explain why public speakers must be audience centered.

2.  Explain what it means to say that audiences are egocentric.

3.  Identify the major demographic traits of audiences.

4.  Identify the major situational traits of audiences.

5.  Use a questionnaire as a method of audience analysis for classroom speeches.

6.  Explain how a speaker can adapt to the audience while preparing the speech and while delivering the speech.

## Chapter Outline

I.   Good speakers are audience-centered *(text pages 90-92)*.
     A.  They understand that the primary purpose of public speaking is to gain a desired response from their listeners.
     B.  They keep three questions in mind as they prepare their speeches:
         1.  Who am I addressing?
         2.  What do I want the audience to know, believe, or do because of my speech?
         3.  How can I most effectively compose and present my speech to accomplish that aim?

II.  It is important for student speakers to approach their classmates as a real audience *(text pages 92-93)*.
   A.  Because the classroom seems like an artificial speaking situation, it is easy for students to lose sight of their classmates as an authentic audience.
   B.  The best student speakers take their audience seriously and treat their classmates as worthy of their best effort.

III. Good speakers understand the psychology of audiences *(text pages 93-94)*.
   A.  A speaker's task is to make the audience want to pay attention to her or his message.
   B.  The auditory perception of audiences is always selective.
      1.  Everything a speaker says is filtered through a listener's frame of reference.
      2.  Every speech contains two messages.
         a.  The message sent by the speaker.
         b.  The message received by the audience.
   C.  Audiences are egocentric.
      1.  They pay closest attention to messages that affect them directly.
      2.  They typically approach speeches by asking, "Why is this important to me?"
   D.  These psychological principles have two important implications for speakers.
      1.  Listeners will judge a speech on the basis of what they already know and believe.
      2.  Speakers must take care to relate their messages to an audience's existing knowledge and beliefs.

IV.  The first stage of audience analysis is examining demographic traits of the audience and how they might affect reception of the speech *(text pages 94-100)*.
   A.  Few things affect a person's outlook more than her or his age.
      1.  Each generation has more-or-less common experiences and values.
      2.  Effective speakers adapt to these experiences and values when addressing an audience.
   B.  Gender issues can have a strong impact on how an audience responds to a speech.
      1.  Women and men in the United States share a broader range of experiences than was the case a few decades ago.
      2.  The composition of audiences has also changed.
         a.  Many audiences that were once predominantly male now include large numbers of women.

        b.    Many audiences that were once predominantly female now include plenty of men.

    3.    To be effective in today's world, public speakers must avoid outdated gender stereotypes and be responsive to *both* the similarities and the differences between men and women.

C.    It is also important to consider the racial, ethnic, or cultural background of audience members.

    1.    This is especially true as the United States becomes more and more a multicultural, multiracial society.

    2.    Almost every audience will contain people whose racial, ethnic, or cultural backgrounds will significantly influence their response to the speaker's message.

    3.    An effective speaker will take account of the different racial, ethnic, or cultural backgrounds of listeners when preparing a speech.

D.    The religious views of the audience need to be considered.

    1.    As the United States becomes more diverse culturally, it is also becoming more diverse religiously.

    2.    A speaker cannot assume that her or his religious views, whatever they may be, will be shared by all members of the audience.

    3.    Failure to consider the religious views of the audience can seriously weaken a speech.

E.    The group membership of an audience is another important factor to consider.

    1.    There are thousands of national, state, and local voluntary associations in the U.S.

    2.    The group affiliations of audience members can provide valuable clues about their interests and attitudes.

F.    There are also a number of other potentially important demographic variables.

    1.    They include occupation, economic position, education, intelligence, and place of residence.

    2.    Special demographic variables for classroom speeches might include year in school, major, extracurricular activities, job aspirations, and living arrangements.

    3.    Anything characteristic of a given audience is potentially important to a speaker addressing that audience.

V.    The second stage of audience analysis is examining features of the audience unique to the speaking situation at hand *(text pages 100-104)*.

A.    The first factor to consider is the size of the audience.

    1.    Larger audiences usually require more formal presentations.

    2.    Audience size may also affect a speaker's language, choice of appeals, and use of visual aids.

B.    The second factor to consider is the physical setting of the speech.

1. The receptivity of listeners is frequently influenced by physical conditions such as the size, seating, and temperature of the room.
2. Speakers should do what they can to control the influence of physical setting on the audience.

C. The third factor to consider is the audience's disposition toward the topic.
   1. A speaker needs to asses the audience's interest in the topic.
      a. Outside the classroom, people seldom expend the time and effort to attend a speech unless they are interested in the topic.
      b. For classroom speeches, it is usually necessary to take special measures to get the audience involved.
   2. A speaker needs to asses the audience's knowledge about the topic.
      a. If the audience knows little about the topic, the speaker will have to talk at a more elementary level.
      b. If the audience knows a lot about the topic, the speaker can take a more advanced approach.
   3. A speaker needs to assess the audience's attitude toward the topic.
      a. If the audience is skeptical about or hostile toward the speaker's views on the topic, the speaker will have to adapt to that skepticism or hostility.
      b. If the audience is favorably disposed toward the speaker's view of the topic, the speaker will usually have an easier task.

D. The fourth factor to consider is the audience's disposition toward the speaker.
   1. An audience's response to a message is invariably colored by their perceptions of the speaker.
   2. The more credible and competent listeners believe a speaker to be, the more likely they are to accept what the speaker says.

E. The fifth factor to consider is the audience's disposition toward the occasion.
   1. The occasion will often determine the audience's expectations about the length and content of the speech.
   2. Speakers who seriously violate these expectations risk alienating the audience.

VI. There are several ways to get demographic and situational information about the audience *(text pages 104-108)*.
   A. For speeches outside the classroom, speakers often make informal inquiries about their audience.

       1.    They may ask the person who invites them to speak to explain the group's history and purpose.

       2.    They may sound out someone else who has addressed the same group.

  B.    For classroom speeches, students often use audience-analysis questionnaires.

       1.    There are three basic types of questions for such questionnaires.

           a.    Fixed-alternative questions offer a choice between two or more specific responses.

           b.    Scale questions allow for a continuum of answers.

           c.    Open-ended questions give maximum leeway in responding.

       2.    There are four guidelines for effective audience-analysis questionnaires.

           a.    They are carefully planned to elicit the necessary information.

           b.    They use all three types of questions to get specific and detailed information.

           c.    They are clear and unambiguous.

           d.    They are relatively brief.

VII.  Once speakers complete their audience analysis, they use that analysis to adapt their speech to their listeners *(text pages 108-111)*.

  A.    Most of the work of audience adaptation takes place before the speech as part of the preparation process.

       1.    A speaker should keep the audience in mind at every stage of speech preparation.

       2.    A speaker should keep the following questions constantly in mind while preparing the speech.

           a.    How is the audience likely to respond to what I will say?

           b.    How can I adjust my message to make it as clear and convincing as possible?

       3.    Adjusting the message to the audience requires two things of a speaker during the process of speech preparation.

           a.    The speaker must anticipate how listeners will respond to the speech.

           b.    The speaker must be creative in thinking of ways to adapt the speech to listeners.

  B.    Audience adaptation also takes place during the presentation of the speech.

       1.    No matter how hard a speaker works ahead of time, things do not always go smoothly on the day of the speech.

           a.    Physical circumstances might be different than anticipated.

           b.    The audience might respond differently than anticipated.

2.   Skillful speakers learn to adapt to these kinds of changes.
   a.   They modify whatever aspect of their speech is necessary to take account of changed physical circumstances.
   b.   They keep an eye out for audience feedback and adjust their remarks accordingly.

## Application Exercises *(from text pages 112-113)*

1.   Advertisers are usually very conscious of their audience. Choose an issue of a popular magazine such as *Time, Newsweek, Sports Illustrated, Cosmopolitan,* or the like. From that issue select five advertisements to analyze. Try to determine the audience being appealed to in each advertisement, and analyze the appeals (verbal and visual) used to persuade buyers. How might the appeals differ if the ads were designed to persuade a different audience?

   **Discussion:** *Because the audience appeal of most magazine advertisements is quite obvious, this exercise usually promotes vigorous class discussion on the principles of audience analysis and adaptation. In addition, it almost always provokes questions about the ethics of audience adaptation. If you use this exercise, be sure to have students bring a copy of their advertisements to class.*

2.   Below are three general speech topics and, for each, two hypothetical audiences to which a speech might be delivered. For each topic, write a brief paragraph explaining how you might adjust your specific purpose and message according to the demographic characteristics of the audience.

   a.   *Topic:*          "Fiber-Optic Technology"

   *Audience #1:*   50% engineering majors, 30% science majors, 20% music majors

   *Audience #2:*   40% English majors, 30% science majors, 30% pre-law majors

   **Discussion:** *Audience #1 will likely be more interested in and knowledgeable about the topic than will audience #2. The speaker addressing audience #2 will have to give special attention to gaining attention, to relating the topic to the audience, and to avoiding technical language.*

b. *Topic:* "Sexual Assault: The Biggest Campus Crime"

*Audience #1:* 80% female, 20% male

*Audience #2:* 80% male, 20% female

**Discussion:** *Although sexual assault is a topic of great interest to both male and female students, the orientations of each toward the topic are usually different. Because women face the threat of sexual assault on a daily basis, a speech to audience #1 might stress steps that women can take to avoid becoming the victims of sexual assault. Because men do not face the same personal threat of sexual assault, a speech to audience #2 might seek to sensitize male listeners to the seriousness of the problem, demonstrate that men are not immune from the problem because their wives, sisters, mothers or girlfriends could become the victims of sexual assault, and explain what steps men can take to make campus a safer place for women students.*

c. *Topic:* "The Watergate Crisis"

*Audience #1:* Day class, 70% age 18 to 22, 30% age 23 and over

*Audience #2:* Evening class, 50% age 35 and over, 30% age 22 to 35, 20% age 18 to 22

**Discussion:** *The Watergate crisis occurred in 1973-1974. Most members of audience #1 are too young to have any recollection of the dramatic events that rocked the nation and forced the resignation of President Richard Nixon. A speech to this group would have to provide basic historical facts about Watergate before taking up more complex issues such as its impact on American politics. Nor can a speaker addressing audience #1 assume that most of his or her listeners will necessarily be interested in the topic.*

*On the other hand, a speaker addressing audience #2 can assume that most listeners have a fair stock of knowledge about the Watergate crisis. Much of the audience lived through the crisis and may recall it rather vividly. They are more likely to be interested in it than audience #1, and they probably will not need much historical background about it. Many of these listeners may also have fairly definite opinions about the crisis and the people involved in it, although the demographic analysis will not reveal what those opinions are. Finally, the speaker will have to take some account of the 20 percent of the audience who are too young to know much about the crisis.*

*Of course, a speaker can assume only so much about an audience from its demographic characteristics—especially on such a complex and controversial topic as Watergate. Thus this example points out the need for situational audience analysis in addition to the demographic analysis. For an alternative to this exercise, see the first entry under Additional Exercises and Activities for this chapter.*

3.    For your next speech, design and circulate among your classmates an audience analysis questionnaire like that discussed on pages 105-108 of the textbook. Use all three kinds of questions explained in the text—fixed-alternative questions, scale questions, and open-ended questions. After you have tabulated the results of the questionnaire, write an analysis explaining what the questionnaire reveals about your audience and what steps you must take to adapt your speech to the audience.

**Discussion:** *Although speakers outside the classroom seldom use questionnaires, this exercise is extremely useful because it requires students to engage in systematic audience analysis. It also requires them to conceive of their classmates as a genuine audience.*

*This exercise works best in conjunction with the first persuasive speech. You can set aside 5 to 10 minutes at the start of several class meetings to allow students to respond to questionnaires, or you can have students fill in the questionnaires at home and return them at the next class meeting. Finally, I would recommend having students turn in the analyses of their questionnaires at the time they turn in their preparation outlines.*

4.    Analyze the speech in the Appendix by Alan Alda ("A Reel Doctor's Advice to Some Real Doctors"). Explain what special steps Alda takes to fit his message to the audience. Be specific in your analysis, and be prepared to discuss your conclusions in class.

**Discussion:**    *Alda's speech provides an excellent model of audience adaptation. Here is a synopsis of the speech:*

*Specific Purpose:  To persuade the graduates of the Columbia College of Physicians and Surgeons to analyze the values they will follow in their careers as doctors.*

*Central Idea:  Be skilled, be learned, be aware of the dignity of your calling—but please don't ever lose sight of your own simple humanity.*

*Method of Organization: Problem-solution*

*Introduction: The introduction runs through paragraph 9. Alda's main task here is to establish his credibility as an actor advising an audience of medical doctors. He begins by confronting the question directly: "Why get someone who only pretends to be a doctor when you could get a real one?" He uses humor to make clear that he has no pretensions of being a doctor, and he spends paragraphs 5-8 discussing Hawkeye Pierce, the television character for which he is famous. In addition to reinforcing Alda's credibility, these paragraphs introduce the kind of doctor Alda will urge his audience to be. Paragraph 9 brings the introduction to an end by announcing the central idea of the speech: "Be skilled, be learned, be aware of the dignity of your calling—but please don't ever lose sight of your own simple humanity."*

*Body: The body of Alda's speech contains two main points. The first begins in paragraph 10 and deals with the problems that keep doctors from being as humane and as compassionate as they should be. Alda finishes discussing this main point with the internal summary in paragraph 20. Paragraph 21 is a transition into the second main point, which begins in paragraph 22. Having defined the problem in main point I, Alda gives a solution in main point II. The solution is to decide "exactly what your values are, and then to figure out how you're going to live by them" (paragraph 22). Alda continues to discuss the solution through paragraph 49.*

*Conclusion: The conclusion, which is quite effective, begins in paragraph 50. Notice especially the last paragraph, which poignantly reinforces the central idea.*

*Audience Adaptation: Alda uses a number of methods to build his credibility and to establish common ground with his audience. They include expressions of humility (paragraphs 1-3, 50); humor (paragraphs 2-3, 11, 23, 26, 28, 39); expressions of confidence in himself (paragraph 4); drawing on the audience's positive attitudes toward Hawkeye Pierce (paragraph 5); noting the similarities between actors and doctors (paragraphs 11-12, 19); and complimenting the audience (paragraphs 14-15, 51). It is worth noting that most of these appear in the first half of the speech, before Alda concentrates on giving advice to his audience.*

5. Read the speech in the Appendix by Barbara Bush ("Choices and Change"). Focus on how Bush adapts her message to her audience in light of the controversy that preceded her speech. Be prepared to discuss your ideas in class.

**Discussion:** *Barbara Bush's commencement speech at Wellesley College is an excellent study in audience analysis and adaptation. As the headnote in the textbook explains, the choice of Bush as speaker touched off a protest among roughly one-quarter of Wellesley's graduating seniors. The protest in turn sparked a national controversy involving students, educators, politicians, and newspaper editorialists. When Bush rose to speak, she faced an immediate audience that had been polarized by the controversy and many members of which were skeptical, some even hostile, to her appearance at Wellesley.*

*Instead of pretending there was no controversy, Bush acknowledged it and turned it to her advantage with a deft blend of humor and good will. She did not abandon her own views on the issues facing women in American society, but neither did she disparage listeners who held different views. The result is a speech that students find interesting both for its approach to audience adaptation and for its message about the role of women in the United States. Expect a lively discussion on both aspects of the speech.*

*Have students prepare their analysis based on the transcript of the speech in the textbook. Then, before discussing the speech in class, show students the videotape of the speech from "Commencement Speeches at Wellesley College, June 1, 1990," which is part of the videotape supplement to* The Art of Public Speaking. *If you show the videotape, take advantage of the opportunity to discuss how Bush's delivery helps or hinders the presentation of her message to the audience at Wellesley. Here is a synopsis of the speech:*

*Introduction: The introduction consists of paragraph 1, in which Bush acknowledges other dignitaries as well as members of her audience. Christine Bicknell, whom Bush calls her "new best friend" was the student speaker who had preceded her on the podium. I do not know the reason for the "best friend" statement.*

*Body: The body runs from paragraph 2 through paragraph 17 and contains two main points. The first is developed in paragraphs 2-7. In this section of the speech, Bush praises Wellesley's commitment to diversity, but she does not define diversity in racial, ethnic, or sexual terms. Rather, she characterizes it in general terms as requiring the effort "to learn about and respect difference, to be compassionate with* one another, to cherish our own identity, and to accept unconditionally the same in others" (paragraph 7). This is a crucial move, for it allows Bush to identify with a value shared by most of her listeners while at the same time implying that the people opposed to her appearance have not been acting in the true spirit of diversity.

Any potential conflict over this move, however, is quickly dissipated by Bush's good-natured treatment, in paragraph 8, of the fact that Alice Walker had been the senior class' first choice for commencement speaker. In the second half of paragraph 8, Bush introduces her second main point—that Wellesley's seniors will have crucial choices to make as they begin the journey for their own true colors.

As Bush develops this point in paragraphs 9-17, she urges her listeners to make three choices—to get involved in major social issues (paragraph 10), to keep in mind that life is supposed to be fun (paragraphs 11-12), and to cherish their human relationships with family and friends (paragraphs 13-16). Bush spends most of her time on the third choice, and in doing so presents a number of lines that were widely quoted afterward by commentators on the speech.

Paragraph 17 brings the second main point to a close and contains the best known line of the speech, in which Bush says: "Somewhere out in this audience may even be someone who will one day follow in my footsteps, and preside over the White House as the president's spouse. And I wish him well!" Although Bush had used this line in previous speeches, it was new to the audience at Wellesley, and they responded with cheering and prolonged applause. Paragraph 17 is also noteworthy for the way it links the two main points of the speech by referring back to the story in main point one about where the mermaids stand.

Conclusion: The conclusion consists of paragraph 18, in which Bush states that the controversy over her appearance is over but that the conversation on women's issues is only beginning. After thanking the seniors for the "courtesy and honor" of addressing them, Bush closes by saying to the seniors, "may your future be worthy of your dreams."

## Additional Exercises and Activities

1.    Below are six specific purpose statements for classroom speeches. For each specific purpose statement, lead a class discussion that seeks to answer the question: "What steps would a speaker with this specific purpose statement need to take to adapt her or his speech to the interests, knowledge, and attitudes of this class?"

    a.    To inform my audience how they can protect their apartment or dorm room against burglaries.

    b.    To inform my audience about the principles of aerodynamics that allow an airplane to fly.

    c.    To inform my audience about the causes, symptoms, and treatment of eating disorders.

    d.    To persuade my audience that the Social Security system should be replaced with a national system of individual retirement accounts.

    e.    To persuade my audience that capital punishment should be abolished in all parts of the United States.

    f.    To persuade my audience to participate in intramural sports.

    **Discussion:** *This is an excellent alternative (or supplement) to Exercise 2 on pages 112-113 of the textbook. While that exercise asks students to generalize about hypothetical listeners, this exercise gets them thinking about a specific real audience—their speech class. As a result, it has two benefits. One, of course, is to expand their understanding of the factors involved in audience analysis and adaptation in general. The second is to give them insight into the audience they will be addressing in their classroom speeches.*

    *This exercise can be conducted entirely in class or, to save time, it can be given to students as a homework assignment. To facilitate classroom discussion, the six specific purpose statements are also available as part of the transparency supplement that accompanies* The Art of Public Speaking.

2.    You may wish to have your students prepare a formal demographic analysis of the class. One method is to lead a class discussion in which students create the items for a demographic audience analysis questionnaire. Another method is to give students a questionnaire format to follow. A sample is reproduced on page 134.

> **Discussion:** *Although the demographic questionnaire is not as useful for students as creating a situational audience analysis questionnaire, it is a good way to begin to get them attuned to the process of audience analysis. You should be aware, however, that some schools have deemed demographic questionnaires to be an invasion of students' privacy. If you have any doubts about the situation at your school, be sure to check before distributing the questionnaire.*

3.    Have students prepare an Audience Analysis and Adaptation Worksheet (see pages 135-136) in conjunction with one or more of their speeches. Hand out the worksheets early, so students can use them throughout the speech preparation process. You can have the students turn in their worksheets at the same time as their initial preparation outlines, or you can require that they be turned in on the day of each student's speech.

> **Discussion:** *This is a relatively detailed worksheet, but if students use it conscientiously, it will help them become much more aware of the factors involved in audience analysis and adaptation. To help ensure that students take the worksheet seriously, you should probably make it a graded assignment. Some teachers simply include the worksheet as part of the overall grade for the speech; others assign a separate grade for the worksheet.*

# Questionnaire for Demographic Audience Analysis

1.  Age _____

2.  Sex:  Male _____     Female _____

3.  Relationship status: Married _____        Single _____

    Divorced _____        Engaged _____

    Widowed _____        Domestic partnership _____

4.  Religion _____

5.  Race/Ethnic Background _____

6.  Year in school:      First-year _____        Sophomore _____

    Junior _____        Senior _____

7.  Major (declared or anticipated): _____

8.  Home town: _____

    Population: _____

9.  Campus organizations to which you belong: _____

    _____

10. Off-campus organizations to which you belong: _____

    _____

11. Jobs you have held: _____

    _____

    _____

# Audience Analysis and Adaptation Worksheet
## Part I

**Speaker** _____   **Topic** _____

What is the audience for this speech? _____

_____

What is the specific purpose of this speech? _____

_____

In choosing a specific purpose, how can you narrow the topic so it will be appropriate to this audience?

_____

_____

**Demographic audience analysis:**  What special adaptation is necessary in the speech because of the audience's

    age _____

    sex _____

    religion _____

    racial or ethnic background _____

    group membership _____

    other (specify) _____

**Situational audience analysis:**  What special adaptation is necessary in the speech because of the audience's

    size _____

    response to the physical setting _____

    knowledge about the topic _____

    interest level in the topic _____

    attitude toward the topic _____

    disposition toward the speaker _____

    disposition toward the occasion _____

(continued in Part II)

# Audience Analysis and Adaptation Worksheet
# Part II

**Speaker** _____  **Topic** _____

**Adaptation in the speech:** Answer each of the following questions.

What device(s) did you use in the introduction to gain attention from this audience?

_____

_____

What steps did you take to relate the topic directly to this audience in the introduction?

_____

_____

What are the main points of the speech? Why did you develop these particular main points for this audience?

_____

_____

_____

_____

What decisions did you make in choosing supporting materials for this audience?

_____

_____

What special steps did you take to make your language clear and appropriate to this audience?

_____

_____

What adjustments did you make in delivery—rate of speech, volume, tone of voice, gestures, etc.—to communicate your ideas to this audience?

_____

_____

_____

# Extra Teaching and Learning Resources

## General

Atlas, James. "Beyond Demographics." *Atlantic* (October 1984), 49-58.

Brookhiser, Richard. "The Melting Pot is Still Simmering." *Time* (March 1, 1993), p. 72.

Canary, Daniel J., and Hause, Kimberley S. "Is There Any Reason to Research Sex Differences in Communication?" *Communication Quarterly*, 41 (1993), 129-144.

DeRosa, DeAnna, and Wilcox, Dennis L. "Gaps are Narrowing Between Female and Male Students." *Public Relations Review*, 15 (1989), 80-90.

Eagly, Alice H., and Chaiken, Shelly. *The Psychology of Attitudes*. Fort Worth, Texas: Harcourt Brace Jovanovich, 1993.

Fowles, Jib. "Advertising's Fifteen Basic Appeals." In Robert Atwan, Barry Orton, and William Vesterman (eds.), *American Mass Media: Industries and Issues*. New York: Random House, 1986, pp. 43-54.

Fuchs, Lawrence H. *The American Kaleidoscope: Race, Ethnicity, and the Civic Culture*. Hanover, N.H.: University Press of New England, 1990.

Greenwald, A.G., and Leavitt, C. "Audience Involvement in Advertising: Four Levels." *Journal of Consumer Research*, 11 (1984), 581-592.

Gudykunst, William B., and Young, Yun Kim. *Communicating with Strangers: An Approach to Intercultural Communication*, 2nd ed. New York: McGraw-Hill, 1992.

Ivy, Diana K., and Backlund, Phil. *Exploring GenderSpeak: Personal Effectiveness in Gender Communication*. New York: McGraw-Hill, 1994.

Klopf, Donald W. *Intercultural Encounters: The Fundamentals of Intercultural Communication*, 2nd ed. Englewood, Colo.: Morton Publishing, 1991.

Loeb, Paul. "Most Students Today Are Individualists, Not Activists." *Utne Reader* (May/June 1990), 56-62.

Lustig, Myron W., and Koester, Jolene. *Intercultural Competence: Interpersonal Communication Across Cultures*. New York: HarperCollins, 1993.

McGuire, William J. "Attitudes and Attitude Change." In Gardner Lindzey and Elliot Aronson (eds.), *Handbook of Social Psychology*. New York: Random House, 1985, II, 233-346.

Pavlik, John. "Audience Complexity as a Component of Campaign Planning." *Public Relations Review*, 14 (1988), 12-21.

Raines, Claire, and Bradford, Lawrence J. *Twenty-Something: Managing and Motivating Today's New Work Force*. New York: Mass Media Limited, 1992.

Samovar, Larry A., and Porter, Richard E. *Communication Between Cultures*. Belmont, Calif.: Wadsworth, 1991.

Shankar, Archana Daya. "Issues of Ethnic Diversity in the Basic Course." In Lawrence J. Hugenberg, Pamela L. Gray, and Douglas M. Trank (eds.), *Teaching and Directing the Basic Communications Course*. Dubuque, Iowa: Kendall/Hunt, 1993, pp. 291-298.

*Time* (Fall 1993). Special issue devoted to "The New Face of America."

Wood, Julia T. *Gendered Lives: Communication, Gender, and Culture*. Belmont, Calif.: Wadsworth, 1994.

Wright, Rudy R. *The Meeting Spectrum: An Advanced Guide for Meeting Professionals*. San Diego, Calif.: Rockwood Enterprises, 1988, Chapter 16.

## Classroom Activities and Assignments

Downey, Sharon D. "Audience Analysis Exercise." In Stephen E. Lucas (ed.), *Selections from the Speech Communication Teacher, 1986-1991*. New York: McGraw-Hill, 1992, pp. 12-13.

Garbowitz, Fred. "Changing Classroom Populations Call for Increased Diversity." In Stephen E. Lucas (ed.), *Selections from the Speech Communication Teacher, 1986-1991*. New York: McGraw-Hill, 1992, pp. 26-27.

Hawkinson, Ken. "Two Exercises on Diversity and Gender." *Speech Communication Teacher*, 8 (Fall 1993), 2-4.

Hill, L. Brooks, and Javidi, Manoocher. "The Needs of the International Student." In Lawrence J. Hugenberg, Pamela L. Gray, and Douglas M. Trank (eds.), *Teaching and Directing the Basic Communications Course*. Dubuque, Iowa: Kendall/Hunt, 1993, pp. 263-270.

Langley, Darrell C. "The Heckling Speech." In Stephen E. Lucas (ed.), *Selections from the Speech Communication Teacher, 1986-1991*. New York: McGraw-Hill, 1992, p. 67.

McClarty, Wilma. "Audience Analysis: Go and Tell." *Speech Communication Teacher*, 8 (Fall 1993), pp. 4-5.

McKinney, Bruce C. "Audience Analysis Exercise." In Stephen E. Lucas (ed.), *Selections from the Speech Communication Teacher, 1986-1991*. New York: McGraw-Hill, 1992, p. 13.

Mohsen, Raed A. "Out on Campus: A Challenging Public Speaking Experience." *Speech Communication Teacher*, 7 (Summer 1993), 10-11.

Neumann, David. "Selecting Messages: An Exercise in Audience Analysis." In Stephen E. Lucas (ed.), *Selections from the Speech Communication Teacher, 1986-1991*. New York: McGraw-Hill, 1992, p. 14.

Ross, Charlynn. "The Challenging Audience Exercise." In Stephen E. Lucas (ed.), *Selections from the Speech Communication Teacher, 1986-1991*. New York: McGraw-Hill, 1992, p. 69.

Ross, Charlynn. "Suggestions for Teaching International Students." In Stephen E. Lucas (ed.), *Selections from the Speech Communication Teacher, 1986-1991*. New York: McGraw-Hill, 1992, pp. 28-29.

Rowan, Katherine. "The Speech to Explain Difficult Ideas." In Stephen E. Lucas (ed.), *Selections from the Speech Communication Teacher, 1986-1991*. New York: McGraw-Hill, 1992, pp. 69-71.

Schumer, Allison. "Helping International Students Adapt to American Communication Norms." In Stephen E. Lucas (ed.), *Selections from the Speech Communication Teacher, 1986-1991*. New York: McGraw-Hill, 1992, p. 30.

Stern, Rick. "Audience Spinouts." In Stephen E. Lucas (ed.), *Selections from the Speech Communication Teacher, 1986-1991*. New York: McGraw-Hill, 1992, pp. 14-15.

Wilson, Wendy L. "Sex Role Stereotypes: What Do We See in Them?" *Speech Communication Teacher*, 3 (Winter 1989), 15.

## Films and Videos

"A World of Gestures." University of California Extension Center for Media and Independent Learning (1991). 28 minutes.

"American Tongues." Center for New American Media (1986). 40 minutes.

"Cross-Cultural Communication in Diverse Settings." Insight Media (1992). 60 minutes.

"Diversity Series." Quality Media Resources (1993). Four-module set; 20 minutes per module.

"Doing Business Internationally." CRM Films (1992). 43 minutes.

"How to Get Your Point Across in 30 Seconds or Less." Coronet/MTI Film and Video (1986). 30 minutes.

"Managing Diversity." CRM Films (1991). 22 minutes.

"The Public Speaker and the Audience." RMI Media Productions (1986). 28 minutes.

"The Speaker's Purpose and Occasion." RMI Media Productions (1986). 30 minutes.

# Chapter 6 Gathering Materials

## Chapter Objectives

*After reading this chapter, students should be able to:*

1.  Explain how drawing on their own knowledge and experience can enrich their speeches.

2.  Delineate the three stages of interviewing and explain the responsibilities of the interviewer at each stage.

3.  Explain the major resources available for researching speeches in the library.

4.  Follow the five tips for doing research discussed in the chapter.

## Chapter Outline

I.   A speaker's own knowledge and experience can be a valuable resource for information on a speech topic *(text pages 116-117)*.
     A.  We usually speak best about topics with which we are familiar.
     B.  Supplementing facts and figures from books with personal experience can add color and emotion to a speech.

II.  Interviewing people with specialized knowledge is another way to gather materials for a speech *(text pages 117-122)*.
     A.  The first stage in the interviewing process takes place before the interview.
         1.  The interview process begins when a speaker formulates a purpose for the interview.
         2.  Once the purpose of the interview is clear, a speaker must decide whom to interview and set up an appointment with that person.

3. Next the speaker needs to consider whether or not to tape record the interview.
   a. There are two advantages to using a tape recorder.
      (1) The interviewer can concentrate on listening and asking questions rather than taking notes.
      (2) A tape recording provides an exact record of the interview.
   b. There are two disadvantages to using a tape recorder.
      (1) Some interviewees are uncomfortable with a tape recorder.
      (2) It takes a great deal of time after the interview to distill notes from the tape recording.
   c. A tape recorder should never be used without the consent of the person being interviewed.
4. The most important task before the interview is preparing the questions to be asked.
   a. Effective interviewers write out their questions in advance of the interview.
   b. They go into the interview with a list of specific, thoughtful queries.
B. The second stage of the interview process takes place during the interview itself.
   1. It is important to dress appropriately and to show up on time.
   2. It is a good idea at the outset to restate the purpose of the interview so as to refresh the interviewee's memory.
   3. If the interviewee consents to being tape recorded, the equipment should be set up quickly and inconspicuously.
   4. The most important part of the interview is asking the questions.
      a. Effective interviewers keep on track by making sure they cover the questions on their prearranged list.
      b. At the same time, they take advantage of opportunities to ask follow-up questions or to pursue new information.
   5. In addition to asking good questions, the interviewer must listen carefully to the answers.
      a. Effective interviewers will ask for clarification if an answer is unclear.
      b. They will also double check if they have questions about a quotation.
   6. Finally, the interviewer should try not to exceed the stipulated time period for the interview.
C. The third stage of the interview process takes places after the interview.
   1. While the interview is still fresh, the researcher should review her or his notes.

        a.    Effective interviewers concentrate on reviewing the main points of the interview.

        b.    They also focus on specific details that may be useful in the speech.

    2.    As soon as possible after the interview, the researcher should transcribe ideas and information from the interview onto index cards that can be sorted along with other materials gathered in the research process.

III.   Speakers can write away for research materials *(text page 123)*.

   A.   Special interest groups, corporations, and government agencies all offer free or inexpensive publications.

   B.   Addresses can be obtained through the *Encyclopedia of Associations*, available at most libraries.

IV.   Library research is the major source of material for most speeches *(text pages 123-134)*.

   A.   Librarians are an excellent resource.

    1.    They can help students locate specific information.

    2.    They can also direct students to specialized research sources.

   B.   Catalogues list all the books and periodicals in the library and where they are located.

    1.    Card catalogues have information on small paper cards.

    2.    Computer catalogues store information on electronic databases.

   C.   The reference section contains a wealth of information about almost any topic.

    1.    Encyclopedias provide accurate, objective information on a wide range of topics.

        a.    General encyclopedias offer short articles about all branches of human knowledge.

        b.    Special encyclopedias are devoted to specific subjects and are more detailed than general encyclopedias.

    2.    Yearbooks are annual publications that are invaluable for current information.

        a.    *Statistical Abstracts* is the standard source for numerical information on life in the United States.

        b.    *The World Almanac and Book of Facts* includes data from international sources.

        c.    *Facts on File* covers national and international news events.

    3.    Dictionaries offer a wide range of information about language.

        a.    Some dictionaries, such as *Webster's*, define words currently in use.

        b.    Others, such as the *Oxford English Dictionary*, provide histories of words or phrases.

4.    Books of quotations can be useful, especially for introductions and conclusions.
    a.    The best all-purpose book of quotations is *Bartlett's Familiar Quotations*.
    b.    There are also many specialized books of quotations.
5.    Biographical aids provide information about contemporary and historical figures.
    a.    Works such as *Who's Who in America, International Who's Who,* and *Current Biography* focus on contemporary figures.
    b.    Works such as the *Dictionary of American Biography* and *Notable American Women* focus on historical figures.
6.    Atlases and gazetteers provide geographical information.
    a.    Atlases contain maps, charts, and tables about all parts of the world.
    b.    Gazetteers follow the same alphabetical format as dictionaries, but all the entries deal with geographical topics.
7.    Periodical indexes are indispensable for finding articles in magazines and journals.
    a.    General indexes such as the *Reader's Guide to Periodical Literature* provide up-to-date listings of articles in general-interest publications.
    b.    Special indexes provide guides to scholarly or highly specialized publications.
8.    Newspaper indexes are crucial for research on many topics.
    a.    Most major U.S. newspapers are indexed.
    b.    In addition, there are special newspaper indexes such as *NewsBank Index* and *Editorials on File* that catalogue selected articles and editorials.

D.    Computerized research services can also help locate material for speeches.
1.    Computer research services can quickly locate obscure or highly specialized materials on current topics.
2.    They are usually limited, however, to materials published in the past ten or fifteen years.

V.    Regardless of which resources speakers rely on in gathering speech materials, there are several ways to make their research more efficient *(text pages 134-138)*.
A.    It is imperative that speakers begin their research early.
1.    Starting early helps ensure that there will be adequate time to conduct thorough research.
2.    Starting early also allows the speaker time to think about and organize materials gathered during the research process.

B.   Speakers should create a preliminary bibliography of research sources.
1.   A preliminary bibliography lists every source that looks as if it might be helpful in preparing the speech.
2.   It is longer than the final bibliography, which lists only those sources that are actually used in the speech.
C.   Speakers can save time and energy by taking research notes efficiently.
1.   They should record notes on index cards, which can be easily sorted in organizing the speech.
2.   They should include the source and a heading for each note.
3.   They should use a single card for each note.
4.   They should distinguish between direct quotations, paraphrases, and their own ideas.
5.   They should take plenty of notes.
D.   The research process is most productive when speakers think about their materials as they research.
1.   Doing research is more than a mechanical routine.
2.   It involves creativity to find interesting information.
3.   It involves critical thinking in assessing research materials and their relationship to the speech topic.

## Application Exercises *(from text pages 140-141)*

1.   Plan to conduct an interview for one of your classroom speeches. Be sure to follow the guidelines for effective interviewing discussed in the chapter. Afterward, evaluate the interview. Did you prepare for it adequately? Did you get the information you wanted? What would you do differently if you could conduct the interview again?

**Discussion:** *This exercise is most applicable if you assign students to conduct a research interview for one of their speeches. Having students write evaluations of their interviews requires them to think systematically about the interview process.*

2.   Your library probably has the *Encyclopedia of Associations* in its reference section. Using the *Encyclopedia*, find the names and addresses of three organizations you might write to for information about one of your speech topics.

**Discussion:** *Most students are not aware of the* Encyclopedia of Associations. *This exercise gives them a chance to see how helpful it can be.*

3.   In the *Readers' Guide to Periodical Literature* or one of the special indexes listed on pages 130-131, find three articles on the subject of your next speech. Prepare a preliminary bibliography card for each article, and track down the articles in the stacks or in the periodicals section of the library.

> **Discussion:** *It is astounding how many college students have never used special indexes or the* Readers' Guide to Periodical Literature. *This exercise is meant to remedy that situation and, like the preceding exercises, also gets students started on researching their next speech.*

4.   This exercise is designed to give you firsthand acquaintance with some of the major reference works available to you. Your task is to answer each of the following questions. Some of the questions indicate where you will find the answer, and some do not. If necessary, recheck the chapter to see which reference works are most likely to supply the answers. For each question, record both your answer and where you found it.

a.   According to *Facts on File*, what did four girls in Great Britain win from their parents during the week of December 31, 1992?

> *(Four girls in Great Britain won "divorces" from their parents during the week of December 31, 1992.* Facts on File Yearbook, 1992, *page 991.)*

b.   Who said, "Who knows what women can be when they are finally free to become themselves"?

> *(Betty Friedan said, "Who knows what women can be when they are finally free to become themselves."* Bartlett's Familiar Quotations, *15th edition, page 898.)*

c.   In what year was nineteenth-century Native American leader Pushmataha elected chief of his Choctaw tribe?

> *(Pushmataha was elected chief of his tribe in 1805.* Dictionary of American Biography, *Volume 8, page 274.)*

d.   According to volume 64 of *Education Index*, what journal published an article entitled "Lost in the Crowd?" in July 1992 about class size in colleges and universities?

> *("Lost in the Crowd" was published in* The Times Higher Education Supplement *of July 17, 1992.* Education Index, *Volume 64, page 73.)*

e.  From what school and in what year did American family studies researcher Li-Ying Hilary Wang receive her Ph.D.?

*(Li-Ying Hilary Wang earned her Ph.D. at Cornell University in 1991. Who's Who of American Women, 1993-1994, page 1015.)*

f.  According to the *Oxford English Dictionary*, what is the original meaning of the word "assassin"?

*(The original meaning of the word "assassin" was a "hashish-eater," referring to "Moslem fanatics in the time of the Crusades who were sent forth by their sheikh . . . to murder the Christian leaders." From this the word came generally to mean one who undertakes to put another to death by treacherous violence.* Oxford English Dictionary, *Volume 1, page 499.)*

g.  Which issue of the *New York Times* in 1992 carried an article on the Pennsylvania State University's professional golf management program?

*(An article on Penn State University's golf management program appeared in the* New York Times *on March 15, 1992.* New York Times Index, *1992, page 919.)*

h.  According to the *Encyclopedia of Religion and Ethics*, who was most responsible for starting Sunday schools in England?

*(The person most responsible for starting Sunday schools in England was Robert Raikes, editor of the* Gloucester Journal. Encyclopedia of Religion and Ethics, *Volume 12, page 112.)*

i.  What percentage of the United States adult population performed volunteer work in 1989?

*(In 1989, 20.4 percent of the U.S. adult population performed volunteer work.* Statistical Abstract of the United States, *1992, page 374.)*

j.  According to the 1993 edition of *Current Biography*, what was sportscaster Bob Costas's first professional job?

*(In his first professional job, Bob Costas announced games for the Syracuse Blazers, a minor-league hockey team.* Current Biography Yearbook, *1993, page 125).*

**Discussion:** *This is an excellent way to acquaint students with reference sources they otherwise might not employ. Under ideal circumstances, each student would complete the exercise working alone. Practically, however, this is seldom possible. One alternative is to divide the class into groups and have each group be responsible for tracking down answers. This can be followed by a class discussion comparing the groups' answers. Another alternative is to assign each student two or three specific questions to answer. Whichever method you use, you will probably need more than the ten questions included in the textbook. Therefore, three more sets of questions are included among the Additional Exercises and Activities below.*

*If you assign this exercise, it is probably a good idea to alert the librarians in the reference section a few days ahead of time. They may also appreciate receiving a copy of the exercise. This will allow them to make whatever special preparations may be necessary to help your students.*

# Additional Exercises and Activities

1.  Arrange for your students to take a tour of the campus library. Students should read Chapter 6 before the tour, and they should be assigned application exercises from the chapter after the tour.

    **Discussion:** *Because so many students do not know how to use the library efficiently, this activity is extremely beneficial. Not only are most libraries pleased to conduct such a tour, but they are quite adept at orienting it to the specific needs of individual classes. Arrange the tour two or three weeks in advance. Then contact the library a few days before the tour to indicate whether your students are mostly freshmen, sophomores, juniors, or seniors; what research tasks they will face in preparing their speeches; and any special features of the library you wish to have stressed on the tour. Students usually find the tour so helpful that, at the end of the term or semester, they often rank it—and the development of their research skills—among the most valuable aspects of their speech class.*

2.   Answer each of the following questions. Some of the questions indicate where the answer can be found, and some do not. If necessary, recheck Chapter 6 of the textbook to see in which reference sources you are most likely to find the answers. For each question, record both your answer and where you found it, following the format on page 140 of the textbook.

   a.   According to the 1992 *World Almanac and Book of Facts*, who was named the "Top Hero" of young America in *World Almanac*'s twelfth annual poll, taken in 1991?

   b.   In an editorial of January 12, 1993, reprinted in *Editorials on File*, the *St. Petersburg Times* quoted EPA administrator William K. Reilly on the risks of second-hand smoke. What did Reilly say?

   c.   According to the *Encyclopedia of World Art*, when did the use of stained glass as an art form first become widespread?

   d.   What occupation is listed for Vera Cooper Rubin in  *Who's Who of American Women, 1993-1994*?

   e.   What is the title of the article on the marketing of olive oil listed in Volume 35 of *Business Periodicals Index*?

   f.   Who said, "Absence makes the heart grow fonder"?

   g.   According to the 1993 *Statistical Abstract of the United States*, how many nuclear power plants were there in the U.S. in 1965? In 1992?

   h.   What was the original name of the famous 19th-century American woman abolitionist known as Sojourner Truth? In what year did she take the name Sojourner Truth?

   i.   When and where was Israeli leader Shimon Peres born?

   j.   According to the 1993 *Facts on File Yearbook*, who received the Pulitzer Prize for general nonfiction that year? What was the title of the winning book?

**Answers to Additional Exercise 2:**

a.   According to the 1992 *World Almanac and Book of Facts*, who was named the "Top Hero" of young America in *World Almanac*'s annual poll for 1991?

*(General H. Norman Schwarzkopf was young America's "Top Hero" in 1991.* World Almanac and Book of Facts, 1992, *page 32.)*

b.   In an editorial of January 12, 1993, reprinted in *Editorials on File*, the *St. Petersburg Times* quoted EPA administrator William K. Reilly on the risks of second-hand smoke. What did Reilly say?

*(Reilly said: "The risks associated with environmental tobacco smoke are at least an order of magnitude greater than they are for virtually any chemical or risk that EPA regulates."* Editorials on File, 1993, *page 55.)*

c.   According to the *Encyclopedia of World Art*, when did the use of stained glass as an art form first become widespread?

*(The use of stained glass as an art form first became widespread in the 12th century.* Encyclopedia of World Art, *Volume 13, page 350.)*

d.   What occupation is listed for Vera Cooper Rubin in *Who's Who of American Women, 1993-1994*?

*(Vera Cooper Rubin is listed as a research astronomer.* Who's Who of American Women, 1993-1994, *page 845.)*

e.   What is the title of the article on the marketing of olive oil listed in Volume 35 of *Business Periodicals Index*?

*(The title of the article is "Oil Snobs." It was published in* Forbes, *March 29, 1993.* Business Periodicals Index, *Volume 35, page 2229.)*

f.   Who said, "Absence makes the heart grow fonder"?

*("Absence makes the heart grow fonder" comes from the ancient Roman writer Sextus Propertius.* Bartlett's Familiar Quotations, *15th edition, page 112.)*

g. According to the 1993 *Statistical Abstract of the United States*, how many nuclear power plants were there in the U.S. in 1965? In 1992?

*(In 1965 there were 6 nuclear power plants in the U.S. In 1992 there were 109.* Statistical Abstract of the United States, 1993, *page 588.)*

h. What was the original name of the famous 19th-century American woman abolitionist known as Sojourner Truth? In what year did she take the name Sojourner Truth?

*(Sojourner Truth's original name was Isabella. She took the name Sojourner Truth in 1843.* Notable American Women, *Volume 3, pages 479-480.)*

i. When and where was Israeli leader Shimon Peres born?

*(Shimon Peres was born in Poland in 1923.* International Who's Who, *1993-1994, page 1218.)*

j. According to the 1993 *Facts on File Yearbook*, who received the Pulitzer Prize for general nonfiction that year? What was the title of the winning book?

*(The 1993 Pulitzer Prize for general nonfiction went to Garry Wills for* Lincoln at Gettysburg: The Words that Remade America. Facts on File Yearbook, 1993, *page 275.)*

3.   Answer each of the following questions. Some of the questions indicate where the answer can be found, and some do not. If necessary, recheck Chapter 6 of the textbook to see in which reference works you are most likely to find the answers. For each question, record both your answer and where you found it, following the format on page 140 of the textbook.

a.   Which issue of the *New York Times* in 1992 carried an article about plans to renovate and enlarge the Pentagon building in Washington, D.C.?

b.   In what year did modern American historian Mary Ritter Beard publish *Woman as a Force in History*?

c.   According to *Facts on File Yearbook,* what was the top-grossing film in the United States and Canada for the week of November 27-December 3, 1992?

d.   What is the first definition of "rhetoric" listed in the *Oxford English Dictionary*?

e.   According to Volume 20 of the *Social Sciences Index*, what journal published an article about Egghead Software, Inc., in October 1992 entitled "Over Easy"?

f.   In what state is the Cheeseman Dam located and when was it completed?

g.   According to the 1993 *Current Biography Yearbook*, how many copies of John Grisham's books are in print?

h.   What companies are listed in the 1994 *World Almanac and Book of Facts* as the three leading advertisers in the United States for 1990-1991?

i.   According to the *McGraw-Hill Encyclopedia of Science and Technology*, who were two of the earliest writers on the subject of extraterrestrial intelligence?

j.   Where did novelist Stephen King attend college and when did he graduate?

**Answers to additional exercise 3:**

a. Which issue of the *New York Times* in 1992 carried an article about plans to renovate and enlarge the Pentagon building in Washington, D.C.?

   *(The article was published in the* New York Times *on March 22, 1992.* New York Times Index, 1992, *page 919.)*

b. In what year did modern American historian Mary Ritter Beard publish *Woman as a Force in History*?

   *(Mary Ritter Beard published* Woman as a Force in History *in 1946.* Notable American Women: The Modern Period, *page 72. This is a 1980 addition to the original three-volume* Notable American Women, *which was published in 1971.)*

c. According to *Facts on File Yearbook*, what was the top-grossing film in the United States and Canada for the week of November 27-December 3, 1992?

   *(The top grossing film in the United States and Canada for the week of November 27-December 3, 1992, was* Home Alone 2. Facts on File Yearbook, 1992, *p. 947.)*

d. What is the first definition of "rhetoric" listed in the *Oxford English Dictionary*?

   *(The first definition of "rhetoric" in the* Oxford English Dictionary *is as follows: "The art of using language so as to persuade or influence others; the body of rules to be observed by a speaker or writer in order that he may express himself with eloquence."* Oxford English Dictionary, 2nd edition, Volume 13, page 857.)*

e. According to Volume 20 of the *Social Sciences Index*, what journal published an article about Egghead Software, Inc., in October 1992 entitled "Over Easy"?

   *(The article "Over Easy" about Egghead Software, Inc., was published in the* Economist *of October 3, 1992.* Social Sciences Index, *Volume 20, page 205.)*

f.   In what state is the Cheeseman Dam located and when was it completed?

*(The Cheeseman Dam is located in Colorado; it was completed in 1904.*
Webster's New Geographical Dictionary, *1988 edition, page 247.)*

g.   According to the 1993 *Current Biography Yearbook*, how many copies of John Grisham's books are in print?

*(There are 22 million copies of John Grisham's books in print.* Current Biography Yearbook, 1993, *page 221.)*

h.   What companies were listed in the 1994 *World Almanac and Book of Facts* as the three leading advertisers in the United States for 1990-1991?

*(The three leading advertisers in the U.S. for 1990-1991 were Procter & Gamble, Philip Morris, and General Motors.* World Almanac and Book of Facts, 1994, *page 299.)*

i.   According to the *McGraw-Hill Encyclopedia of Science and Technology*, who were two of the earliest writers on the subject of extraterrestrial intelligence?

*(Two of the earliest writers on the subject of extraterrestrial intelligence were Metrodorus of Chios, who wrote in the fifth century B.C., and Lucretius, who wrote in the first century B.C.* McGraw-Hill Encyclopedia of Science and Technology, *7th edition, Volume 6, page 576.)*

j.   Where did novelist Stephen King attend college and when did he graduate?

*(Stephen King graduated from the University of Maine in 1970.* Who's Who in America, 1994, *Volume 1, page 1881.)*

4. Answer each of the following questions. Some of the questions indicate where the answer can be found, and some do not. If necessary, recheck Chapter 6 of the textbook to see in which reference works you are most likely to find the answers. For each question, record both your answer and where you found it, following the format on page 140 of the textbook.

  a. What award did Peruvian diplomat Javier Perez de Cuellar win in 1992?

  b. According to *Facts on File*, who was tennis star Monica Seles playing—and in what city—when she was stabbed at courtside on April 30, 1993?

  c. How does the *International Encyclopedia of the Social Sciences* define "social movements"?

  d. According to *Webster's New Geographical Dictionary*, what did early Spanish explorers believe about the Cibola region in present day New Mexico?

  e. Where did American political activist Ethel Rosenberg die in 1953?

  f. According to the 1993 *Statistical Abstract of the United States*, how many academic libraries were there in the U.S. as of 1991?

  g. What are the origins of the word "moonshine"—as explained by William Morris and Mary Morris in their *Morris Dictionary of Word and Phrase Origins*?

  h. According to *Grove's Dictionary of Music and Musicians*, what is the regal and when was it invented?

  i. Under the category "College Students" in the 1993 *NewsBank Index*, information is indexed about speech codes at five different schools. What are the schools?

  j. According to the *McGraw-Hill Encyclopedia of Science and Technology*, how many species of cockroaches are there in the world?

**Answers to additional exercise 4:**

a.   What award did Peruvian diplomat Javier Perez de Cuellar win in 1992?

*(In 1992 Javier Perez de Cuellar won the Four Freedoms Award, which is presented by the Franklin Delano Roosevelt Institute.* International Who's Who, 1993-1994, *page 1218.)*

b.   According to *Facts on File Yearbook*, who was tennis star Monica Seles playing—and in what city—when she was stabbed at courtside on April 30, 1993?

*(Seles was playing Magdalena Maleeva of Bulgaria when she was stabbed in Hamburg, Germany.* Facts on File Yearbook, 1993, *page 341.)*

c.   How does the *International Encyclopedia of the Social Sciences* define "social movements"?

*(The* International Encyclopedia of the Social Sciences *defines "social movements" as "a wide variety of collective attempts to bring about a change in certain social institutions or to create an entirely new order."* International Encyclopedia of the Social Sciences, *Volume 14, pages 438-439.)*

d.   According to *Webster's New Geographical Dictionary*, what did early Spanish explorers believe about the Cibola region in present day New Mexico?

*(Early Spanish explorers believed the Cibola region contained vast treasures.* Webster's New Geographical Dictionary, *1988 edition, page 266.)*

e.   Where did American political activist Ethel Rosenberg die in 1953?

*(Convicted of a conspiracy to commit espionage, Ethel Rosenberg died in the electric chair at Sing Sing prison.* Notable American Women: The Modern Period, *page 601. This is a 1980 addition to the original three-volume* Notable American Women, *which was published in 1971.)*

f.   According to the 1993 *Statistical Abstract of the United States*, how many academic libraries were there in the U.S. as of 1991?

*(As of 1991 there were 4,613 academic libraries in the U.S. Statistical Abstract of the United States, 1993, page 186.)*

g.   What are the origins of the word "moonshine"—as explained by William Morris and Mary Morris in their *Morris Dictionary of Word and Phrase Origins*?

*(Here is what the Morrises say about the origins of "moonshine":*

> *"The general belief is that* moonshine *as a name for illegally made whiskey originated because the distillers did their work under cover of night so as not to be detected by revenue agents. However, there is evidence in a dictionary published in London by the Rev. John Ash in 1785 that the word* moonshine *already existed and referred to liquor illegally smuggled by night from France to England."*

*William Morris and Mary Morris, Dictionary of Word and Phrase Origins, Second Edition, page 393.)*

h.   According to Volume 18 of *Biography Index*, what is the title of the article about Georgia O'Keeffe published in *Art News* in April 1992?

*(In April 1992 Art News published an article on Georgia O'Keeffe titled "Days with Georgia." Biography Index, Volume 18, page 295.)*

i.   Under the category "College Students" in the 1993 *NewsBank Index*, information is indexed about speech codes at five different schools. What are the schools?

*(The schools are University of Connecticut, Kean College, North Carolina State University, University of Pennsylvania, and Vanderbilt University. NewsBank Index, 1993, page 131.)*

j.   According to the *McGraw-Hill Encyclopedia of Science and Technology*, how many species of cockroaches are there in the world?

*(There are approximately 2,500 species of cockroaches. McGraw-Hill Encyclopedia of Science and Technology, 7th edition, Volume 4, page 89.)*

# Extra Teaching and Learning Resources

## Library Research

Berkman, Robert I. *Find It Fast: How to Uncover Expert Information on Any Subject.* New York: Harper and Row, 1987.

Engeldinger, Eugene A. "Bibliographic Instruction and Critical Thinking: The Contribution of the Annotated Bibliography." *Reference Quarterly*, 28 (1988), 195-202.

Gates, Jean Key. *Guide to the Use of Libraries and Information Sources*, 7th ed. New York: McGraw-Hill, 1994.

Harris, Sherwood. *The New York Public Library Book of How and Where to Look It Up.* Englewood Cliffs, N.J.: Prentice-Hall, 1991.

Katz, William A. *Introduction to Reference Work.* 5th ed. New York: McGraw-Hill, 1987.

McCormack, Mona. *The New York Times Guide to Reference Materials*, rev. ed. New York: Dorsett Press, 1988.

## Interviewing

Douglas, Jack D. *Creative Interviewing.* Beverly Hills, Calif.: Sage, 1985.

Hunt, Gary, and Eadie, William. *Interviewing: A Communication Approach.* New York: Holt, Rinehart and Winston, 1987.

Perry, Patrick. "The 'Perfect' Interview." *The Writer* (December 1988), 18-21.

Simons, Mary Crescenzo. "The Q's and A's of Interviewing: Ask Questions that Require More Than a Yes-or-No Answer." *The Writer* (August 1988), 19-23.

Stewart, Charles J. "Teaching Interviewing." In John A. Daly, Gustav W. Friedrich, and Anita L. Vangelisti (eds.), *Teaching Communication: Theory, Research, and Methods.* Hillsdale, N.J.: Lawrence Erlbaum, 1990, pp. 157-167.

Stewart, Charles J., and Cash, William B. *Interviewing: Principles and Practices*, 6th ed. Dubuque, Iowa: W. C. Brown, 1991.

## Classroom Activities and Assignments

Garrett, Roger L. "Helping Students Discover Interviewing Skills." In Stephen E. Lucas (ed.), *Selections from the Speech Communication Teacher, 1986-1991.* New York: McGraw-Hill, 1992, pp. 37-38.

Hankins, Gail. "Gathering Materials: A Three-Course Solution to a One-Course Problem." *Speech Communication Teacher* (Summer 1992), 1-2.

Hugenberg, Lawrence W., and O'Neill, Daniel J. "Researching National Issues Forum Topics." *Speech Communication Teacher* (Fall 1991), 1-2.

Sellnow, Timothy L. "An Oral History Exercise for the Self-Evaluation of Interview Skills." *Speech Communication Teacher* (Winter 1992), 11.

Wright, Mark H., and Wilson, Susan R. "An Interview Analysis Project for Public Speaking Classes." *Speech Communication Teacher* (Spring 1993), 5-6.


## Films and Videos

"Crediting Your Sources." RMI Media Productions (1991). 30 minutes.

"Learning to Use the Library." RMI Media Productions (1991). 30 minutes.

# Chapter 7 Supporting Your Ideas

## Chapter Objectives

*After reading this chapter, students should be able to:*

1. Explain why speakers need strong supporting materials for their ideas.

2. Distinguish among extended examples, brief examples, and hypothetical examples.

3. Explain how to use examples effectively in a speech.

4. Identify three questions for judging the reliability of statistics.

5. Discuss how to use statistics effectively in a speech.

6. Distinguish between peer testimony and expert testimony and explain the proper use of testimony in a speech.

## Chapter Outline

I. Speeches need strong supporting materials to bolster the speaker's point of view *(text pages 144-145)*.
   A. A speech composed of unsupported assertions may leave an audience skeptical and unconvinced.
   B. Specific and credible details are more convincing than are unsupported generalizations.

II.  The use of supporting materials is closely related to critical thinking *(text pages 145-146)*.
    A.  Choosing the supporting materials for a speech requires critical thinking.
        1.  Speakers must determine which ideas need to be supported given the audience, topic, and purpose.
        2.  Speakers must do research to find materials that will support their ideas clearly and creatively.
        3.  Speakers must evaluate their supporting materials to make sure they really do back up their ideas.
    B.  Assessing the quality of supporting materials in a speech requires critical thinking.
        1.  Speakers must make sure their supporting materials are accurate.
        2.  Speakers must make sure their supporting materials are relevant.
        3.  Speakers must make sure their supporting materials come from reliable sources.

III.  Examples are the first major kind of supporting material *(text pages 146-150)*.
    A.  Examples are an excellent way to get an audience involved with a speech.
        1.  They provide concrete details that make ideas specific, personal, and lively.
        2.  Researchers have found that examples have more impact on an audience's beliefs than any other kind of supporting material.
    B.  There are three types of examples—brief, extended, and hypothetical.
        1.  Brief examples are specific instances that a speaker refers to in passing.
            a.  They are often employed when a speaker wants to quickly illustrate a point.
            b.  They are sometimes used when a speaker is introducing a topic.
            c.  They are also effective when stacked up to reinforce a speaker's point.
        2.  Extended examples are longer and more detailed than brief examples.
            a.  They are often called illustrations, narratives, or anecdotes.
            b.  Because they tell a story vividly and dramatically, they are an excellent way to pull listeners into a speech.
        3.  Hypothetical examples describe an imaginary situation.
            a.  They are especially effective for relating a general principle directly to the audience.
            b.  Whenever a speaker uses a hypothetical example, it should be supplemented with statistics or testimony to show that the example could really occur.

C.   There are several tips for using examples effectively.
   1.   A speaker should use examples to clarify ideas.
   2.   A speaker should use examples to reinforce ideas.
   3.   A speaker should use examples to personalize ideas.
   4.   A speaker should use extended examples that are vivid and richly textured.
   5.   A speaker should practice delivery to enhance the impact of extended examples.

IV.   Statistics are the second major kind of supporting material *(text pages 150-159)*.
   A.   When used properly, statistics are an effective way to support a speaker's ideas.
      1.   Like brief examples, statistics can be cited in passing to clarify or strengthen a speaker's points.
      2.   Statistics can also be used in combination to show the magnitude or seriousness of an issue.
   B.   Because statistics can be easily manipulated and distorted, speakers should evaluate their statistics carefully.
      1.   Speakers need to make sure their statistics are representative of what they claim to measure.
      2.   Speakers need to understand the differences among basic statistical measures such as the mean, the median, and the mode.
         a.   The mean—popularly called the average—is determined by summing all the items in a group and dividing by the number of items.
         b.   The median is the middle figure in a group once the figures are put in order from highest to lowest.
         c.   The mode is the number that occurs most frequently in a group of numbers.
      3.   Speakers need to determine whether their statistics come from reliable sources.
   C.   There are several tips for using statistics effectively.
      1.   Statistics should be used to quantify ideas.
         a.   The main value of statistics is to give ideas numerical precision.
         b.   Research has shown that statistics can greatly enhance the impact of examples by quantifying the speaker's point.
      2.   Statistics should be used sparingly.
         a.   Cluttering a speech with too many numbers can make it dull and uninteresting.
         b.   Effective speakers include statistics only when they are needed.

3. The source of statistics should be identified in the speech.
   a. Critical listeners understand that statistics can easily be manipulated.
   b. Research indicates that speakers are more persuasive to careful listeners when they identify the sources of their statistics.
4. Statistics should be explained and made meaningful to the audience.
   a. Statistics don't speak for themselves.
   b. They need to be interpreted and related to the audience.
   c. This is especially important when dealing with large figures that may be remote from the audience's frame of reference.
5. Complicated statistics should be rounded off.
   a. Detailed figures can be too lengthy and involved to be readily understood by listeners.
   b. Unless there is a strong reason to give exact numbers, lengthy figures should be rounded off for the audience.
6. Statistical trends should be clarified with visual aids.
   a. It is often difficult for listeners to grasp the meaning of statistical trends when they are presented verbally.
   b. Effective speakers frequently use graphs and other visual aids to make their statistics easier to comprehend.
D. Statistics can be found in many sources.
   1. Newspapers, magazines, and scholarly journals, are good sources of statistics.
   2. Works such as *Statistical Abstract* and *Statistical Yearbook* are devoted exclusively to statistics.

V. Testimony is the third basic kind of supporting material *(text pages 159-164)*.
   A. Testimony can be highly effective when used in a speech.
      1. Listeners are often influenced by people who have special knowledge or experience on a topic.
      2. By quoting or paraphrasing such people, speakers can give their ideas greater strength and impact.
   B. There are two kinds of testimony—expert testimony and peer testimony.
      1. Expert testimony comes from people who are acknowledged authorities in their fields.
         a. This type of testimony provides credibility when the speaker is not an expert on the speech topic.
         b. Expert testimony is especially important when the topic is controversial or when the audience is skeptical about the speaker's point of view.
      2. Peer testimony comes from ordinary people who have firsthand experience with a topic.

        a.    This type of testimony gives a more personal viewpoint than can be gained by expert testimony.

        b.    It usually has much greater authenticity and emotional impact than does expert testimony.

C.    Testimony can be presented by quoting or by paraphrasing.

    1.    One way to present testimony is by quoting word for word.

        a.    Quotations are most effective when they are brief.

        b.    Quotations arc most cffcctivc whcn thcy convey the speaker's meaning better than the speaker's own words.

        c.    Quotations are most effective when they are eloquent, witty, or compelling.

    2.    Another way to present testimony is by paraphrasing.

        a.    Paraphrasing is preferable when the wording of a quotation is obscure or awkward.

        b.    Paraphrasing is preferable when the quotation is longer than two or three sentences.

D.    There are several tips for using testimony effectively.

    1.    Speakers should quote or paraphrase accurately.

    2.    Speakers should use testimony from qualified sources.

    3.    Speakers should use testimony from unbiased sources.

    4.    Speakers should identify the people being quoted or paraphrased.

# Application Exercises *(from text pages 169-170)*

1.    Each of the following statements violates at least one of the criteria for effective supporting materials discussed in the chapter. Identify the flaw (or flaws) in each statement.

    a.    According to a poll conducted for Hardee's restaurants, most people prefer the taste of Hardee's fried chicken over the taste of Kentucky Fried Chicken.

        **Discussion:** *Because Hardee's is a competitor of Kentucky Fried Chicken, it can hardly be considered an objective source of polling data on the question of whose fried chicken most people prefer. Although it is possible that Hardee's could hire a research firm that would conduct a scientifically valid survey, a survey conducted by an independent consumer group would be a more credible source in this case.*

    b.    It's just not true that violence on television has an influence on crimes by young people. All my friends watch television, and none of us has ever committed a violent crime.

**Discussion:** *The example cited here may well be unrepresentative of young people in general. The experience of the speaker and his or her friends is not a sufficient basis for reaching a sweeping conclusion about the impact of television on crimes by young people.*

c. According to statistics compiled by the Board of Regents, the median salary for professors at our state university is $44,850. This shows that professors average almost $45,000 a year in salary.

**Discussion:** *The speaker is confusing the median salary with the mean, which is popularly called the average. The median is the middle figure in a group once the numbers are arranged from highest to lowest and may differ considerably from the "average."*

d. The Department of Health and Human Services reports that single parents now head 25 percent of families with children under age 18 in the United States. A staggering 54 percent of these families live below the poverty line, compared with 18 percent of all families with children. For families headed by females, the figure is 47 percent compared with 19 percent for families headed by males. By the year 2000, 50 percent of U.S. families may be headed by single parents.

**Discussion:** *This statement compresses so many statistics into a brief span that even the most attentive listener would have trouble sorting them out. The speaker would be better off saying something like: "According to the Census Bureau, 25 percent of all U.S. families with school-age children are headed by single parents. More than half of these families live below the poverty line, especially if the single parent is a woman. Even more distressing, the problem will get worse by the year 2000."*

e. As Kevin Costner said in a recent interview, America must act now to protect its national parks. If we do not take action right away, Costner said, the park system may be permanently damaged.

**Discussion:** *Although he is certainly a concerned citizen, Kevin Costner is not a highly qualified source on the U.S. park system. The speaker would be better off citing someone who is an authority in the area.*

f. A random poll of 265 people taken recently in Washington, D.C., showed that 78 percent of those interviewed opposed term limitations on U.S. Senators and Representatives. Clearly, then, the American people oppose such limitations.

**Discussion:** *A random poll of 265 people in Washington, D.C., cannot be considered representative of the opinion of "the American people." The sampling is too small and too restricted in the range of people polled. Because Washington, D.C., is the seat of the federal government, people in that city are probably less likely than those elsewhere to favor limitations on the number of terms that can be served by members of the Senate and the House of Representatives. Yet another problem is that the source of the "random poll" is not identified.*

g.    In the words of one expert, "Genetic screening for job applicants is scientifically unreliable and legally questionable. Not only are the tests highly inaccurate, but they pose a serious threat to a potential employee's right to privacy."

**Discussion:** *The speaker does not identify "one expert" or present the expert's credentials as an authority on the topic.*

h.    According to the U.S. Census Bureau, the average annual income of Americans who do not graduate from high school is $5,904. For those with a high-school diploma the average is $12,924 a year. College graduates average $25,392 a year, while people with a master's degree average $33,864.

**Discussion:** *This is a highly instructive set of statistics from a reliable source, but the speaker should round off the numbers. There is no reason to give exact figures down to the dollar. In fact, by not rounding off, the speaker actually dilutes the impact of the figures. It would be more effective to say that people in the U.S. who do not graduate from high school earn $5,900 a year, people with a high-school diploma earn almost $13,000, college graduates earn $25,000, and people with a master's degree earn almost $34,000.*

2.    Analyze the speech in the Appendix by Steven Harris ("Family Medical Histories: A Proven Lifesaver"). Identify the main points of the speech and the supporting materials used for each. Evaluate the speaker's use of supporting materials in light of the criteria discussed in this chapter.

**Discussion:** *By analyzing the use of supporting materials in a speech, students often get a better idea of how to use supporting materials in their own speeches. "Family Medical Histories: A Proven Lifesaver" has a variety of supporting materials and illustrates how they can be employed to clarify and bolster a speaker's ideas. It also has enough gaps in its supporting materials for students to discuss how the speaker could have employed* them more effectively. In addition to having students read the speech, you may want to show the videotape of it, which is available as part of the instructional supplement to The Art of Public Speaking. Here is a synopsis of the speech:

*Specific Purpose: To persuade my audience that they should make a family medical history.*

*Central Idea: Because so many diseases have genetic origins, a family medical history is often of vital importance in helping to ensure proper medical diagnosis and treatment.*

*Method of Organization: Problem-Solution*

*Introduction: The introduction consists of paragraphs 1-3. The story of Gilda Radner in paragraph 1 is an excellent attention-getter and provides a striking illustration of why a person should know her or his family medical history. In paragraph 2 the speaker indicates the importance of the topic and relates it to his audience. Paragraph 3 provides a clear preview statement of the main points to be covered in the body of the speech. All in all, this is a fine introduction except for its lack of a statement establishing the speaker's credibility. Although it is clear from the rest of the speech that the speaker has done a thorough job of research, he should have made reference to his research in the introduction.*

*Body: There are two main points in the body of this speech. The first deals with the need for family medical histories and is developed in paragraphs 4-9. The speaker begins by showing the large number of diseases with genetic links (paragraphs 4-5). He then explains that the medical community has not placed as much importance as it should on family history in diagnosing and treating patients (paragraphs 6-9).*

*The second main point presents the speaker's solution and runs from paragraph 10 through paragraph 13. After an excellent transition, the speaker notes that he will focus in his solution on what individuals can do to help doctors provide accurate diagnoses of genetically based medical conditions. He then explains, in paragraphs 11-13, how to create a family medical history. His explanation is clear, specific, and detailed enough to give the audience a good sense of exactly what is involved. As you will see if you view the speech on videotape, the speaker used a striking visual aid in this section of the speech so his listeners could see what a family medical tree might look like.*

*Conclusion: The conclusion consists of paragraph 14, in which the speaker summarizes his main points and reinforces the central idea by referring to the UCLA School of Public Health's 50 Simple Things You Can Do to Save Your Life. He then gives the speech a sense of psychological unity by alluding back to his opening example of Gilda Radner. The closing line is somewhat dramatic and ends the speech by once again relating the topic directly to the audience.*

*Supporting Materials: The speaker uses one extended example—the story of Gilda Radner in paragraph 1, which introduces the topic and dramatizes the need to know one's family medical history. The story of Radner's tragic death hangs over the entire speech and is mentioned again by the speaker in his conclusion.*

*Unfortunately, the speaker did not have time to present a second extended example—this time of someone whose life had been saved by creating a family medical history. Although this would have been very helpful in demonstrating the practicality of the speaker's solution, it was more important that he include the opening example. If a speaker has time for only one extended example, as is frequently the case in classroom speeches, he or she can usually get the greatest rhetorical mileage out of the example by presenting it in the introduction.*

*The speaker uses statistics more than any other kind of supporting material. In paragraph 1 he mentions the survival rates for ovarian cancer as part of the Gilda Radner story. In paragraphs 4-5 he gives figures from U.S. News and World Report and researchers at the University of Utah to support his point that hereditary factors play an important role in many diseases. In paragraphs 8-9 he presents the results of two studies published in the New York State Journal of Medicine to illustrate the fact that doctors often do not include family history as part of their patients' medical records.*

*The only instance of testimony occurs at the end of paragraph 9, where the speaker quickly cites the Hereditary Cancer Institute at Creighton University in support of his claim that only a small minority of doctors take hereditary factors into account when diagnosing and treating patients. Not only would a stronger citation have been more effective here, but the speech as a whole would have been improved if the speaker had included more testimony in support of his position. Although he uses a fair number of statistics, he should have provided at least a couple quotations from highly qualified medical experts to bolster his view of the problem and of the practicality of his solution.*

# Additional Exercises and Class Activities

1.  Have students prepare and present a one-point speech in which they state their point, support it with three pieces of supporting material, and then summarize the point. The speech should be 1-2 minutes in length and should be accorded the same weight in grading as a homework assignment.

    > **Discussion:** *If done properly, this can be an excellent way to give students an extra oral performance while at the same time helping them learn to use supporting materials effectively. Students should be allowed—indeed, encouraged—to use materials from the major speech assignment on which they are currently working. For example, if you deal with Chapter 7 during the unit on persuasive speaking, urge students to develop their one-point speech using materials that will appear in their persuasive speech. Some teachers require that students use all three kinds of supporting materials in the speech; others require that they use at least two. In most cases, the entire class will be able to present their speeches in a single session.*

2.  Evaluate the use of supporting materials in the following speech excerpt. Be sure to deal with *all* the supporting materials in each paragraph, and *be specific* in assessing their strengths and weaknesses.

    > According to emergency medicine specialist Dr. Randall Sword, emergency rooms will handle more than 160 million cases this year alone. This means that one out of every 16 Americans will spend time in an emergency room this year. Unfortunately, the National Academy of Sciences states that "emergency medical care is one of the weakest links in the delivery of health care in the nation." In fact, medical researchers estimate that 5,000 deaths annually from poisoning, drowning, and drug overdoses, as well as 20 percent of all deaths from automobile accidents, would not have happened if the victims had received prompt and proper emergency room care.
    >
    > One cause of this problem is that many doctors are not properly trained in emergency care. According to *U.S. News and World Report*, fewer than 50 percent of emergency room physicians have completed special emergency training courses. A survey by Frey and Mangold found that untrained emergency room physicians felt they were unsure how to diagnose or treat many of the extreme abdomen, chest, and cardiac disorders that often appear in hospital emergency rooms.

Another cause of the problem is that precious time is often wasted on useless paperwork before vital emergency treatment begins. Several years ago, a man driving by an elementary school in my hometown had a heart attack and crashed into a school yard. Seven children were taken to the emergency room three blocks away, but the real tragedy had not yet begun. Once in the emergency room, the children were denied treatment until their parents were contacted and the admitting forms were filled out. By the time the forms were completed, two of the children had died.

**Discussion:** *This speech excerpt is brief enough to be used as a classroom activity. One approach is to divide the class into groups of four to five students each. Give each group ten minutes to read and analyze the excerpt, and then have each group make a two-minute report to the class assessing the strengths and weaknesses of the supporting materials in the excerpt. Another approach, of course, is to give the excerpt to each student individually. In either case, you should be able to generate an effective class discussion. Here is a brief analysis of the excerpt:*

*Paragraph One: The statistic in sentence 1 comes from a credible source. In sentence 2 the speaker does a nice job of showing what the statistic means for the U.S. public in general, though she might also have related it directly to her audience by stating how many of them would probably require emergency care during the year. The quotation from the National Academy of Sciences is excellent, and it is followed by statistics showing the seriousness of the problem. The statistics, however, should have been attributed to a specific source, rather than to unidentified "medical researchers."*

*Paragraph Two: The supporting materials in this paragraph are certainly relevant to the speaker's claim that doctors are not properly trained in emergency care. The statistics in sentence 2 are from a credible source, and the source is clearly identified. Unfortunately, in sentence 3 the speaker does not identify Frey and Mangold or their qualifications with respect to the topic.*

*Paragraph Three: While the extended example in this paragraph is dramatic, vivid, and relevant to the speaker's point, the speaker should have provided statistics or testimony to show that the example is not atypical.*

3.    Have students analyze the speech in Part V of this manual by Susan Zaeske ("Warning: Household Chemicals," pages 373-376). Have students focus their analysis on the speaker's use of supporting materials.

> **Discussion:**   *A persuasive speech on a question of policy, "Warning: Household Chemicals" gives students additional work in analyzing the use, and occasional misuse, of supporting materials. For a full discussion of the speech, see pages 377-380 of this manual.*

# Extra Teaching and Learning Resources

## General

Badzinski, Diane M. "Message Cues and Narrative Comprehension: A Developmental Study." *Communication Quarterly*, 40 (1992), 228-238.

Brown, Mary Helen. "Defining Stories in Organizations: Characteristics and Functions." In James A. Anderson, ed., *Communication Yearbook 13*. Newbury Park, Calif.: Sage, 1990, pp. 162-190.

Fisher, Walter R. *Human Communication as Narration: Toward a Philosophy of Reason, Value, and Action*. Columbia: University of South Carolina Press, 1989.

Hardwig, John. "Relying on Experts." In Trudy Govier (ed.), *Selected Issues in Logic and Communication*. Belmont, Calif.: Wadsworth, 1988, pp. 125-137.

Herrick, James A. *Critical Thinking: The Analysis of Arguments*. Scottsdale, Ariz.: Gorsuch Scarisbrick, 1991.

Hollihan, Thomas A., and Riley, Patricia. "The Rhetorical Power of a Compelling Story: A Critique of a 'Toughlove' Parental Support Group." *Communication Quarterly*, 35 (1987), 13-25.

Kellerman, Kathy. "The Concept of Evidence: A Critical Review." *Journal of the American Forensics Association*, 16 (1980), 159-172.

Kazoleas, Dean C. "A Comparison of the Persuasive Effectiveness of Qualitative versus Quantitative Evidence: A Test of Explanatory Hypotheses." *Communication Quarterly*, 41 (1993), 40-50.

Kirkwood, William G. "Parables as Metaphors and Examples." *Quarterly Journal of Speech*, 71 (1985), 422-440.

Koballa, Thomas R., Jr. "Persuading Teachers to Reexamine the Innovative Elementary Science Programs of Yesterday: The Effect of Anecdotal versus Data-Summary Conclusions." *Journal of Research in Science Teaching*, 23 (1986), 437-449.

Langellier, Kristin M. "Personal Narratives: Perspectives on Theory and Research." *Text and Performance Quarterly*, 9 (1989), 243-276.

Lewis, William F. "Telling America's Story: Narrative Form and the Reagan Presidency." *Quarterly Journal of Speech*, 73 (1987), 280-302.

Paulos, John Allen. "Counting on Dyscalculia." *Discover* (March 1994), 30-36.

Paulos, John Allen. *Innumeracy: Mathematical Illiteracy and Its Consequences.* New York: Hill and Wang, 1988.

Reinard, John C. "The Empirical Study of the Persuasive Effects of Evidence: The Status after Fifty Years of Research." *Human Communication Research*, 15 (1988), 3-59.

Reynolds, Rodney A., and Burgoon, Michael. "Belief Processing, Reasoning, and Evidence." In Robert N. Bostrom (ed.), *Communication Yearbook 7.* Beverly Hills, Calif.: Sage, 1983, pp. 83-104.

Rosteck, Thomas. "Narrative in Martin Luther King's *I've Been to the Mountaintop.*" *Southern Communication Journal*, 58 (1992), 22-32.

Runyon, Richard P. *How Numbers Lie: A Consumer's Guide to the Fine Art of Numerical Deception.* Lexington, Mass.: Lewis, 1981.

Stuckey, Mary E. "Anecdotes and Conversations: The Narrational and Dialogic Styles of Modern Presidential Communication." *Communication Quarterly*, 40 (1992), 45-55.

## Classroom Activities and Assignments

Dittus, James K. "Grade Begging as an Exercise in Argumentation." *Speech Communication Teacher* (Summer 1992), 5.

Kauffman, James. "Collecting and Evaluating Evidence." *Speech Communication Teacher* (Winter 1992), 12.

Newburger, Craig. "Testing Students' Ability to Distinguish Facts from Inferences." *Speech Communication Teacher* (Winter 1994), 13-14.

## Films and Videos

"A Case Study for Critical Thinking: Vietnam." Insight Media (1987). 52 minutes.

"Crediting Your Sources." RMI Media Productions (1991). 30 minutes.

"Critical Thinking: How to Evaluate Information and Draw Conclusions." Insight Media (1986). 47 minutes.

"Planning Your Speech." Coronet/MTI Film and Video (1976). 13 minutes.

"Presenting an Argument." Films for the Humanities (1992). 20 minutes.

# Chapter 8 Organizing the Body of the Speech

## Chapter Objectives

*After reading this chapter, students should be able to:*

1. Explain why it is important to organize speeches clearly and coherently.

2. Identify the five major patterns of organizing main points in a speech.

3. Discuss the guidelines given in the text for organizing main points.

4. Explain the four kinds of speech connectives and their roles in a speech.

## Chapter Outline

I. The ability to organize one's ideas clearly and coherently is a vital skill *(text pages 174-175)*.
   A. Clear organization is essential to effective public speaking.
      1. Research shows that well-organized speeches are easier for listeners to comprehend.
         a. Listeners demand coherence from speakers.
         b. Because listeners get only one chance to grasp the ideas in a speech, it is crucial that those ideas be clearly structured.
      2. Research shows that listeners find speakers who give well-organized speeches more competent and trustworthy.
   B. Clear organization is also connected to critical thinking.
      1. Organizing speeches helps students understand the relationships between ideas.
      2. The skills of critical thinking used in organizing speeches will benefit students in many aspects of their lives.

II. The main points are the most important element in organizing the body of a speech *(text pages 175-185)*.
   A. Because main points are the central features in the body of a speech, they should be selected carefully.
      1. Sometimes the main points are evident from a speaker's specific purpose statement.
      2. Often they emerge as the speaker researches the topic.
   B. Speeches should have a limited number of main points.
      1. Most speeches contain from two to five main points.
         a. Students do not have time in classroom speeches to develop more than five main points.
         b. No matter how long a speech may be, it should have a limited number of main points or the audience will have trouble sorting them out.
      2. If a speaker discovers that she or he has too many main points, the points should be condensed into a few broad categories.
   C. Main points should be organized strategically to achieve the speaker's purpose.
      1. When arranged chronologically, main points follow a time sequence.
         a. Chronological order is used when a speaker recounts a series of historical events in the order they happened.
         b. Chronological order is also effective for speeches that explain a process or that demonstrate how to do something.
      2. When arranged spatially, main points follow a directional pattern.
         a. Main points in spatial order proceed from top to bottom, right to left, east to west, or some other route.
         b. Like chronological order, spatial order is used most often in informative speeches.
      3. When arranged causally, main points show a cause-and-effect relationship.
         a. Speeches with causal organization have two main points
            (1) One main point deals with the causes of an event.
            (2) The other main point deals with the effects of an event.
         b. Causal order is flexible enough to be used for informative and persuasive speeches alike.
      4. Main points can also be organized in problem-solution order.
         a. The first point main point of a problem-solution speech shows the existence of a problem.
         b. The second main point presents a solution to the problem.
         c. Problem-solution order is most effective for persuasive speeches.
      5. Main points are most often arranged in topical order.
         a. Speeches that follow topical order break the speech topic into its constituent parts.

                (1)    A speech on fireworks might focus on four different kinds of fireworks.

                (2)    A speech on Babe Didrikson might focus on the three major sports in which she excelled.

        b.    The main points should divide the topic logically and consistently.

        c.    Topical order works equally well for informative and persuasive speeches.

  D.    There are three tips for preparing effective main points.

      1.    Speakers should keep their main points separate and distinct.

        a.    Each main point should focus on a single idea.

        b.    Each main point should be worded clearly.

      2.    Speakers should try to use parallel wording in their main points.

        a.    Parallel wording makes main points easier to understand.

        b.    Parallel wording makes main points stand out from the details of the speech.

      3.    Speakers should balance the amount of time devoted to each main point.

        a.    Each main point needs to receive enough emphasis to be clear and convincing.

        b.    The time devoted to each main point does not need to be equal, but it should usually be roughly balanced.

III.    Once the main points of a speech are in strategic order, a speaker must make sure that the supporting materials are effectively organized *(text pages 185-187)*.

  A.    It is crucial that supporting materials be well organized because misplaced supporting materials are confusing to listeners.

  B.    Details and evidence need to be directly relevant to the main points they support.

IV.    Speakers should use connectives to strengthen their organization in the body of the speech *(text pages 187-191)*.

  A.    Connectives are words or phrases that join one thought to another and indicate the relationship between them.

      1.    Connectives are like ligaments and tendons in the human body.

      2.    They hold the speech together, making it unified and coherent.

  B.    There are four types of connectives.

      1.    Transitions indicate when a speaker has completed one thought and is moving on to another.

        a.    Technically, transitions state *both* the thought a speaker has completed and the thought she or he is about to develop.

        b.    Without transitions, a speech will seem disjointed and uncoordinated.

2. Internal previews let the audience know what the speaker will take up next.
   a. Internal previews are more detailed than transitions.
   b. They are rarely necessary for every main point.
3. Internal summaries remind listeners of what they have just heard.
   a. Internal summaries are especially useful when a speaker finishes a complex or important point.
   b. They clarify and reinforce the speaker's ideas.
4. Signposts are brief statements that indicate exactly where a speaker is in the speech or that focus attention on key ideas.
   a. Signposts can be numerical ("First," "Second," "Third," etc.).
   b. Questions also work well as signposts.
   c. So do phrases such as "Be sure to keep this in mind," "Above all, you need to know," and the like.

## Application Exercises *(from text pages 192-193)*

1. Identify the organizational method used in each of the following sets of main points.

   I. Cesar Chavez is best known for his efforts to protect the rights of Hispanic farm workers in California.
   II. Cesar Chavez was also a tireless advocate for Hispanic racial and cultural pride in general.

   *(topical)*

   I. The outermost section of the ancient Egyptian burial tomb was the entrance passage.
   II. The next section of the Egyptian burial tomb was the antechamber.
   III. The third section of the Egyptian burial tomb was the treasury.
   IV. The innermost section of the Egyptian burial tomb was the burial chamber.

   *(spatial)*

   I. Sickle-cell anemia is a hereditary blood disease caused by abnormal blood cells.
   II. The effects of sickle-cell anemia include liver damage, blindness, paralysis, and early death.

   *(causal)*

I. Rodeos began in the Old West as contests of skill among cowboys during cattle roundups.
II. By 1920 rodeos had become a popular spectator sport for the general public.
III. Today rodeos combine traditional western events with a circuslike atmosphere and the marketing techniques of big business.

*(chronological)*

I. A shortage of trained nurses has become a serious problem at hospitals throughout the United States.
II. The problem can be solved by offering nurses better salaries and improved working conditions.

*(problem-solution)*

2. What organizational method (or methods) might you use to arrange main points for speeches with the following specific purpose statements?

To inform my audience about the major events in the development of the civil rights movement from 1955 to 1970.

To inform my audience of the causes and effects of the erosion of America's seacoasts.

To inform my audience about the educational philosophy of Maria Montessori.

To inform my audience about the geographical regions of the Philippines.

To persuade my audience that our state legislature should enact tougher legislation to deal with the continuing problem of child abuse.

To inform my audience about the major kinds of symbols used in traditional Native American art.

**Discussion:** *Here are suggestions for organizational methods that could be used for each of these specific purpose statements:*

To inform my audience about the major events in the development of the civil rights movement from 1955 to 1970.

*(The most obvious choice for a speech with this specific purpose would be chronological order, but it could also be arranged topically.)*

To inform my audience of the causes and effects of the erosion of America's seacoasts.

> *(A speech with this specific purpose would probably be structured in causal order.)*

To inform my audience about the educational philosophy of Maria Montessori.

> *(A speech with this specific purpose would most likely be organized topically, with each main point dealing with a different aspect of Montessori's educational philosophy.)*

To inform my audience about the geographical regions of the Philippines.

> *(A speech with this specific purpose would probably be organized spatially, though it could also be structured topically.)*

To persuade my audience that our state legislature should enact tougher legislation to deal with the continuing problem of child abuse.

> *(Based on the methods of organization discussed in this chapter, a speech with this specific purpose would most likely be arranged in problem-solution order. In Chapter 15, we shall discuss more specialized methods for organizing persuasive speeches.)*

To inform my audience about the major kinds of symbols used in traditional Native American art.

> *(Although a speech with this specific purpose would probably be arranged in topical order, it might be organized chronologically if the speaker were to deal with the changes in Native American art symbols over the years.)*

3.  Turn to the outline of main points and supporting materials for the speech about hypnosis on pages 185-186. Create appropriate transitions, internal summaries, internal previews, and signposts for the speech.

> **Discussion:** *The purpose of this exercise is to give students practice in thinking about where connectives are needed in a speech and in creating the appropriate connectives. The exercise seems to work best when used as an in-class activity. Divide the class into groups, and have each group perform the exercise. Follow this with a class discussion in which each group presents its handiwork.*

## Additional Exercises and Class Activities

1.   Below is a speech outline with eight main points. Reorganize the outline so as to reduce the original eight main points to two main points, each with four subpoints. Use the new main points and subpoints to fill in the blank outline at the bottom of this page.

I.     The deficit in the federal budget could be lessened by cutting defense spending.

II.    The deficit in the federal budget could be lessened by raising income taxes.

III.   The deficit in the federal budget could be lessened by imposing a luxury tax on nonessential items.

IV.    The deficit in the federal budget could be lessened by cutting welfare spending.

V.     The deficit in the federal budget could be lessened by cutting foreign aid.

VI.    The deficit in the federal budget could be lessened by stricter enforcement of income tax collection.

VII.   The deficit in the federal budget could be lessened by adding a tax surcharge for upper-income families.

VIII.  The deficit in the federal budget could be lessened by cutting aid to states and cities.

I.

   A.

   B.

   C.

   D.

II.

   A.

   B.

   C.

   D.

**Discussion:** *When reorganized, the outline should look like the one printed below, though subpoints need not be in the same order as written here. The important matter is that students see how the eight original points can be regrouped as subpoints under two main points. To facilitate class discussion, this exercise is also available as part of the transparency supplement that accompanies* The Art of Public Speaking.

I.    One way to reduce the deficit in the federal budget is by cutting spending.
    A.    Defense spending could be cut.
    B.    Welfare spending could be cut.
    C.    Foreign aid could be cut.
    D.    Aid to states and cities could be cut.

II.   Another way to reduce the deficit in the federal budget is by increasing revenue.
    A.    Income taxes could be raised.
    B.    The collection of income taxes could be more strictly enforced.
    C.    A luxury tax could be imposed on nonessential items.
    D.    A tax surcharge on upper-income families could be instituted.

2.    Have students read the sample speech with commentary at the end of Chapter 16 of the textbook ("The Dangers of Chewing Tobacco," pages 390-394). Assign students three tasks: (1) Pick out the main points of the speech; (2) Identify its method of organization; (3) Locate places where it uses connectives and, in each case, identify the kind of connective used—transition, internal preview, internal summary, or signpost.

**Discussion:** *This exercise can be done with almost any of the speeches in the Appendix of the textbook or in Part V of this manual. I recommend "The Dangers of Chewing Tobacco" because it is especially rich in its use of connectives. Other excellent choices are "A Friend in Need," which appears on pages 459-462 of the textbook, and "Seatbelts: A Habit That Could Save Your Life," which appears on pages 361-363 of this manual and can be readily copied for distribution to students.*

*Regardless of the speech you assign, this exercise usually works best when it is given as a homework assignment followed by a class discussion. Be sure, in the discussion, to ask students to assess how well the speaker uses connectives and to identify places where additional connectives would have enhanced the clarity or coherence of the speech.*

3.    Identify the organizational method used in each of the following sets of main points.

I.    Early people did not have money, but used a system of exchange based on the barter of goods and services.
II.    Coin money was invented in ancient Turkey, China, and India before the birth of Christ.
III.    Paper money began in China about 600 A.D. but did not become popular in the West until the 1600s.
IV.    Today almost every country has an official currency tied to the international rate of exchange.

I.    Genetic engineering is producing new plant hybrids that will vastly increase world agricultural production.
II.    Genetic engineering is producing breakthroughs in medicine that will allow people to live healthier lives.
III.    Genetic engineering is producing bacteria that will help clean up industrial pollutants.

I.    Gambling addiction is an increasingly serious problem throughout the United States.
II.    The problem of gambling addiction can best be solved by a combination of education and rehabilitation.

I.    There are several causes for the destruction of the rain forests in South America.
II.    If the destruction of the rain forests continues, the effects will have global impact.

I.    The top layer of the earth is a rocky "skin" called the crust.
II.    Beneath the crust is a thick layer of rock called the mantle.
III.    The next lower section is a mass of melted rock called the outer core.
IV.    At the center of the earth is a solid mass called the inner core.

**Discussion:** *This complements exercise 1 on pages 192-193 of the textbook and gives students additional work in understanding the methods of organization discussed in this chapter. To facilitate class discussion, this exercise is also available as part of the transparency supplement that accompanies* The Art *of Public* Speaking. *Here are answers to the exercise.*

I.   Early people did not have money, but used a system of exchange based on the barter of goods and services.
II.  Coin money was invented in ancient Turkey, China, and India before the birth of Christ.
III. Paper money began in China about 600 A.D. but did not become popular in the West until the 1600s
IV.  Today almost every country has an official currency tied to the international rate of exchange.

*(chronological)*

I.   Genetic engineering is producing new plant hybrids that will vastly increase world agricultural production.
II.  Genetic engineering is producing breakthroughs in medicine that will allow people to live healthier lives.
III. Genetic engineering is producing bacteria that will help clean up industrial pollutants.

*(topical)*

I.   Gambling addiction is an increasingly serious problem throughout the United States.
II.  The problem of gambling addiction can best be solved by a combination of education and rehabilitation.

*(problem-solution)*

I.   There are several causes for the destruction of the rain forests in South America.
II.  If the destruction of the rain forests continues, the effects will have global impact.

*(causal)*

I.   The top layer of the earth is a rocky "skin" called the crust.
II.  Beneath the crust is a thick layer of rock called the mantle.
III. The next lower section is a mass of melted rock called the outer core.
IV.  At the center of the earth is a solid mass called the inner core.

*(spatial)*

# Extra Teaching and Learning Resources

## General

Corbett, Edward P.J. *Classical Rhetoric for the Modern Student*, 3rd ed. New York: Oxford University Press, 1990, Chapter 3.

Daniels, Tom D., and Whitman, Richard F. "The Effects of Message Introduction, Message Structure, and Verbal Organizing Ability Upon Learning of Message Information." *Human Communication Research*, 7 (1981), 147-160.

D'Arcy, Jan. *Technically Speaking: Proven Ways to Make Your Next Presentation a Success*. New York: American Management Association, 1992, Chapter 11.

Fritz, Paul A., and Weaver, Richard L., II. "Teaching Critical Thinking in the Basic Speaking Course: A Liberal Arts Perspective." *Communication Education*, 35 (1986), 174-182.

Hauser, Margaret Fitch. "Message Structure, Inference Making, and Recall." In Robert N. Bostrom (ed.), *Communication Yearbook 8*. Beverly Hills, Calif.: Sage, 1984, pp. 278-292.

Hoffman, Regina M. "Temporal Organization as a Rhetorical Resource." *Southern Communication Journal*, 57 (1992), 194-204.

Sussman, Lyle. "Managing to Speak by Managing the Speech." *Personnel*, 65 (1988), 60-64.

## Classroom Activities and Assignments

Avadian, Brenda, and Thanos, Marilyn. "Speechmapping: The Road Through Speech Preparation and Delivery." In Stephen E. Lucas (ed.), *Selections from the Speech Communication Teacher, 1986-1991*. New York: McGraw-Hill, 1992, pp. 51-52.

Blom, Patricia. "Using Group Activities in Basic Public Speaking." In Stephen E. Lucas (ed.), *Selections from the Speech Communication Teacher, 1986-1991*. New York: McGraw-Hill, 1992, pp. 52-53.

Brown, Kevin James. "'Spidergrams': An Aid for Teaching Outlining and Organization." In Stephen E. Lucas (ed.), *Selections from the Speech Communication Teacher, 1986-1991*. New York: McGraw-Hill, 1992, pp. 53-54.

Ensign, Russell L. "The 'Arrow through Ass's Ribs' Outline: A Teaching Aid for the Basic Course." *Speech Communication Teacher* (Fall 1993), 10-11.

Hufman, Melody. "The Maze as an Instrument for Public Speaking." *Communication Education*, 34 (1985), 63-68.

McClish, Glen. "The 'Authorial Conversion' Structure in Oral Argument." *Speech Communication Teacher* (Spring 1993), 10-11.

Mino, Mary. "Structuring: An Alternate Approach for Developing Clear Organization." In Stephen E. Lucas (ed.), *Selections from the Speech Communication Teacher, 1986-1991*. New York: McGraw-Hill, 1992, pp. 55-56.

Schnell, Jim. "The Developmental Speech Sequence Model (DSSM)." In Stephen E. Lucas (ed.), *Selections from the Speech Communication Teacher, 1986-1991*. New York: McGraw-Hill, 1992, p. 56.

## Films and Videos

"Be Prepared to Speak." Kantola-Skeie Productions (1985). 27 minutes.

"Organizing the Speech." RMI Media Productions (1986). 28 minutes.

"Planning Your Speech." Coronet/MTI Film and Video (1976). 13 minutes.

# Chapter 9 Beginning and Ending the Speech

## Chapter Objectives

*After reading this chapter, students should be able to:*

1.  Identify the four objectives of a speech introduction.

2.  Explain seven methods that can be used to gain attention in an introduction.

3.  Identify the major functions of a speech conclusion.

4.  Explain the methods a speaker can use to fulfill the functions of a conclusion.

## Chapter Outline

I.   Speeches need effective introductions and conclusions *(text page 196)*.
     A.  An effective introduction gets the speaker off on the right foot.
         1.  It creates a favorable first impression with the audience.
         2.  It boosts a speaker's self-confidence for the rest of the speech.
     B.  An effective conclusion ends the speech on a strong note.
         1.  It gives the speaker one last chance to emphasize his or her main points.
         2.  It creates a favorable final impression.

II.  There are four objectives of a speech introduction *(text pages 196-208)*.
     A.  The first objective is to gain the attention and interest of the audience.
         1.  One method of gaining attention is to relate the topic to the audience.
             a.  People pay attention to things that affect them directly.

  b. No matter what other interest-arousing lures a speaker uses, she or he should *always* relate the topic to the audience.

2. A second method of gaining attention is to state the importance of the topic.
  a. An audience is not likely to be interested in a topic they regard as unimportant.
  b. Whenever a speaker discusses a topic whose importance may not be clear to the audience, the speaker should think about ways to demonstrate its importance in the introduction.

3. A third method of gaining attention is to startle the audience.
  a. This method can be highly effective.
  b. It important, however, that the startling material be directly related to the speech.

4. A fourth method of gaining attention is to arouse the curiosity of the audience.
  a. People are curious.
  b. Their interest can be engaged with a series of statements that whet their curiosity about the subject of the speech.

5. A fifth method of gaining attention is to question the audience.
  a. A speaker can use either a single question or a series of questions.
  b. The question or questions should be firmly related to the content of the speech.

6. A sixth method of gaining attention is to begin with a quotation.
  a. A well-chosen quotation can add depth, human interest, or humor to an introduction.
  b. The quotation will be most effective if it is no longer than a sentence or two.

7. A seventh method of gaining attention is to tell a story.
  a. Because all people enjoy stories, this may be the most effective method of beginning a speech.
  b. For this method to work, the story must be delivered well.

8. Other methods of gaining attention include referring to the occasion, inviting audience participation, using audio equipment or visual aids, relating to a previous speaker, and beginning with humor.
  a. All of these methods can be effective depending on the audience, the topic, and the occasion.
  b. Unlike the first seven methods of gaining attention, these additional methods are used more frequently in speeches outside the classroom than in the classroom.

B. The second objective of a speech introduction is to reveal the topic of the speech.
 1. An effective introduction clearly states the speech topic to avoid confusing the audience.

2.   Even if the audience already knows the topic, a speaker should usually restate it during the introduction.
C.   The third objective of a speech introduction is to establish the credibility and good will of the speaker.
1.   Credibility is a matter of being perceived by the audience as qualified to speak on a particular topic.
a.   Credibility can be based on research or firsthand experience.
b.   Whatever the source of a speaker's credibility, she or he should let the audience know.
2.   Establishing good will is a matter of showing that the speaker has the audience's best interests in mind.
a.   Creating good will is especially crucial for speakers outside the classroom who may be identified with causes that arouse hostility among the audience.
b.   Creating good will can also be a concern for students who advocate highly unpopular positions in their classroom speeches.
D.   The fourth objective of a speech introduction is to preview the body of the speech.
1.   A preview statement tells an audience what to listen for in the rest of the speech.
2.   Because they generally come at the end the introduction, preview statements provide a smooth lead-in to the body of the speech.
3.   Previews are also an opportunity to present special information, such as definitions of terms, that the audience will need to understand the rest of speech.

III.   There are five tips for preparing an effective introduction *(text pages 208-209)*.
A.   The introduction should usually be relatively brief.
B.   Speakers should keep an eye out for potential introductory material as they research the speech.
C.   Speakers should be creative when devising their introductions.
D.   Speakers should not be concerned with the exact wording of the introduction until the body of the speech is finished.
E.   The introduction should be worked out in detail so it can be delivered effectively.

IV.   A speech conclusion has two primary functions *(text pages 209-214)*.
A.   The first function is to signal the end of the speech.
1.   Abrupt endings leave listeners surprised and unfulfilled.
2.   One way to signal the end of a speech is with a brief verbal cue such as "In conclusion" or "One last thought."
3.   Another way to signal the end is by the speaker's manner of delivery.

        a.    In a crescendo ending, the speech builds in force until it reaches a zenith of power and intensity.

        b.    In a dissolve ending, the final words fade like a spotlight on a concert singer, bringing the speech to an emotional close.

B.    The second function of a conclusion is to reinforce the audience's understanding of or commitment to the central idea of the speech.

    1.    There are four methods of accomplishing this.

        a.    One method is to summarize the main points of the speech.

        b.    A second method is to conclude with a quotation.

        c.    A third method is to end with a dramatic statement.

        d.    A fourth method is to refer back to the introduction of the speech.

    2.    These methods can be used separately or in combination to create an effective conclusion.

V.    There are four tips for preparing an effective conclusion *(text pages 214-215)*.

A.    Speakers should keep an eye out for potential concluding materials as they research the speech.

B.    Speakers should conclude with a bang instead of a whimper.

C.    Speakers should not be long-winded in the conclusion.

D.    Speakers should prepare the content and delivery of their conclusions with special care.

## Application Exercises *(from text page 216)*

1.    Here are six speech topics. Explain how you might relate each to your classmates in the introduction of a speech.

| | |
|---|---|
| Social Security | laughter |
| illiteracy | steroids |
| soap operas | blood donation |

**Discussion:** *Students often have great difficulty deciding how to relate their speech topics directly to their classmates. This exercise is designed to give them some practice, and it works equally well as a homework assignment, as a group activity in class, or simply as the basis for a general class discussion. After the class deals with each item, you may want to read your students the following excerpts from the introductions of student speeches on each of the six topics.*

Social
Security:     *Many of you may think, "What does Social Security have to do with me? I'm young, healthy, and nowhere near retirement age."*

*But Social Security has a lot to do with you. If you don't have a job today, you will in a couple of years. And when you do, you will pay Social Security taxes. How much will you pay? That depends on how much you earn. If you earn $40,000, you will pay more than $3,000 a year in Social Security taxes. At present tax rates, that comes to more than $125,000 in the course of your working career. You should know where your money goes and whether you will ever benefit from it.*

illiteracy:     *Imagine that you are in France visiting some friends. Because your friends are busy, you offer to go to the grocery store—even though you don't know a word of French. At the store, you look for what you need, but none of the cans or boxes have pictures on them. You come out of the store thinking you have bought a box of cereal and a can of soup, but when you get to your friends' house, you discover that you have a box of laundry detergent and a can of dog food.*

*Although this scenario is admittedly far-fetched, it should give you some idea of how frustrating it is to look at a bunch of letters and not know what they mean. This is the same frustration that millions of adults in the United States experience every day because they are functionally illiterate.*

soap operas:  *Are you an addict? Do you need a daily fix to keep going? Are you hooked on one of the modern college students' most popular escapes from reality?*

*I'm talking, of course, about soap operas. Once the exclusive domain of housewives and secretaries, soap operas now have a huge audience among America's college students. According to Newsweek magazine, students across the land are watching soap operas in record numbers. I don't know about you, but in my experience getting a front-row seat for Days of Our Lives in the dorms or the student union is just as tough as getting a seat on the fifty-yard line for football or at center court for basketball!*

laughter:     *The neural circuits in your brain begin to reverberate. Chemical and electrical impulses start flowing rapidly through your body. Your pituitary gland is stimulated. Hormones and endorphins race through your blood.*

*Your body temperature rises by half a degree. Your pulse and blood pressure increase. Your arteries and chest muscles contract, your vocal chords quiver, and your face contorts. Pressure builds in your lungs. Your lower jaw suddenly becomes uncontrollable and breath bursts from your mouth at seventy miles per hour.*

*This is surely no laughing matter. Or is it? It is! This is a medical description of what happens in your body during a burst of laughter. It sounds dreadful, but we all know it feels great.*

steroids:    *Imagine that you're one of an elite group of students fighting for a spot at the top of your class. You're fully aware of the implications of an upcoming exam. If you blow it, you lose your rank. However, a good grade virtually assures you of prestige and a comfortable job.*

*So you look for that extra edge—a little something to push your already strained mind further. If there were a pill that would increase your mental sharpness for a short period of time and ensure you a high score on the exam, chances are many of you would consider taking it.*

*Amateur and professional athletes are faced with a similar dilemma every day of their competitive lives. In the never-ending search for the extra edge in sports, many athletes have given in to the lure of anabolic steroids.*

blood
donation:    *Picture this: You're walking home from class with your best friend. You begin to cross College Avenue. All of a sudden, out of nowhere comes a car that doesn't stop for the red light. Your friend is hit. It happened so fast that all you know is your friend is down and can't move.*

*The ambulance arrives and takes your friend to the hospital. At the hospital you find out your friend has serious internal bleeding and desperately needs blood. One major problem—at this time there is no blood available in your friend's blood type. Your throat tightens up. You naturally thought there was always enough blood. Now you find out there isn't.*

*Even though this situation is hypothetical, it is far from impossible. A poster from the Red Cross sums this up well: "Blood is like a parachute. If it's not there when you need it, chances are you'll never need it again."*

2.    Think of a speech topic (preferably one for your next speech in class). Create an introduction for a speech dealing with any aspect of the topic you wish. In your introduction be sure to gain the attention of the audience, to reveal the topic and relate it to the audience, to establish your credibility, and to preview the body of the speech.

> **Discussion:** *This exercise is designed to give students practice developing a complete introduction. For an alternative activity, see the second entry under Additional Exercises and Activities in this chapter.*

3. Using the same topic as in Exercise 2, create a speech conclusion. Be sure to let your audience know the speech is ending, to reinforce the central idea, and to make the conclusion vivid and memorable.

> **Discussion:** *This exercise is designed to give students practice in developing a complete conclusion. For an alternative activity, see the second entry under Additional Exercises and Activities, below.*

## Additional Exercises and Class Activities

1. Show students the material on introductions and conclusions from "Introductions, Conclusions, and Visual Aids: A Videotape Supplement to *The Art of Public Speaking*," which accompanies the textbook. As students view the tape, have them evaluate which introductions and conclusions are most effective and why. Follow the tape with a class discussion.

> **Discussion:** *It is one thing to read sample introductions and conclusions in a book; it is another to present them in a speech. By viewing videotape, students can see what effective introductions and conclusions look like with respect to delivery as well as content. Developed exclusively to accompany* The Art of Public Speaking, *"Introductions, Conclusions, and Visual Aids" consists of excerpts from a variety of speeches that illustrate concepts discussed in the book. Students usually find it highly instructive.*

2. Divide the class into groups of 3 to 5 students. Assign each group a topic on which it must prepare a complete introduction and conclusion. Give the groups 20 minutes to work on their introductions and conclusions. Each group should pick one of its members to deliver its introduction and conclusion to the class.

> **Discussion:** *This is an effective alternative to exercises 2 and 3 above. By working in groups, students can use brainstorming to devise more creative introductions and conclusions. Presenting the introductions and conclusions orally allows the whole class to participate in a discussion about the strengths and weaknesses of each group's results.*

3.  Here are four complete introductions from classroom speeches. Each has at least one flaw that keeps it from fulfilling all the functions of a good introduction. In each case identify the flaw (or flaws) and make specific suggestions for improving the introduction.

a.  What tiny crystal fortified the coffers of many ancient empires and laid waste to others? What mineral has the power to create and the power to destroy? What is "good as gold" when scarce and "cheap as dirt" when abundant?

   The answer to all of these questions is salt, the spice of life. Today I would like to look at the importance of salt in history, at how we spice up our lives with salt today, and at the role salt will probably play in the future.

b.  We have so much unused human potential. By improving the use of your time, you can have much more time for social activities. You can use your mental processes more fully, thereby improving your grades. You can also increase your physical stamina and improve your health. We must learn to know our bodies.

c.  A six-year-old collie lay battered and helpless by the side of the road. The car that hit her had broken her pelvis, dislocated her hip, and smashed her jaw. It had also blinded her, and she whimpered in pain and fear.

   Unfortunately, this true story happens much too frequently because of the growing problem of pet overpopulation. Having grown up on a farm with animals of all kinds, I care deeply about their welfare, and I have become aware through my veterinary courses of how serious the problem of pet overpopulation is.

d.  Every problem has at least two sides. When one side is right, and the other side is wrong, the problem is easy to solve. But what if both sides have merit in their arguments? How do you solve these problems?

   Balancing the rights of everyone in an adoption is one of these problems. The parents who give up the child have a right that all the information they disclose be kept confidential, while the adopted child has a right to know about the identity of his or her natural parents.

   Today I'd like to explore this problem with you and look at one approach to solving it.

**Discussion:** *This is an excellent exercise because it gets students to focus on all four objectives of a speech introduction. Here is a brief analysis of each of the introductions in the exercise.*

a.   *This introduction uses a series of questions to get attention, introduces the topic clearly, and has a concise preview statement. Its most obvious flaw is a lack of material establishing the speaker's credibility. It might also be improved by relating the topic of salt directly to the audience at the outset.*

b.   *By relating to the audience, this introduction does a fair job of capturing attention—but that is all. It does not reveal the topic of the speech, establish the credibility of the speaker, or preview the main points of the speech.*

c.   *This introduction does an excellent job of gaining attention, of introducing the topic of pet overpopulation, and of establishing the speaker's credibility. It is flawed, however, by its lack of a preview statement. As with the introduction on salt, it also could be strengthened if it related the topic directly to the audience.*

d.   *This introduction does a good job of revealing the topic and previewing the main points of the speech. It does nothing to establish the speaker's credibility, and it is weak as an attention-getter.*

4.   Have the class pay special attention to their classmates' introductions and conclusions during the next round of speeches. Afterward, have the class select the three most effective introductions and conclusions.

**Discussion:**   *This is a good way to review the principles of effective introductions and conclusions. Surprisingly, students usually tend to agree about the most effective introductions and conclusions. To avoid hurt feelings, though, it is a good idea not to rank-order the three top choices.*

# Extra Teaching and Learning Resources

## General

Boyd, Stephen D. "Creating a Quality Conclusion." *Public Relations Journal* (September 1990), 34-35.

Daniels, Tom D., and Whitman, Richard F. "The Effects of Message Introduction, Message Structure, and Verbal Organizing Ability Upon Learning of Message Information." *Human Communication Research*, 7 (1981), 147-160.

Ehrilch, Henry. *Writing Effective Speeches*. New York: Paragon House, 1992, Chapters 10-11.

Magee, Mary F., and Davies, Melinda M. "Crafting a Powerhouse Introduction." *Training and Development Journal* (October 1989), 25-27.

Reinhardt, Christine. "A Thousand Points to Write: Peggy Noonan on Getting a Speech Started—and Keeping It Going." *Working Woman* (November 1990), 120, 166, and 169.

Zinsser, William. *On Writing Well*, 4th ed. New York: HarperCollins, 1990, Chapters 10-11.

## Classroom Activities and Assignments

Avadian, Brenda, and Thanos, Marilyn. "Speechmapping: The Road Through Speech Preparation and Delivery." In Stephen E. Lucas (ed.), *Selections from the Speech Communication Teacher, 1986-1991*. New York: McGraw-Hill, 1992, pp. 51-52.

Hibben, Jean. "Eliminating the 'My Speech is About' Introduction." *Speech Communication Teacher* (Fall 1992), 11.

Schnell, Jim. "The Developmental Speech Sequence Model (DSSM)." In Stephen E. Lucas (ed.), *Selections from the Speech Communication Teacher, 1986-1991*. New York: McGraw-Hill, 1992, p. 56.

## Films and Videos

"Be Prepared to Speak." Kantola-Skeie Productions (1985). 27 minutes.

"Introductions, Conclusions, and Visual Aids: A Videotape Supplement to *The Art of Public Speaking*." McGraw-Hill, 1992. 58 minutes.

"Organizing the Speech." RMI Media Productions (1986). 28 minutes.

"Planning Your Speech." Coronet/MTI Film and Video (1976). 13 minutes.

# Chapter **10** Outlining the Speech

## Chapter Objectives

*After reading this chapter, students should be able to:*

1.  Explain why it is important to outline speeches.

2.  Explain the differences between a preparation outline and a speaking outline.

3.  Construct a preparation outline following the guidelines presented in the book.

4.  Construct a speaking outline following the guidelines presented in the book.

## Chapter Outline

I.  Outlines are essential to effective speeches *(text page 220)*.
    A.  An outline helps a speaker place related items together.
    B.  An outline helps a speaker ensure that ideas flow from one to another.
    C.  An outline helps create a coherent structure for the speech.

II.  Creating a preparation outline is a vital step in putting a speech together *(text pages 220-227)*.
    A.  A preparation outline is a detailed outline used to plan a speech.
    B.  The process of writing a preparation outline requires that a speaker bring together all the elements of the speech.
        1.  What will be said in the introduction.
        2.  How main points will be stated and supported.
        3.  What will be said in the conclusion.
    C.  There are eight guidelines for effective preparation outlines.
        1.  The preparation outline should include the speaker's specific purpose statement.

    a.    The specific purpose statement should be written before the text of the outline itself.

    b.    Including the specific purpose statement makes it easier to judge how well the speech accomplishes the speaker's aim.

2.    The preparation outline should include the speaker's central idea.

    a.    The central idea can follow the specific purpose as an independent element of the outline.

    b.    It can also be identified in the body of the outline.

3.    The preparation outline should clearly label the introduction, body, and conclusion of the speech.

    a.    This ensures that the speech indeed has an introduction, body, and conclusion.

    b.    It also helps guarantee that each part of the speech meets its objectives.

    c.    Labels for the introduction, body, and conclusion are stated separately from the system of symbolization used in the outline.

4.    The preparation outline should have a consistent pattern of symbolization and indentation.

    a.    In the most common system of outlining, main points are identified by Roman numerals and are indented equally.

    b.    Subpoints are identified with capital letters and are indented equally.

    c.    There may also be sub-subpoints and even sub-sub-subpoints.

    d.    Using a consistent pattern of symbolization and indentation provides a clear visual framework that shows the relationships among the ideas in the speech.

5.    The preparation outline should state main points and subpoints in full sentences.

    a.    Using full sentences clearly identifies the content of each point.

    b.    Using full sentences helps ensure that a speaker has thought out the points fully.

6.    The preparation outline should label transitions, internal summaries, and internal previews.

    a.    This helps make sure that the speech has sufficient transitions, internal summaries, and internal previews.

    b.    Labels for these elements are not included in the system of symbolization of the outline.

7.    The preparation outline should include a bibliography.

    a.    The bibliography is a list of all the sources used in preparing the speech.

    b.    Students should check with their teacher to see if they must follow a specific format for the bibliography.

8.    The preparation outline may also include a title for the speech.

a.   Students should check with their teacher to see if a title is required.

b.   If a title is required, it should be brief, attract the attention of the audience, and encapsulate the main thrust of the speech.

III.   Once the preparation outline is completed, a speaking outline can be drawn up *(text pages 228-233)*.

A.   A speaking outline is a brief outline used to deliver a speech.

B.   The primary purpose of a speaking outline is to help a speaker remember what to say.

1.   It includes key words and phrases from the preparation outline.

2.   It includes essential statistics and quotations the speaker does not want to forget.

3.   It includes cues to direct and sharpen a speaker's delivery.

C.   Speaking outlines are especially effective for extemporaneous speeches.

1.   An extemporaneous speech is thoroughly prepared and practiced in advance.

2.   The specific wording, however, is selected as the speech is being delivered.

3.   Most classroom speeches are delivered extemporaneously.

D.   There are four guidelines for effective speaking outlines.

1.   The speaking outline should follow the same visual framework used in the preparation outline.

a.   Using the same symbolization and indentation as in the preparation outline makes the speaking outline easier to prepare.

b.   It also makes it easier for the speaker to see where she or he is in the speech at any given moment.

2.   The speaking outline should be plainly legible.

a.   A speaking outline is worthless unless it is instantly readable at a distance.

b.   Using dark ink, large letters, and leaving extra space helps make the speaking outline more readable.

3.   The speaking outline should be as brief as possible.

a.   Detailed notes often prevent a speaker from maintaining eye contact with the audience.

b.   The best rule is that a speaking outline should contain the minimum necessary to jog a speaker's memory and keep him or her on track.

4.   The speaking outline should include cues for delivering the speech.

a.   One technique is to highlight key ideas that require special vocal emphasis.

b.   Another is to jot down prompts for delivery such as "slow down," "pause," and "louder."

# Application Exercises *(from text pages 234-235)*

1. In the left-hand column below is a partially blank outline from a speech about sleep deprivation. In the right-hand column, arranged in random order, are the subpoints to fill in the outline. Choose the appropriate subpoint for each blank in the outline.

| *Outline* | *Subpoints* |
|---|---|
| I. Most Americans do not get the sleep they need on a regular basis. | Sleep deprivation has been linked to a number of health problems. |
| A. | The *Times* also blames falling asleep at the wheel for 6,500 U.S. traffic deaths each year. |
| B. | The typical adult needs about eight hours of sleep each night to function effectively during the day. |
| 1. | Second, it increases the risk of heart disease. |
| 2. | The same study showed that 20 percent of the population gets less than six hours sleep a night. |
| II. Sleep deprivation is a major cause of traffic accidents and deaths. | The statistics linking sleep deprivation to traffic accidents and deaths are alarming. |
| A. | Yet most Americans consistently get less than eight hours sleep a night. |
| 1. | First, it weakens the immune system. |
| 2. | Sleep deprivation is second only to alcohol as the leading cause of traffic accidents and deaths. |
| B. | *Newsweek* reports that "sleep deprivation has become one of the most pervasive health problems facing the U.S." |
| III. Sleep deprivation also contributes to poor personal health. | A Stanford study showed that over half the population gets less than seven hours sleep a night. |
| A. | Third, it contributes to gastrointestinal illness. |
| B. | The *Los Angeles Times* reports that drowsiness causes 200,000 auto accidents each year. |
| 1. | |
| 2. | |
| 3. | |

**Discussion:** *This is an excellent exercise to help students develop outlining skills. In case you wish to assign more than one such exercise, there are two scrambled outlines among the Additional Exercises and Activities (pages 204-207), and three more among the essay exam questions in Chapter 10 of the* Test Bank.

*When filled in, the outline on sleep deprivation should look like the following. To facilitate class discussion, the outline is also available as part of the transparency supplement to* The Art of Public Speaking.

I.   Most Americans do not get the sleep they need on a regular basis.
    A.   The typical adult needs about eight hours of sleep each night to function effectively during the day.
    B.   Yet most Americans consistently get less than eight hours sleep a night.
        1.   A Stanford study showed that over half the population gets less than seven hours sleep a night.
        2.   The same study showed that 20 percent of the population gets less than six hours sleep a night.

II.  Sleep deprivation is a major cause of traffic accidents and deaths.
    A.   The statistics linking sleep deprivation to traffic accidents and deaths are alarming.
        1.   The *Los Angeles Times* reports that drowsiness causes 200,000 auto accidents each year.
        2.   The *Times* also blames falling asleep at the wheel for 6,500 U.S. traffic deaths each year.
    B.   Sleep deprivation is second only to alcohol as the leading cause of traffic accidents and deaths.

III. Sleep deprivation also contributes to poor personal health.
    A.   *Newsweek* reports that "sleep deprivation has become one of the most pervasive health problems facing the U.S."
    B.   Sleep deprivation has been linked to a number of health problems.
        1.   First, it weakens the immune system.
        2.   Second, it increases the risk of heart disease.
        3.   Third, it contributes to gastrointestinal illness.

2.   Following the format used in the sample preparation outline on pages 225-227, outline the sample speech at the end of Chapter 14 ("Dandelions: The Uncommon Weed"). Be sure to include a specific purpose statement, to identify the central idea, to label the introduction, body and conclusion, to use a consistent pattern of symbolization and indentation, to state the main points and subpoints in full sentences, and to label transitions and internal summaries.

**Discussion:** *This exercise serves two purposes. First, it gives students a chance to practice using the outline format explained in the book. As a result, it usually improves the quality of the students' initial preparation outlines. Second, this exercise is a capstone to Chapters 8-10. It requires students to work with all of the organizational elements discussed in the last three chapters—to delineate the introduction, body, and conclusion; to distinguish main points from supporting materials; to identify connectives; and the like. By analyzing how these elements work in a single speech, students should get a better sense of how to construct their own speeches.*

*This exercise works best when it is assigned to students to complete at home in preparation for class discussion. Allow at least 30 minutes to discuss the outline in class. Go through the speech step by step, asking students what they identified as the specific purpose, central idea, introduction, main points, connectives, etc. Expect a lively discussion and plenty of questions.*

*A complete preparation outline of the speech follows. To facilitate class discussion, the outline is also available as part of the transparency supplement that accompanies* The Art of Public Speaking. *To help students see the relationship among main points, subpoints, etc., the outline consists of several color-coded transparencies that cumulatively present the different elements in the outline.*

### "Dandelions: The Uncommon Weed"

*Specific Purpose:*   To inform my audience about the medical and culinary uses of dandelions.

*Central Idea:*   Despite its reputation as an irritating weed, the dandelion's medical and culinary properties make it a very useful plant.

*Introduction:*

I.   What starts out yellow and ends up as a fluffy white ball?
    A.   If I told you it was *Taraxacum Officinale*, would that ring a bell?
    B.   What if I told you it was of the *Compositae* family?

II.   The subject I am speaking about is none other than the common, ordinary dandelion.

III.   Homeowners regard the dandelion as the most troublesome of all weeds.

IV.  However, I have learned from botany class and from further research that the dandelion has wide medical and culinary uses.

V.  Today I will explain these uses to you.

(*Transition:* We'll start by looking at the dandelion's medicinal value.)

*Body*

I.  The dandelion has a number of medicinal uses.
  A.  Its scientific name, *Taraxacum Officinale*, testifies to its value as a medicine.
    1.  *Taraxacum* refers to medical properties of a plant found in Persia.
    2.  *Officinale* indicates that a plant species is used by pharmacists.
  B.  Throughout history, dandelions have been used to cure medical ailments.
    1.  Used by ancient Egyptians to treat stomach and kidney disorders.
    2.  Cures recorded by Arabian physicians in tenth century.
    3.  In sixteenth-century England dandelion waters used to treat illness among nobility.
  C.  Today scientists know that dandelions have great medicinal value.
    1.  According to Mea Allen, author of *Weeds*, dandelions contain chemicals that stimulate blood circulation, the liver, the digestive organs, and the bladder and kidneys.
    2.  Audrey Hatfield, in her book *How to Enjoy Your Weeds*, says dandelion tea helps relieve many conditions.
      a.  Liver and lung disorders.
      b.  Anemia.
      c.  Mild laxative.
      d.  Aids digestion.
      e.  Eczema, scurvy, and other skin conditions.
    3.  The dandelion is so valuable in treating medical ailments that 100,000 pounds are imported into the U.S. each year.

(*Transition*: If you have no interest in using dandelions for your health, you can still find them of use in the kitchen.)

II.  Dandelions have many culinary uses.
  A.  Dandelions have been used as food for thousands of years.
    1.  Were among the original bitter herbs of Passover.
    2.  English have used them in salads since the Middle Ages.
    3.  Many ethnic groups in the United States eat dandelions.
  B.  All parts of the dandelion can be used to make a variety of delicious foods.
    1.  Leaves can be added to salads.

2. Roots may be roasted and used as coffee substitute.
3. Flowers can be steeped to produce wine.
4. Entire plant may be used to make beer.
C. In addition to being tasty, dandelions are extremely nutritious.
    1. According to Peter Gail, professor of economic botany at Cleveland State University, "The dandelion's nutrient qualities read almost like a One-A-Day vitamin."
    2. Dandelion greens are especially nutritious.
        a. Fifty percent more vitamin C than tomatoes.
        b. Twice as much protein as eggplant.
        c. Double the fiber of asparagus.
        d. As much iron as spinach.
        e. More potassium than bananas.
D. All of this may sound strange to you, but not to the people of Vineland, New Jersey, Dandelion Capital of the World.
    1. Dandelions are a million-dollar crop in Vineland.
        a. Sell for $1.25 a pound at start of season.
        b. Most of crop ends up in Baltimore, Philadelphia, and New York City.
    2. Every March, Vineland hosts a seven-course dandelion dinner.
        a. Consists entirely of foods made from dandelions.
        b. Tickets sell for $25 apiece.
        c. People come from as far away as Ohio.
    3. Former mayor Patrick Fiorilli says: "In your yard, you go out and pull the dandelions out of the grass. Our farmers pull the grass out of the dandelions."

*Conclusion*

I. As we have seen, the dandelion is a very misunderstood plant.
A. The dandelion is not simply an irritating weed.
B. With many medicinal and culinary uses, it is one of the most underrated plants in the world.
II. Hopefully, in the future more people will recognize that this "common" weed is a truly uncommon plant.

3. From the preparation outline you constructed in Exercise 2, create a speaking outline that you might use in delivering the speech. Follow the guidelines for a speaking outline discussed in this chapter.

> **Discussion:** *This exercise helps clarify the differences between a preparation outline and a speaking outline and gives students practice in creating a speaking outline. Whether or not you have students complete this exercise at home, you can follow class discussion of the preparation outline for "Dandelions: The Uncommon Weed" by discussing what a speaking outline for the same speech might include.*

# Additional Exercises and Class Activities

1. In the left-hand column below is a partially blank outline from a speech about suicide among college students. In the right-hand column, arranged in random order, are the subpoints to fill in the outline. Choose the appropriate subpoint for each blank in the outline.

| *Outline* | *Subpoints* |
|---|---|
| I. Suicide among college students is a serious problem. | Even on our campus the rate of suicide and attempted suicide is quite high. |
|   A. | There are also more subtle warning signs that a person may try to commit suicide. |
|   B. | There are excellent services available on campus and in the community to help potential suicide victims. |
|   C. | In town students can go to the Suicide Prevention Center. |
|     1. | One warning sign is loss of appetite. |
|     2. | Identifying potential suicide victims is easier than you think. |
| II. We can help solve the problem by knowing how to identify potential suicide victims and whom to contact about helping them. | Dean Howard also said that for every known suicide attempt, two or three more go unnoticed. |
|   A. | According to the National Institute of Mental Health, suicide is the fastest growing cause of death for people aged 17 to 24 nationwide. |
|     1. | In an interview with Roger Howard, associate dean of students, I learned that last year there were over 60 known suicide attempts on our campus. |
|     2. | A second warning sign is prolonged depression. |
|       a. | The National Institute of Mental Health says 80 percent of the people who commit suicide tell someone ahead of time that they are going to kill themselves. |
|       b. | A third warning sign is giving away one's possessions. |
|       c. | Last year 10,000 young Americans committed suicide. |
|   B. | On campus students can go to the University Counseling Service. |
|     1. | |
|     2. | |

**Discussion:** *When filled in, the outline should look like the one below. (The order of points IA and IB can be reversed without damaging the students' answers.) To facilitate class discussion, the outline is available as part of the transparency supplement that accompanies* The Art of Public Speaking.

I.   Suicide among college students is a serious problem.

    A.   According to the National Institute of Mental Health, suicide is the fastest growing cause of death for people aged 17 to 24 nationwide.

    B.   Last year 10,000 young Americans committed suicide.

    C.   Even on our campus the rate of suicide and attempted suicide is quite high.

        1.   In an interview with Roger Howard, associate dean of students, I learned that last year there were over 60 known suicide attempts on our campus.

        2.   Dean Howard also said that for every known suicide attempt, two or three more go unnoticed.

II.  We can help to solve the problem by knowing how to identify potential suicide victims and whom to contact about helping them.

    A.   Identifying potential suicide victims is easier than you might think.

        1.   The National Institute of Mental Health says that 80 percent of the people who commit suicide tell someone ahead of time that they are going to kill themselves.

        2.   There are also more subtle warning signs that a person may try to commit suicide.

            a.   One warning sign is loss of appetite.

            b.   A second warning sign is prolonged depression.

            c.   A third warning sign is giving away one's possessions.

    B.   There are excellent services on campus and in the community to help potential suicide victims.

        1.   On campus students can go to the University Counseling Service.

        2.   In town students can go to the Suicide Prevention Center.

2.   In the left-hand column below is a blank outline from a speech about the achievements of Booker T. Washington. In the right-hand column, arranged in random order, are the main points and subpoints to fill in the outline. Choose the appropriate main point or subpoint for each blank in the outline.

| *Outline* | *Main Points and Subpoints* |
|---|---|
| I. | All told, Washington delivered some 4,000 public speeches during his 30-year career as an orator. |
| A. | Some people praise the speech as a brilliant example of audience adaptation in a very difficult situation. |
| 1. | Washington is also known as one of the ablest speakers in American history. |
| 2. | When Washington founded Tuskegee Institute in 1881, the school had only one dilapidated building and an enrollment of 40 students. |
| B. | Today, Tuskegee Institute remains a leader in applied research and practical education. |
| II. | Washington's most famous speech is his "Atlanta Exposition Address" of 1895. |
| A. | The growth of Tuskegee Institute under Washington's guidance was nothing short of phenomenal. |
| B. | To this day, Washington's speech at Atlanta remains highly controversial. |
| 1. | Booker T. Washington is best known for founding Tuskegee Institute in Alabama. |
| 2. | By the time Washington died in 1915, Tuskegee Institute occupied 2,000 acres of land, enrolled 1,500 students, and boasted a faculty of 200 instructors. |
| a. | Other people condemn the speech for failing to denounce racial segregation and inequality. |
| b. | In the "Atlanta Exposition Address" Washington urged blacks to strive for economic advancement rather than to agitate for immediate social equality. |

**Discussion:** *When filled in, the outline should look the one below. To facilitate class discussion, the outline is available as part of the transparency supplement that accompanies* The Art of Public Speaking.

I.  Booker T. Washington is best known for founding Tuskegee Institute in Alabama.

    A.   The growth of Tuskegee Institute under Washington's guidance was nothing short of phenomenal.

        1.   When Washington founded Tuskegee Institute in 1881, the school had only one dilapidated building and an enrollment of 40 students.

        2.   By the time Washington died in 1915, Tuskegee Institute occupied 2,000 acres of land, enrolled 1,500 students, and boasted a faculty of 200 instructors.

    B.   Today, Tuskegee Institute remains a leader in applied research and practical education.

II.  Booker T. Washington is also known as one of the ablest speakers in American history.

    A.   All told, Washington delivered some 4,000 public speeches during his 30-year career as an orator.

    B.   Washington's most famous speech is his "Atlanta Exposition Address" of 1895.

        1.   In the "Atlanta Exposition Address" Washington urged blacks to strive for economic advancement rather than to agitate for immediate social equality.

        2.   To this day, Washington's speech at Atlanta remains highly controversial.

            a.   Some people praise the speech as a brilliant example of audience adaptation in a very difficult situation.

            b.   Other people condemn the speech for failing to denounce racial segregation and inequality.

# Extra Teaching and Learning Resources

## General

Brody, Marjorie, and Kent, Shawn. *Power Presentations: How to Connect with Your Audience and Sell Your Ideas*. New York: Wiley, 1993, Chapter 10.

Ehrlich, Henry. *Writing Effective Speeches*. New York: Paragon House, 1992, Chapter 17.

Valenti, Jack. *Speak Up with Confidence: How to Prepare, Learn, and Deliver Effective Speeches*. New York: Morrow, 1982, Chapter 4.

## Classroom Activities and Assignments

Avadian, Brenda, and Thanos, Marilyn. "Speechmapping: The Road Through Speech Preparation and Delivery." In Stephen E. Lucas (ed.), *Selections from the Speech Communication Teacher, 1986-1991*. New York: McGraw-Hill, 1992, pp. 51-52.

Brown, Kevin James. "'Spidergrams': An Aid for Teaching Outlining and Organization." In Stephen E. Lucas (ed.), *Selections from the Speech Communication Teacher, 1986-1991*. New York: McGraw-Hill, 1992, pp. 53-54.

Ensign, Russell L. "The 'Arrow through Ass's Ribs' Outline: A Teaching Aid for the Basic Course." *Speech Communication Teacher* (Fall 1993), 10-11.

McClish, Glen. "The 'Authorial Conversion' Structure in Oral Argument." *Speech Communication Teacher* (Spring 1993), 10-11.

Mino, Mary. "Structuring: An Alternate Approach for Developing Clear Organization." In Stephen E. Lucas (ed.), *Selections from the Speech Communication Teacher, 1986-1991*. New York: McGraw-Hill, 1992, pp. 55-56.

Schnell, Jim. "The Developmental Speech Sequence Model (DSSM)." In Stephen E. Lucas (ed.), *Selections from the Speech Communication Teacher, 1986-1991*. New York: McGraw-Hill, 1992, p. 56.

# Chapter 11 Using Language

## Chapter Objectives

*After reading this chapter, students should be able to:*

1. Explain why the effective use of language is vital to a public speaker.

2. Explain the differences between denotative and connotative meaning.

3. Explain the importance of using language accurately in public speeches.

4. Identify three methods public speakers can use to help ensure that their language will be clear to listeners.

5. Explain how public speakers can use imagery and rhythm to help bring their ideas to life.

6. Explain why public speakers need to avoid sexist language and identify four ways they can do so.

## Chapter Outline

I. Language is important *(text pages 238-240)*.
   A. Contrary to popular belief, language does not simply mirror reality.
   B. Language helps create our sense of reality by giving meaning to events.
      1. Language is not neutral.
      2. The words we use to label an event determine to a great extent how we respond to it.
   C. Words are vital to thinking itself.
      1. Thought and language are closely linked.
      2. On most occasions when we are looking for "just the right word," what we are really looking for is just the right idea.
   D. Words are the tools of a speaker's craft.
      1. Different words have different uses—just like the tools of any profession.
      2. Public speakers must choose the right words for the job they want to do.

II.  Words have two kinds of meaning—denotative and connotative *(text pages 240-241).*
    A.  Denotative meaning is precise, literal, and objective.
        1.  It describes the object, person, or idea referred to.
        2.  One way to think of a word's denotative meaning is as its dictionary definition.
    B.  Connotative meaning is more variable, figurative, and subjective.
        1.  It is what the word suggests or implies.
        2.  Connotative meaning includes all the ideas, feelings, and emotions associated with the word.
    C.  Choosing words skillfully for their denotative and connotative meanings is a crucial part of the speaker's art.

III.  Public speakers need to use language accurately *(text pages 241-242).*
    A.  Using language accurately is as vital to a speaker as using numbers accurately is to an accountant.
        1.  Speakers need to be sensitive to the shades of meaning of different words.
        2.  Speakers should not use a word unless they are confident of its meaning.
    B.  Speakers who have serious aspirations should develop a systematic plan for improving their vocabulary.

IV.  Public speakers need to use language clearly *(text pages 243-248).*
    A.  Because listeners cannot turn to a dictionary or reread a speaker's words to discover their meaning, a speaker's meaning must be immediately comprehensible.
    B.  One way to ensure that a speaker's meaning is clear is to use familiar words.
        1.  A major barrier to clear speech is using stuffy, unfamiliar words when ordinary, familiar ones will do the job better.
        2.  Familiar words allow a speaker's meaning to come across without forcing the audience to perform mental gymnastics.
        3.  Even when dealing with technical topics, effective speakers find ways to explain their ideas in language that is familiar to the audience.
    C.  A second way to ensure that a speaker's meaning is clear is to use concrete words.
        1.  Concrete words refer to tangible objects and are more specific than abstract words.
        2.  Listeners are more likely to be interested in and to remember concrete words.
    D.  A third way to ensure that a speaker's meaning is clear is to eliminate linguistic clutter.
        1.  "Clutter" refers to the habit of using many more words than is necessary to express a speaker's meaning.

2. Cluttered speech forces listeners to hack through a tangle of words to discover the speaker's meaning.
3. Clear speakers keep their language lean and lively, clean and crisp.

V. Public speakers need to use language vividly *(text pages 248-254)*.
A. Effective speakers use imagery to express their ideas vividly.
1. One way to generate imagery is to use concrete words.
a. Because concrete words call up mental impression of sights, sounds, touch, smell, and taste, they are the key to effective imagery.
b. By using concrete words a speaker can create vivid images that pull listeners irresistibly into the speech.
2. A second way to generate imagery is through the use of simile.
a. Simile is an explicit comparison between things that are essentially different yet have something in common.
b. A simile always contains the words "like" or "as"—as in "Air pollution is eating away at the monuments in Washington, D.C., like a giant Alka-Seltzer tablet."
3. A third way to generate imagery is through the use of metaphor.
a. Metaphor is an implicit comparison between things that are essentially different yet have something in common.
b. Unlike simile, metaphor does not contain the words "like" or "as"—as in "America's cities are the windows through which the world looks at American society."
B. Effective speakers use rhythm to enhance the vividness of their discourse.
1. Language has a rhythm created by the choice and arrangement of words.
a. Speakers, like poets, sometimes seek to exploit the rhythm of language.
b. By catching listeners up in an arresting string of sounds, speakers can strengthen the impact of their words.
2. There are four basic stylistic devices for enhancing the rhythm of a speech.
a. The first device is parallelism—the similar arrangement of a pair or series of related words, phrases, or sentences.
b. The second device is repetition—repeating the same word or set of words at the beginning or end of successive clauses or sentences.
c. The third device is alliteration—repeating the initial consonant sound in close or adjoining words.
d. The fourth device is antithesis—juxtaposing contrasting ideas, usually in parallel structure.

VI. Public speakers need to use language appropriately *(text pages 254-256)*.
    A.   A speaker's language should be appropriate to the occasion.
        1.   Language that is appropriate for some occasions may not be appropriate for others.
        2.   Effective speakers adjust their language to the formality and etiquette of the occasion.
    B.   A speaker's language should be appropriate to the audience.
        1.   Language that is appropriate for some audiences may not be appropriate for others.
            a.   Technical language may be fine for an audience of specialists, but it would not be suitable for a general audience.
            b.   Profanity or off-color language might be fine for a comedian in a night-club, but most listeners would find it offensive in a formal public speech.
            c.   Most listeners are also offended by name-calling and other forms of abusive language.
        2.   As a general rule, speakers should bend over backward to avoid language that might confuse or offend their audience.
    C.   A speaker's language should be appropriate to the topic.
        1.   When speaking to inform, for example, straightforward, descriptive language is usually most appropriate.
        2.   When speaking to commemorate, on the other hand, special language devices such as metaphor, antithesis, and alliteration would be quite suitable.
    D.   A speaker's language should be appropriate to the speaker himself or herself.
        1.   Every speaker has her or his own language style.
        2.   Effective speakers develop their language styles over many years of trial, practice, and error.

VII. Public speakers are more effective when they avoid sexist language *(text pages 256-259)*.
    A.   Avoiding sexist language is a matter of accuracy in public speaking.
        1.   In today's world, most gender stereotypes are outdated and incorrect.
        2.   Being accurate in such matters is just as important as being accurate in other aspects of language.
    B.   Avoiding sexist language is also vital to audience adaptation.
        1.   Almost every audience a speaker addresses will include people—men and women alike—who are offended by sexist language.
        2.   In this respect, as in others, an effective speaker will adjust to the values and expectations of the audience.
    C.   There are four nonsexist usages that have become so widely accepted that no aspiring speaker can afford to ignore them.

1. The first usage is to avoid the generic "he."
2. The second usage is to avoid "man" when referring to both men and women.
3. The third usage is to avoid stereotyping jobs and social roles by gender.
4. The fourth usage is to avoid unnecessary or patronizing gender labels.
D. If speakers have questions about sexist and nonsexist usages, they should consult one of the many guidebooks to nonsexist language.

# Application Exercises *(from text pages 261-262)*

1. Arrange each of the sequences below in order, from the most abstract word to the most concrete word.

   a. housing complex, building, dining room, structure, apartment

      *(structure, building, housing complex, apartment, dining room)*

   b. *Mona Lisa*, art, painting, creative activity, portrait

      *(creative activity, art, painting, portrait,* Mona Lisa*)*

   c. Communication Department, university, educational institution, Stanford, school

      *(educational institution, school, university, Stanford, Communication Department)*

   d. automobile, vehicle, Ferrari, transportation, sports car

      *(transportation, vehicle, automobile, sports car, Ferrari)*

2. In each of the following sentences, select the most appropriate word to complete the statement.

   a. subsidy, award, contribution, present

      Tanya received a special ____*award*____ from the city for her heroism in saving a drowning child.

      According to *USA Today*, a tie is the most popular ____*present*____ for a man's birthday.

      Many farmers get a government ____*subsidy*____ for not planting certain crops.

      Einstein's theory of relativity was a major ____*contribution*____ to the development of modern physics.

b.   fact, evidence, proof, data

To get a refund, a customer must provide ____*proof*____ of purchase.

The statistical ____*data*____ show that more and more college students are working their way through school.

It is a scientific ____*fact*____ that the earth revolves around the sun.

In the jury's mind, the _____*evidence*_____ clearly showed that the defendant was guilty.

3.   Rewrite each of the following sentences using clear, familiar words.

a.   Some students were not cognizant of the fact that the professor made a modification in the assignment subsequent to the last class meeting.

*(Some students did not know the professor changed the assignment after class.)*

b.   My employment objective is to attain a position of maximum financial reward.

*(I want a job that pays well.)*

c.   All professors at this school are expected to achieve high standards of excellence in their instructional duties.

*(All professors here are expected to be good teachers.)*

d.   The burglar evaded security personnel and is no longer on the premises.

*(The burglar escaped.)*

e.   In the eventuality of a fire, it is imperative that all persons evacuate the building without undue delay.

*(In case of fire, get out of the building as quickly as possible.)*

4.   Each of the statements below uses one or more of the following stylistic devices—metaphor, simile, parallelism, repetition, alliteration, antithesis. Identify the device (or devices) used in each statement.

a.   "It will be up to you who are graduating today to take from Harvard not just knowledge, but wisdom; not just intelligence, but humanity; not just a drive for self-fulfillment, but a sense of service and a taste for hard work." (Colin Powell)

*(repetition and parallelism)*

b.    "The vice presidency is the sand trap of American politics. It's near the prize, and designed to be limiting." (Howard Fineman)

*(metaphor)*

c.    "For too long American leadership has waffled and wiggled and wavered." (Bill Bradley)

*(alliteration)*

d.    "America is not like a blanket—one piece of unbroken cloth, the same color, the same texture, the same size. America is more like a quilt—many patches, many sizes, and woven and held together by a common thread." (Jesse Jackson)

*(simile, repetition, parallelism)*

5.    Analyze Martin Luther King's "I Have a Dream" (Appendix, pages 450-454). Identify the methods King uses to make his language clear, vivid, and appropriate. Look particularly at King's use of familiar words, concrete words, imagery, and rhythm.

> **Discussion:** *King's speech usually works quite well for study in the classroom. Because it is so famous, students look forward to reading it; yet it is short enough for them to do a thorough job of analysis. Also, the speech is so rich in its use of language that students can readily identify the major techniques King uses to make his ideas clear and compelling.*
>
> *Have students prepare their analysis as a homework assignment based on the transcript of the speech in the textbook. Then, before discussing the speech in class, show students the videotape of the speech from Volume I of the* Great Speeches *series that accompanies* The Art of Public Speaking. *If you show the videotape, take advantage of the opportunity to discuss how King's masterful delivery reinforces the impact of his words. Here is a synopsis of the speech.*
>
> *Specific Purpose: To reinforce the commitment of the audience to the principles of the nonviolent civil rights movement.*
>
> *Central Idea: By continued nonviolent protest, African Americans will achieve their full citizenship rights.*
>
> *Method of Organization: Topical*

*Introduction: The opening sentence constitutes the introduction of King's speech. Such a perfunctory introduction is unusual, but it was appropriate in King's situation. The audience had been waiting all afternoon to hear King speak. He did not need any special devices to secure their attention or to build his credibility. The speech might have been improved by an explicit preview statement, but the opening paragraph implies that King will focus on the meaning and importance of "the greatest demonstration for freedom in the history of our nation."*

*Body: There are four main sections in the body of the speech. The first runs from paragraph 2 through paragraph 8. In this section King addresses the nation at large and develops two subpoints. In paragraphs 3-6 he bemoans the "shameful condition" of American blacks, who still face poverty, segregation, and discrimination 100 years after the Emancipation Proclamation. In paragraphs 7-8 King reminds the nation of "the fierce urgency of now" and warns that continued protest will "shake the foundations of our nation until the bright day of justice emerges."*

*The second section of the body consists of paragraphs 9-14, in which King speaks primarily to his followers. He develops four subpoints: (1) In paragraphs 9-10 he urges black Americans to maintain their commitment to nonviolent methods of protest. (2) In paragraph 11, which received more applause than any other part of the speech, King reaffirms the need for blacks and whites to work together for freedom and equality. (3) In paragraph 12 King again stresses that African Americans cannot be satisfied until their grievances are resolved. (4) In paragraphs 13-14 King acknowledges that many African Americans have suffered "trials and tribulations" in their quest for freedom, but he urges them to keep the faith that their situation "can and will be changed."*

*The third section of the body consists of paragraphs 15-21, in which King dramatizes his "dream" of all Americans living in freedom and brotherhood. This is the most famous section of the speech, but the ideas were not new. King had said much the same thing, including repetition of the phrase "I Have a Dream," in a speech at Detroit two months earlier.*

*The fourth section of the speech consists of paragraphs 22-29. Here King reaffirms his belief that "we will be free one day." He recites the first verse of "My Country 'Tis of Thee," builds into the series of sentences beginning with "Let freedom ring," and then moves into the emotionally charged final paragraph.*

*Conclusion:* "I Have a Dream" is one of those speeches in which it is almost impossible to identify a discrete conclusion. The speech builds steadily to the powerful closing lines without a discernible shift from body to conclusion. The important question when judging a speech is not "Does the speech have a conclusion?" but "Does the speech conclude effectively?" In King's case the answer to the latter question is unequivocally yes.

*Language:* The most important feature of King's language is his use of familiar, concrete words. From beginning to end, he relies on words and phrases that create sharp, vivid images—"flames of withering injustice," "manacles of segregation and chains of discrimination," "sunlit path of racial justice," "whirlwinds of revolt," "heightening Alleghenies of Pennsylvania." This kind of language helps King make tangible the abstract principles of liberty and equality.

This is best seen in the "dream" section (paragraphs 15-21). Dreams are visual phenomena, and King's "dream" is strikingly visual. Instead of talking in vague terms about the ideals of freedom and justice, he makes those ideals concrete. Listening to him, we can almost see the sons of former slaves and the sons of former slave owners sitting down together on the red hills of Georgia. We can feel the sweltering heat of Mississippi and the cool breezes of the oasis of freedom and justice it will become. We can picture little black boys and black girls joining hands in Alabama with little white boys and white girls. By making his "dream" so vivid, King communicates it much more effectively than he could have through abstract language.

King's speech is also notable for its heavy use of metaphor. Most obvious is the extended metaphor of the "promissory note" or "bad check" in paragraphs 4-6, but there are also a number of brief metaphors scattered throughout the speech (see especially paragraphs 2-3, 7-9, 13, and 22) as well as a brace of similes in paragraph 2.

It is important to note that most of the metaphors and similes occur in pairs and are arranged to emphasize progress from a negative condition to a positive condition. For example: "It came as a joyous daybreak to end the long night of their captivity" (paragraph 2); ". . . to rise from the dark and desolate valley of segregation to the sunlit path of racial justice" (paragraph 7); ". . . to lift our nation from the quicksands of racial injustice to the solid rock of brotherhood" (paragraph 7); "The whirlwinds of revolt will continue to shake the foundations of our nation until the bright day of justice emerges" (paragraph 8); ". . . transform the jangling discords of our nation into a beautiful symphony *of brotherhood" (paragraph 22). These metaphors strengthen King's message that continued protest will change things for the better.*

*King also relies heavily on repetition and parallelism to reinforce his ideas and accent the cadence of his speech. There are eight major units of repetition and parallelism: (1) The "One hundred years later . . ." series in paragraph 3; (2) The "Now is the time . . ." series in paragraph 7; (3) The "We must . . ." and "We must not . . ." series in paragraphs 9 and 10; (4) The "We can never be satisfied . . ." and "We cannot be satisfied . . ." series in paragraph 12; (5) The "Go back to . . ." series in paragraph 14; (6) The "I have a dream . . ." series in paragraphs 15 through 21; (7) The "to . . . together" series in paragraph 22; (8) The "Let freedom ring . . ." series in paragraphs 24 through 28.*

*Finally, one can observe the heavy religious tone of King's speech. Not only are there a number of explicit religious references, but many of King's words and images are Biblical in origin. For example, "It came as a joyous daybreak to end the long night of their captivity" (paragraph 2) brings forth images of the exodus of the Jews from ancient Egypt. The phrase "until justice rolls down like waters and righteousness like a mighty stream" (paragraph 12) echoes the words of the prophet Amos. Similarly, King's statement in paragraph 21 that "every valley shall be exalted, every hill and mountain shall be made low, the rough places will be made plane and the crooked places will be made straight, and the glory of the Lord shall be revealed, and all flesh shall see it together" is repeated almost verbatim from the Old Testament book of Isaiah.*

## Additional Exercises and Activities

1.   Have students analyze the speech in Chapter 17 of the textbook by Ryan Saurer ("James ᛖCool Papaᛖ Bell," pages 409-410). Students should focus their analysis on how Saurer utilizes imagery, parallelism, repetition, and other resources of language to enhance the impact of his ideas.

*Discussion: "James ᛖCool Papaᛖ Bell" is an excellent speech to study in conjunction with Chapter 11—especially if you do not deal with it as part of the section on commemorative speaking in Chapter 17. It is particularly valuable as a complement to Application Exercise 5, above, in which students analyze Martin Luther King's "I Have a Dream."*

*Although most students are fascinated by the stylistic brilliance of King's masterpiece, they are often so overwhelmed by it that they cannot envision themselves emulating King's use of language in their own speeches. "James 'Cool Papa' Bell," however, is a classroom speech and it shows how students can use the same devices as King to elevate and enliven their discourse. For a synopsis of "James 'Cool Papa' Bell," see pages 320-321 of this manual. If you discuss the speech in class, you may also want to show the videotape of it, which is available as part of the instructional supplement to* The Art of Public Speaking.

2.  Distribute copies of "Hail to the Heroes," by James Davis, which appears on pages 406-407 of this manual. Have students focus on how Davis uses imagery, repetition, parallelism, and other resources of language to enhance the impact of his ideas.

> **Discussion:** *A student commemorative speech, "Hail to the Heroes" is a rich text to study for its use of language. As with Ryan Saurer's speech on "James 'Cool Papa' Bell" (see the previous Additional Exercise/Activity), it illustrates how students can use the resources of language to elevate and polish their discourse. For a synopsis of the speech, see page 408 of this manual.*

3.  Have students compose one page of prose in which they use all the resources of language discussed in the textbook—imagery, simile, metaphor, antithesis, alliteration, etc.—to describe a scene or to capture an emotion. Possible topics include:

| | |
|---|---|
| the beach at sunset | my happiest moment |
| walking in the forest | my most fearful experience |
| a rainy night | my favorite person |
| life in the city | my most embarrassing moment |
| a boisterous party | my worst experience |
| any special location | my favorite childhood memory |

> **Discussion:** *Encourage students to be as "literary" or "poetic" as they wish in this exercise. Some will go overboard and become excessively maudlin or melodramatic, but some will create surprisingly effective and moving prose. If you have students present orally what they have written, this exercise can also provide an additional brief speaking opportunity in class.*

4.    In each of the following sentences, select the most appropriate word to complete the statement:

a.    insisted, persisted, urged, persevered

I _____ her to treat her roommates more kindly.

Though he tried to prove his innocence, the district attorney _____ in believing him guilty.

Despite the difficulty of the job, she _____ until she completed it.

He _____ that gun control legislation will do little to reduce crimes of violence.

b.    guess, prediction, estimate, forecast

I just read the *Wall Street Journal*'s _____ for the economy next year.

Will you turn on the television and get the weather _____ for tomorrow?

It's always a good idea to get a written _____ before taking your car in for repairs.

Chien doesn't have the foggiest idea how many jelly beans are in the jar. He's just making a _____.

c.    snap, tap, clap, slap

I knew someone was following me through the woods when I heard a twig _____ behind me.

The insistent _____ of the flag against the pole increased the drama of the military funeral.

Sheila walked with so much spring in her step you could hear her feet _____ on the sidewalk.

All at once we heard a tremendous _____ of thunder.

d.    necessary, compulsory, unavoidable, irresistible

The final exam in this course is _____.

Milos tried to turn down the offer of a free Caribbean cruise, but in the end he found it simply _____.

Proper clothing is _____ to survival in the Arctic.

Because Crystal's train was late, her failure to keep the appointment was really _____.

**Discussion:** *This is an enjoyable exercise that increases students' awareness of the importance of careful, accurate word choice. The correct answers follow. To facilitate class discussion, this exercise is available as part of the transparency supplement that accompanies* The Art of Public Speaking.

a. insisted, persisted, urged, persevered

I __urged__ her to treat her roommates more kindly.

Though he tried to prove his innocence, the district attorney __persisted__ in believing him guilty.

Despite the difficulty of the job, she __persevered__ until she completed it.

He __insisted__ that gun control legislation will do little to reduce crimes of violence.

b. guess, prediction, estimate, forecast

I just read the *Wall Street Journal*'s __prediction__ for the economy next year.

Will you turn on the television and get the weather __forecast__ for tomorrow?

It's always a good idea to get a written __estimate__ before taking your car in for repairs.

Chien doesn't have the foggiest idea how many jelly beans are in the jar. He's just making a __guess__.

c. snap, tap, clap, slap

I knew someone was following me through the woods when I heard a twig __snap__ behind me.

The insistent __slap__ of the flag against the pole increased the drama of the military funeral.

Sheila walked with so much spring in her step you could hear her feet __tap__ on the sidewalk.

All at once we heard a tremendous __clap__ of thunder.

d. necessary, compulsory, unavoidable, irresistible

The final exam in this course is __compulsory__.

Milos tried to turn down the offer of a free Caribbean cruise, but in the end he found it simply __irresistible__.

Proper clothing is __necessary__ to survival in the Arctic.

Because Crystal's train was late, her failure to keep the appointment was really __unavoidable__.

5.   Have students identify the flaw in each of the following metaphors and rewrite each sentence to make it clear and consistent.

a.   The safety of all Central America will be jeopardized unless we stop the Communists in their tracks before they get under full sail.

**Discussion:**  *"In their tracks" suggests that the Communists are running, while "under full sail" suggests that they are sailing. The sentence should be rewritten so as to avoid mixing metaphors. For example: "The safety of all Central America will be jeopardized unless we stop the Communists in their tracks before they reach full speed."*

b.   The Senator hopes to use his victory in the California primary as a springboard to rekindle his campaign.

**Discussion:**  *The only conceivable way one could use a "springboard" to "rekindle" a campaign is by burning the springboard. The mixed metaphor could be avoided by having the Senator use his victory in the California primary as a "spark to rekindle his campaign" or as a "springboard to boost his campaign."*

c.   Although the Irish began at the bottom of the social ladder, they have now achieved a niche in the backbone of the nation.

**Discussion:**  *The mixing of "social ladder" and "backbone of the nation" is ludicrous. One alternative would be: "Although the Irish began at the bottom of the social ladder, they have now climbed many rungs higher." Actually, this sentence would be most improved by avoiding metaphor altogether. For example: "Although the Irish began life in America with few advantages, they have made many important contributions to the nation."*

d.   College professors should not draw the ivory towers around themselves as some sort of sacred cloak.

**Discussion:**  *What an interesting image—a college professor wrapped in an ivory tower! Like the last sentence, this one would be much improved if the speaker did not strain for a metaphor. If the ivory tower metaphor were kept, a better sentence would be: "College professors should not try to avoid social responsibility by hiding in the ivory towers."*

6. The following paragraph is filled with verbal clutter. Following the model on page 247 of the textbook, edit the paragraph so as to eliminate the unnecessary words. You should be able to find fifty to sixty such words. If you don't find that many, go back to the paragraph and edit it again.

Imagine the thought of burning up a priceless, invaluable painting by Rembrandt just in order to stay warm for ten minutes. Sounds really crazy, doesn't it? But that is comparable to just what is happening right now in the Amazon rain forest of Brazil. In 1970 the president of Brazil began to start a 14,000-mile network of highways to open up the huge, vast area of the rain forest to settlement by poor, poverty-stricken Brazilians. Unfortunately, the project has been nothing but a disaster from the very beginning. Working in the hot, torrid, steamy jungle caused many fatal deaths among the workers. Soon a whole lot of foreign businesses began to get themselves involved in the project. Now the whole thing is utterly out of hand. Today there is a very real danger that the whole ecological balance of the rain forest will be irrevocably destroyed completely and altogether. This will have important and serious future implications in terms of what it means not only for Brazil, but for all of the rest of South America.

**Discussion:** *This exercise is especially helpful if you have students prepare a manuscript speech. It works well as an in-class exercise, since it can be completed fairly quickly. To give students additional practice in clearing the underbrush out of their prose, this exercise can be supplemented with Additional Exercise/Activity 7 below. Here is what the paragraph looks like when it has been edited to eliminate the clutter. To facilitate class discussion, the edited paragraph is available as part of the transparency supplement that accompanies* The Art of Public Speaking.

Imagine ~~the thought of~~ burning ~~up~~ a priceless, ~~invaluable~~ painting by Rembrandt just ~~in order~~ to stay warm for ten minutes. Sounds ~~really~~ crazy, doesn't it? But that is comparable to ~~just~~ what is happening ~~right now~~ in the Amazon rain forest of Brazil. In 1970 the president of Brazil began ~~to start~~ a 14,000-mile network of highways to open ~~up~~ the ~~huge,~~ vast ~~area of the~~ rain forest to settlement by poor, ~~poverty-stricken~~ Brazilians. Unfortunately, the project has been ~~nothing but~~ a disaster from the ~~very~~ beginning. Working in the ~~hot, torrid, steamy~~ jungle caused many ~~fatal~~ deaths among the workers. Soon ~~a whole lot of~~ foreign businesses began to get ~~themselves~~ involved in the project. ~~Now the whole thing is utterly out of hand.~~ Today there is ~~a very real~~ danger that the ~~whole~~ ecological balance of the rain forest will be irrevocably destroyed ~~completely and altogether.~~ This will have important ~~and serious future~~ implications ~~in terms of what it means~~ not only for Brazil, but for all of ~~the rest of~~ South America.

7. The following paragraph is filled with verbal clutter. Following the model on page 247 of the textbook, edit the paragraph so as to eliminate the unnecessary words. You should be able to find forty to fifty such words. If you don't find that many, go back to the paragraph and edit it again.

Rock music is such a big and important part of our lives today that it is extremely difficult to imagine a time in which people lived without it. But there was once such a time. It was only forty years ago. The early 1950s were a time of bubble gum and soda pop—a pure and simple age. Then a new kind of music started coming on the scene like a huge tidal wave pouring onto a calm and quiet beach. A whole lot of young performers were appearing who were revolutionizing the shape of American popular music. Bill Haley, Chuck Berry, Elvis Presley, Fats Domino, Little Richard, Jerry Lee Lewis—the list is a long one that goes on and on. But one rock and roll performer stands out above the rest as the most original and innovative of them all. His name? Buddy Holly.

**Discussion:** *Like the previous Additional Exercise/Activity, this works well as an in-class activity and is especially helpful if you have students prepare a manuscript speech. Here is what the paragraph looks like when it has been edited to eliminate the clutter. To facilitate class discussion, the edited paragraph is available as part of the transparency supplement that accompanies* The Art of Public Speaking.

Rock music is such a big ~~and important~~ part of our lives ~~today~~ that it is *hard* ~~extremely difficult~~ to imagine a time ~~in which~~ *when* people lived without it. But there was ~~once~~ such a time. ~~It was only forty years ago.~~ The early 1950s were a time of bubble gum and soda pop—a pure and simple age. Then a new kind of music *emerging* ~~started coming on the scene~~ like a ~~huge~~ tidal wave *engulfing* ~~pouring onto a calm and~~ quiet beach. ~~A whole lot of~~ *Many* young performers ~~were appearing who~~ were revolutionizing ~~the shape of~~ American popular music. Bill Haley, Chuck Berry, Elvis Presley, Fats Domino, Little Richard, Jerry Lee Lewis—the list ~~is a long one that~~ goes on and on. But one ~~rock and roll~~ performer stands out ~~above the rest~~ as the most ~~original and~~ innovative of ~~them~~ all. His name? Buddy Holly.

# Extra Teaching and Learning Resources

## General

Bryson, Bill. *The Mother Tongue: English and How It Got That Way*. New York: Morrow, 1990).

Cmiel, Kenneth. *Democratic Eloquence: The Fight Over Popular Speech in Nineteenth-Century America*. New York: Morrow, 1990.

Gozzi, Raymond, Jr. *New Words and a Changing American Culture*. Columbia, S.C.: University of South Carolina Press, 1990.

Lucas, Stephen E. "The Stylistic Artistry of the Declaration of Independence." *Prologue: Quarterly of the National Archives*, 22 (1990), 24-43.

Lutz, William. *Doublespeak*. New York: Harper and Row, 1989.

McArthur, Tom (ed.). *The Oxford Companion to the English Language*. Oxford: Oxford University Press, 1992.

McCrone, John. *The Ape That Spoke: Language and the Evolution of the Human Mind*. New York: Morrow, 1991.

McCrum, Robert, Cran, William, and MacNeil, Robert. *The Story of English*. New York: Viking, 1986.

Tarver, Jerry. "Words in Time: Some Reflections on the Language of Speech." *Vital Speeches*, 54 (1988), 410-412.

Williams, Joseph. *Style: Ten Lessons in Clarity and Grace*, 4th ed. New York: HarperCollins, 1993.

Zinsser, William. *On Writing Well*, 4th ed. New York: HarperCollins, 1990.

## Figures of Speech

Corbett, Edward P. J. *Classical Rhetoric for the Modern Student*. 3rd ed. New York: Oxford University Press, 1990, Chapter 4.

Lakoff, George, and Johnson, Mark. *Metaphors We Live By*. Chicago: University of Chicago Press, 1980.

Quinn, Arthur. *Figures of Speech: Sixty Ways to Turn a Phrase*. Salt Lake City: Gibbs M. Smith, 1982.

## Nonsexist Language

Cameron, Deborah (ed.). *The Feminist Critique of Language: A Reader*. London: Routledge, 1990.

Ivy, Diana K., and Backlund, Phil. *Exploring Gender Speak: Personal Effectiveness in Gender Communication*. New York: McGraw-Hill, 1994.

Maggio, Rosalie. *The Bias-Free Word Finder: A Dictionary of Nondiscriminatory Language*. Boston: Beacon Press, 1991.

Miller, Casey, and Swift, Kate. *The Handbook of Nonsexist Writing for Writers, Editors, and Speakers*, 2nd ed. New York: Lippincott and Crowell, 1988.

Miller, Casey, and Swift, Kate. *Words and Women: New Language in New Times*. (New York, 1991).

Wood, Julia T. *Gendered Lives: Communication, Gender, and Culture*. Belmont, Calif.: Wadsworth, 1994.

## Classroom Activities and Assignments

Adams, John C. "Earstorming." *Speech Communication Teacher* (Spring 1992), 3.

Bozik, Mary, and Beall, Melissa. "Modeling Metaphorical Thinking." *Speech Communication Teacher* (Winter 1994), 1-3.

Hochel, Sandra. "Language Awareness and Assessment." In Stephen E. Lucas (ed.), *Selections from the Speech Communication Teacher, 1986-1991*. New York: McGraw-Hill, 1992, p. 39.

Jensen, Marvin D. "Revising Speech Style." In Stephen E. Lucas (ed.), *Selections from the Speech Communication Teacher, 1986-1991*. New York: McGraw-Hill, 1992, pp. 39-41.

Lamoureux, Edward Lee. "Practicing Creative Word Choice with Dialogic Listening." In Stephen E. Lucas (ed.), *Selections from the Speech Communication Teacher, 1986-1991*. New York: McGraw-Hill, 1992, pp. 41-42.

McGrath, Richard. "The Slang Game." In Stephen E. Lucas (ed.), *Selections from the Speech Communication Teacher, 1986-1991*. New York: McGraw-Hill, 1992, pp. 42-43.

Pinker, Steven. *The Language Instinct: How the Mind Creates Language*. New York: Morrow, 1994.

Rowley, Edwin N. "More Than Mere Words." *Speech Communication Teacher,* (Fall 1992), 5.

## Films and Videos

"American Tongues." Center for New American Media (1986). 40 minutes.

"Choosing the Ideas and Words." RMI Media Productions (1986). 28 minutes.

"Doublespeak." Films for the Humanities (1989). 28 minutes.

"Language." Insight Media (1990). 30 minutes.

"Language and Communication." Insight Media (1983). 30 minutes.

"Sexism in Language." Films for the Humanities (1993). 20 minutes.

"The Language of Leadership: The Winston Churchill Method." Films for the Humanities (1993). 60 minutes.

"Verbal Communication: The Power of Words," revised version. CRM Films (1992). 22 minutes.

"What Do You Mean?" Insight Media (1983). 30 minutes.

# Chapter 12 Delivery

## Chapter Objectives

*After reading this chapter, students should be able to:*

1. Explain why good delivery is important to successful speaking.

2. Explain the major characteristics of effective speech delivery.

3. Identify the four methods of delivering a speech.

4. Explain the eight aspects of voice usage that are crucial to public speaking.

5. Discuss the four aspects of nonverbal communication that are most important to a public speaker.

6. Explain the five-step method presented in the chapter for practicing extemporaneous speech delivery.

## Chapter Outline

I.   Good delivery can make the difference between a successful speech and an unsuccessful speech *(text pages 266-276)*.
  A.   In addition to having something to say, a speaker must also know *how* to say it.
    1.   A wonderfully written speech can be destroyed by poor delivery.
    2.   Even a mediocre speech will be more effective if it is delivered well.
  B.   Good delivery is an art.
    1.   It conveys the speaker's message clearly, interestingly, and without distracting the audience.

2.   Most audiences prefer delivery that combines a certain degree of formality with the best attributes of good conversation—directness, vocal and facial expressiveness, and a lively sense of communication.

II.  There are four basic methods of delivering a speech *(text pages 267-270).*
  A.  Some speeches are read verbatim from a manuscript.
    1.  Manuscript speeches are often used in situations that require absolute accuracy of wording or that impose strict time limits upon the speaker.
    2.  Speakers should take several steps when speaking from a manuscript.
      a.  They should rehearse the speech aloud to make sure it sounds natural.
      b.  They should work on establishing eye contact with the audience.
      c.  They should make sure the final copy of the manuscript is legible at a glance.
      d.  They should concentrate on *talking with* the audience rather than *reading to* them.
  B.  Some speeches are recited from memory.
    1.  Nowadays it is customary to deliver only the shortest speeches from memory.
    2.  When delivering a speech from memory, the speaker should learn it so thoroughly that she or he can concentrate on communicating with the audience rather than on remembering specific words.
  C.  Some speeches are delivered impromptu.
    1.  Impromptu speeches are presented with little or no immediate preparation.
    2.  When speakers find themselves faced with an impromptu speaking situation, they should follow four simple steps to organize their thoughts quickly.
      a.  First, they should state the point to which they are responding.
      b.  Second, they should state the point they want to make.
      c.  Third, they should use whatever support they have—examples, statistics, or testimony—to prove their point.
      d.  Fourth, they should summarize their point.
    3.  In addition, an impromptu speaker should consider the following suggestions.
      a.  If there is sufficient time, quickly jot down brief a outline to remember what to say.
      b.  Try to remain calm and assured regardless of how nervous you might be.
      c.  Maintain strong eye contact with the audience.

        d.    Concentrate on speaking at a clear, deliberate pace.

        e.    Use signposts ("first," "second," etc.) to help the audience keep track of your ideas.

D.    Some speeches are delivered extemporaneously.

    1.    Extemporaneous speeches are carefully prepared and practiced in advance.

    2.    They are presented from a set of notes, but the exact wording is chosen at the moment of delivery.

    3.    There are several advantages to extemporaneous delivery.

        a.    It gives greater control over ideas and language than impromptu delivery.

        b.    It allows for greater spontaneity and directness than memorized or manuscript delivery.

        c.    It encourages conversational vocal qualities, natural gestures, and strong eye contact.

    4.    Most classroom speeches are delivered extemporaneously.

    5.    At the end of this chapter, students will find a five-step method for practicing extemporaneous delivery.

III.   Effective speakers learn to control their voices to enhance the impact of their message *(text pages 270-277)*.

A.    The volume of a speaker's voice is basic to effective delivery.

    1.    If a speaker talks too softly, he or she will not be heard.

    2.    If a speaker talks too loudly, he or she will be thought boorish.

    3.    Whether speaking with or without a microphone, a speaker must adjust her or his volume to the acoustics of the room and the size of the audience.

B.    The pitch of a speaker's voice has an impact on delivery.

    1.    Pitch is the highness or lowness of a speaker's voice.

    2.    Speakers who do not change their pitch speak in a monotone, which makes their voice flat and lifeless.

    3.    Effective speakers vary their pitch to generate interest and to convey meaning and emotion.

C.    The rate of a speaker's voice will affect the outcome of a speech.

    1.    Rate refers to the speed at which a person speaks.

    2.    Although most people in the United States speak at a rate between 120 and 150 words per minute, there is no uniform rate for effective speechmaking.

    3.    The most appropriate rate depends on the speaker's voice, the mood the speaker is trying to create, the audience, and the occasion.

    4.    Two obvious faults to avoid are speaking so slowly that listeners get bored or so fast that they lose track of the message.

D. Effective pauses can contribute greatly to a speaker's impact.
    1. Pauses can be used to signal the end of a thought unit, to give an idea time to sink in, or to lend dramatic impact to a statement.
    2. Novice speakers can develop their use of pauses by practice and by observing experienced speakers.
    3. Above all, a speaker should avoid vocalized pauses.
        a. Vocalized pauses include statements such as "like," "er," "uh," or "um."
        b. Research shows that too many vocalized pauses reduce a speaker's credibility and persuasiveness.
E. Vocal variety is one of the most important elements in effective delivery.
    1. Vocal variety refers to modulations in the rate, pitch, volume, and timing of a speaker's voice.
    2. Speakers who lack vocal variety come across as flat, dull, and uncommunicative.
    3. Speakers who possess strong vocal variety come across as lively, dynamic, and communicative.
F. Pronunciation is another vocal feature that influences the outcome of a speech.
    1. Errors in pronunciation can reduce a speaker's credibility.
    2. If a speaker has doubts about how to pronounce a word, she or he should check the pronunciation in a dictionary or with another person.
G. Articulation also has an impact on how a speech is received.
    1. Articulation refers to how crisply and distinctly we form particular speech sounds.
    2. Some errors in articulation are caused by physical problems such as a cleft palate, a misaligned jaw, or a poorly fitted dental plate.
    3. Most errors in articulation are caused by laziness—by failing to produce speech sounds clearly and precisely.
    4. Articulation errors caused by physical problems often require the aid of a certified speech therapist.
    5. Articulation errors caused by laziness can be remedied by diagnosing the errors and working to correct them.
H. A speaker's dialect can influence how the speech is received.
    1. Dialects are accents, grammatical patterns, and vocabulary distinctive to particular regions or ethnic groups.
    2. Although no dialect is inherently superior or inferior to another, heavy use of dialect in public speaking can be troublesome if the audience does not share the dialect in question.
    3. Regional or ethnic dialects usually do not pose a problem if listeners are familiar with the dialect and find it appropriate to the occasion.

IV. Effective speakers learn to use nonverbal communication to enhance the impact of their message *(text pages 277-282)*.
  A. Nonverbal communication can play a major role in the outcome of a speech.
    1. Researchers estimate that hundreds of thousands of messages are conveyed through bodily movement.
    2. Studies show that in some situations nonverbal communication accounts for much of the meaning communicated by a speaker.
  B. Four aspects of nonverbal communication are especially important for public speakers.
    1. The first aspect is personal appearance.
      a. Listeners always see a speaker before they hear the speaker.
      b. Just as speakers adapt to the audience and occasion in other respects, so should they take care to dress and groom appropriately.
    2. The second aspect is bodily action.
      a. Public speakers need to avoid distracting bodily actions such as fidgeting with notes, leaning on the lectern, and shifting weight from one foot to the other.
      b. Effective speakers learn to control these actions so as to keep attention focused on the message of the speech.
      c. Effective speakers are also aware of their actions before and after the speech as well as during it.
        (1) Before the speech, they walk confidently to the lectern, establish eye contact with the audience, and look poised and confident regardless of how nervous they may be.
        (2) After the speech, they give their closing line a few moments to sink in, calmly gather up their notes, and maintain their confident demeanor while returning to their seat.
    3. The third aspect is gestures.
      a. Some accomplished speakers gesture a great deal; others hardly at all.
      b. The cardinal rule is that whatever gestures a speaker does make should not draw attention to themselves or distract from the message of the speech.
      c. Gestures should appear natural and spontaneous, clarify or reinforce the speaker's ideas, and be appropriate to the audience and occasion.
    4. The fourth aspect is eye contact.
      a. Audiences often look at a speaker's eyes for clues about the speaker's truthfulness, intelligence, and feelings.

   b. Although customs of eye contact in interpersonal communication vary from culture to culture, there is fairly wide agreement across cultures on the importance of eye contact in public speaking.

   c. Research shows that in the United States speakers who fail to establish eye contact are perceived as ill at ease and often as insincere or dishonest.

   d. Establishing eye contact is one of the quickest ways to establish a communicative bond with an audience.

     (1) Eye contact helps capture an audience's attention.

     (2) Eye contact helps establish the speaker's credibility.

     (3) Eye contact allows speakers to see and respond to feedback.

V. Speakers can improve their speech delivery by following a five-step method *(text pages 282-283)*.

  A. First, the speaker should go over her or his preparation outline aloud.

   1. This allows the speaker to judge how the written outline translates into spoken discourse.

   2. It also gives the speaker a chance to clarify and revise the speech as necessary.

  B. Second, the speaker should prepare a speaking outline.

   1. Preparing a speaking outline increases the speaker's familiarity with the speech.

   2. The speaking outline should conform to the guidelines presented in Chapter 10.

  C. Third, the speaker should practice the speech aloud several times using only the speaking outline.

   1. At this stage, the speaker should not worry about getting everything in the speech just right.

   2. The aim is to gain control of the ideas and structure of the speech, not to learn it word for word.

  D. Fourth, the speaker should polish and refine the delivery.

   1. Practicing in front of a mirror is one way to check on nonverbal communication such as gestures and eye contact.

   2. Tape recording the speech is an excellent way to gauge such things as rate, pauses, articulation, and vocal variety.

   3. A few practice sessions in front of other people—friends, family, roommates, etc.—can be especially valuable.

  E. Fifth, the speaker should give the speech a dress rehearsal under conditions as close as possible as those he or she will face during the actual speech.

   1. Some students like to try the speech in an empty classroom a day or two before the speech is due.

2. It is important that the dress rehearsal incorporate every aspect of the speech, including visual aids.
F. In order for this method to be effective, speakers must start early.
   1. A single practice session—no matter how long—is rarely enough.
   2. Student speakers should give themselves *at least* a couple of days, preferably more, to gain command of the speech and its presentation.

## Application Exercises *(from text pages 284-286)*

1. Radio and television announcers must have outstanding articulation. One way they develop it is by practicing tongue twisters. Try these. Start by saying them slowly and firmly, so that each sound is clearly formed. Gradually increase to your normal rate of speech.

   a. Which wily wizard wished wicked wishes for Willy?

   b. The sixth sick Sheik's sheep is sick.

   c. Fetch me the finest French-fried freshest fish that Finney fries.

   d. Shy Sarah saw six Swiss wrist watches.

   e. One year we had a Christmas brunch with Merry Christmas mush to munch. But I don't think you'd care for such. We didn't like to munch mush much.

   **Discussion:** *Try this as an in-class activity. It's enjoyable and it helps make students aware of the need for precise articulation. Here are a few other tongue-twisters to use:*

   f. The view from the veranda gave forth a fine vista of waves and leafy foliage.

   g. She sells seashells on the seashore.

   h. While we waited for the whistle on the wharf, we whittled vigorously on the white weatherboards.

   i. Grass grew green on the graves in Grace Gray's grandfather's graveyard.

   j. Pete Briggs pats pigs.
   Briggs pats pink pigs.
   Briggs pats big pigs.
   Pete Briggs is a pink pig, big pig patter.

   k. Amidst the mists and coldest frosts,
   With stoutest wrists and loudest boasts,
   He thrusts his fists against the posts,
   And still insists he sees the ghosts.

2. An excellent way to improve your vocal variety is to read aloud selections from poetry that require emphasis and feeling. Choose one of your favorite poems that falls into this category, or else find one by leafing through a poetry anthology. Practice reading the selection aloud. As you read, use your voice to make the poem come alive. Vary your volume, rate, and pitch. Find the appropriate places for pauses. Underline the key words or phrases you think should be stressed. Modulate your tone of voice; use inflection for emphasis and meaning.

   For this to work, you must overcome your fear of sounding affected or "dramatic." Most beginning speakers do better if they exaggerate changes in volume, rate, pitch, and expression. This will make you more aware of the many ways you can use your voice to express a wide range of moods and meanings. Besides, what sounds overly "dramatic" to you usually does not sound that way to an audience. By adding luster, warmth, and enthusiasm to your voice, you will go a long way toward capturing and keeping the interest of your listeners.

   If possible, practice reading the selection into a tape recorder. Listen to the playback. If you are not satisfied with what you hear, practice the selection some more and record it again.

   > **Discussion:** *Beginning speakers are often much less animated delivering a speech than in ordinary conversation. This is due partly to inexperience, partly to nervousness, partly to fear of sounding affected. But whatever the cause, the result is dull and lifeless delivery.*
   >
   > *This exercise is designed to help students over this barrier. At the start of the course they are likely to feel more comfortable using their voices expressively when reciting poetry than when delivering a speech. As they work with their poems, they often become more accustomed to modulating their voices to enhance the meaning of the words. As a capstone to the exercise, have students present their poems orally in class.*

3. Watch a ten-minute segment of a television drama with the sound turned off. What do the characters say with their dress, gestures, facial expressions, and the like? Do the same with a television comedy. How do the nonverbal messages in the two shows differ? Be prepared to report your observations in class.

   > **Discussion:** *This exercise attunes students to the dimensions and effects of nonverbal communication, and it usually generates a lively class discussion. It works best if you assign particular programs for the entire class to watch.*

4.    Attend a speech on campus. You may choose either a presentation by a guest speaker from outside the college or a class session by a professor who has a reputation as a good lecturer. Prepare a brief report on the speaker's vocal and nonverbal communication.

In your report, first analyze the speaker's volume, pitch, rate, pauses, vocal variety, pronunciation, and articulation. Then evaluate the speaker's personal appearance, bodily action, gestures, and eye contact. Explain how the speaker's delivery added to or detracted from what the speaker said. Finally, note at least two techniques of delivery used by the speaker that you might want to try in your next speech.

**Discussion:** *This exercise provides for an out-of-class speech observation. You may want to have students write a brief paper reporting their observations; you may prefer that they use an observation form such as the one provided on the next page.*

## Additional Exercises and Activities

1.    Lead a class discussion in which students develop a set of criteria for effective speech delivery. After the discussion, codify the criteria into an evaluation form that can be used by the class for the remainder of the term.

**Discussion:** *Although this exercise takes an entire class period, it can be quite helpful. At the start of the discussion, tell students that they should draw the criteria not only from the textbook, but also from their own experience. Although most of the class may not have much background as public speakers, they all have considerable experience as consumers of speeches (in classroom lectures, if nowhere else). As a result, they are already fairly expert in detecting delivery behaviors that enhance or inhibit effective communication.*

*By combining what they have read in the textbook with what they have learned from experience, most classes put together an excellent set of criteria for speech delivery. Moreover, because they have generated the evaluation form themselves, students are more committed to it. For a more complete discussion of how this kind of exercise works in the classroom, see Lynne Webb, "A Student-Devised Evaluation Form,"* Speech Communication Teacher, *9 (Spring 1989), 5-7, reprinted in Stephen E. Lucas (ed.),* Selections From the Speech Communication Teacher, 1986-1991, *which is part of the instructional supplement that accompanies* The Art of Public Speaking.

# Out-of-Class Speech Observation—Delivery

*Your name* _____ *Speaker* _____

Where was the speech presented? _____

What was the occasion for the speech? _____

**VOCAL COMMUNICATION:**  *Record your observations about each of the following aspects of the speaker's voice.*

Volume _____

Pitch _____

Rate _____

Pauses _____

Vocal variety _____

Pronunciation _____

Articulation _____

**NONVERBAL COMMUNICATION:**  *Record your observations about each of these aspects of the speaker's nonverbal communication.*

Personal appearance _____

Bodily action _____

Gestures _____

Eye contact _____

**OVERALL EVALUATION OF DELIVERY:**  *Explain how the speaker's delivery added to or detracted from the message.*

_____

_____

**WHAT IT MEANS FOR ME:**  *Explain at least two techniques of delivery used by the speaker that you might want to try in your next speech.*

_____

_____

_____

2.  Show students one or more selections from the videotapes of student speeches that accompany *The Art of Public Speaking*. Use the videotapes to illustrate points about effective and ineffective speech delivery.

    **Discussion:** *It is extremely difficult to teach delivery from a textbook. Perhaps the greatest benefit of using videotapes in the speech classroom is that they help students see in action the principles of delivery discussed in the textbook. Any of the speeches on the videotapes that accompany* The Art of Public Speaking *can be used for this purpose, and you will want to choose speeches that illustrate most clearly the points you emphasize in your classes.*

    *For the convenience of instructors, several of the student speeches available on videotape are also printed in the fifth edition of* The Art of Public Speaking. *These speeches include "Dandelions: The Uncommon Weed" (pages 329-331), "The Dangers of Chewing Tobacco" (pages 390-394), "James 'Cool Papa' Bell" (pages 409-410), "The Hidden World of Perfumes" (pages 444-447), "Family Medical Histories: A Proven Lifesaver" (pages 454-456), and "A Friend in Need" (pages 459-462). For more information on individual speeches, consult the synopses in this manual (see the Table of Contents) and the handbooks that accompany the videotapes.*

3.  Show students a videotape of a speech. After a couple of minutes turn off the sound and have students concentrate on the nonverbal cues sent by the speaker's appearance, bodily action, gestures, and eye contact. After a couple of minutes turn the sound back on so students can concentrate on the interaction of the speaker's vocal and nonverbal communication.

    **Discussion:** *This is an easy way to illustrate the wide range of nonverbal cues sent by a speaker. To their surprise, students can usually tell from the nonverbal cues alone whether the speaker is intent on communicating with the audience or is simply going through the motions. To save time, try combining this activity with the preceding exercise.*

4.  Assign one or more rounds of impromptu speeches. Speeches should be one and a half minutes to two minutes in length. Encourage students to follow the guidelines for impromptu speaking discussed on pages 268-269 of the textbook.

    **Discussion:** *When you announce this assignment, most students will act as if you had condemned them to a fate worse than death. Yet for most students, impromptu speeches, if handled properly by the instructor, can be an enormously valuable confidence builder.*

One way to approach impromptu speeches is to assign two or three at various intervals throughout the term. Another approach is to devote as many as three consecutive days to impromptu speeches, with each student in the class giving a speech on each day. The latter approach works particularly well because it gives students a chance to become comfortable with the impromptu situation. With each succeeding day, students gain poise and confidence. By the third day, many are so relaxed—and are giving such good speeches—that they ask to do more impromptu presentations. Another benefit of this approach is that students get so used to speaking without notes that their skills of extemporaneous speaking also improve dramatically—especially with respect to eye contact, gestures, and vocal variety.

If you assign two or more consecutive days of impromptu speaking, try to schedule them about two-thirds of the way through the term. If you assign them too early, students will not have learned enough about speechmaking in general to have a solid foundation for giving impromptu speeches. In addition, impromptu speaking involves considerable psychological risk on the part of students. The more comfortable students are with their classmates, the more willing they are to take the necessary risk. If you assign a series of impromptu speeches too early in the semester, students may recoil from the assignment rather then benefitting from it.

Although impromptu speeches can be used as a graded assignment, most teachers use them as an informal, non-graded speaking experience. Because students are usually apprehensive about speaking impromptu—especially initially—you should do all you can to maintain a low-key, supportive atmosphere.

One of the major questions with respect to impromptu speaking is how to select topics. When faced with impromptu speaking situations outside the classroom, students will speak about issues of immediate concern to their job, their church, their community, and the like. One way to approximate this experience is to develop a topic for each student based on one of her or his previous classroom speeches.

For example, if a student has given an informative speech on the benefits of learning CPR, you might assign him or her the following topic: "Doesn't learning CPR take a lot of time and money. Besides, I have never come across a person having a heart attack or drowning. It all seems like a lot of bother for something most people will never use. Is it really that important to know CPR?"

Or if a student has given a persuasive speech urging the audience to help save the Brazilian rain forests, you might give her or him this topic: "Of course, it would be nice to save the rain forests of South America, but who are we to tell Brazilians what to do with their land? After all, the United States uses more natural *resources per capita than any other country in the world. Aren't we being hypocritical in asking Brazil to save the rain forests while we continue our dependence on foreign oil?"*

*Now you have created a situation analogous to one people often face in real life—defending their position on a subject with which they are already familiar. Students should feel free to use material from their previous speech in the impromptu speech—indeed, they should be encouraged to do so.*

*If you conduct a second round of impromptu speeches, again give students a choice of topics that will allow them to draw on familiar ideas and experiences. Some possibilities include: (1) What is your favorite—or least favorite—hobby/academic subject/sport/ time of year, etc.? Why? (2) What are two or three things that really annoy you? (3) What is the most—or least—favorite aspect of your college experience so far? (4) If you could change any single aspect of college life at this school, what would it be? (5) What do you think it means to be successful in life? (6) What is the most fulfilling or rewarding aspect of your life to date? These topics are so universal that students will have no difficulty finding one on which to speak.*

*If you hold a third round of speeches, you can use the same set of topics— just make sure each student chooses a different individual topic from the one he or she chose in the second round. You can also devise new topics of a similar nature for the third round. You might even require that each student supply one or two topics that can go into the pool of possible topics for the entire class. This works especially well when students have responded positively to the first two days of impromptu speeches.*

*Regardless of the kinds of topics you use, give each student a few minutes to prepare the speech. You can do this by having the first 3-4 speakers choose their topics at the beginning of class. Then, as each speaker finishes, have a new student select his or her topic. If the speeches are to be two minutes in length, give the speakers time signals when they have one minute to go and then again when they have 30 seconds left. If you have an especially large class, you may have to reduce the length of the speeches to ensure that all students have an opportunity to perform on each day of impromptu speeches.*

*For other approaches to impromptu speaking, see the articles on this subject in Stephen E. Lucas (ed.),* Selections from the Speech Communication Teacher, 1986-1991, *which is part of the instructional supplement that accompanies* The Art of Public Speaking.

5. Divide the class into groups of three to five students. Assign each group a short children's story to present at the next class session. In presenting the story, each group is to act as if its audience were a ward of small children at a local hospital. Tell the students they must exaggerate their voice, their gestures, their facial expressions, and their bodily actions just as they would if they were actually telling the story to a group of children. Presentations should be 5-7 minutes in length, and each group should get together for an hour or so the evening before the assignment is due to assign speaking parts and to rehearse its presentation.

> **Discussion:** *This exercise can work very well to help students use their voices and bodies expressively to communicate with an audience. By role playing as if they were addressing an audience of small children, many students feel less inhibited than if they were "actually" addressing their peers. They also tend to feel less intimidated speaking as members of groups. Indeed, a side benefit of this exercise is that it can help break down barriers among members of the class—especially if it is assigned fairly early in the quarter or semester.*
>
> *Good candidates for children's stories include such time-honored classics as "The Three Little Pigs," "Little Red Riding Hood," "Goldilocks," and "The Gingerbread Man"—all of which contain vivid action and dramatic dialogue. There are also a number of more contemporary stories that work quite well, including "The Tawny Scrawny Lion," Charlotte Zolotow's "Mister Rabbit and the Lovely Present," Maurice Sendak's "Pierre" and "Where the Wild Things Are," and Dr. Seuss's "The Cat in the Hat" and "Horton the Elephant."*
>
> *To help ensure that all students participate fully in this exercise, many teachers assign some sort of minor grade to each group's presentation.*

6. Arrange to videotape at least one round of informative or persuasive speeches. Meet individually with each student to review her or his tape. Stop the tape periodically to point out what the speaker does particularly well and to indicate where improvement is needed.

> **Discussion:** *This can be extraordinarily valuable for students because it gives them a chance to hear and see themselves as others hear and see them. It also gives you a chance to give each student a constructive "blow-by-blow" critique of his or her speech. At first students are somewhat apprehensive about being videotaped. But once they see how valuable it is, they often request to have the next speech taped as well.*

# Extra Teaching and Learning Resources

## Voice

Buller, David B., LePoire, Beth A., and Aune, R. Kelly. "Social Perceptions as Mediators of the Effect of Speech Rate Similarity on Compliance." *Human Communication Research*, 19 (1992), 286-311.

Crannell, Kenneth C. *Voice and Articulation*, 2nd ed. Belmont, Calif.: Wadsworth, 1991.

Hahner, Jeffrey C., Sokoloff, Martin A., and Salisch, Sandra L. *Speaking Clearly: Improving Voice and Diction*, 4th ed. New York: McGraw-Hill, 1993.

McCallion, Michael. *The Voice Book: For Actors, Public Speakers, and Everyone Who Wants to Make the Most of Their Voice*. New York: Theatre Arts Books, 1988.

*NBC Handbook of Pronunciation*, 4th ed. New York: HarperCollins, 1991.

Randall, J. "Voice Power: How to Sound as Professional as You Look." *Executive Female* (March-April 1988), 51-53.

Ray, George B. "Vocally Cued Personality Prototypes: An Implicit Personality Theory." *Communication Monographs*, 53 (1986), 266-276.

## Nonverbal Communication

Axtell, Roger E. *Gestures: The Do's and Taboos of Body Language Around the World*. New York: Wiley, 1991.

Burgoon, Judee K., Buller, David B., and Woodall, W. Gill. *Nonverbal Communication: The Unspoken Dialogue*. New York: HarperCollins, 1990.

Burgoon, Judee K., Birk, Thomas, and Pfau, Michael. "Nonverbal Behaviors, Persuasion, and Credibility." *Human Communication Research*, 17 (1990), 140-169.

DeVito, Joseph, and Hecht, Michael L. (eds.). *The Nonverbal Communication Reader*. Prospect Heights, Ill.: Waveland, 1990.

Knapp, Mark L. "Teaching Nonverbal Communication." In John A. Daly, Gustav W. Friedrich, and Anita L. Vangelisti (eds.). *Teaching Communication: Theory, Research, and Methods*. Hillsdale, N.J.: Lawrence Erlbaum, 1990, pp. 129-144.

Knapp, Mark L., and Hall, Judith A. *Nonverbal Communication in Human Interaction*, 3rd ed. Fort Worth, Texas: Holt, Rinehart and Winston, 1992.

Malandro, Loretta A., Barker, Larry L., and Barker, Deborah Ann. *Nonverbal Communication*, 2nd ed. New York: Random House, 1989.

Manusov, Valerie. "Perceiving Nonverbal Messages: Effects of Immediacy and Encoded Intent on Receiver Judgments." *Western Journal of Speech Communication*, 55 (1991), 235-253.

Patterson, Miles L., Churchill, Mary E., Burger, Gary K., and Powell, Jack L. "Verbal and Nonverbal Modality Effects on Impressions of Political Candidates: Analysis from the 1984 Presidential Debates." *Communication Monographs*, 59 (1992), 231-242.

Streek, Jurgen. "Gesture as Communication I: Its Coordination with Gaze and Speech." *Communication Monographs*, 60 (1993), 275-299.

Townsend, John. "Paralinguistics: It's Not What You Say, It's the Way That You Say It." *Management Decision* (May 1988), 36-40.

Trimby, Madeline J. "What Do You Really Mean?" *Management World* (July-August 1988), 12-13.

## Classroom Activities and Assignments—General

Gaulard, Joan M. "To Read, To Memorize, or To Speak." In Stephen E. Lucas (ed.), *Selections from the Speech Communication Teacher, 1986-1991*. New York: McGraw-Hill, 1992, pp. 23-24.

Mills, Daniel D. "Tag Team Championship: Improving Delivery Skills." In Stephen E. Lucas (ed.), *Selections from the Speech Communication Teacher, 1986-1991*. New York: McGraw-Hill, 1992, p. 24.

Murray, Patricia. "The Objective Game." In Stephen E. Lucas (ed.), *Selections from the Speech Communication Teacher, 1986-1991*. New York: McGraw-Hill, 1992, pp. 24-25.

Snyder, Lee. "Twenty-Five Speeches an Hour." In Stephen E. Lucas (ed.), *Selections from the Speech Communication Teacher, 1986-1991*. New York: McGraw-Hill, 1992, p. 25.

## Classroom Activities and Assignments—Nonverbal Communication

Johnson, Craig. "People's Court Comes to the Classroom." In Stephen E. Lucas (ed.), *Selections from the Speech Communication Teacher, 1986-1991*. New York: McGraw-Hill, 1992, p. 49.

Rollman, Steven A. "Classroom Exercises for Teaching Nonverbal Communication." In Stephen E. Lucas (ed.), *Selections from the Speech Communication Teacher, 1986-1991*. New York: McGraw-Hill, 1992, pp. 49-50.

Schnell, James A. "Experiential Learning of Nonverbal Communication in Popular Magazine Advertising." In Stephen E. Lucas (ed.), *Selections from the Speech Communication Teacher, 1986-1991.* New York: McGraw-Hill, 1992, p. 50.

Valentine, Carol Ann, and Arnold, William E. "Nonverbal Scavenger Hunt." *Speech Communication Teacher* (Winter 1992), 14-15.

## Classroom Activities and Assignments—Speech Anxiety

Adams, Lori. "Speech Anxiety Simulation." *Speech Communication Teacher* (Fall 1992), 13.

Ayres, Joe, Hopf, Theodore S., and Ady, Jeff. "Coping with Speech Anxiety." In Stephen E. Lucas (ed.), *Selections from the Speech Communication Teacher, 1986-1991.* New York: McGraw-Hill, 1992, pp. 62-63.

Isaacson, Zelda. "Paradoxical Intention: A Strategy to Alleviate the Anxiety Associated with Public Speaking." *Speech Communication Teacher* (Summer 1993), 13-14.

Langdon, Harry. "A Course on Stage Fright." In Stephen E. Lucas (ed.), *Selections from the Speech Communication Teacher, 1986-1991.* New York: McGraw-Hill, 1992, pp. 63-64.

Mino, Mary. "Building Confidence Through Oral Interpretation." *Speech Communication Teacher* (Winter 1994), 10-11.

Stowell, Jessica. "Free Writing to Deal with Speech Anxiety." *Speech Communication Teacher* (Spring 1992), 15.

## Classroom Activities and Assignments—Impromptu Speeches

Beauchene, Kathleen. "Using Quotations as Impromptu Speech Topics." In Stephen E. Lucas (ed.), *Selections from the Speech Communication Teacher, 1986-1991.* New York: McGraw-Hill, 1992, p. 72.

Bytwerk. Randall. "The 'Just a Minute' Impromptu Exercise." In Stephen E. Lucas (ed.), *Selections from the Speech Communication Teacher, 1986-1991.* New York: McGraw-Hill, 1992, pp. 72-73.

Markham, Reed. "Power Minutes." In Stephen E. Lucas (ed.), *Selections from the Speech Communication Teacher, 1986-1991.* New York: McGraw-Hill, 1992, pp. 74-75.

McClarty, Wilma. "Nomination Speech: The Ideal Date." In Stephen E. Lucas (ed.), *Selections from the Speech Communication Teacher, 1986-1991.* New York: McGraw-Hill, 1992, pp. 75-76.

McKinney, Bruce C. "The 'Jeopardy' of Impromptu Speaking." In Stephen E. Lucas (ed.), *Selections from the Speech Communication Teacher, 1986-1991*. New York: McGraw-Hill, 1992, pp. 76-77.

Purdy, Ed. "Painless Impromptu Speaking." In Stephen E. Lucas (ed.), *Selections from the Speech Communication Teacher, 1986-1991*. New York: McGraw-Hill, 1992, p. 77.

Schumer, Allison. "Structure and Substance in a One-Minute Speech." In Stephen E. Lucas (ed.), *Selections from the Speech Communication Teacher, 1986-1991*. New York: McGraw-Hill, 1992, pp. 77-78.

Stahl, Michael G., and Adams, Lori. "Two Takes on Impromptu Speaking Topics: Retiring the Hat." *Speech Communication Teacher* (Winter 1994), 4-6.

Sugimoto, Naomi. "Impromptu Fortune-Telling Exercise." *Speech Communication Teacher* (Fall 1993), 5.

Wall, Jeanette. "Me? Give an Impromptu Speech? No Way!" In Stephen E. Lucas (ed.), *Selections from the Speech Communication Teacher, 1986-1991*. New York: McGraw-Hill, 1992, pp. 78-79.

Wilks, Dorothy. "Two Birds with One Stone." In Stephen E. Lucas (ed.), *Selections from the Speech Communication Teacher, 1986-1991*. New York: McGraw-Hill, 1992, p. 79.

## Films and Videos

"A World of Gestures." University of California Extension Center for Media and Independent Learning (1991). 28 minutes.

"American Tongues." Center for New American Media (1986). 40 minutes.

"Be Prepared to Speak." Kantola-Skeie Productions (1985). 27 minutes.

"Body Language." Insight Media (1986). 30 minutes.

"Communication: The Nonverbal Agenda," revised version. CRM Films (1988). 20 minutes.

"Delivering the Speech." RMI Media Productions (1986). 28 minutes.

"First Impressions: The Sales Connection." Insight Media (1992). 30 minutes.

"How to Get Your Point Across in 30 Seconds or Less." Coronet/MTI Film and Video (1986). 30 minutes.

"Making Your Point Without Saying a Word." Insight Media (1990). 27 minutes.

"Nonverbal Communication." Insight Media (1991). 27 minutes.

"Nonverbal Communication: Eye Contact and Kinesics." RMI Media Productions (1986). 28 minutes.

"Nonverbal Communication: Paralanguage and Proxemics." RMI Media Productions (1986). 28 minutes.

Peters, Tom. "Ten Vital Rules for Giving Incredible Speeches and Why They're Irrelevant." Video Publishing House (1990). 32 minutes.

"Presentation Excellence." Video Publishing House (1984). 77 minutes.

"Speak for Yourself: A Dynamic Vocal Workout." Insight Media (1989). 25 minutes.

"Speaking Effectively to One or One Thousand," revised edition. CRM Films (1992). 21 minutes.

"The Anatomy of Eloquence." Insight Media (1990). 31 minutes.

"The Human Voice." University of California Extension Center for Media and Independent Learning (1993). 30 minutes.

"When You Have to Get Up and Talk." BBP (1985). 24 minutes.

# Chapter

# 13 Using Visual Aids

## Chapter Objectives

*After reading this chapter, students should be able to:*

1. Explain the three major advantages of using visual aids in a speech.

2. Identify the kinds of visual aids available for use in speeches.

3. Apply the guidelines given in the chapter for using visual aids effectively.

## Chapter Outline

I. Visual aids offer a speaker several advantages *(text pages 290-291)*.
   A. Visual aids strengthen the clarity of a speaker's message.
   B. Visual aids increase the interest of a speaker's information.
   C. Visual aids make a speaker's message easier for listeners to retain.
   D. Visual aids enhance a speaker's credibility.
   E. Visual aids can substantially improve a speaker's persuasiveness.

II. There are many different kinds of visual aids *(text pages 291-301)*.
   A. Objects can work extremely well as visual aids.
      1. Showing the object being discussed is a fine way to clarify a speaker's ideas and give them dramatic impact.
      2. Unfortunately, many objects cannot be used in speeches because they are too large, too small, unavailable, etc.
   B. Models provide an excellent alternative to objects.
      1. One type is a small-scale model of a large object.
      2. Another type is a large-scale model of a small object.
      3. A third type is a life-size model.

C.   Photographs are another kind of visual aid.
   1.   Photographs can be of great advantage to a speaker.
   2.   To be effective, however, they must be significantly enlarged so the audience can see them.
D.   Drawings can provide superb alternatives to photographs.
   1.   Drawings, including diagrams, sketches, and maps, offer the advantage of being inexpensive.
   2.   They can also be specifically designed for the speech so as to illustrate the speaker's points precisely.
E.   Graphs are a good way to clarify and simplify statistics.
   1.   Line graphs are best for illustrating statistical trends.
   2.   Pie graphs are well suited for demonstrating distribution patterns.
   3.   Bar graphs are effective for showing comparisons between two or more items.
F.   Charts are a good choice when a speaker needs to summarize large blocks of information.
   1.   They can be used to present a larger number of categories than can be shown on a bar graph.
   2.   They can be used to summarize the steps of a process.
   3.   Than can be used to present information the audience may want to write down.
G.   When used properly, slides and videotapes can be extremely effective as visual aids.
   1.   The detail, vividness, and immediacy of slides and videotapes are hard to match.
   2.   The most effective way to use slides in classroom speeches is usually to convert them to transparencies, which can be shown with an overhead projector.
   3.   Videotape is only effective when it is edited skillfully and is integrated smoothly into the speech.
   4.   When using either slides or videotape, the speaker should practice with the projector or playback equipment ahead of time so it will work flawlessly during the speech.
H.   Computer-generated graphics can provide dramatic, professional-looking visual aids.
   1.   Computer-generated graphics can include anything from simple diagrams to sophisticated charts and graphs.
   2.   For classroom speeches, computer-generated graphics are usually presented on transparencies that are shown with an overhead projector.
I.   Transparencies are an effective way to present a wide variety of visual aids.
   1.   Transparencies can be made from many types of visual aids, including photographs, drawings, and computer-generated graphics.

2.   Transparencies are inexpensive, easy to produce, and provide a strong visual image.

3.   When preparing transparencies, a speaker must make sure any writing is large enough to be seen clearly from the back of the room.

4.   The speaker should use the overhead projector when rehearsing the speech to make sure the transparencies are well coordinated with the rest of the presentation.

J.   Sometimes the speaker can use her or his own body as a visual aid.

1.   This occurs most often in speeches of demonstration, in which a speaker shows how to do something.

2.   Doing a demonstration well requires practice to coordinate the speaker's actions with his or her words.

III.   There are nine tips for using visual aids effectively *(text pages 302-306)*.

A.   Speakers should avoid using the chalkboard for visual aids.

1.   Writing on the chalkboard has the disadvantage of requiring speakers to turn their backs to the audience.

2.   Even if visual aids are drawn on the chalkboard in advance, they usually lack the vividness or neatness of aids presented on poster board or a transparency.

3.   If writing on the chalkboard is unavoidable, a speaker must make sure any handwriting is clear and large enough for everyone to read.

B.   Speakers should prepare visual aids in advance.

1.   Advance preparation gives the speaker time to devise a creative and attractive visual aid.

2.   It also allows the speaker to practice the speech with the visual aid.

C.   Speakers should ensure that their visual aids are large enough.

1.   A visual aid is useless if the audience cannot see it.

2.   When preparing drawings, charts, graphs, or transparencies, speakers must guard against the tendency to write or draw too small.

3.   Speakers can check the visibility of their visual aids by getting as far away from them as the most distant listener will be sitting.

D.   Speakers should display visual aids where listeners can see them.

1.   Good speech preparation includes checking where a speaker will display her or his visual aids.

2.   Once the speaker has chosen a suitable location for the aid, the speaker must be sure to stand where all listeners can see the aid during the speech.

E.   Speakers should avoid passing visual aids among the audience.

1.   Once visual aids get into the hands of the audience, people pay more attention to the visuals than to the speaker.

2.  This is also true of handouts, which can easily distract an audience's attention from the speaker.
3.  If a speaker wants the audience to have information to take home, it should be passed out after the speech.

F.  Speakers should display visual aids only while discussing them.
  1.  Visual aids become distracting when they are displayed throughout the speech.
  2.  To avoid distracting the audience, a speaker should cover or remove visual aids when they are not in use.

G.  Speakers should talk to their audiences, not to their visual aids.
  1.  It is easy to break eye contact with the audience when presenting a visual aid.
  2.  Effective speakers glance periodically at their visual aids, but also keep eye contact with the audience to get feedback about how the aid is coming across.

H.  Speakers should explain their visual aids clearly and concisely.
  1.  A visual aid is only as useful as the explanation that goes with it.
  2.  Unfortunately, speakers often rush over their visual aid too quickly.
  3.  Instead, they should describe the major features of the aid and spell out its meaning for the audience.

I.  Speakers should practice with their visual aids when rehearsing the speech.
  1.  More than one speaker has ruined the effect of a visual aid by not practicing with it before the speech.
  2.  Effective speakers work out in advance how they will set up, explain, and remove their visual aids so the speech flows smoothly.

## Application Exercises *(from text page 307)*

1.  Watch a "how-to" type of television program (a cooking or gardening show, for example) or the weather portion of a local newscast. Notice how the speaker uses visual aids to help communicate the message. What kind or kinds of visual aids are used? How do they enhance the clarity, interest, and retainability of the speaker's message? What would the speaker have to do to communicate the message effectively without visual aids?

    **Discussion:** *This exercise helps attune students to the advantages and logistics of using visual aids in a speech. It works best if you assign a single program for the entire class to watch, so there is a common basis for class discussion. As an alternative, you can videotape segments of several programs yourself and show them to the class.*

2. Consider how you might use visual aids to explain each of the following:

   a. How to perform the Heimlich maneuver to help a choking victim.

   b. The location of the five boroughs of New York City.

   c. The proportion of the electorate that votes in major national elections in the United States, France, Germany, England, and Japan, respectively.

   d. Where to write for information about student loans.

   e. The wing patterns of various species of butterflies.

   f. The increase in the amount of money spent by Americans on health care since 1965.

   g. How to change a bicycle tire.

   h. The basic equipment and techniques of rock climbing.

   **Discussion:** *This exercise is designed to get students thinking about how they might use visual aids in their classroom speeches. Handle the class discussion as a kind of brainstorming session and encourage students to be creative in their suggestions for visual aids. As the discussion progresses, you can also draw attention to the guidelines for using visual aids effectively.*

3. Plan to use visual aids in at least one of your classroom speeches. Be creative in devising your aids, and be sure to follow the guidelines discussed in the chapter for using them. After the speech, analyze how effectively you employed your visual aids, what you learned about the use of visual aids from your experience, and what changes you would make in using visual aids if you were to deliver the speech again.

   **Discussion:** *Some teachers assign a round of speeches—usually informative—in which students must use visual aids. Such an assignment has several advantages. First, it gives students practical experience in creating and using visual aids. Second, it often reduces nervousness—because the visual aid heightens audience interest, helps divert the gaze of listeners from the speaker, and makes the speaker feel less self-conscious. Third, it encourages students to get away from their notes and to speak extemporaneously while explaining the visual aid.*

# Additional Exercises and Class Activities

1.  Develop a file of old visual aids you can bring to class to demonstrate for students the characteristics of effective and ineffective visual aids. Have the students identify which aids work well, which do not, and why. Ask students for ways to improve the ineffective visual aids.

    > **Discussion:** *When it comes to teaching students about visual aids, a picture is truly worth a thousand words. Bringing old visual aids to class is an excellent teaching device you can use to help students understand how to use visual aids in their speeches. This allows them to see how large the print or drawing must be, how important it is to keep the aid clean and uncluttered, how using bright, contrasting colors brings aids to life, how visual aids don't explain themselves, etc. It also allows you to illustrate the proper techniques for setting up and displaying visual aids, for explaining the point made by an aid, for communicating directly with the audience while discussing an aid, and so forth.*
    >
    > *Developing a file of visual aids is not very difficult. Simply collect the aids from your students after their speeches. Keep the aids in your office, so they will be at hand when you need to use them. After a few classes, you'll find that you have more than enough aids to demonstrate just about any point you wish to make. Some course directors keep a central file of visual aids from which instructors can draw as the need arises.*

2.  Show students the visual aids section from the "Introductions, Conclusions, and Visual Aids" videotape that accompanies *The Art of Public Speaking*. As students view the tape, have them evaluate which speakers use visual aids most effectively. Follow the tape with a class discussion.

    > **Discussion:** *It is one thing to create a good visual aid; it is another to use the aid effectively. By viewing speeches on videotape, students can see how visual aids should be integrated into an oral presentation. Developed exclusively to accompany* The Art of Public Speaking, *"Introductions, Conclusions, and Visual Aids" contains excerpts from a variety of speeches that illustrate concepts discussed in the book. One section of the tape is devoted to visual aids, and students usually find it highly instructive.*

# Extra Teaching and Learning Resources

## General

Adler, Ronald B. *Communicating at Work: Principles and Practices for Business and the Professions*, 4th ed. New York: McGraw-Hill, 1992, Chapter 12.

Antonoff, Michael. "Presentations that Persuade." *Personal Computing* (July 1990), 60-68.

Baird, Russell N., Turnbull, Arthur T., and McDonald, Duncan. *The Graphics of Communication: Media, Methods, and Technology*, 6th ed. Fort Worth, Texas: Harcourt Brace Jovanovich, 1993.

Bohn, Emil, and Jabusch, David. "The Effect of Four Methods of Instruction on the Use of Visual Aids in Speeches." *Western Journal of Speech Communication*, 46 (1982), 253-265.

Brody, Marjorie, and Kent, Shawn. *Power Presentations: How to Connect with Your Audience and Sell Your Ideas*. New York: Wiley, 1993, Chapter 23.

D'Arcy, Jan. *Technically Speaking: Proven Ways to Make Your Next Presentation a Success*. New York: American Management Association, 1992, Chapter 10.

Lefferts, Robert. *Elements of Graphics: How to Prepare Charts and Graphs for Effective Reports*. New York: Harper and Row, 1981.

LeRoux, Paul. "The Fine Art of Show-and-Tell." *Working Woman* (September 1985), 126-130.

O'Malley, Christopher. "Making Quick Presentations: How to Get Better Visuals in Minutes." *Personal Computing* (December 1985), 76-83.

Rigden, John S. "The Lost Art of Oratory: Damn the Overhead Projector." *Physics Today* (March 1990), 73-75.

Satterthwaite, Les. *Instructional Media: Materials, Production, and Utilization*, 2nd ed. Dubuque, Iowa: Kendall/Hunt, 1991.

Treece, Malra. *Successful Communication for Business and the Professions*, 6th ed. Boston: Allyn and Bacon, 1993.

Tufts, Edward R. *The Visual Display of Quantitative Information*. Cheshire, Conn.: Graphics Press, 1983.

Vassallo, Wanda. *Speaking with Confidence: A Guide for Public Speakers*. White Hall, Va.: Betterway Publications, 1990, Chapter 5.

Vogel, Douglas R., Dickson, Gary W., and Lehman, John A. *Persuasion and the Role of Visual Presentation Support: The UM/3M Study*. (Minneapolis: University of Minnesota School of Management, 1986).

Wilks, Dorothy. "Two Birds with One Stone." In Stephen E. Lucas (ed.), *Selections from the Speech Communication Teacher, 1986-1991*. New York: McGraw-Hill, 1992, p. 79.

Wright, Rudy A. *The Meeting Spectrum: An Advanced Guide for Meeting Professionals*. San Diego, Calif.: Rockwood Enterprises, 1988, Chapters 12-13.

Zelazny, Gene. *Say It with Charts: The Executive's Guide to Successful Presentations in the 1990s*, 2nd ed. Burr Ridge, Ill.: Irwin Professional Publishing, 1991.

## Films and Videos

"Aids to Speaking." Coronet/MTI Film and Video (1979). 15 minutes.

"How to Get Your Point Across in 30 Seconds or Less." Coronet/MTI Film and Video (1986). 30 minutes.

"Introductions, Conclusions, and Visual Aids: A Videotape Supplement to *The Art of Public Speaking*." McGraw-Hill, 1992. 58 minutes.

# Chapter 14  Speaking to Inform

## Chapter Objectives

*After reading this chapter, students should be able to:*

1.  Explain the four kinds of informative speeches discussed in the chapter.

2.  Apply the five guidelines for informative speaking offered in the chapter.

## Chapter Outline

I.  Speaking to inform is one of the most important skills a student can develop *(text page 310)*.
    A.  Informative speaking is vital to success in business.
        1.  In one survey, informative speaking was ranked as the most important speech skill in the workplace.
        2.  In another survey, 62 percent of the respondents said they used informative speaking "almost constantly."
    B.  Nor are people in business the only ones who rely on informative speaking.
        1.  There are endless situations in which people need to inform others.
        2.  The ability to convey knowledge and understanding will prove valuable to students throughout their lives.
    C.  There are three criteria for effective informative speaking.
        1.  The information should be communicated accurately.
        2.  The information should be communicated clearly.
        3.  The information should be made meaningful and interesting to the audience.

II.    Informative speeches can be classified into four types *(text pages 311-320)*.
    A.    Some informative speeches are about objects.
        1.    Speeches about objects describe something that is visible, tangible, and stable in form.
            a.    Objects may have moving parts or be alive.
            b.    They may include places, structures, animals, even people.
        2.    Speeches about objects need to be sharply focused.
            a.    A speaker cannot convey everything about an object in a brief speech.
            b.    It is important to choose a specific purpose that is not too broad to be achieved in the allotted time.
        3.    Speeches about objects can use a variety of organizational patterns.
            a.    A speech about the history or evolution of an object would be arranged in chronological order.
            b.    A speech about the main features of an object might be arranged in spatial order.
            c.    Most informative speeches about objects will fall into topical order.
    B.    Some informative speeches are about processes.
        1.    A process is a systematic series of actions that leads to a specific result or product.
        2.    Speeches about processes explain how something is made, describe how something is done, or convey how something works.
        3.    There are two kinds of informative speeches about processes.
            a.    One type explains a process so the audience will understand it better.
            b.    The other type explains a process so the audience will be able to perform the process themselves.
        4.    Speeches about processes often require visual aids.
            a.    Charts are an effective way to outline the steps of a process.
            b.    In some cases, the speaker will need to demonstrate the steps or techniques of the process.
        5.    Speeches about processes require careful organization.
            a.    Speeches that explain a process step by step are arranged in chronological order.
            b.    Speeches that focus on the major principles or techniques involved in performing the process are usually arranged in topical order.
            c.    Whichever method of organization is used, each step in the process must be clear and easy for listeners to follow.
    C.    Some informative speeches are about events.
        1.    Speeches about events can deal with any kind of happening or occurrence.

        a.    The occurrence may be historical in nature—such as the Battle of Little Big Horn or the civil rights movement.

        b.    The occurrence may be everyday in nature—such as modern dance or chronic fatigue syndrome.

    2.    There are many ways to organize a speech about an event.

        a.    Speeches that recount the history of an event are arranged in chronological order.

        b.    Speeches that analyze the causes and effects of an event are arranged in causal order.

        c.    Speeches that deal with particular elements of an event are usually arranged in topical order.

D.    Some informative speeches are about concepts.

    1.    Speeches about concepts convey information concerning beliefs, theories, principles, or other abstract subjects.

    2.    Speeches about concepts are usually arranged in topical order.

        a.    One common approach is to enumerate the main features or aspects of the concept.

        b.    A more complex approach is to define the concept, identify its major elements, and illustrate it with specific examples.

        c.    Yet another approach is to explain competing schools of thought about the concept.

    3.    Speeches about concepts are often more complex than other kinds of informative speeches.

        a.    When discussing concepts, a speaker should avoid technical language and define terms clearly.

        b.    A speaker should also use examples and comparisons to make concepts understandable to listeners.

E.    The lines dividing speeches about objects, processes, events, and concepts are not absolute.

    1.    Most topics can fit into more than one category depending on how the speech is developed.

    2.    The most important thing is that speakers decide how they want to handle a topic and then develop the speech accordingly.

III.  There are five guidelines for effective informative speaking *(text pages 320-328)*.

    A.    Informative speakers should be wary of overestimating what the audience knows.

        1.    In most cases, the audience will be only vaguely knowledgeable about the speaker's topic.

        2.    The speaker cannot assume the audience will know what he or she means.

        3.    To avoid misunderstanding, the speaker must explain ideas thoroughly and clearly.

4. One way to do this is to consider whether the speech will be clear to someone who is hearing about the topic for the first time.
5. Informative speakers should keep in mind the journalists' code: "Never *over*estimate the knowledge of your audience; never *under*estimate the intelligence of your audience."

B. Informative speakers should find ways to relate the subject directly to the audience.
1. Informative speakers must recognize that what is fascinating to them may not be fascinating to everybody.
2. Effective informative speakers work to get the audience interested—and to keep them interested.
   a. They begin with a creative introduction that connects the topic with the interests and concerns of the audience.
   b. They find ways throughout the body of the speech to talk about the topic in terms of their listeners.

C. Informative speakers should avoid being too technical.
1. An informative speech may be overly technical because the subject matter is too specialized for the audience.
2. An informative speech may also be overly technical because of the speaker's use of jargon or obscure language.
3. Effective informative speakers select topics that are not too technical for the audience.
4. Effective informative speakers recognize that language appropriate for an audience of specialists may well be confusing to a general audience.

D. Informative speakers should avoid abstractions.
1. Replacing tedious abstractions with specific details makes an informative speech more compelling.
2. One way to avoid abstractions is through description.
   a. Colorful descriptions of external events can draw listeners into the speech.
   b. Description can also be used to communicate internal feelings vividly and engagingly.
3. A second way to avoid abstractions is with comparisons.
   a. Comparisons allow a speaker to explain new ideas in concrete, familiar terms.
   b. Effective informative speakers are adept at using comparisons to draw listeners into the speech.
4. A third way to avoid abstractions is with contrast.
   a. Like comparison, contrast can put abstractions into concrete terms.
   b. Contrast is also an excellent way to give listeners a sense of perspective on concepts and events.

E. Informative speakers should personalize their ideas.
1. Nothing enlivens an informative speech more than personal illustrations.
2. Whenever possible, informative speakers should try to dramatize their ideas in human terms.
3. The best way to accomplish this is with examples—real or hypothetical—that personalize the subject matter.

## Application Exercises *(from text page 333)*

1. Below is a list of subjects for informative speeches. Your task is two-fold: (1) Select four of the topics and prepare a specific purpose statement for an informative speech about each of the four. Make sure that your four specific purpose statements include at least one that deals with its topic as an object, one that deals with its topic as a process, one that deals with its topic as an event, and one that deals with its topic as a concept. (2) Explain what method of organization you would most likely use in structuring a speech about each of your specific purpose statements.

| | |
|---|---|
| computers | sports |
| animals | music |
| science | cultural customs |
| education | technology |
| television | hobbies |

**Discussion:** *This exercise gets students to work on developing specific purpose statements for informative speeches. It also leads them to apply what is said in the text about methods of organizing informative speeches. If you include Chapter 4, Selecting a Topic and Purpose, or Chapter 8, Organizing the Body of the Speech, in the unit on informative speaking, you may wish to forego this exercise in favor of the exercises in Chapters 4 and 8.*

2. Analyze the speech in the Appendix by Kyle Knoeck ("The Hidden World of Perfumes," pages 444-447). Identify the specific purpose, central idea, main points, and method of organization. Evaluate the speech in light of the guidelines for informative speaking discussed in this chapter.

**Discussion:** *Clear, entertaining, and sharply organized, "The Hidden World of Perfumes" shows how students can apply the guidelines for informative speaking presented in the chapter. It is also available as part of the videotape supplement to* The Art of Public Speaking. *Here is a brief synopsis of the speech.*

*Specific Purpose:*  *To inform my audience about the production and uses of perfumes in today's world.*

*Central Idea:*  *A complex blend of many ingredients, the most important of which are essential oils, perfumes are being put to number of new uses in today's commercial world.*

*Method of Organization:  Topical*

*Introduction:   The introduction consists of paragraphs 1-5. In addition to gaining attention, the comparison in paragraphs 1-2 between the cost of petroleum and the cost of perfume indicates the importance of the topic. So too does the statement in paragraph 3 that perfumes have been used by humankind for at least 4,000 years. In paragraph 4 the speaker uses a touch of humor to establish his credibility and to relate the subject directly to his listeners. The droll tone of this paragraph is appropriate for the topic and crops up again in several places throughout the speech. Paragraph 5 provides a succinct preview statement and a strong lead-in to the body of the speech.*

*Body:  Arranged in topical order, the body contains two main points, the first of which deals with the ingredients of perfumes (paragraphs 6-12). After explaining the nature of essential oils, the key ingredients in any perfume (paragraph 7), the speaker distinguishes among three kinds of essential oils—those that come from animal products (paragraph 8), those that come from flowering plants (paragraphs 9-10), and those that come from synthetic ingredients (paragraph 11). The speaker then completes his first main point by relating how essential oils are combined with other ingredients—usually alcohol—to produce the final product (paragraph 12).*

*An excellent transition in paragraph 13 moves the speaker into his second main point, which deals with the new commercial applications of perfumes generated by research on the links between perfume and human behavior (paragraphs 14-18). The speaker begins by summarizing some of the major findings of that research (paragraph 14). He then explains how businesses are experimenting with perfumes to improve customer sales and worker productivity (paragraphs 15-16). He brings the body of the speech to a close by examining some of the ethical and health issues raised by the new commercial applications of perfume (paragraphs 17-18).*

*Although a speech on the topic of perfumes could easily become either too technical or too trivial for a classroom presentation, the speaker steers between both of these potential pitfalls. With few exceptions, he avoids technical language and explains his ideas in clear, familiar, everyday terms. He provides a wealth of fascinating supporting materials from reliable sources, and he consistently identifies his sources for the audience. Nor does he make the mistake of overestimating his audience's knowledge of the topic. Throughout the body of the speech, he explains ideas clearly, fully, and credibly.*

*Conclusion:  The conclusion consists of the last two paragraphs. After a quick summary of his main points in paragraph 19, the speaker adroitly ties the entire speech together in paragraph 20 by referring back to ideas he had broached in the introduction about the cost of perfume and its use in a wide range of commercial products. The closing words—about the use of perfumes in cattle feed—ends the speech on a clever note.*

## Additional Exercises and Class Activities

1.  Show the class one or more informative speeches from the videotapes of student speeches that accompany *The Art of Public Speaking*. Use the videotapes to illustrate points about effective informative speaking.

    **Discussion:**  *There are several excellent student informative speeches on the videotape supplement to* The Art of Public Speaking. *Two of those speeches—"The Hidden World of Perfumes" and "Dandelions: The Uncommon Weed"—are printed in this edition of the textbook. Also available on the videotape is "Nothing to Sneeze At," which is printed on pages 350-352 of this manual. For more information about individual speeches, consult the handbook that accompanies the informative speech videotape.*

2.  Popular nonfiction writing often provides helpful models of informative discourse on technical topics. Have each student select an article of interest from the medicine, science, or business section of *Time* or *Newsweek*. The student should prepare a brief report on the article answering each of the following:

    a.  How effectively does the author use definition, explanation, description, comparison, contrast, and examples to make the subject clear and interesting to ordinary readers? Identify two particular techniques used in the article that you might want to try in your next informative speech.

    b.  Are there some points in the story that you don't fully understand? If so, what information might the author have supplied to make the points clear to you?

    c.  Assume you will be giving a speech on the same topic as the article. What specific steps would you take to relate the topic directly to your classmates? To make it fully understandable to them? Consider not only what you might say in your speech, but also how you might use visual aids to enhance what you say.

**Discussion:** *This can be a very helpful exercise if you have students give more than one informative speech or if you are teaching an advanced public speaking class. Because of its complexity, it does not work well when beginning speakers are preparing their first informative speech.*

3.    Divide the class into groups of three to four students each. Have each group select one of the topics listed below (or other topics of your choosing). Each group has 15 minutes to work out a two-minute explanation designed for an audience that knows absolutely nothing about the topic. Each group should select one of its members to present the explanation orally to the class.

How to tie a shoe lace
How to change a car tire
The basic rules of baseball
How to bathe a dog
How to program a VCR
The rules of gin rummy

**Discussion:** *This exercise drives home the complexity of giving information to listeners who are not already familiar with the topic. Like the preceding activity, it is usually too demanding for novice speakers who are working on their first informative speech. It can work very well in an advanced public speaking class or in the later stages of an introductory class with very good students.*

4.    Distribute copies of "Nothing to Sneeze At," by Jeff Moran, which appears on pages 350-352 of this manual. Have students analyze the speech in light of the criteria for informative speaking presented in this chapter of the textbook.

**Discussion:** *A top-notch informative speech, "Nothing to Sneeze At" is interesting, clearly organized, fits well with the guidelines for informative speaking discussed in the chapter, and is short enough to be discussed in a single class session. It is also available as part of the videotape supplement to* The Art of Public Speaking. *For a synopsis of the speech, see pages 353-355 of this manual.*

5.    Distribute copies of "The Heimlich Maneuver," by Kelly Marti, which appears on pages 356-358 of this manual. Have students analyze the speech in light of the criteria for informative speaking presented in the chapter.

**Discussion:** *"The Heimlich Maneuver" is an outstanding informative speech. Excerpts from it can also be used as the basis for in-class exercises or examination questions. For a guide to the speech, see pages 359-360 of this manual.*

6.  Distribute copies of "The Mahatma and Satyagraha," by Walter Stromer, which appears on pages 395-400 of this manual. Have students analyze the speech in light of the criteria for informative speaking presented in the chapter.

> **Discussion:** *Longer and more complex than the other informative speeches in the book or the instructor's manual, "The Mahatma and Satyagraha" is a fine example of a public lecture. It is a clear, thoughtful, and highly instructive exposition of the life and principles of the great Indian leader Mohandas Gandhi. For a guide to the speech, see pages 401-402 of this manual.*

# Extra Teaching and Learning Resources

## General

Brinton, Alan. "On Viewing Knowledge as Rhetorical." *Central States Speech Journal*, 36 (1985), 270-281.

Frandsen, Kenneth D., and Clement, Donald A. "The Functions of Human Communication in Informing: Communicating and Processing Information." In Carroll C. Arnold and John Waite Bowers (eds.), *Handbook of Rhetorical and Communication Theory*. Boston: Allyn and Bacon, 1984, pp. 338-399.

Clarke, John H. "Building a Lecture that Really Works." *Education Digest*, 53 (1987), 52-55.

Jansen, Sue Curry. "Power and Knowledge: Toward a New Critical Synthesis." *Journal of Communication*, 33 (1983), 342-354.

Knapp, Mark L., Stohl, Cynthia, and Reardon, Kathleen K. "Memorable Messages." *Journal of Communication*, 31 (1981), 27-41.

Lang, Annie. "Effects of Chronological Presentation of Information on Processing and Memory for Broadcast News." *Journal of Broadcasting and Electronic Media*, 33 (1989), 441-452.

Robertson, Douglas S. "The Information Revolution." *Communication Research*, 17 (1990), 235-254.

Salmon, Charles T. "Message Discrimination and the Information Environment." *Communication Research*, (1985), 363-372.

Weimer, Walter B. "Why All Knowing Is Rhetorical." *Journal of the American Forensic Association*, 20 (1983), 63-71.

Wismer, Robert D. "Making an Effective Technical Presentation." *Research-Technology Management* (July-August 1989), 9-10.

Zinsser, William. *On Writing Well*, 4th ed. New York: HarperCollins, 1990.

## Classroom Activities and Assignments

Adler, Barbara. "A Speech About a Great American Speech." In Stephen E. Lucas (ed.), *Selections from the Speech Communication Teacher, 1986-1991*. New York: McGraw-Hill, 1992, p. 65.

Fregoe, David H. "Informative vs. Persuasive Speaking: The Objects Game." In Stephen E. Lucas (ed.), *Selections from the Speech Communication Teacher, 1986-1991*. New York: McGraw-Hill, 1992, pp. 57-58.

Rowan, Katherine. "The Speech to Explain Difficult Ideas." In Stephen E. Lucas (ed.), *Selections from the Speech Communication Teacher, 1986-1991*. New York: McGraw-Hill, 1992, pp. 69-71.

Schumer, Allison. "Custom Comparison Speeches." In Stephen E. Lucas (ed.), *Selections from the Speech Communication Teacher, 1986-1991*. New York: McGraw-Hill, 1992, p. 71.


## Films and Videos

"Critical Thinking: How to Evaluate Information and Draw Conclusions." Insight Media (1986). 47 minutes.

"Informing People." Films for the Humanities (1992). 20 minutes.

"Reporting and Briefing." Coronet/MTI Film and Video (1979). 16 minutes.

# Chapter 15 Speaking to Persuade

## Chapter Objectives

*After reading this chapter, students should be able to:*

1.  Clarify the differences between an informative speech and a persuasive speech and explain why speaking to persuade is especially challenging.

2.  Explain what it means to say that audiences engage in a mental dialogue with the speaker as they listen to a persuasive speech.

3.  Discuss the concept of target audience and its role in persuasive speaking.

4.  Define a question of fact and give an example of a specific purpose statement for a persuasive speech on a question of fact.

5.  Define a question of value and give an example of a specific purpose statement for a persuasive speech on a question of value.

6.  Define a question of policy and give an example of a specific purpose statement for a persuasive speech on a question of policy.

7.  Explain the difference between passive agreement and immediate action as goals for persuasive speeches on questions of policy.

8.  Explain the three basic issues of need, plan, and practicality and their importance in persuasive speeches on questions of policy.

9.  Discuss the four methods of organization used most often in persuasive speeches on questions of policy.

10. Identify the five steps in Monroe's motivated sequence.

# Chapter Outline

I.   Persuasion is a psychological process *(text pages 337-341)*.
    A.   Persuasive speaking occurs in situations where disagreement exists.
        1.   In some situations, two or more points of view may be completely opposed.
        2.   In other situations, the disagreement may be a matter of degree.
        3.   Without some disagreement, there would be no need for persuasion.
    B.   Of all the types of public speaking, persuasion is the most complex and the most challenging.
        1.   Persuasive speeches often deal with controversial topics that involve people's most basic attitudes, values, and beliefs.
        2.   No matter how skilled a speaker may be, some listeners are so committed to their own ideas that they cannot be persuaded to the speaker's point of view.
        3.   For this reason, persuasive speakers must enter a speech situation with realistic goals.
            a.   If listeners are not strongly committed one way or another on the speech topic, a speaker can realistically hope to move some of them toward her or his viewpoint.
            b.   If listeners are strongly opposed to a speaker's message, the speaker can consider the speech a success if it moves even a few to reexamine their views.
    C.   When processing persuasive messages listeners engage in a mental give-and-take with the speaker.
        1.   Listeners do not sit passively and soak in everything a speaker says.
            a.   As they listen, they assess the speaker's credibility, delivery, supporting materials, language, and the like.
            b.   They may argue, inside their own minds, with the speaker.
        2.   Effective persuasive speakers regard their speeches as a kind of mental dialogue with the audience.
            a.   When preparing the speech, they try to put themselves in the place of the audience and imagine how they will respond.
            b.   Above all, they try to anticipate audience objections and to answer them in the speech.
    D.   It is often helpful for persuasive speakers to think in terms of reaching their target audience.
        1.   The target audience is the part of the whole audience a speaker most wants to reach with his or her message.
        2.   In most situations, the target audience consists of uncommitted listeners, listeners who are inclining toward agreement with the speaker, and listeners who disagree with the speaker but who are open to persuasion.

3. Once a speaker knows where the target audience stands, she or he can adapt the speech to fit the values and concerns of the target audience.

4. Concentrating on the target audience, however, does not mean the speaker should exclude other listeners.
    a. Targeting one portion of the audience does not give speakers license to ignore or insult the rest of their listeners.
    b. A speaker must always keep in mind the ideas and feelings of the entire audience.

II. Some persuasive speeches deal with questions of fact *(text pages 341-343)*.
   A. Persuasive speeches on questions of fact seek to persuade an audience to accept the speaker's view of the facts on a particular issue.
      1. Some questions of fact can be answered with certainty—for example, how far is it from New York to London?
      2. Other questions of fact cannot be answered with certainty—for example, will the economy be better or worse next year?
   B. A persuasive speech on a question of fact is different from an informative speech.
      1. The aim of an informative speech is to give information as impartially as possible, not to argue for a particular point of view.
      2. Unlike speeches to inform, persuasive speeches on questions of fact take a partisan view of the information and try to persuade the audience to accept the speaker's view about that information.
         a. The legal system is a good model for understanding persuasive speeches on questions of fact.
         b. In a trial, the competing attorneys will try to persuade the jury that the facts of the case prove either the guilt or the innocence of the defendant.
   C. Most persuasive speeches on questions of fact are organized topically.
      1. In such speeches, each main point will present a reason why the audience should agree with the speaker.
      2. As in other speeches using topical order, persuasive speeches on questions of fact should subdivide the topic logically and consistently.

III. Some persuasive speeches deal with questions of value *(text pages 343-346)*.
   A. Questions of value require judgments based on a person's beliefs about what is right or wrong, good or bad, moral or immoral, etc.
   B. When dealing with a question of value, a speaker needs to justify her or his value judgment in light of a clearly defined set of standards.
      1. The first step is to define the speaker's standards for value judgment.
      2. The second step is to judge the subject of the speech against those standards.

C.   Speeches on questions of value are usually organized topically.
1.   The first main point establishes the standards for the speaker's value judgment.
2.   The second main point applies those standards to the speech topic.

IV.   Most persuasive speeches deal with questions of policy *(text pages 346-351)*.
A.   Questions of policy deal with specific courses of action.
1.   They inevitably involve questions of fact.
2.   They may also involve questions of value.
3.   But they always go beyond questions of fact or value to decide whether something should or should not be done.
B.   There are two types of persuasive speeches on questions of policy.
1.   One type seeks to gain passive agreement that a policy is desirable, necessary, and practical.
a.   The speaker's aim is to affect the thinking of listeners.
b.   The speaker does not try to get listeners to take action in support of the policy.
2.   The second type seeks to motivate the audience to take immediate action.
a.   The speaker's aim is to get the audience to do something in support of the policy.
b.   When seeking immediate action, speakers should make their recommendations for action as specific as possible.
C.   Persuasive speeches on questions of policy must address three basic issues—need, plan, and practicality.
1.   The first basic issue is need.
a.   Speakers who advocate a change in policy must prove there is a need for the change.
b.   Speakers who oppose a change in policy will try to show there is no need for change.
2.   The second basic issue is plan.
a.   After showing the need for change, a persuasive speaker must offer a specific plan—policy—that will solve the need.
b.   The speaker should be as specific as time allows in identifying the major features of the plan.
3.   The third basic issue is practicality.
a.   Speakers who advocate a new policy must show their plan is workable and will solve the need without creating new problems.
b.   Speakers who oppose a shift in policy will argue that a proposed plan is impractical and will create more problems than it will solve.
4.   The amount of time devoted to need, plan, and practicality in any given speech will depend on the topic and the audience.

V.  Four patterns of organization are especially effective for persuasive speeches on questions of policy *(text pages 351-357)*.
   A.  The first pattern is problem-solution order.
       1.  Speeches that advocate a change in policy often fall naturally into problem-solution order.
           a.  The first main point shows the need for a new policy by proving the existence of a serious problem.
           b.  The second main point presents a plan for solving the problem and demonstrates its practicality.
       2.  Problem-solution order can also be used in speeches opposing a change in policy.
           a.  The first main point shows that there is *no* need for change.
           b.  The second main point shows that even if there were a need, the proposed new policy would not solve it and would create serious problems of its own.
   B.  The second pattern is problem-cause-solution order.
       1.  Speeches following this method of organization have three main points.
           a.  The first main point shows the existence of a problem.
           b.  The second main point analyzes the causes of the problem.
           c.  The third main point presents a solution to the problem.
       2.  Problem-cause-solution order makes it easier to check whether the proposed solution will get at the causes of the problem, rather than merely controlling its symptoms.
   C.  The third pattern is comparative advantages order.
       1.  This pattern of organization is most effective when the audience already agrees there is a need for a new policy.
       2.  Rather than dwelling on the need, the speaker devotes each main point to explaining why his or her plan is preferable to other solutions.
   D.  The fourth pattern is Monroe's motivated sequence.
       1.  The motivated sequence has five steps that follow the psychology of persuasion.
           a.  The first step is to gain the attention of the audience.
           b.  The second step is to show the need for a change.
           c.  The third step is to satisfy the sense of need by presenting a plan that will remedy the need.
           d.  The fourth step is to visualize the benefits and practicality of the plan.
           e.  The fifth step is to urge the audience to take action in support of the plan.
       2.  Because it is psychologically based, the motivated sequence is especially valuable for persuasive speeches that seek immediate action.

## Application Exercises *(from text pages 363-364)*

1.  Look back at the story of Ramon Trujillo at the beginning of this chapter (page 336). Like Ramon, most people do a certain amount of persuading every day in normal conversation. Keep a journal of your communication activities for an entire day, making special note of all instances in which you tried to persuade someone else to your point of view. Choose one of those instances and prepare a brief analysis of it.

    In your analysis, answer the following questions: (1) Who was the audience for your persuasive effort? (2) What was the "specific purpose" and "central idea" of your persuasive message? (3) Did you rehearse your persuasive message ahead of time, or did it arise spontaneously from the situation? (4) Were you successful in achieving your "specific purpose"? (5) If you faced the same situation again, what strategic changes would you make in your persuasive effort?

    > **Discussion:** *This exercise emphasizes the extent to which most people engage in persuasion as part of normal conversation. It also provides a good springboard for discussion about the similarities between the kind of informal persuasive "speeches" we all give every day and the formal persuasive speeches students will present in class. Students should find that the strategic thinking they put into planning a formal persuasive speech is similar in many ways to the strategic thinking they use when trying to persuade someone in ordinary conversation.*

2.  Below are four specific purposes for persuasive speeches. In each case explain whether the speech associated with it concerns a question of fact, a question of value, or a question of policy. Then rewrite the specific purpose statement to make it appropriate for a speech about one of the other two kinds of questions. For instance, if the original purpose statement is about a question of policy, write a new specific purpose statement that deals with the same topic as either a question of fact or a question of value.

    a.  To persuade my audience to donate time as a community volunteer.

    b.  To persuade my audience that violence on television is a major cause of violent behavior in society.

    c.  To persuade my audience that a national sales tax should be adopted to help balance the federal budget.

    d.  To persuade my audience that it is unethical for businesses to use genetic testing in screening potential employees.

**Discussion:** *This exercise works extremely well to help students understand the differences among questions of fact, value, and policy. Two possible variations follow each of the statements in the exercise.*

a. To persuade my audience to donate time as a community volunteer. *(question of policy)*

   *Question of fact: To persuade my audience that there is a serious shortage of community volunteers in our locality.*

   *Question of value: To persuade my audience that they have a moral obligation to help people less fortunate than themselves.*

b. To persuade my audience that violence on television is a major cause of violent behavior in society. *(question of fact)*

   *Question of value: To persuade my audience that the federal government has a moral duty to monitor the amount of violence in television programming.*

   *Question of policy: To persuade my audience that further reforms should be enacted to reduce the amount of violence on television programs designed for children.*

c. To persuade my audience that a national sales tax should be adopted to help balance the federal budget. *(question of policy)*

   *Question of fact: To persuade my audience that a major source of new revenue is needed to balance the federal budget.*

   *Question of value: To persuade my audience that a national sales tax is an equitable way to help balance the federal budget.*

d. To persuade my audience that it is unethical for businesses to use genetic testing in screening potential employees. *(question of value)*

   *Question of fact: To persuade my audience that genetic testing is not always accurate in predicting whether people will contract particular diseases or come down with other medical conditions.*

   *Question of policy: To persuade my audience that businesses should be prohibited from using genetic testing as a method of screening potential employees.*

3.   Choose a topic for a persuasive speech on a question of policy. Create two specific purpose statements about that topic—one for a speech to gain passive agreement, another for a speech to motivate immediate action. Once you have the specific purpose statements, explain how the speech seeking immediate action would differ in its structure and persuasive appeals from the speech seeking passive agreement.

**Discussion:**   *Understanding the distinction between seeking passive agreement and immediate action is crucial for effective persuasive speeches on questions of policy. This exercise helps students understand that distinction and the impact it has on the organization and strategy of a speech to persuade. The exercise works best when it is given as a homework assignment so students have plenty of time to work out their answers.*

*As an alternative, the exercise can also be used as the basis for a small-group activity in class. Divide the class into groups and have each come up with its own answers. Designate one person to present the result of each group's work to the class.*

*Here, as a general guide, is what the results might look like for a speech on the topic of cardiopulmonary resuscitation (CPR).*

a.   *Specific purpose statement for a speech seeking passive agreement:  To persuade my audience that everyone should learn CPR.*

b.   *Specific purpose statement for a speech seeking immediate action:  To persuade my audience to enroll in a CPR class at the Red Cross.*

c.   *Structure of the speech seeking passive agreement:  This speech would most likely be organized either in topical order (in which case each main point would explain a reason why everyone should learn CPR) or in problem-solution order (in which case the first main point would show why the lack of general CPR training is a problem and the second main point would present the speaker's plan to solve the problem).*

d.   *Structure of the speech seeking immediate action:  This speech could be organized in problem-solution order, but if it were, the speaker would have to be sure to include a call to action as part of the solution. A more effective organizational pattern might be Monroe's motivated sequence, which is specifically designed for speeches that aim to motivate listeners to take immediate action.*

e. *Persuasive appeals of the speech seeking passive agreement: This speech would focus on convincing the audience that it would be desirable for everyone to have training in CPR, but it would not try to persuade the audience to go out and learn CPR. As a result, the speaker could deal with the topic at a general level without having to confront the audience's objections to taking a CPR class themselves.*

f. *Persuasive appeals of the speech seeking immediate action: A speaker cannot motivate an audience to immediate action without relating the topic directly to the audience and providing motivational appeals showing why they must change their behavior. It is also crucial that the speaker deal with the audience's potential reasons for not taking action—cost, lack of time, inconvenience, etc.*

   *In the case of a speech on CPR, the speaker would need to show not just that there is a significant problem that can be solved by learning CPR, but also that it is necessary and practical for the listeners themselves to learn CPR. The speaker would have to anticipate the objections listeners might have to enrolling in a CPR class (too little time, not enough money, etc.) and answer those objections in the speech. The speaker might also rely more on emotional appeal in the speech seeking immediate action than in the speech seeking passive agreement. (See Chapter 16, pages 385-390, of the textbook for a discussion of emotional appeal in persuasive speaking.)*

4. Analyze the sample speech with commentary at the end of this chapter ("The Problem with Pennies," pages 358-361). Because this is a speech on a question of policy, pay special attention to how the speaker deals with the three basic issues of need, plan, and practicality. Does the speaker present a convincing case that a serious problem exists? Does she offer a clear plan to solve the problem? Does she demonstrate that the plan is practical?

   **Discussion:** *"The Problem with Pennies" is an excellent persuasive speech on a question of policy and provides an instructive model for students who are preparing their own speeches. The commentary that accompanies the speech on pages 358-361 of the textbook points out a number of its major features. Here is a synopsis that gives special attention to how the speaker deals with the issues of need, plan, and practicality.*

   *Specific Purpose: To persuade my audience that pennies should be eliminated from the United States money supply.*

*Central Idea: Because pennies cause problems for individuals, businesses, and the economy as a whole, they should be eliminated from the U.S. money supply.*

*Method of Organization:  Problem-solution.*

*Need:  The speaker deals with the need for a change in the first main point of the body, which runs from paragraph 4 through paragraph 8. In paragraphs 4-5 she shows that pennies are such an annoyance that many people simply don't use them. After citing the results of her class survey, in which two-thirds of the class said they found pennies bothersome, the speaker presents a series of specific situations in which pennies are a nuisance. Her repeated use of "you" in paragraph 4 gives the speech a personal tone and relates it directly to the audience. So, too, does the story from writer Noel Gunther in paragraph 5 about his experience collecting pennies while in college.*

*In paragraph 6 the speaker claims that pennies are a nuisance for businesses as well as for individuals. She supports the claim with an arresting set of figures from* Fortune *magazine and the National Association of Convenience Stores. Here, as elsewhere, the speaker's evidence is from reliable sources which she identifies for the audience.*

*Paragraphs 7 and 8 present a combination of statistics and testimony to demonstrate the problems created for the nation as a whole by keeping pennies in circulation. The evidence in paragraph 8 is particularly strong and builds cumulatively to the statement, based on testimony from U.S. Treasury officials, that "it costs our society considerably more than a penny to transact a penny's worth of business." All in all, the need section of this speech is extremely well developed.*

*Plan:  After a transition in paragraph 9, the speaker moves to her second main point, in which she presents her plan and demonstrates its practicality. The plan has four steps, which are presented in paragraphs 10-13. Each step is explained clearly and concisely so that listeners will understand exactly what the speaker is proposing. This is especially notable in paragraphs 10 and 11. Notice how much less effective the speech would have been if the speaker had failed in those paragraphs to explain the procedures by which purchases and sales taxes will be rounded off to the nearest nickel.*

*Practicality: The speaker demonstrates the practicality of her plan in paragraphs 14 and 15. Dealing with questions of practicality is especially crucial in a speech such as "The Problem with Pennies," in which listeners are likely to be skeptical about a speaker's plan. As discussed in the textbook (pages 338-339), persuasive speakers must think of their speech as a kind of mental dialogue with the audience. The speaker must anticipate the possible objections listeners will raise to the speaker's point of view and answer those objections in the speech.*

*"The Problem with Pennies" provides an excellent example of how to do this. In paragraph 14 the speaker reasons analogically in showing that her plan is similar to that by which half-pennies were abolished during the nineteenth century. "None of us miss the half-cent," she explains, "and in a few years none of us will miss the penny." (For a discussion of analogical reasoning and its role in persuasive speaking, see Chapter 16, pages 384-385, of the textbook.)*

*In paragraph 15 the speaker deals with possible reservations about the feasibility of rounding off purchases to the nearest nickel by showing that most people already do exactly that when they use the "Take a Penny, Leave a Penny" containers at local convenience stores. It is also important to note how the speaker relates her ideas in paragraphs 14 and 15 directly to her audience by using words such as "us," "we," and "you." Because the speaker is trying to answer the objections of her immediate listeners, it only makes sense for her to bring her ideas home to those listeners in personal terms.*

5. Select a television commercial that is organized according to Monroe's motivated sequence. Prepare a brief analysis in which you (a) identify the target audience for the commercial, and (b) describe each step in the motivated sequence as it appears in the commercial.

> **Discussion:** *Although this exercise does not deal directly with public speaking, it is a splendid way to get students to think about Monroe's motivated sequence and the structure of persuasive messages in general—and it almost always produces a lively class discussion. It works best when given as a homework assignment, so students have plenty of time to think about and to analyze the commercials they select. When discussing the commercials in class, be sure to make connections between the organization of the commercials and the organization of a speech.*

## Additional Exercises and Class Activities

1.    Below are eight statements. Explain whether each statement deals *primarily* with a question of fact, a question of value, or a question of policy.

   a.    President Franklin D. Roosevelt knew in advance about the Japanese plan to attack Pearl Harbor and allowed it to happen.

   b.    If Franklin D. Roosevelt knew in advance about the Japanese plan to attack Pearl Harbor, he was wrong in allowing it to happen.

   c.    Using lie detector tests as screening devices for jobs in private business is a violation of the employee's right to privacy.

   d.    The use of lie detector tests for screening employees in private business should be banned by law.

   e.    A federal law should be passed requiring that anti-lock brakes be standard on all new cars sold in the United States.

   f.    If anti-lock brakes were standard equipment on all cars sold in the United States, we could reduce the number of traffic fatalities by 5,000 lives every year.

   g.    Colorizing classic movies such as *Casablanca* violates the artistic integrity of such movies.

   h.    Congress should protect the artistic integrity of movies such as *Casablanca* by passing a law prohibiting the colorization of classic American films.

**Discussion:** *These statements are somewhat more complex than those in Exercise 1 on page 363 of the textbook. Dealing with them provides valuable extra work for students in distinguishing among questions of fact, value, and policy. It also helps demonstrate how one kind of question can have strong implications for a speech on one of the other types of questions. To facilitate class discussion, this exercise—including answers—is available as part of the overhead transparency supplement that accompanies* The Art of Public Speaking.

a. President Franklin D. Roosevelt knew in advance about the Japanese plan to attack Pearl Harbor and allowed it to happen.

   *(question of fact)*

b. If Franklin D. Roosevelt knew in advance about the Japanese plan to attack Pearl Harbor, he was wrong in allowing it to happen.

   *(question of value)*

c. Using lie detector tests as screening devices for jobs in private business is a violation of the employee's right to privacy.

   *(question of value)*

d. The use of lie detector tests for screening employees in private business should be banned by law.

   *(question of policy)*

e. A federal law should be passed requiring that anti-lock brakes be standard on all new cars sold in the United States.

   *(question of policy)*

f. If anti-lock brakes were standard equipment on all cars sold in the United States, we could reduce the number of traffic fatalities by 5,000 lives every year.

   *(question of fact)*

g. Colorizing classic movies such as *Casablanca* violates the artistic integrity of such movies.

   *(question of value)*

h. Congress should protect the artistic integrity of movies such as *Casablanca* by passing a law prohibiting the colorization of classic American films.

   *(question of policy. Although defining "artistic integrity" and deciding what constitutes a "classic" film both involve value judgments, the statement is concerned primarily with advocating a congressional policy preventing colorization.)*

2. Conduct a class discussion on the ethics of persuasive speaking. Among the issues to consider are: (1) Is it ethical for one person to try to persuade another? (2) What is the most ethical approach for a speaker to take when trying to persuade an audience? (3) To what extent should a persuasive speaker reveal her or his true motives to the audience? (4) Are there any situations in which it would be ethical for a speaker to distort the truth in order to persuade an audience? (5) Is it ethical for a speaker to use emotional appeal to sway listeners?

> **Discussion:** *Questions of ethics can arise every time a speaker seeks to persuade an audience. By dealing with the issue at the start of the unit on persuasive speaking, instructors can emphasize to students the importance of keeping a firm ethical rudder in their speeches. It may be helpful to have students review Chapter 2 of the textbook ("Ethics and Public Speaking") in preparation for discussion. It may also be helpful to hand out copies of the Checklist for Ethical Public Speaking from page 83 of this manual.*
>
> *Although this exercise can work very well early in the unit on persuasion, some instructors prefer to discuss ethics in conjunction with the next chapter of the textbook ("Methods of Persuasion"), which contains a section devoted to the ethics of emotional appeal (pages 389-390). For a similar exercise in Chapter 16, see page 296 of this manual.*

3. Show the class one or more persuasive speeches from the videotapes of student speeches that accompany *The Art of Public Speaking*. Use the videotapes to illustrate points about effective persuasive speaking.

> **Discussion:** *The videotape supplement to* The Art of Public Speaking *contains several student persuasive speeches that can be used for classroom analysis and discussion. Three of the persuasive speeches on the videotape—"The Dangers of Chewing Tobacco," "A Friend in Need," and "Family Medical Histories: A Proven Lifesaver"—are printed in this edition of the book. For more information about individual speeches, consult the guide that accompanies the videotape.*

4. Distribute copies of "Drinking and Boating: A Deadly Combination," by Sheila Mir, which appears on pages 367-369 of this manual. Have students analyze the speech in light of the criteria for persuasive speeches on questions of policy presented in the chapter.

**Discussion:** *A persuasive speech on a question of policy, "Drinking and Boating: A Deadly Combination" is an excellent speech for analysis and discussion. Because of its clear organization, strong use of evidence, and attention to all three basic issues of need, plan and practicality, it provides a good model for students who are preparing their own persuasive speeches. For a full discussion of the speech, see pages 370-372 of this manual.*

5.  Hand out copies of "David—And a Lot of Other Neat People," by Kathy Weisensel, which is printed on pages 381-384 of this manual. Have students analyze the speech in light of the criteria for persuasive speeches on questions of fact presented in the chapter.

    **Discussion:** *"David—And a Lot of Other Neat People" is a persuasive speech on a question of fact. Concisely organized and keenly argued, it builds a strong case against the misconceptions many people hold about mental retardation. For a full discussion of the speech, see pages 385-386 of this manual.*

6.  Distribute copies of "Ghosts," by Ken Lonnquist, which is printed on pages 387-391 of this manual. Have students analyze the speech in light of the criteria for persuasive speeches on questions of value discussed in the chapter.

    **Discussion:** *"Ghosts" is a persuasive speech on a question of value. Delivered in an introductory argumentation and debate class at the University of Wisconsin-Madison, it is considerably more complex than the typical classroom speech. The speaker's purpose was to convince his classmates that abortion is morally wrong, and he knew from his audience analysis that all but one of his listeners opposed his position.*

    *Because the topic of the speech is so controversial, it invariably sparks a heated class discussion. If that discussion is to be most productive, however, it needs to focus primarily on the speaker's techniques rather than on his position regarding abortion. If you assign the speech, urge students to put aside their personal opinions about abortion and to analyze the speech in light of questions such as the following:*

    *(1)  Is the introduction well suited to the speaker's task of gaining good will and establishing common ground with his audience?*

    *(2)  What kind of reasoning does the speaker rely on most of all throughout the speech?*

(3)   *Although the speech deals with a question of value, its persuasiveness rests largely on the speaker's ability to convince his listeners about a question of fact. What is that question of fact? How effectively does the speaker deal with it given the opposition of his listeners?*

(4)   *How effectively does the speaker use the resources of language discussed in Chapter 11—imagery, metaphor, parallelism, repetition, etc.—to express his ideas? What are the "ghosts" to which he refers throughout the speech? Is this an appropriate image for the speech, or does it distract attention from the major issue?*

*For full commentary on the speech, see pages 392-394 of this manual.*

# Extra Teaching and Learning Resources

## General

Bettinghaus, Edwin P., and Cody, Michael J. *Persuasive Communication*, 4th ed. New York: Holt, Rinehart and Winston. 1987.

Cialdini, Robert B. *Influence: The New Psychology of Modern Persuasion*. New York: Morrow, 1993.

Clark, Ruth Anne. *Persuasive Messages*. New York: Harper and Row, 1984.

Dillard, James Price. "Self-Inference and Foot-in-the Door Technique." *Human Communication Research*, 16 (1990), 422-447.

Eagly, Alice H., and Chaiken, Shelly. *The Psychology of Attitudes*. Fort Worth, Texas: Harcourt Brace Jovanovich, 1993.

Goldfaden, Gloria. "Winning Hearts and Minds." *The Humanist* (November-December 1988), 13.

Johnston, Deirdre D. *The Art and Science of Persuasion*. Dubuque, Iowa: W.C. Brown, 1994.

Larson, Charles U. *Persuasion: Reception and Responsibility*, 6th ed. Belmont, Calif.: Wadsworth, 1992.

Littlejohn, Stephen W., and Jabusch, David M. *Persuasive Transactions*. Glenview, Ill.: Scott Foresman, 1987.

McGuire, William J. "Attitudes and Attitude Change." In Gardner Lindzey and Elliot Aronson (eds.), *Handbook of Social Psychology*, 3rd ed. New York: Random House, 1985, II, 233-346.

McVey, Stephanie. "Giving Presentations That Persuade." *Management World* (January-February 1989), 6-8.

Miller, Gerald R., Burgoon, Michael, and Burgoon, Judee K. "The Functions of Human Communication in Changing Attitudes and Gaining Compliance." In Carroll C. Arnold and John Waite Bowers (eds.), *Handbook of Rhetorical and Communication Theory*. Boston: Allyn and Bacon, 1984, pp. 400-474.

O'Keefe, Daniel J. *Persuasion: Theory and Research*. Newbury Park, Calif.: Sage, 1990.

Perloff, Richard M. *The Dynamics of Persuasion*. Hillsdale, N.J.: Lawrence Erlbaum, 1993.

Petty, Richard E., and Cacioppo, John T. *Communication and Persuasion: Central and Peripheral Routes to Attitude Change*. New York: Springer-Verlag, 1986.

Petty, Richard E., and Cacioppo, John T. "The Elaboration Likelihood Model of Persuasion." In Leonard T. Berkowitz (ed.), *Advances in Experimental and Social Psychology*, Vol. 19. New York: Academic Press, 1986, pp. 123-205.

Reardon, Kathleen Kelley. *Persuasion in Practice*. Newbury Park, Calif.: Sage, 1991.

Simons, Herbert. *Persuasion: Understanding, Practice, and Analysis*, 2nd ed. New York: Random House, 1986.

## Classroom Activities and Assignments

Fregoe, David H. "Informative vs. Persuasive Speaking." In Stephen E. Lucas (ed.), *Selections from the Speech Communication Teacher, 1986-1991*. New York: McGraw-Hill, 1992, pp. 57-58.

Garrett, Roger L. "The Premises of Persuasion." In Stephen E. Lucas (ed.), *Selections from the Speech Communication Teacher, 1986-1991*. New York: McGraw-Hill, 1992, pp. 58-59.

Langley, C. Darrell. "The Heckling Speech." In Stephen E. Lucas (ed.), *Selections from the Speech Communication Teacher, 1986-1991*. New York: McGraw-Hill, 1992, p. 67.

MacDonald, Madlyne A. "The Key to Persuasion." In Stephen E. Lucas (ed.), *Selections from the Speech Communication Teacher, 1986-1991*. New York: McGraw-Hill, 1992, pp. 59-60.

McKinney, Bruce C. "Audience Analysis Exercise." In Stephen E. Lucas (ed.), *Selections from the Speech Communication Teacher, 1986-1991*. New York: McGraw-Hill, 1992, p. 13.

Mohsen, Raed A. "Out on Campus: A Challenging Public Speaking Experience." *Speech Communication Teacher* (Summer 1993), 10-11.

Ross, Charlynn. "The Challenging Audience Exercise." In Stephen E. Lucas (ed.), *Selections from the Speech Communication Teacher, 1986-1991*. New York: McGraw-Hill, 1992, p. 69.

Schreir, Howard N. "Analyzing Persuasive Tactics." In Stephen E. Lucas (ed.), *Selections from the Speech Communication Teacher, 1986-1991*. New York: McGraw-Hill, 1992, p. 61.

## Films and Videos

"A Case Study for Critical Thinking: Vietnam." Insight Media (1987). 52 minutes.

"Critical Thinking: How to Evaluate Information and Draw Conclusions." Insight Media (1986). 47 minutes.

"Endless Persuasion." (1977). RMI Media Productions. 28 minutes.

"Persuasive Speaking." Esquire (1982). 60 minutes.

"Psycho-Sell: Advertising and Persuasion." Insight Media (1991). 25 minutes.

"Speaking Persuasively." (1977). RMI Media Productions. 28 minutes.

"When You Buy: How Ads Persuade." Insight Media (1989). 33 minutes.

# Chapter 16 Methods of Persuasion

## Chapter Objectives

*After reading this chapter, students should be able to:*

1.  Explain the role of speaker credibility in persuasive speaking.

2.  Define the differences among initial credibility, derived credibility, and terminal credibility.

3.  Discuss three ways a speaker can enhance her or his credibility during a persuasive speech.

4.  Explain why it is important for persuasive speakers to use evidence in their speeches.

5.  Discuss the four tips presented in the chapter for using evidence in persuasive speeches.

6.  Define reasoning from specific instances and explain the guidelines given in the chapter for using this method of reasoning.

7.  Define reasoning from principle and explain the guidelines a speaker should follow when employing reasoning from principle.

8.  Define causal reasoning and explain the two common errors speakers need to avoid when using causal reasoning.

9.  Define analogical reasoning and explain how to judge the validity of an analogy.

10. Explain the role of emotional appeal in persuasive speaking and discuss when it is ethical for a speaker to employ emotional appeal.

11. Identify three methods a speaker can use to generate emotional appeal when speaking to persuade.

## Chapter Outline

I.  There is a perpetual interest in the methods of persuasion *(text page 368)*.
    A.  People have been studying the strategies and tactics of successful persuasion for thousands of years.
    B.  Scholars generally agree that listeners are persuaded by a speaker for one or more of four reasons.
        1.  Because they perceive the speaker as having high credibility.
        2.  Because they are won over by the speaker's evidence.
        3.  Because they are convinced by the speaker's reasoning.
        4.  Because their emotions are touched by the speaker's ideas or language.

II. A speaker's credibility plays an important role in persuading the audience *(text pages 368-373)*.
    A.  Credibility is the audience's attitude toward or perception of the speaker.
        1.  The more favorably listeners view a speaker, the more likely they are to accept what the speaker says.
        2.  A speaker's credibility will vary from audience to audience and topic to topic.
            a.  The same speaker may have high credibility for one audience and low credibility for another.
            b.  A speaker may also have high credibility on one topic and low credibility on another.
    B.  A speaker's credibility is affected by two primary factors—competence and character.
        1.  Competence refers to how an audience regards a speaker's intelligence, expertise, and knowledge of the subject.
        2.  Character refers to how an audience regards a speaker's sincerity, trustworthiness, and concern for the well-being of the audience.
    C.  There are three types of credibility.
        1.  Initial credibility is the audience's perception of the speaker before the speech begins.
        2.  Derived credibility is produced by everything a speaker says and does during the speech.
        3.  Terminal credibility is the audience's perception of the speaker at the end of the speech.

D. There are three strategies speakers can use to enhance their credibility.
   1. Speakers can enhance their credibility by explaining their competence.
      a. They can stress their research on the speech topic.
      b. They can stress special knowledge of the topic gained through personal experience.
   2. Speakers can enhance their credibility by establishing common ground with the audience.
      a. Establishing common ground means showing respect for and identifying with the audience's values and beliefs.
      b. Establishing common ground is especially important in the introduction of a persuasive speech.
   3. Speakers can enhance their credibility by delivering their speeches fluently, expressively, and with conviction.
      a. There is substantial research showing that fluent, animated delivery greatly enhances a speaker's credibility.
      b. Speaking with genuine conviction also does a great deal to strengthen a speaker's credibility.

III. A speaker's use of evidence plays an important role in persuading the audience *(text pages 373-377)*.
  A. Evidence consists of examples, statistics, and testimony used to prove or disprove something.
  B. To be persuasive, speakers must support their views with evidence.
   1. Careful listeners are skeptical of unsupported claims and generalizations.
   2. Strong evidence is particularly important when the speaker is not recognized as an expert on the speech topic.
   3. Strong evidence is also crucial when the target audience opposes the speaker's point of view.
      a. Skeptical listeners will mentally create counterarguments to "answer" what the speaker says.
      b. The speaker's success will depend partly on how well she or he anticipates these internal responses and gives evidence to refute them.
  C. There are four tips persuasive speakers should follow to use evidence effectively.
   1. Persuasive speakers should use specific evidence.
      a. Research indicates that evidence is more persuasive when it is stated in specific rather than general terms.
      b. Specific evidence also enhances a speaker's credibility by demonstrating his or her grasp of the topic.
   2. Persuasive speakers should use novel evidence.
      a. Studies show that evidence will be more persuasive when it is new to the audience.

        b.    Presenting an audience new facts and figures requires resourceful research, but it is well worth the effort.

    3.    Persuasive speakers should use evidence from credible sources.

        a.    There is a good deal of research indicating that listeners find evidence from competent, credible sources more persuasive than evidence from less qualified sources.

        b.    Listeners are especially skeptical about evidence from sources that appear to be biased or self-interested.

    4.    Persuasive speakers should make clear the point of their evidence.

        a.    Studies have shown that speakers cannot count on listeners to draw, on their own, the conclusion a speaker wants them to reach.

        b.    In most situations, persuasive speakers need to be sure to state the point they are trying to make with their evidence.

IV.  A speaker's reasoning plays an important role in persuading the audience *(text pages 377-385).*

  A.  Reasoning is the process of drawing a conclusion based on evidence.

  B.  Public speakers have two major concerns with respect to reasoning.

    1.    The first is to make sure the speaker's reasoning is sound.

    2.    The second is to get listeners to agree with the speaker's reasoning.

  C.  Persuasive speakers often use reasoning from specific instances.

    1.    When speakers reason from specific instances, they progress from a number of particular facts to a general conclusion.

    2.    Speakers should follow three guidelines when reasoning from specific instances.

        a.    They need to beware of hasty generalizations based on insufficient evidence.

        b.    They need to be careful with their wording so as not to overstate the facts.

        c.    They need to reinforce their argument with statistics or testimony.

  D.  Persuasive speakers often use reasoning from principle.

    1.    When speakers reason from principle, they move from a general principle to a specific conclusion.

    2.    Speakers should follow two basic guidelines when reasoning from principle.

        a.    They need to make certain the audience will accept the general principle.

        b.    They also need to make sure the audience will accept the minor premise.

  E.  Persuasive speakers often use causal reasoning

    1.    Causal reasoning tries to establish the relationship between causes and effects.

2. Speakers should follow two guidelines when using causal reasoning.
   a. They should avoid the fallacy of false cause.
      (1) This fallacy is often known by its Latin name, *post hoc, ergo propter hoc*, which means "after this, therefore because of this."
      (2) Speakers who commit this fallacy assume that because one event comes after another, the first event must necessarily be the cause of the second.
   b. Speakers should also avoid the fallacy of assuming that events have only one cause.
      (1) Most events have several causes.
      (2) Speakers need to be wary of oversimplifying complex causes or attributing a complex effect to a single cause.
F. Persuasive speakers often use analogical reasoning.
   1. Analogical reasoning compares two similar cases to draw the conclusion that what is true in one case will also be true in the other.
   2. The most important guideline for speakers using analogical reasoning is to make sure the two cases being compared are essentially alike.
      a. If the cases being compared are essentially alike, the analogy is valid.
      b. If the cases being compared are not essentially alike, the analogy is invalid.

V. A speaker's emotional appeals play an important role in persuading the audience *(text pages 385-390)*.
   A. Emotional appeals—often called motivational appeals—are intended to make listeners feel sad, angry, guilty, fearful, reverent, or the like.
   B. Effective persuasion often requires emotional appeal.
      1. Few people are moved to change their attitudes or take action when they are bored or complacent.
      2. As George Campbell wrote in his *Philosophy of Rhetoric*, "When persuasion is the end, passion also must be engaged."
   C. Speakers can generate emotional appeal in three ways.
      1. One way to generate emotional appeal is with emotionally charged language.
         a. Language can generate strong responses in an audience by evoking emotions attached to particular words and phrases.
         b. Speakers should be careful, however, of calling attention to their emotional appeals with a sudden barrage of emotional language that is inconsistent with the rest of the speech.
      2. A second way to generate emotional appeal is with vivid examples.

      a.    Vivid, richly textured examples allow emotional appeal to grow naturally out of the content of the speech.

      b.    Examples add impact, bring ideas home to listeners in personal terms, and make the speech more compelling.

    3.    A third way to generate emotional appeal is to speak with sincerity and conviction.

      a    The strongest source of emotional appeal is the conviction and sincerity of the speaker.

      b.    Speakers who feel the emotion themselves will communicate that emotion through everything they say and do in the speech.

D.    Because emotional appeals have so much potential power, they need to be used with a strong sense of ethical responsibility.

    1.    Emotional appeals can be abused by unscrupulous speakers for detestable causes.

    2.    Emotional appeals can also be used by principled speakers for noble causes.

    3.    Ethical speakers make sure their emotional appeals are appropriate to the speech topic.

      a.    Emotional appeals are often necessary when a speaker is trying to persuade an audience to take action.

      b.    Emotional appeals are usually inappropriate when a speaker is discussing a question of fact.

    4.    Even when trying to move listeners to action, a speaker should never substitute emotional appeals for evidence and reasoning.

      a.    Persuasive speeches should always be built on a firm foundation of facts and logic.

      b.    Speakers need to develop a good case based on reason *and* kindle the emotions of the audience.

    5.    When using emotional appeals, persuasive speakers should also keep in mind the guidelines for ethical speechmaking discussed in Chapter 2.

## Application Exercises *(from text pages 395-397)*

1.    Research has shown that a speaker's initial credibility can have great impact on how the speaker's ideas are received by listeners. Research has also shown that a speaker's credibility will vary from topic to topic and audience to audience. In the left-hand column below is a list of well-known public figures. In the right-hand column is a list of potential speech topics. Assume that each speaker will be addressing your speech class.

    For each speaker, identify the topic in the right-hand column on which she or he would have the highest initial credibility for your class. Then explain how the speaker's initial credibility might be affected if the speaker were discussing the topic in the right-hand column directly across from her or his name.

| *Speaker* | *Topic* |
|---|---|
| Hillary Rodham Clinton | African Americans: The Next Agenda |
| George Bush | Women in the Mass Media |
| Barbara Walters | Reforming the American Presidency |
| Jesse Jackson | Talk Shows: Who Needs Them? |
| David Letterman | The American Health Care Revolution |

**Discussion:**  *This exercise is almost certain to provoke a lively discussion and is a fine way to launch a class discussion on the importance of credibility in persuasive speaking. Here are some plausible responses to the questions about each of the speakers listed in the exercise:*

*Hillary Rodham Clinton:  Most students would find Clinton most credible if she were speaking on "The American Health Care Revolution," a subject to which she has devoted considerable energy. Students who oppose the Clinton health care program might argue that Hillary Clinton is not a credible source, but there is a difference between gauging the credibility of a speaker and assessing her or his stand on the issues. It is possible to acknowledge a speaker's credibility and still disagree with that speaker's point of view.*

*If Hillary Clinton were speaking on the topic across from her name—"African Americans: The Next Agenda"—she would almost surely be seen as having less credibility than on the topic of health care. The speaker in the exercise who would have the highest credibility on this topic would be Jesse Jackson.*

*George Bush:  Bush's credibility would be highest if he were speaking on "Reforming the American Presidency." As a former President, he is intimately familiar with the nature of the presidency and would doubtless have thoughts as to how it might be strengthened. Other speakers listed in the exercise might also be seen as having substantial credibility on this topic—most notably, Jesse Jackson and Hillary Clinton—but neither would be able to speak about the presidency from quite the same personal perspective as George Bush.*

*On the other hand, Bush would doubtless have much less credibility on the topic across from his name—"Women in the Mass Media." Most people would likely find his views on the mass media in general colored by partisan motives (as would be the case with any political figure). In addition, as the 1992 presidential election showed, many women see Bush as unconcerned about their needs and aspirations. Of all the speakers listed in the exercise, Barbara Walters would almost surely have the highest credibility on the subject of women in the mass media.*

*Barbara Walters:  As a broadcast journalist and a woman, Barbara Walters' credibility would be strongest if she were speaking on "Women in the Mass Media." Hillary Clinton's views on this topic might be well regarded by some listeners, but she lacks Walters' many years working in the mass media. David Letterman, of course, has plenty of experience with television, but as a comedian and talk-show host, he would have difficulty establishing his credibility as a serious speaker on almost any subject other than comedy or talk shows.*

*If Barbara Walters were speaking on the topic across from her name—"Reforming the American Presidency"—she would have some credibility, but nowhere near as much as a television reporter who specializes in political issues. As we saw earlier, George Bush is the speaker listed in the exercise to whom most listeners would likely accord the highest credibility on the topic of the presidency.*

*Jesse Jackson:   Although Jackson would be seen by many audiences as a credible speaker on both health care and the presidency, the topic listed in the exercise on which he would have the highest credibility is unquestionably "African Americans: The Next Agenda." This would be true both for listeners who are strong backers of Jackson and for listeners who are not. Jackson's status as the most prominent spokesperson for African Americans is widely acknowledged across racial, social, and political lines.*

*If Jackson were speaking on the topic opposite his name—"Talk Shows: Who Needs Them"—his credibility would not be any lower than that of most people listed in the exercise. The question of who needs talk shows does not require extraordinary expertise or experience. It is, in fact, so minor in comparison to questions such as health care, the presidency, or the future of African Americans that it is almost ludicrous to think of a major public figure such as Jackson addressing the topic.*

*David Letterman:  As popular as David Letterman is with college students, it is hard to imagine that many would find him a credible speaker on the subject of health care—or, for that matter, on any of the other topics listed in the exercise except for "Talk Shows: Who Needs Them?" Just as it would seem preposterous for a figure of Jesse Jackson's standing to speak on an entertainment topic such as talk shows, it would seem equally out of character for a comedian such as Letterman to give a serious speech on a topic of major political or economic consequence. No matter well informed he might be on the topic, he would have to work very hard to be taken seriously.*

2.   Identify the kind of reasoning used in each of the following statements. What weaknesses, if any, can you find in the reasoning of each?

a.   According to a study by the American Medical Association, men with bald spots have three times the risk of heart attack as men with a full head of hair. Strange as it may seem, it looks as if baldness is a cause of heart attacks.

**Discussion:** *This statement is an example of causal reasoning. It is flawed by the fallacy of false cause. The fact that men with bald spots have three times the risk of heart attack does not mean their baldness is a cause of their heart attacks. If there is any connection between baldness and heart attacks, it is that both are brought on by similar factors—stress, heredity, diet, etc.—but medical researchers do not yet have an answer to this question.*

b.   Contrary to what the chemical industry argues, limiting pesticide use does not threaten the food supply. Sweden has cut back on pesticides by 50 percent over the last few years with almost no decrease in its harvest. The Campbell Soup Company uses no pesticides at all on tomatoes grown in Mexico, and they reap as much fruit as ever. Many California farmers who practice pesticide-free agriculture have actually experienced increases in their crop yields.

**Discussion:**  *This statement is an example of reasoning from specific instances. Whether it is flawed depends on whether the three specific instances mentioned in the statement are representative of what happens in most cases in which farmers reduce their use of pesticides. And that cannot be determined in the absence of further evidence. One way to provide that evidence would be to follow the three instances with expert testimony that limiting pesticide use does not threaten the food supply. Another way would be to offer statistics showing that in a wide number of cases farmers have reduced their use of pesticides without reducing their crop yields. Even then, however, a skeptical listener (or a representative of the pesticide industry) could argue that the testimony is not conclusive or that the statistics are not sufficient to prove the speaker's point beyond doubt.*

c.   The United States Constitution guarantees all citizens the right to bear arms. Gun control legislation infringes on the right of citizens to bear arms. Therefore, gun control legislation is contrary to the Constitution.

**Discussion:**  *This statement is an example of reasoning from principle. The reasoning is valid in that the movement from the general principle (The U.S. Constitution guarantees all citizens the right to bear arms) to the minor premise (Gun control legislation infringes on the right of citizens to bear arms) to the conclusion (Therefore, gun control legislation is contrary to the Constitution) is logically valid.*

*Logical validity, however, is judged by the form of an argument, not by its content. If the conclusion has been correctly inferred from the premises, the argument is valid regardless of whether or not the premises are true. It is possible to have a valid argument from principle that is patently unsound. For example:*

a.   *All movie stars live in Hollywood.*

b.   *Tommy Lee Jones is a movie star.*

c.   *Therefore, Tommy Lee Jones lives in Hollywood.*

*This is a valid argument. If it is true that all movie stars live in Hollywood, and if it is also true that Tommy Lee Jones is a movie star, then it must be true that Tommy Lee Jones lives in Hollywood. In fact, however, it is not true that all movie stars live in Hollywood. Many live outside Hollywood; Tommy Lee Jones lives in Texas. Even though the argument is valid, it is not sound.*

*A sound argument from principle is one in which the reasoning is valid and all of the premises are true. For example:*

a.   *To be elected President of the United States a person must be at least 35 years of age.*

b.   *Bill Clinton was elected President of the United States.*

c.   *Therefore, Bill Clinton is at least 35 years of age.*

*In this case, the reasoning is valid and the premises are true. The conclusion is sound.*

*What about the argument regarding gun control? Is it sound as well as valid? That depends upon how one interprets the meaning of the clause of the U.S. Constitution ensuring citizens the right to bear arms. If one interprets that clause as meaning that all citizens have the right to own any kind of gun they please, then gun control legislation would certainly be contrary to the Constitution. If one interprets the right to bear arms in an eighteenth-century context as meaning that all citizens have the right to maintain their own* weapons so as to be able to serve in the militia—a situation that is not relevant to U.S. life in the twentieth century—then gun control legislation might not be contrary to the Constitution.

*The persuasiveness of the argument in any given situation will depend on the ability of the speaker to convince the audience that he or she has the "correct" interpretation of the clause of the Constitution that guarantees citizens the right to bear arms. As with the example of reasoning from specific instances presented earlier, this case demonstrates that reasoning is not always a cut-and-dried matter.*

d.   Almost every industrialized nation in the world except for the United States has a national curriculum and national tests to help ensure that schools throughout the country are meeting high standards of education. If such a system can work elsewhere, it can work in the United States as well.

**Discussion:** *This statement is an example of analogical reasoning. Its validity depends upon whether the factors that allow a national curriculum and national testing to work successfully in most industrialized nations are also present in the United States. Advocates of nationalizing the educational system argue that the U.S. is similar enough to most other industrialized countries to conclude, on the basis of their experience, that a national curriculum and national tests would work successfully in the U.S. Opponents of nationalizing the educational system argue that U.S. society and its educational objectives are so unique that it is not possible to conclude, on the basis of other countries' experience, that a national curriculum and national testing can be successfully implemented in the U.S. In my opinion, the evidence is not yet conclusive enough to determine which side is correct. The important point is that students understand how one would judge the validity of the analogy.*

3.   Over the years there has been much debate about the role of emotional appeal in public speaking. Do you believe it is ethical for public speakers to use emotional appeals when seeking to persuade an audience? Do you feel there are certain kinds of emotions to which an ethical speaker should not appeal? Why or why not? Be prepared to explain your ideas in class.

**Discussion:** *Because so much has been written over the years about the ethics of emotional appeal in persuasion, it is often valuable to take some time in class to discuss the issue. The purpose of the discussion is not so much for students to come away with the "correct" answer as it is for them to develop their* *own thinking about the ethics of emotional appeal. Instructors who wish to learn more about this fascinating topic should consult the sources cited under "Emotional Appeal" in the Extra Teaching and Learning Resources for this chapter of the manual.*

4.    Analyze the speech in the Appendix by Sandy Hefty, "A Friend in Need," pages 459-462.). Pay special attention to how the speaker uses the methods of persuasion discussed in this chapter.

> **Discussion:** *"A Friend in Need" is a good persuasive speech on a question of policy. It illustrates many of the methods of persuasion discussed in this chapter and provides a helpful model of how students can use Monroe's motivated sequence to organize persuasive speeches that seek immediate action.*
>
> *Specific Purpose: To persuade my audience to volunteer time to help needy elderly people remain independent in their homes.*
>
> *Central Idea:  By participating in a volunteer program, college students can help needy elderly people continue to live independently in their homes.*
>
> *Method of Organization:  Monroe's motivated sequence*
>
> *Introduction:  The introduction consists of paragraphs 1-5. The opening story about Loretta Olson gets the audience's attention and also contains a gentle trace of humor. When the speech was delivered in class, several members of the audience chuckled as they identified Loretta Olson's forgetfulness with the memory lapses experienced by some of their elderly relatives. In paragraph 2 the speaker effectively explains her personal involvement with the topic and, at the same time, establishes her credibility and good will.*
>
> *In paragraphs 3 and 4 the speaker uses statistics from the U.S. Census Bureau to establish the importance of the topic. Her comparison, in paragraph 4, between the 1.8 million Americans in the 75-plus age group who fall below the poverty line and the combined populations of Seattle, Boston, and Indianapolis is an excellent illustration of how speakers can translate large numbers into figures that are more meaningful to the audience. It is also worth noting how, in paragraph 3, the speaker relates the topic to her audience by mentioning the results of her class survey, which showed that almost all of her classmates had living grandparents.*

Paragraph 5 ends the introduction by stating the speaker's central idea and providing a clear lead-in to the body of the speech.

Body:   After getting the attention of her audience in the introduction, the speaker begins the body of her speech in paragraphs 6 and 7 with the second step in Monroe's motivated sequence—showing the need for a new course of action. In paragraph 6 the speaker explains that many elderly people cannot meet all of their physical needs, and she illustrates the point with an example of an 87-year-old woman whom she helped as a caregiver. Had she had more time, she could have provided more support for this point, but, as in most classroom speeches, she had to develop her points crisply and concisely.

In paragraph 7 the speaker continues with the need step of Monroe's motivated sequence by discussing the tragic problem of suicide among the elderly. After presenting figures from the National Center for Vital Statistics showing that persons age 75 and older have the highest suicide rate in the U.S., she provides testimony from Anthony Boxwell about the causes of suicide among the elderly. As in other parts of the speech, the speaker uses credible evidence and identifies her sources for the audience.

After an excellent transition in paragraph 8, the speaker moves to the satisfaction step of the motivated sequence by explaining, in paragraph 9, how students can participate in volunteer programs to help the elderly. Rather than talking in abstract terms, the speaker relates her plan to her listeners by focusing on state and local programs in which they can get involved. After the speech, she provided her audience a handout identifying volunteer agencies they could contact.

Of course, getting an audience to agree that something should be done and getting an audience to do something are two different matters. In paragraphs 10 and 11, therefore, the speaker turns to the visualization step of the motivated sequence by showing the audience the practicality of getting involved in a volunteer program to help the elderly. She explains that students can readily adapt their volunteer work to their personal schedules, that they will experience substantial personal gratification from volunteering, and even that they might be able to receive financial assistance for their efforts. Had the speaker failed to address these issues, her speech would have been much less effective.

*Conclusion:* The speaker concludes with the final step in Monroe's motivated sequence—an appeal to the audience to take action. After quickly summarizing her main points, she closes with the poignant statement that "Loretta Olson—and millions like her—will be forever thankful for your efforts." The emotional appeal of this line, in combination with the sense of psychological unity gained by referring back to the opening example, closes the speech on a strong note.

5.   Analyze the speech in the Appendix by Mary Fisher ("A Whisper of AIDS," pages 456-459). In your analysis, concentrate on how Fisher builds her credibility, employs evidence and reasoning, and generates emotional appeal. In addition, study how she uses the resources of language discussed in Chapter 11 to bring her message home to listeners.

**Discussion:** One of the most acclaimed public discourses of recent years, Mary Fisher's 1992 address to the Republican National Convention provides a masterful illustration of the art of public speaking. Not only does it utilize many of the methods of persuasion treated in this chapter, but it is strikingly eloquent in its use of the resources of language explored in Chapter 11. It also works well for discussion because it deals with one of the burning issues of our time yet is short enough that students can look closely at its rhetorical methods. The exercise usually works best if you have students prepare their analyses of the speech as a homework assignment, so they will be fully prepared to deal with the speech in class. Here is a synopsis of the speech.

*Specific Purpose:* To persuade my audience to adopt attitudes of awareness toward the AIDS epidemic and of compassion toward people who are HIV-positive.

*Central Idea:* Because AIDS can strike anyone at any time, we must do all we can to combat it and to be compassionate toward people who are HIV-positive.

*Method of organization:* Topical

*Introduction:* The introduction of Fisher's speech consists of paragraphs 1-2, in which she succinctly states her aim to "lift the shroud of silence" that has covered the issue of HIV/AIDS in the Republican Party. Because her speech was preceded by a brief video that established her credentials as a traditional Republican despite her status as HIV-positive, she did not need a longer introduction.

*Body:* The body of the speech falls into four main sections, the first of which runs from paragraph 3 through paragraph 6. In these paragraphs Fisher discusses the seriousness of the AIDS crisis in an effort to convince Republicans that neither they—nor anyone else—is immune from the disease. After giving statistics on the extent of the epidemic, she notes that AIDS is not a political creature—it attacks people regardless of age, gender, race, political affiliation, or sexual orientation. And, she stresses, despite everything that has been done to combat AIDS, "it's the epidemic that is winning."

The second section of the body consists of paragraphs 7-10, in which Fisher issues a call to the Republican Party to treat AIDS victims with the compassion they deserve. People who are HIV-positive, she tells her audience, do not merit shame or condemnation. After praising President and Mrs. Bush for their personal compassion toward her, she urges the Party as a whole to act with similar compassion toward AIDS victims in general. It is not possible, she pointedly remarks, to "praise the American family but ignore a virus that destroys it."

In the third section of the body, paragraphs 11-14, Fisher issues a powerful plea to the nation for awareness. Reasoning analogically, she compares people who shrug their shoulders over AIDS to people who did not protest against Hitler's concentration camps in Nazi Germany. No matter what we may think, she warns, "There is no family or community, no race or religion, no place left in America that is safe." Until the U.S. comes to terms with this fact, she warns, it will continue to be a nation at risk.

The fourth—and longest—section of the body runs from paragraph 15 through paragraph 24. In this section Fisher moves back and forth between personal observations about her condition and her family and comments directed to various portions of her audience. After thanking her family in paragraph 15 for their support and compassion, she speaks in paragraphs 16-17 to HIV-positive people who lack support and compassion. It is not you who should feel shame, she says, but those of us who "tolerate ignorance and practice prejudice."

In paragraphs 18-19 Fisher speaks movingly of her two sons—how she hopes they will remember her and how she hopes they will act with courage and leadership when she is gone. Then Fisher urges her audience to act with courage and leadership as well. Turning in paragraph 20 to AIDS sufferers, she tells them that if they have courage, they will find comfort. In paragraph 21 she calls on people who do not have AIDS to exercise leadership by setting aside "prejudice and politics to make room for compassion and sound policy."

Bringing the speech to an emotional climax, Fisher returns to her children in paragraphs 22-23, addresses them by name, and expresses the hope that they will not suffer shame on her account. Then she moves back to her general audience and appeals one last time for awareness and compassion so "my children will not be afraid to say the word AIDS when I am gone."

Conclusion:　If there is a clearly identifiable conclusion to Fisher's speech, it is the brief words of paragraph 25—"God bless the children, and bless us all"—and even those words are so closely connected to the content of paragraph 24 that they can be considered an extension of that paragraph rather than a distinct conclusion. As with Martin Luther King's "I Have a Dream," the most meaningful question to ask about the end of Fisher's speech is not whether it has an explicit conclusion, but whether it concludes effectively—which it unquestionably does.

Credibility:　Fisher faced two problems with respect to her credibility. The first was to be seen as someone with substantial enough Republican credentials to be taken seriously by the convention audience. Because of the repeated praise of "family values" and the negative tone toward people who are HIV-positive by previous speakers at the convention, there was no guarantee that Fisher's immediate audience would pay much heed to her message.

To boost Fisher's credibility as a Republican, her speech was preceded by a video stressing her family's long-time connections with the Republican Party, including her work as a staff assistant to President Ford and her father's activities as a Republican fund-raiser. During the speech itself, Fisher reminded the audience of her Republican credentials by mentioning her testimony before the platform committee three months earlier (paragraph 1), her family's close relationship with President and Mrs. Bush (paragraph 8), and her commitment to the President's cause (paragraph 10).

Fisher's second concern with respect to credibility was to be seen as a bona fide spokesperson for the AIDS community. The video before her speech helped, as it explained the circumstances by which she had become HIV-positive and projected a positive personal image of her as a mother and as an AIDS activist. Whatever positive impact the film had, however, could easily have been destroyed by a poor speech. As it turned out, everything Fisher said and did *in her address boosted her terminal credibility far above her initial credibility. Perhaps most important in this regard were her lack of self-pity, her compassion and good will, her poignant emotional appeals, and her eloquent language.*

*Evidence and reasoning: Although Fisher does not employ a great deal of statistical evidence, she does present telling figures in paragraphs 3 and 6 about the extent of the AIDS epidemic. These figures are necessary to establish her point that AIDS is on the march in the United States and the world. However, had she presented too many statistics, she would have changed the tone of her speech and may have undermined its personal, emotional appeal.*

*Fisher's strongest use of testimony comes in paragraph 12, in which she quotes Pastor Niemoeller about the consequences of not protesting against the Nazi death camps during World War II. She then uses this quotation as the basis for the analogy, in paragraph 13, between the tragic results of ignoring the concentration camps and the tragic consequences of ignoring the explosive growth of the AIDS epidemic.*

*Fisher uses two extended examples in her speech. The first comes in paragraph 8 and describes the compassionate response she has received from President and Mrs. Bush. The moral, of course, is that Republicans in general should respond compassionately to all people who are HIV-positive. The second extended example occurs in paragraph 15, where Fisher explains the support she has received from her family. She then contrasts that support, in paragraphs 16-17, with the prejudice faced by many people who are HIV-positive.*

*As in both of these examples, most of the evidence is Fisher's speech comes from her personal experience. Not only is this appropriate given her status as HIV-positive, but it is sound rhetorical strategy. To be successful, Fisher had to move the AIDS debate beyond the level of statistics and experts and relate it to the lives of ordinary Americans. By drawing on her own experience, Fisher personalizes the issue and gives it an immediacy it had previously lacked for most of her audience.*

*Emotional appeal: Fisher's speech offers a splendid example of the power of emotional appeal in persuasive speaking. Much of her emotional appeal comes, of course, from the highly personal nature of the speech, which was reinforced by Fisher's direct, unaffected delivery. As we shall see shortly, the eloquence, simplicity, and genuine pathos of Fisher's language also contribute to her emotional appeal.*

*As the speech progresses, Fisher appeals primarily to two contrasting emotions—fear and compassion. The most notable fear appeals are in paragraphs 3-6 and 11-14, in which Fisher explains the brutal reality of the AIDS epidemic and seeks to convince her audience that no one is immune from it. The most extended appeals to compassion are in paragraphs 7-10, 15-17, and 21-25, but the need for compassion runs through the entire speech as a theme in a symphony.*

*Language: As effective as Fisher's speech is in other respects, it is distinguished above all by its use of language. Just as Martin Luther King's "I Have a Dream" stands out from the thousands of speeches delivered during the civil rights movement, so the artistry and eloquence of Fisher's address make it the most memorable public discourse to date of the struggle against AIDS.*

*As in most speeches noted for their eloquence, Fisher's language is clear, familiar, and concrete. She creates sharp visual images—often of great poignancy and emotional power, and often in combination with repetition and parallel structure. Examples of this occur in the affecting imagery of paragraphs 4-5, the "Because I was not . . ." series of paragraph 11, the uncompromising insistence of paragraphs 13-14, and the gentle compassion of paragraph 16. It is also worth noting how Fisher uses repetition and parallelism to build the cadence and power of her address as she builds to her conclusion in paragraphs 19-25.*

*Fisher also makes effective use of antithesis. Thematically she juxtaposes the contrasting impulses of fear and compassion, ignorance and awareness, silence and speech. This thematic antithesis is reinforced by the heavy use of stylistic antithesis. In paragraph 2, for example, Fisher says, "I bear a message of challenge, not self-congratulation. I want your attention, not your applause." In paragraph 6 she cautions that AIDS "is not a distant threat; it is a present danger." In paragraph 10 she counsels that "We cannot love justice and ignore prejudice, love our children and fear to teach them." In paragraph 13 she warns, "If you think you are safe, you are at risk." In paragraph 17 she tells AIDS victims, "It is not you who should feel shame; it is we." Indeed, antithesis occurs so frequently that one can find examples of it throughout the address.*

# Additional Exercises and Class Activities

1.   Analyze each of the following statements. Identify the kind of reasoning used in each and explain what weakness, if any, you see in the reasoning.

   a.   There can be no doubt that the Great Depression was caused by Herbert Hoover. He became President in March 1929, and the stock market crashed just seven months later.

   b.   One non-smoker, interviewed at a restaurant, said, "I can eat dinner just fine even though people around me are smoking." Another, questioned by the Gallup Poll, said she doesn't mind working in an office where people are smoking. A third, responding to a *Los Angeles Times* survey, said, "I don't see what all the fuss is about. My wife has smoked for years and it has never bothered me." We can see, then, that cigarette smoke does not cause a problem for most non-smokers.

   c.   In Scotland adoption records are not sealed, and adults who were adopted as children may routinely obtain their original birth certificates. There is no evidence that this leads to fewer adoptions or unhappy adoptive families in Scotland. Surely, then, we can institute the same policy in the United States without creating serious problems.

   d.   Sex education classes were instituted in the public schools during the early 1960s. The number of teenage pregnancies has risen every year since 1966. It is clear, then, that there would not be so many teenage pregnancies if there were no sex education classes in the schools.

   e.   George Washington, Andrew Jackson, Teddy Roosevelt, and Dwight Eisenhower were all ranked among our ten best presidents in a recent poll. We can see, therefore, that military men make especially good presidents.

   f.   In sport, as in war, there is no substitute for victory.

**Discussion:** *This exercise gives students additional practice in reasoning and supplements exercise 2 on page 396 of the textbook.*

a.   There can be no doubt that the Great Depression was caused by Herbert Hoover. He became President in March 1929, and the stock market crashed just seven months later.

**Discussion:** *This statement is an example of causal reasoning. It is flawed by the fallacy of false cause: post hoc, ergo propter hoc. That the stock market crashed just seven months after Herbert Hoover became President does not mean Hoover caused the Great Depression. The Depression was caused by a number of complex forces, most of which had been in motion well before Hoover became President.*

b.   One non-smoker, interviewed at a restaurant, said, "I can eat dinner just fine even though people around me are smoking." Another, questioned by the Gallup Poll, said she doesn't mind working in an office where people are smoking. A third, responding to a *Los Angeles Times* survey, said, "I don't see what all the fuss is about. My wife has smoked for years and it has never bothered me." We can see, then, that cigarette smoke does not cause a problem for most non-smokers.

**Discussion:** *This statement is an example of reasoning from specific instances. It is flawed by the fallacy of hasty generalization. Three examples are hardly enough to establish that cigarette smoke does not cause a problem for most non-smokers. Certainly it would be no problem for an opposing speaker to marshall the examples of three non-smokers who are bothered by cigarette smoke. Neither speaker, however, should try to carry the point by specific instances alone. Rather, they should produce statistics or testimony to demonstrate that the specific instances are representative of non-smokers in general.*

c.   In Scotland adoption records are not sealed, and adults who were adopted as children may routinely obtain their original birth certificates. There is no evidence that this leads to fewer adoptions or unhappy adoptive families in Scotland. Surely, then, we can institute the same policy in the United States without creating serious problems.

**Discussion:** *This statement is an example of reasoning from analogy. To the best of my knowledge, the analogy is valid. The important point here, however, is that students see that the key to assessing the analogy is determining whether social and family life in Scotland are similar enough to social and family life in the United States to conclude that allowing adopted children in America access to their original birth certificates can be instituted with as few problems as in Scotland.*

d.   Sex education classes were instituted in the public schools during the early 1960s. The number of teenage pregnancies has risen every year since 1966. It is clear, then, that there would not be so many teenage pregnancies if there were no sex education classes in the schools.

**Discussion:** *This statement is an example of causal reasoning. From all appearances, it exhibits the fallacy of* post hoc ergo propter hoc. *Just because the number of teenage pregnancies has risen steadily since the institution of sex education classes does not mean the classes have caused the increased number of pregnancies. In addition, the statement is guilty of assuming that sex education classes are the only cause of the growing number of teenage pregnancies. Even if there is some causal connection between the two, there are unquestionably other causes as well.*

e.   George Washington, Andrew Jackson, Teddy Roosevelt, and Dwight Eisenhower were all ranked among our ten best presidents in a recent poll. We can see, therefore, that military men make especially good presidents.

**Discussion:** *This statement, an example of reasoning from specific instances, is flawed by hasty generalization. Although a recent poll did rank Washington, Jackson, Teddy Roosevelt, and Eisenhower as among our ten best presidents, this is not sufficient evidence to indicate that military men make especially good presidents. For one thing, Roosevelt, although he served briefly in the Spanish-American War, cannot be considered a military man in the same sense as Washington, Jackson, and Eisenhower. For another thing, there have been just as many military men who were undistinguished presidents—William Henry Harrison, Zachary Taylor, and Ulysses S. Grant.*

f.   In sport, as in war, there is no substitute for victory.

**Discussion:** *This statement is an example of reasoning from analogy. It assumes that war and sports are so much alike that what is true of the former is also true of the latter. Although one finds much reasoning like this in society, it is flawed by the fact that war and sports are fundamentally different. The purpose of war is to defeat the enemy. While one purpose of sport is to defeat one's opponent, it also has other purposes—such as improving one's fitness, developing one's skill as an athlete, enjoying the activity for its own sake, etc. These objectives can be achieved even in a losing effort.*

2. Have students analyze "The Dangers of Chewing Tobacco," by Catherine Twohig, which appears on pages 390-394 of the textbook. In their analyses, students should pay special attention to how the speaker uses the methods of persuasion discussed in the chapter.

> **Discussion:** *"The Dangers of Chewing Tobacco" is an excellent persuasive speech that illustrates how students can make effective use of all the methods of persuasion discussed in the textbook. In addition to having students analyze the text of the speech, you may want to show the videotape of it, which is available as part of the instructional supplement to* The Art of Public Speaking. *The commentary that accompanies the speech on pages 390-394 of the book points out a number of its major features. Here is a synopsis that focuses on how the speaker employs the methods of persuasion.*

> *Specific Purpose:   To persuade my audience that the laws governing the sale of chewing tobacco should be strengthened and that professional athletes should refrain from using chewing tobacco during games in order to reduce the problem of chewing tobacco use among young adults.*

> *Central Idea:   The dangers of chewing tobacco pose a serious problem that can be curbed by legislation and by banning the use of chewing tobacco during professional sporting events.*

> *Method of Organization:   Problem-solution*

> *Credibility:   The speaker does an excellent job of establishing her credibility in paragraph 3. Her combination of professional training and personal experience make her a very believable speaker. Moreover, as the speech progresses, her command of the topic and her obvious sincerity reinforce the audience's perception both of her competence and of her good will.*

> *Evidence:   The speaker does an excellent job of using evidence to persuade her listeners. The extended examples of Tom in paragraphs 1-2 and of Sean Marsee in paragraph 9 dramatize the speaker's claim about the dangers of chewing tobacco. Both examples are vivid and richly textured, and both deal with people in the same age group as most members of the speaker's audience. These examples alone make up almost 25 percent of the speech, and they are crucial to its impact. In addition, the speaker uses brief examples to good effect in paragraphs 12 and 14 to demonstrate the practicality of her plan.*

*The speaker's use of examples is complemented by her use of statistics in paragraphs 5, 7, 8, and 12. In each case, the speaker employs statistics from credible sources and identifies those sources for her audience. She also does an excellent job of translating her statistics into human terms. The most dramatic instance of this is the extended example of Sean Marsee in paragraph 9 that gives a personal dimension to the statistics cited in paragraph 8. Less dramatic, but equally effective, is the speaker's method in paragraph 5. After stating that the average age of first use of chewing tobacco is "just ten years old," she explains that this means "many children are chewing tobacco when they are in fourth grade." Then, after noting that 21 percent of kindergartners have tried chewing tobacco, she exclaims, "Children are using chewing tobacco before they can even read the warning labels!"*

*Testimony plays less of a role in this speech than do examples and statistics. The speaker uses testimony in three places. In paragraph 6 she cites the American Dental Society and the American Cancer Society on the multiple dangers of chewing tobacco. In paragraph 11 she cites the Department of Law Enforcement to note that laws regulating the sale of chewing tobacco in Wisconsin have been ineffective. In paragraph 13 she cites a statement from the American Dental Association that the use of chewing tobacco by role models is the primary reason children develop an interest in it. In all three cases, the speaker uses credible sources and identifies them in the speech.*

*Reasoning:  The speaker relies primarily on causal reasoning and analogical reasoning. She uses causal reasoning in paragraphs 6-9, where she argues that chewing tobacco is a cause of tooth decay, tooth loss, gum disease, and oral cancer. She does not claim that chewing tobacco is the sole cause of these conditions, only that it is an important contributing factor. In each case, she supports her claim with credible evidence of a causal connection. The speaker also uses causal reasoning in paragraphs 13-14, when she claims that many children start chewing tobacco because they see athletes chewing. If the athletes stopped chewing in games, she reasons, then children would be less likely to chew themselves.*

*The speaker uses analogical reasoning in paragraph 12. Her argument there is that because tougher laws against selling chewing tobacco have worked in California and other states, similar laws would work in the speaker's state of Wisconsin. Analogical reasoning is often used in this way by speakers to demonstrate the practicality of their proposed policy.*

> *Emotional appeal: For the most part, the speaker allows her emotional appeal to grow naturally out of her speech content. Vivid and richly detailed, the extended examples of Tom (paragraph 1) and Sean Marsee (paragraph 9) help to encourage a strong emotional reaction against chewing tobacco. When the speaker delivered the speech, she used a visual aid to show what Tom's face looked like after his surgery. The visual aid was an oversized color photograph, 11 inches by 17 inches, that had been enlarged for the speaker at a local copy service. To enhance the visibility of the photograph, the speaker mounted it on a large piece of white poster board. The effect was quite dramatic—as can be seen from the videotape of the speech—and powerfully reinforced the emotional impact of the speaker's words.*

> *The speaker also does an excellent job in paragraphs 10 and 15 of relating the examples of Tom and Sean to her listeners and of appealing to the fear that they, or someone they love, could be victimized by chewing tobacco. Finally, if you view the speech on videotape, you will see how forcefully the speaker's own emotion and intensity regarding the topic come across. In the last analysis, here—as in other speeches—the sincerity and conviction of the speaker are the strongest source of emotional appeal.*

3.   Show the class one or more persuasive speeches from the videotape of student speeches that accompany *The Art of Public Speaking*. Use the videotapes to illustrate points about the methods of persuasive speaking.

> **Discussion:** *The videotape supplement to this edition of* The Art of Public Speaking *contains several student persuasive speeches that can be used for classroom analysis and discussion. Three of the persuasive speeches on the videotape—"The Dangers of Chewing Tobacco," "A Friend in Need," and "Family Medical Histories: A Proven Lifesaver"—are printed in this edition of the book. For more information about individual speeches, consult the guide that accompanies the videotape.*

4.   Distribute copies of "Seatbelts: A Habit That Could Save Your Life," by Andrew Kinney, which appears on pages 361-363 of this manual. Have students analyze how the speaker employs the methods of persuasion discussed in the chapter.

> **Discussion:** *A persuasive speech on a question of policy, "Seatbelts: A Habit That Could Save Your Life" is an excellent speech for analysis and discussion, and it is also available on the videotape of sample student speeches that accompanies* The Art of Public Speaking. *For a full discussion of the speech, see pages 364-366 of this manual.*

5.  Distribute copies of "Ghosts," by Ken Lonnquist, which is printed on pages 387-391 of this manual. Have students analyze the speech in light of the methods of persuasion discussed in the chapter.

> **Discussion:** *"Ghosts" is a persuasive speech on a question of value. Delivered in an introductory argumentation and debate class at the University of Wisconsin-Madison, it is considerably more complex than the typical classroom speech. The speaker's purpose was to convince his classmates that abortion is morally wrong, and he knew from his audience analysis that all but one of his listeners opposed his position.*
>
> *Because the topic of the speech is so controversial, it invariably sparks a heated class discussion. If that discussion is to be most productive, however, it needs to focus primarily on the speaker's techniques rather than on his position regarding abortion. If you assign the speech, urge students to put aside their personal opinions about abortion and to analyze the speech in light of questions such as the following:*
>
> *(1) Is the introduction well suited to the speaker's task of gaining good will and establishing common ground with his audience?*
>
> *(2) Although the speech deals with a question of value, its persuasiveness rests largely on the speaker's ability to convince his listeners about a question of fact. What is that question of fact? How effectively does the speaker deal with it given the opposition of his listeners? Does the speaker provide sufficient evidence to establish his claim on the question of fact?*
>
> *(3) What kind of reasoning does the speaker rely on most of all throughout the speech? How well does his reasoning accord with the guidelines presented in the chapter?*
>
> *(4) How effective are the speaker's emotional appeals? Do they develop naturally from the content of the speech? Are they likely to be persuasive to listeners who do not already agree with the speaker's position?*
>
> *(5) How does the speaker use the resources of language discussed in Chapter 11—imagery, metaphor, parallelism, repetition, etc.—to express his ideas? What are the "ghosts" to which he refers throughout the speech? Is this an appropriate image for the speech, or does it distract attention from the major issue?*
>
> *For full commentary on the speech, see pages 392-394 of this manual.*

# Extra Teaching and Learning Resources

## General

Bettinghaus, Edwin P., and Cody, Michael J. *Persuasive Communication*, 4th ed. New York: Holt, Rinehart and Winston. 1987.

Cialdini, Robert B. *Influence: The Psychology of Persuasion*, rev. ed. New York: Quill, 1993.

Dillard, James Price. "Persuasion Past and Present: Attitudes Aren't What They Used to Be." *Communication Monographs*, 60 (1993), 90-97.

Eagly, Alice H., and Chaiken, Shelly. *The Psychology of Attitudes*. Fort Worth, Texas: Harcourt Brace Jovanovich, 1993.

Goldfaden, Gloria. "Winning Hearts and Minds." *The Humanist* (November-December 1988), 13.

McVey, Stephanie. "Giving Presentations that Persuade." *Management World* (January-February 1989), 6-8.

O'Keefe, Daniel J. *Persuasion: Theory and Research*. Newbury Park, Calif.: Sage, 1990.

Perloff, Richard M. *The Dynamics of Persuasion*. Hillsdale, N.J.: Lawrence Erlbaum, 1993.

Petty, Richard E., and Cacioppo, John T. *Communication and Persuasion: Central and Peripheral Routes to Attitude Change*. New York: Springer-Verlag, 1986.

Reardon, Kathleen Kelley. *Persuasion in Practice*. Newbury Park, Calif.: Sage, 1991.

Sonnenberg, Frank. "Presentations that Persuade." *Journal of Business Strategy* (September-October 1988), 55-58.

## Credibility

Decker, Bert. *You've Got to Be Believed to Be Heard*. New York: St. Martin's 1992.

Kenton, Sherron B. "Speaker Credibility in Persuasive Business Communication: A Model Which Explains Gender Differences." *Journal of Business Communication*, 26 (1989), 143-157.

McCroskey, James C. *An Introduction to Rhetorical Communication*, 6th ed. Englewood Cliffs, N.J.: Prentice-Hall, 1993, Chapter 5.

McCroskey, James C., and Young, Thomas J. "Ethos and Credibility: The Construct and Its Measurement after Three Decades." *Central States Speech Journal*, 32 (1981), 24-35.

O'Keefe, Daniel J. *Persuasion: Theory and Research*. Newbury Park, Calif.: Sage, 1990, Chapter 8.

Perloff, Richard M. *The Dynamics of Persuasion*. Hillsdale, N.J.: Lawrence Erlbaum, 1993, Chapter 6.


## Evidence and Reasoning

Allen, Mike. "Meta-Analysis Comparing the Persuasiveness of One-Sided and Two-Sided Messages." *Western Journal of Speech Communication*, 55 (1991), 390-404.

Engel, S. Morris. *With Good Reason: An Introduction to Informal Fallacies*, 4th ed. New York: St. Martin's, 1990.

Govier, Trudy (ed.). *Selected Issues in Logic and Communication*. Belmont, Calif.: Wadsworth, 1988.

Herrick, James A. *Critical Thinking: The Analysis of Arguments*. Scottsdale, Ariz.: Gorsuch Scarisbrick, 1991.

Kahane, Howard. *Logic and Contemporary Rhetoric: The Use of Reason in Everyday Life*, 6th ed. Belmont, Calif.: Wadsworth, 1992.

Kazoleas, Dean C. "A Comparison of the Persuasive Effectiveness of Qualitative versus Quantitative Evidence: A Test of Explanatory Hypotheses." *Communication Quarterly*, 41 (1993), 40-50.

O'Keefe, Daniel J. "The Persuasive Effects of Message Sidedness Variations: A Cautionary Note Concerning Allen's (1991) Meta-Analysis." *Western Journal of Communication*, 57 (1993), 87-97.

Reinard, John C. "The Empirical Study of the Persuasive Effects of Evidence: The Status after Fifty Years of Research." *Human Communication Research*, 15 (1988), 3-59.

Reynolds, Rodney A., and Burgoon, Michael. "Belief Processing, Reasoning, and Evidence." In Robert N. Bostrom (ed.), *Communication Yearbook 7*. Beverly Hills, Calif.: Sage, 1983, pp. 83-104.

Stiff, James B. "Cognitive Processing of Persuasive Message Cues: A Meta-Analytic Review of the Effects of Supporting Information on Attitudes." *Communication Monographs*, 53 (1986), 75-89.

Toulmin, Stephen, Rieke, Richard, and Janik, Allan. *An Introduction to Reasoning*, 2nd ed. New York: Macmillan, 1984.

Vancil, David L. *Rhetoric and Argumentation*. Boston: Allyn and Bacon, 1993.

Ziegelmueller, George W., Kay, Jack, and Dause, Charles A. *Argumentation and Advocacy*, 2nd ed. Englewood Cliffs, N.J.: Prentice-Hall, 1990.

## Emotional Appeals

Boster, Franklin J., and Mongeau, Paul. "Fear-Arousing Persuasive Messages." In Robert N. Bostrom and Bruce Westley (eds.), *Communication Yearbook 8*. Beverly Hills, Calif.: Sage, 1984, pp. 330-375.

Garrett, Mary M. "*Pathos* Reconsidered from the Perspective of Classical Chinese Rhetorical Theories." *Quarterly Journal of Speech*, 79 (1993), 19-39.

Karetz, Jack D. "Rational Arguments and Irrational Audiences: Psychology, Planning, and Public Judgment." *Journal of the American Planning Association*, (1989), 445-456.

Smith, Craig R., and Hyde, Michael J. "Rethinking the 'Public': The Role of Emotion in Being-with-Others." *Quarterly Journal of Speech*, 77 (1991), 446-466.

Waddell, Craig. "The Role of *Pathos* in the Decision-Making Process: A Study in the Rhetoric of Science Policy." *Quarterly Journal of Speech*, 76 (1990), 381-400.

Witte, Kim. "Putting the Fear Back into Fear Appeals: The Extended Parallel Process Model." *Communication Monographs*, 59 (1992), 329-349.

## Classroom Activities and Assignments

Dittus, James K. "Grade Begging as an Exercise in Argumentation." *Speech Communication Teacher* (Summer 1992), 5.

Garrett, Roger L. "The Premises of Persuasion." In Stephen E. Lucas (ed.), *Selections from the Speech Communication Teacher, 1986-1991*. New York: McGraw-Hill, 1992, pp. 58-59.

Johnson, Craig. "Nothing to Fear but Fear . . . Or Is There?" In Stephen E. Lucas (ed.), *Selections from the Speech Communication Teacher, 1986-1991*. New York: McGraw-Hill, 1992, p. 59.

Kauffman, James. "Collecting and Evaluating Evidence." *Speech Communication Teacher* (Winter 1992), 12.

Langley, C. Darrell. "The Heckling Speech." In Stephen E. Lucas (ed.), *Selections from the Speech Communication Teacher, 1986-1991*. New York: McGraw-Hill, 1992, p. 67.

MacDonald, Madlyne A. "The Key to Persuasion." In Stephen E. Lucas (ed.), *Selections from the Speech Communication Teacher, 1986-1991*. New York: McGraw-Hill, 1992, pp. 59-60.

Ross, Charlynn. "The Challenging Audience Exercise." In Stephen E. Lucas (ed.), *Selections from the Speech Communication Teacher, 1986-1991*. New York: McGraw-Hill, 1992, p. 69.

Schreir, Howard N. "Analyzing Persuasive Tactics." In Stephen E. Lucas (ed.), *Selections from the Speech Communication Teacher, 1986-1991*. New York: McGraw-Hill, 1992, p. 61.

## Films and Videos

"A Case Study for Critical Thinking: Vietnam." Insight Media (1987). 52 minutes.

"Credibility." CRM Films (1993). 42 minutes.

"Credibility Factor: What Followers Expect from Leaders." CRM Films (1990). 22 minutes.

"Critical Thinking: How to Evaluate Information and Draw Conclusions." Insight Media (1986). 47 minutes.

"Persuasion Gone Awry." (1977). RMI Media Productions. 28 minutes.

"Persuasive Appeals." (1977). RMI Media Productions. 28 minutes.

"Persuasive Speaking." Esquire (1982). 60 minutes.

"Presenting an Argument." Films for the Humanities (1992). 20 minutes.

"Psycho-Sell: Advertising and Persuasion." Insight Media (1991). 25 minutes.

"The Language of Leadership: The Winston Churchill Method." Films for the Humanities (1993). 60 minutes.

"When You Buy: How Ads Persuade." Insight Media (1989). 33 minutes.

# Chapter 17  Speaking on Special Occasions

## Chapter Objectives

*After reading this chapter, students should be able to:*

1.  Explain the guidelines for an effective speech of introduction.

2.  Discuss the purpose and major themes of a speech of presentation.

3.  Discuss the purpose and major themes of a speech of acceptance.

4.  Indicate the fundamental purpose of a commemorative speech and explain why a successful commemorative speech depends so much on the creative use of language.

5.  Explain how an after-dinner speech differs from a speech to inform or to persuade.

## Chapter Outline

I.  Many special occasions provide opportunities for speechmaking *(text page 402)*.
    A.  Ceremonies such as weddings, funerals, and dedications often include speeches.
    B.  So do retirements, graduations, award presentations, retirements, and affairs of state.

C.    Speeches are part of what makes these occasions special and memorable.
D.    The primary aim of speeches on special occasions is neither to inform nor to persuade but to fulfill the special needs of the occasion.

II.    Speeches of introduction present a speaker to an audience *(text pages 402-405)*.
    A.    A good speech of introduction achieves three goals.
        1.    It builds enthusiasm for the upcoming speaker.
        2.    It generates interest in the speaker's topic.
        3.    It establishes a welcoming climate that will boost the speaker's credibility.
    B.    There are several guidelines for speeches of introduction.
        1.    Speeches of introduction should be brief.
            a.    Long speeches of introduction irritate the audience.
            b.    Long speeches of introduction distract attention from the main speaker.
            c.    Under normal circumstances, a speech of introduction should be no more than two or three minutes in length.
        2.    Speeches of introduction should be completely accurate.
            a.    Errors in a speech of introduction embarrass both the introducer and the main speaker.
            b.    Nothing is more important in a speech of introduction than pronouncing the main speaker's name correctly.
        3.    Speeches of introduction should be adapted to the occasion.
            a.    Formal occasions require formal speeches of introduction.
            b.    Informal occasions allow for casual speeches of introduction.
        4.    Speeches of introduction should be adapted to the main speaker.
            a.    An introduction that leaves the main speaker uncomfortable has failed in part of its purpose.
            b.    Overpraising the main speaker—especially for his or her speaking skills—can be a problem.
            c.    Potentially embarrassing remarks about the main speaker's personal life are always inappropriate.
        5.    Speeches of introduction should be adapted to the audience.
            a.    If the main speaker is not well known to the audience, the speech of introduction will need to explain a bit about her or his achievements and qualifications.
            b.    If the main speaker is well known to the audience, the speech of introduction should take account of that knowledge.

6.   Speeches of introduction should try to create a sense of anticipation and drama.
    a.   One way to achieve this is to save the main speaker's name until the last moment of the speech.
    b.   Another way is to deliver the speech of introduction skillfully with sincerity and enthusiasm.

III.   Speeches of presentation are given when someone receives a gift or an award *(text pages 405-406)*.
    A.   Speeches of presentation should usually be fairly brief.
        1.   At times, they can be only a few lines long.
        2.   They can also run to four or five minutes in length.
    B.   The main purpose of a speech of presentation is to explain why the recipient is receiving the award.
        1.   The speech should point out the achievements for which the recipient is receiving the award.
        2.   The speech should discuss the recipient's achievements in a way that will make them meaningful to the audience.
    C.   If the recipient won the award in a competition, the speech of presentation should consider praising the other competitors as well.

IV.   Speeches of acceptance give thanks for a gift or an award *(text pages 406-407)*.
    A.   A speech of acceptance should thank the people who are bestowing the gift or award.
    B.   A speech of acceptance should also acknowledge the people who helped the recipient win the award.

V.   Commemorative speeches are addresses of praise or celebration *(text pages 407-410)*.
    A.   Commemorative speeches pay tribute to a person, a group of people, an institution, or an idea.
        1.   Eulogies, Fourth of July speeches, testimonial addresses, and dedications are examples of commemorative speeches.
        2.   The fundamental purpose of a commemorative speech is to inspire the audience—to heighten their admiration for the person, institution, or idea being praised.
    B.   Although it usually presents information about its subject, a commemorative speech is different from an informative speech.
        1.   The aim of an informative speech is to communicate information clearly and accurately.

2. The aim of a commemorative speech is to express feelings and arouse sentiments.

C. Commemorative speeches depend above all on the creative and subtle use of language.

    1. Some of the most memorable speeches in history are commemorative addresses that we continue to find meaningful because of their eloquent expression.

    2. Two aspects of language use are especially important for commemorative speeches.

        a. The first is avoiding clichés and trite sentiments.

        b. The second is utilizing stylistic devices such as those discussed in Chapter 11 to enhance the imagery, rhythm, and creativity of the speech.

VI. After-dinner speeches are a kind of speech to entertain *(text pages 410-413)*.

A. After-dinner speeches are a long and well-established tradition.

    1. As a formal genre, they developed in England during the early nineteenth century.

    2. Nowadays "after-dinner" speeches are often given at breakfast or lunch gatherings, as well as in the evening.

B. After-dinner speeches are lighter in tone than other types of speeches.

    1. Almost any topic can be appropriate if the speaker approaches it in a lighthearted manner.

    2. An after-dinner speech should not be technical or argumentative.

    3. Supporting materials should be chosen primarily for their entertainment value rather than for their persuasive strength.

    4. Listeners are looking for a good-natured talk that treats the topic imaginatively, even whimsically.

C. Although light in tone, after-dinner speeches require careful preparation.

    1. They should be clearly organized around a central theme.

    2. They should be adroitly delivered to produce the desired impact on the audience.

D. Humor can be an important part of after-dinner speeches.

    1. Many after-dinner speeches are distinguished by their use of humor.

    2. It is not necessary, however, to be a stand-up comic to be a successful after-dinner speaker.

        a. The purpose of humor in an after-dinner speech is more to provoke smiles or chuckles than to convulse the audience with a string of one-liners.

b.    Ideally, humor in an after-dinner speech grows naturally out of the speech materials and provides insight into the topic.

c.    Many excellent after-dinner speeches contain no humor.

(1)    Speakers who are not comfortable working for a laugh should not try to force humor into their speeches.

(2)    If they deal with the topic creatively, select interesting supporting materials, and use language creatively, they will do just fine.

## Application Exercises  *(from text page 415)*

1.    Attend a speech on campus. Pay special attention to the speech introducing the main speaker. How well does it fit the guidelines discussed in this chapter?

> **Discussion:**  *If you use this exercise, you may want to have students complete an evaluation form similar to the one on the next page of this manual.*

2.    Observe several speeches of presentation and acceptance—at a campus awards ceremony or on a television program such as the Academy Awards, Grammy Awards, Emmy Awards, or Tony Awards. Which speeches do you find most effective? Least effective? Why?

> **Discussion:**  *This exercise works especially well if your class meets the day after a program such as the Academy Awards. While watching the program, each student should select his or her candidate for the best acceptance speech. After discussing all of the speeches in class, have students vote for the best acceptance speech. This often produces a spirited discussion while students defend their candidates for the best speech.*

# Out-of-Class Observation
# Speech of Introduction

Your name _____

Name of speaker you observed _____

Where was the speech presented? _____

Who was the speaker introducing? _____

*Evaluate the speech of introduction as follows:*

1. How long was the speech? Was it too long? Too short? About right? Explain.

2. As far as you can tell, was the speech accurate in its remarks about the main speaker? Explain.

3. Was the speech well adapted to the occasion? Explain.

4. Was the speech well adapted to the main speaker? Explain.

5. Was the speech well adapted to the audience? Explain.

6. Did the speech create a sense of anticipation and drama about the main speaker? Explain.

3.   Analyze the commemorative speech by Ryan Saurer ("James 'Cool Papa' Bell," pages 409-410). Assess the speech in light of the criteria for commemorative speaking presented in the chapter.

> **Discussion:** *"James 'Cool Papa' Bell" is a fine commemorative speech. Bell's achievements as a baseball player will probably be appreciated most by students who are fans of the game, but the speech transcends baseball to focus on the larger issue of racism in U.S. society and Bell's refusal to be ground down by it. The speech also illustrates the differences between a commemorative speech and an informative speech. Although the speaker provides information about Bell, he does not seek to present a full view of Bell's life or even of his career as a baseball player. Rather, he focuses on Bell's most praiseworthy qualities and seeks to enhance his listeners' appreciation of those qualities. In addition to discussing this speech in class, you may also want to show the videotape of it, which is available as part of the instructional supplement to* The Art of Public Speaking. *Here is a synopsis of the speech.*

> *Introduction:   The introduction consists of paragraphs 1-2. The speaker begins by arousing curiosity about the topic of his speech. He then reveals that his subject is James "Cool Papa" Bell, who played his entire baseball career in the Negro League because the major leagues were still segregated. The last sentence of paragraph 2 identifies Bell as the finest player in the Negro League and provides a deft lead-in to the body of the speech.*

> *Body:   Composed of paragraphs 3-8, the body of the speech develops three main points. The first is that Bell was the fastest baseball player of all time (paragraphs 3-4). The second is that Bell played the game with a style all his own (paragraphs 5-6). The third—and most important—is that Bell was a pioneer who helped pave the way for Jackie Robinson and other African Americans who would later play Major League Baseball (paragraphs 7-8).*

> *Throughout the body of the speech, the speaker provides well-chosen supporting materials to illustrate Bell's athleticism and character. The speaker also makes effective use of the resources of language discussed in Chapter 11 to elevate and polish the style of the speech. At the end of paragraph 4, for example, he employs alliteration in the sentence, "But no one made fun of his slender size as he swiftly and smoothly stole second or scored from first on a single."*

> *In paragraph 8 the speaker uses repetition and parallelism to emphasize the extent to which Bell was victimized by*

racism—"racism that kept him from playing in the same league as white players, racism that kept him from being in the same record book as white players, racism that kept him from earning the same money as white players." The dexterity of this passage, in combination with its sharp message about the evils of racism, gives the speaker's words special force.

*Conclusion:* The conclusion consists of the final paragraph. After subtly announcing that the speech is coming to an end by saying, "So let's take a few moments . . . ," the speaker closes by reminding the audience of Bell's accomplishments as "the speedy baseball star, the stylish innovator, the man who fought racism just by going to work everyday." The parallel structure of these phrases enhances the cadence of the speaker's delivery, while the final words—"the man who fought racism just by going to work everyday"—provide a sense of drama and reinforce what the speaker sees as Bell's most important attainment.

4. Have students analyze the after-dinner speech by Julie Daggett, ("The Horror of It All," pages 412-413). Evaluate the speech in light of the criteria for after-dinner speaking presented in the chapter.

**Discussion:** "The Horror of It All" shows how students can use humor, personal experience, vivid language, and clever phraseology to create a first-rate after-dinner speech. Although the speech produced few gales of laughter when delivered in class, it did evoke a number of knowing smiles and chuckles as students identified some of their own experiences with those of the speaker. At the same time, it indirectly made a serious point about horror films and their potential impact on children and adults alike. Here is a brief synopsis of the speech.

*Introduction:* The requirements of an introduction in an after-dinner speech are slightly different from those of a persuasive or informative speech. Detailed preview statements are seldom employed in after-dinner speeches. Nor is there often a need in such speeches to establish the speaker's credibility or to gain the good will of hostile listeners. The two objectives that must be accomplished in the introduction of an after-dinner speech are to gain attention and to reveal the topic. In "The Horror of It All," both objectives are achieved in paragraph 1. The opening story does an excellent job of getting the audience involved in the speech, while the last sentence states succinctly that the topic is the speaker's "love/hate relationship with horror movies."

*Body:   Although after-dinner speeches are often more loosely structured than other kinds of speeches, they still need to follow some discernible order rather than simply rambling from point to point. "The Horror of It All" is arranged in chronological order. After beginning the body in paragraph 2 with her "scaredy-cat tendencies" as a young child, the speaker moves to her fascination with* The Exorcist *as she was growing up and to various episodes that illustrate how the movie industry fed her "passion for terror" during "the next several years" (paragraphs 3-5) until she finally decided to give up horror films after being scared out of her wits watching television with her mother (paragraphs 6-7). Throughout the body, ideas are presented clearly and without clutter. Each episode is explained in sharp, vivid language, and the humor emerges naturally and easily from the speaker's descriptions.*

*Conclusion:   In after-dinner speeches, there is seldom a clear break between the body and the conclusion. Nor is there a need to summarize the main points or to alert the audience with phrases such as "In closing." The primary purpose of the conclusion in an after-dinner speech is to bring the speech to a satisfying end. As in other kinds of speeches, this can be accomplished with a story, a quotation, or a clever or dramatic phrase. Also as in other kinds of speeches, it is often helpful to pull the whole speech together by referring back to the introduction.*

*In "The Horror of It All," the conclusion consists of the final paragraph. The repetition of the phrase "It's been two years now . . ." in the first two sentences brings the speaker up to the present and completes the chronological movement of the speech. The reference to Bette Davis recalls the opening example and gives the speech a strong sense of psychological unity. The last three sentences end the speech on an entertaining note while simultaneously reinforcing the tension about the speaker's susceptibility to horror movies that is at the heart of the speech.*

# Additional Exercises and Class Activities

1.   During the final round of speeches, have each student prepare a two-minute speech of introduction for one of their classmates' speeches. The speech should conform with the guidelines for speeches of introduction presented in this chapter, and it should be delivered in class immediately before the speech it is introducing.

**Discussion:** *This assignment gives students practice in creating and presenting a speech of introduction. Assign the speeches well enough in advance that students have a chance to interview the speakers they are introducing. Also assign the speeches of introduction so that no student is delivering both a speech of introduction and a major speech on the same day.*

2.  Assign a speech in which each student introduces a famous person to the class. Tell students they should imagine themselves being able to invite any well-known figure, living or dead, to speak to the class on any topic of the student's choice. The task of each student is to prepare a 2-minute speech introducing his or her chosen person to the class. In their speeches, students should (a) provide some biographical information about the person and her or his contributions, (b) identify the topic of the person's speech, (c) explain why the person's speech topic is important for this audience. Speeches should follow the guidelines for speeches of introduction discussed in the chapter.

**Discussion:** *Like the previous activity, this assignment gives students practice in creating and presenting a speech of introduction. Unlike a speech introducing one of their classmates, however, this speech requires library research so students can learn more about the person they are introducing. Indeed, one of the benefits of this assignment is that students gain experience using the biographical aids available in the reference section of the library (see pages 126-134 of the textbook).*

*When making this assignment, it is extremely important to encourage students to be creative in their speeches. Otherwise, you are likely to get a series of dull recitations summarizing information from* Who's Who, Current Biography, Notable American Women, *and the like. For the most part, though, students are enthusiastic about this assignment, which provides a nice alternative to the usual informative and persuasive speeches. Because this presentation is only two minutes long, all students should be able to deliver their speeches in a single class session.*

*To help students prepare, you may want to show the speeches of introduction by Nan Keohane, President of Wellesley College, for Barbara Bush and Raisa Gorbachev on "Commencement Speeches at Wellesley College, June 1, 1990," which is part of the videotape supplement to* The Art of Public Speaking.

*For additional discussion, see Randall E. Majors, "Practical Ceremonial Speaking: Three Speech Activities,"* Speech Communication Teacher, *(Winter 1989), 2-3, from which this assignment is adapted. Professor Majors' article is reprinted in Stephen E. Lucas (ed.),* Selections from the Speech Communication Teacher, 1986-1991, *which is part of the instructional supplement to* The Art of Public Speaking.

3.    Distribute copies of "Hail to the Heroes," by James Davis, which appears on pages 406-407 of this manual. Have students analyze the speech in light of the criteria for commemorative speaking discussed in the textbook.

> **Discussion:**   *A first-rate commemorative speech, "Hail to the Heroes" is also rich in its use of the resources of language presented in Chapter 11. For a full discussion of the speech, see page 408 of this manual.*

4.    Distribute copies of "My Grandfather," by Kim Lacina, which appears on pages 403-404 of this manual. Have students analyze the speech in light of the criteria for commemorative speaking presented in the chapter.

> **Discussion:**   *"My Grandfather" is an excellent commemorative speech that illustrates how students can use the resources of language to reach high levels of eloquence. For a full discussion of the speech, see page 405 of this manual.*

## Extra Teaching and Learning Resources

### General

Collins, Patrick. "Once More Unto the Speech." *Punch* (September 18, 1991), 18-19.

Ehrilch, Eugene, and Hawes, Gene R. *Speak for Success*. New York: Bantam, 1984, Chapter 13.

Ehrilch, Henry. *Writing Effective Speeches*. New York: Paragon House, 1992, Chapter 13.

Gardner, Gerald. *Speech Is Golden*. New York: St. Martin's Press, 1992, Chapter 9.

Humes, James C. *Roles Speakers Play*. New York: Harper and Row, 1976.

Kelley, Joseph J., Jr. *Speech Writing: A Handbook for All Occasions*. New York: Plume, 1980, Chapter 7.

Vassallo, Wanda. *Speaking with Confidence: A Guide for Public Speakers*. Crozet, Va.: Betterway Publications, 1990, Chapter 8.

### Classroom Activities and Assignments

Lamansky, Martin. "Getting to Know My Hero: The Speech of Tribute." *Speech Communication Teacher* (Winter 1993), 10.

Majors, Randall E. "Practical Ceremonial Speaking: Three Speech Activities." In Stephen E. Lucas (ed.), *Selections from the Speech Communication Teacher, 1986-1991.* New York: McGraw-Hill, 1992, p. 68.

Poyner, Barry Cole. "Adding a Ceremonial Touch." *Speech Communication Teacher* (Fall 1992), 12.

Sikes, Shirley. "Introducing the Speaker." *Speech Communication Teacher* (Fall 1991), 14.

Walter, Suzanne. "Introduction of a Speaker: Multipurpose and Multicultural." *Speech Communication Teacher* (Spring 1993), 3.

# Chapter 18 Speaking in Small Groups

## Chapter Objectives

*After reading this chapter, students should be able to:*

1. Identify the four kinds of leadership that may occur in a small group.

2. Distinguish among the procedural needs, task needs, and maintenance needs of a small group.

3. Explain the five major responsibilities of every participant in a small group.

4. Identify the five stages of the reflective-thinking process and discuss the major tasks of a group at each stage.

5. Explain the methods for presenting orally the findings of a small group.

## Chapter Outline

I. Speaking in small groups is an important form of communication *(text pages 418-419)*.
   A. Small groups exist in virtually every area of life, including business, education, government, religion, community organizations, and volunteer associations.
   B. As its name implies, a small group is limited in size.
      1. Most experts set the maximum number of members at eight.
      2. The group must be small enough to allow free discussion among all members.
   C. This chapter deals with a particular kind of small group—the problem-solving small group.

1. A problem-solving small group is formed to solve a particular problem.
2. Speaking in a problem-solving small group involves many skills similar to those used in public speaking.

II. To be productive, a small group needs effective leadership *(text pages 419-421)*.
   A. There are several kinds of leadership in a small group.
      1. In some groups, there is no specific leader.
         a. When the need for leadership arises, any member can provide it.
         b. At times, every member of the group will fulfill leadership functions.
      2. In some groups, there is an implied leader.
         a. The implied leader might have the highest rank in the group.
         b. The implied leader may be the person with the most experience and expertise on the topic.
      3. In some groups, there is an emergent leader.
         a. Emergent leaders are people who, by their ability or personality, take on a leadership role.
         b. Ideally, the emergent leader will be constructive in helping the group achieve its objectives.
      4. Some groups have a designated leader.
         a. A designated leader is assigned or elected when the group is formed.
         b. Formal committees usually have a designated leader as chairperson.
   B. Small groups have three kinds of leadership needs.
      1. Procedural needs are the "housekeeping" requirements of the group.
         a. They include organizing meetings, setting agendas, taking notes, preparing handouts, and the like.
         b. Procedural needs can be met by a designated leader or can be apportioned among all group members.
      2. Task needs are substantive actions that help the group complete its project.
         a. Task needs include analyzing the issues facing the group, collecting information, keeping the group on task, helping the group reach consensus, and the like.
         b. If these needs are not met, the group will not be successful in achieving its objectives.
      3. Maintenance needs involve interpersonal relations within the group.
         a. They include creating a supportive environment for the group, managing conflict among group members, helping the group feel good about its accomplishments, and the like.

b.   Because interpersonal problems can interfere with a group's performance, effective leaders need to be keenly attentive to maintenance needs.

III.   Regardless of a small group's leadership, every member of a group has five responsibilities *(text pages 422-427)*.
   A.   Members should commit themselves to the goals of the group.
      1.   For a group to succeed, members must align their personal goals with the group's goals.
      2.   Hidden agendas—in which individuals put personal goals over those of the group—are especially damaging.
   B.   Members should fulfill their individual assignments.
      1.   Division of labor is one of the advantages of working in a small group.
      2.   A group can only be effective if each member fulfills his or her specific duties.
      3.   No matter what other assignments they may have, all members of a small group have one vital assignment—listening.
         a.   Effective listening prevents confusion about what is happening in the group.
         b.   Effective listening allows each member to evaluate the merits of other members' ideas or suggestion.
         c.   Effective listening establishes a positive climate for discussion.
   C.   Members should avoid interpersonal conflicts.
      1.   Personal disagreements decrease a group's effectiveness.
      2.   Disagreements among group members should be kept on a task level, rather than on a personal level.
   D.   Members should encourage full participation in the group.
      1.   One way to encourage participation is by listening attentively to other members.
      2.   A second way to encourage participation is by inviting quiet members to speak.
      3.   A third way to encourage participation is by offering supportive comments to other members.
   E.   Members should work to keep the group's discussion on track.
      1.   Members need to make sure the discussion is proceeding in an orderly fashion from one issue to another.
      2.   Members also need to make sure the group does not make hasty or ill-considered decisions.

IV.   The reflective-thinking method is an effective procedure for organizing discussion in a problem-solving small group *(text pages 427-433)*.
   A.   The first step in the reflective-thinking method is defining the problem.

1. Before a group can make progress, it must know precisely what problem it is trying to solve.
2. The best way to define the problem is to phrase it as a question of policy.
3. A group should follow four guidelines when phrasing the question for discussion.
    a. It should make the question as clear and specific as possible.
    b. It should phrase the question so as to allow for a wide variety of answers.
    c. It should avoid biased or slanted questions.
    d. It should pose only a single question.

B. The second step in the reflective-thinking process is analyzing the problem.
1. Too often groups try to map out solutions before they have a firm grasp of the problem.
2. If a group analyzes the problem thoroughly, it will be in a much better position to devise a workable solution.
3. When analyzing the problem, a group should pay special attention to two questions.
    a. How severe is the problem?
    b. What are the causes of the problem?

C. The third step in the reflective-thinking method is establishing criteria for the solution.
1. It is vital that a group set up criteria before discussing solutions.
2. Setting up criteria gives the group a way to judge the appropriateness and practicality of potential solutions.

D. The fourth step in the reflective-thinking method is generating potential solutions.
1. At this stage, the group's goal is to come up with the widest possible range of solutions.
2. Brainstorming is an effective way to generate potential solutions.
    a. Each member of the group lists all the possible solutions he or she can think of.
    b. The group creates a master list of all the members' potential solutions.
    c. The group then discusses the ideas, adding any new suggestions to the master list.

E. The fifth step in the reflective-thinking method is selecting the best solution.
1. The group should assess each potential solution in light of the criteria established for an ideal solution.
2. In doing so, the group should try to reach consensus.
    a. A consensus decision is one that all members accept.
    b. Consensus decisions usually result in superior decisions and increased unity within the group.

V.   Once a group has reached a decision, it needs to present its
     recommendations clearly and convincingly *(text pages 433-435)*.
     A.   Although a group's recommendations are usually presented formally in
          writing, the written report is often supplemented with—or sometimes
          replaced by—an oral presentation.
     B.   One kind of oral presentation is an oral report.
          1.   An oral report is much the same in content as a written report.
          2.   In most cases, one member of the group delivers the oral report.
          3.   An oral report should be approached like any other speech.
     C.   A symposium is a second kind of oral presentation.
          1.   A symposium consists of a moderator and several speakers seated
               in front of an audience.
               a.   The moderator introduces the topic and the speakers.
               b.   Each speaker delivers a prepared speech on a single aspect
                    of the group's work.
          2.   The speeches in a symposium should be carefully planned to
               cover all important aspects of the group's project.
     D.   A panel discussion is a third kind of oral presentation.
          1.   A panel discussion is essentially a conversation in front of an
               audience.
               a.   Panel discussions have a moderator who introduces the
                    panelists and keeps the discussion on track.
               b.   Panelists speak briefly, informally, and impromptu.
          2.   Like other forms of speechmaking, a panel discussion requires
               serious preparation.
               a.   Although panelists speak impromptu, they need to study the
                    topic and map out their ideas ahead of time.
               b.   The moderator needs to establish an agenda for the
                    discussion and make sure all panelists get to voice their
                    ideas.

# Application Exercises *(from text pages 436-437)*

1.   Identify the flaw (or flaws) in each of the following questions for a problem-
     solving group discussion. Rewrite each question so it conforms with the criteria
     discussed in the chapter for effective discussion questions.

     a.   Should all students be required to take two years of a foreign language
          to graduate from college?

          **Discussion:** *This question can be answered with a simple yes or
          no. It should be rephrased to allow for a wide variety of answers.
          For example: "What should be the foreign language requirements
          for graduation from college?"*

b.   What should be done to prevent the outrageously cruel and inhumane treatment of animals in laboratory experiments?

**Discussion:**  *This question is biased or slanted. It should be rewritten more objectively. For example, "What should be the guidelines for using animals in laboratory experiments?"*

c.   What should be done about child abuse?

**Discussion:**  *This question is too broad and ambiguous. It should be rewritten so as to be clear and specific. For example: "What should be done by courts and law enforcement agencies to help reduce the problem of child abuse?"*

d.   What should our state government do to control the cost of welfare and to combat unemployment?

**Discussion:**  *This question poses two questions. It should be rewritten to ask a single question. For example: "What should our state government do to control the cost of welfare?" Or: "What should our state government do to combat unemployment?"*

e.   Should the federal government institute a system of standardized national tests for all school children?

**Discussion:**  *This question can be answered with a simple yes or no. It should be rewritten to allow for a wide variety of answers. For example: "What should the federal government do to improve the quality of education in the United States?"*

2.   If possible, arrange to observe a problem-solving small group in action. You might attend a meeting of your city council, the school board, the zoning commission, a local business, a church committee. To what extent does the discussion measure up to the criteria of effective discussion presented in this chapter? What kind of leadership does the group have, and how well does the leader (or leaders) fulfill the group's procedural needs, task needs, and maintenance needs? How do the other members meet their responsibilities? What aspects of the meeting are handled most effectively? Which are handled least effectively?

**Discussion:**  *This exercise gives students the opportunity to observe a small group in action. You may want to have students write a brief paper reporting their observations. Or you may want to arrange for the entire class to observe the same group meeting, so as to provide a common basis for class discussion.*

3.  Identify a relatively important decision you have made in the last year or two. Try to reconstruct how you reached that decision. Now suppose you could remake the decision following the reflective-thinking method. Map out exactly what you would do at each stage of the method. Do you still reach the same decision? If not, do you believe the reflective-thinking method would have led you to a better decision in the first place?

    **Discussion:** *This exercise requires students to sort out the steps of the reflective-thinking method and to apply them to the students' own decision making. Not only does this help familiarize students with the steps of the method, but it makes the point that the reflective-thinking method is not restricted to group discussion.*

4.  Attend a symposium or panel discussion on campus. Prepare a brief analysis of the proceedings. First, study the role of the moderator. How does she or he introduce the topic and the participants? What role does the moderator play thereafter? Does she or he guide and focus the panel discussion? Does she or he summarize and conclude the proceedings at the end?

    Second, observe the participants. Are the speeches in the symposium well prepared and presented? Which speaker (or speakers) do you find most effective? Least effective? Why? Do participants in the panel discussion share talking time? Does their discussion appear well planned to cover major aspects of the topic? Which panelist (or panelists) do you find most effective? Least effective? Why?

    **Discussion:** *This can be handled much like Exercise 2. The questions in the exercise can also be used as the basis for evaluating symposia or panel discussions presented in class.*

## Additional Exercises and Class Activities

1.  Have students perform the exercise "Lost on the Moon," as follows:*

    First, divide the class into groups of 4 to 6 members, and have each member complete the "Lost on the Moon" Individual Worksheet on page 333. Allow ten minutes for this part of the exercise.

    Second, have each group discuss their individual answers and try to reach a consensus ranking of the 12 items. Each group should complete the "Lost on the Moon" Group Worksheet on page 334. Allow 25 minutes for this portion of the exercise.

    Then proceed to the third step, on pages 335-336.

---

*Adapted from Jay Hall, "Decisions, Decisions, Decisions," *Psychology Today*, 5 (November 1971), 51-54, 86-88.

# "Lost on the Moon" Individual Worksheet

*Instructions:*

Your spaceship has just crash-landed on the lighted surface of the moon. You were scheduled to rendezvous with a command ship 200 miles away, also on the lighted side of the moon, but the rough landing has ruined your ship and destroyed all the equipment on board, except for the 12 items listed below.

Your crew's survival depends on reaching the command ship, so you must choose the most critical items available for the 200-mile trip. Your task is to rank the 12 items according to their importance in allowing your crew to survive the 200-mile journey to the command ship. In the column titled "Your rank," place the number 1 by the most important item, the number 2 by the second most important item, and so on through number 12, the least important.

You have ten minutes to complete this worksheet.

| Item | Your rank | NASA rank | Difference |
|------|-----------|-----------|------------|
| box of matches | | | |
| food concentrate | | | |
| fifty feet of nylon rope | | | |
| parachute silk | | | |
| two .45 caliber pistols | | | |
| solar-powered portable heating unit | | | |
| two 100-pound tanks of oxygen | | | |
| map of the moon's constellation | | | |
| self-inflating life raft | | | |
| magnetic compass | | | |
| five gallons of water | | | |
| solar-powered FM receiver-transmitter | | | |

## "Lost on the Moon" Group Worksheet

*Instructions:*

Your task is to reach a consensus ranking of the 12 items needed to survive the journey to the command ship 200 miles away. This means that the ranking for each of the 12 items should be agreed upon by each member of the group before it becomes a part of the group's decision. Here are some guides to use in reaching consensus:

1.  Don't argue stubbornly for your own point of view just because it is yours. Listen to other members of the group and be willing to change your views on the basis of reason and logic.

2.  On the other hand, don't change your mind simply to avoid disagreement. Seek out differences of opinion and try to get every member involved in the decision-making process. The more information you have, the better chance you will have of making a sound decision.

3.  Avoid such techniques as majority vote, averaging, flipping coins, and bargaining.

After your group has reached consensus on how to rank the 12 items, fill in the "Group rank" column below. You have 25 minutes to complete this phase of the exercise.

| Item | Group rank | NASA rank | Difference |
|---|---|---|---|
| box of matches | | | |
| food concentrate | | | |
| fifty feet of nylon rope | | | |
| parachute silk | | | |
| two .45 caliber pistols | | | |
| solar-powered portable heating unit | | | |
| two 100-pound tanks of oxygen | | | |
| map of the moon's constellation | | | |
| self-inflating life raft | | | |
| magnetic compass | | | |
| five gallons of water | | | |
| solar-powered FM receiver-transmitter | | | |

For the third step of the exercise, have students compute their individual and group scores, as follows:

    a.    Provide students the correct ranking for each item, as given by NASA. Students should write this ranking in the column headed "NASA rank" on each of the two worksheets.

| Item | NASA rank | NASA's rationale |
|---|---|---|
| box of matches | 12 | No oxygen on moon to sustain flame |
| food concentrate | 4 | Efficient means of supplying energy requirements |
| fifty feet of nylon rope | 6 | Useful in scaling cliffs, tying injured together |
| parachute silk | 7 | Protection from sun's rays |
| two .45 caliber pistols | 9 | Possible means of self-propulsion |
| solar-powered portable heating unit | 10 | Not needed—temperature on the lighted side of the moon can exceed 100° C |
| two 100-pound tanks of oxygen | 1 | Most pressing survival need because of lack of oxygen on the moon |
| map of the moon's constellation | 3 | Primary means of navigation |
| self-inflating life raft | 8 | Some value for shelter or carrying. Also, $CO^2$ bottle in military raft may be used for propulsion. |
| magnetic compass | 11 | Worthless for navigation because magnetic field on the moon is not polarized |
| five gallons of water | 2 | Replacement for tremendous loss of liquid on lighted side of moon |
| solar-powered FM receiver-transmitter | 5 | For communication with command ship, but FM requires line-of-sight transmission and short ranges |

b.   For each item on both worksheets students should enter the difference between their individual ranking or group ranking and the NASA ranking. It makes no difference which ranking is higher. For example, if the individual or group ranking is 12 and the NASA ranking is 8, the difference is 4. Likewise, if the individual ranking is 8 and the NASA ranking is 12, the difference is 4.

c.   The total score for each worksheet is figured by adding all the numbers in the "Difference" column on each sheet.

Fourth, have students compare their individual scores with the group score. Also have students compare the average individual score of all members of each group with the group score. In almost every case the group's score will be better—closer to NASA's rankings—than either the individual scores or the average individual score of the group's members.

Fifth, conduct a general class discussion of the results and of the decision-making procedures used in the groups.

> **Discussion:** *This is an excellent exercise to acquaint students with the processes and benefits of small-group discussion. Students see how a small group can provide resources that allow it to improve upon the individual decisions of its members. Students also get firsthand experience in the difficult task of trying to reach consensus in a small group. In fact, because this exercise provokes so many questions and comments from students, you can use the general class discussion afterward to highlight any number of specific points about decision-making in small groups.*

2.   Have students perform the "Hostages" exercise, as follows:*

First, divide the class into groups of 4 to 6 members, and have each member complete the "Hostages" Individual Worksheet on pages 337-338. Allow ten minutes for this part of the exercise.

Second, have each group discuss their individual answers and try to reach a consensus ranking of the eight hostages. Each group should complete the "Hostages" Group Worksheet on page 339. Allow 20 minutes for this part of the exercise.

Third, have each group report its rankings to the rest of the class. Afterward, conduct a general class discussion of the results and of the decision-making procedures used in the groups.

---

*Adapted from Anne L. Haehl, "Adapting to Non-Traditional Students," *Speech Communication Teacher* (Winter 1988), 12-13. Used with permission of Anne L. Haehl and the Speech Communication Association.

# "Hostages" Individual Worksheet

*Instructions:*

A plane has been hijacked! The hijackers offer to release four passengers to the U.S embassy. In return for this gesture, the government of a neutral country will agree to allow the plane to land at its airport and refuel.

The captors insist, however, that U.S. authorities select the four to be released from the following list. The President has given your group the job of making the selection. If you do not select the people, the hijackers are perfectly willing to allow the plane to run out of gas and crash, killing all passengers. You must reach a decision by consensus, and you must do so within the next half hour.

You may assume the terrorists are honest about releasing those who are chosen to be released. You do not know what will happen to those who remain on the plane, but given what is known about this particular terrorist group, you expect most or all of the remaining hostages probably will die.

Quickly rank the following passengers in the order in which you would choose them to be released. In the column titled "Your rank," place the number 1 by the hostage you would save first, the number 2 by the one you would save second, and so on through number 8, the hostage you would save last.

You have ten minutes to complete this part of the exercise, after which you will discuss the matter with your group and reach an agreement.

| *Hostages* | *Your rank* |
|---|---|

1. Brenda Jones, age 27, has three children by three different fathers, none of whom she has married. She loves her children, however, and has resolved to get her life together for the children's sake. Her mother is caring for them so Brenda can attend a six-week training program for women who lack job skills. _____

2. Fr. John O'Brien, 65 years old, is in excellent health. A Roman Catholic priest, he has dedicated his life to working with the poor in an inner-city ghetto. He is taking this flight to arrange for funding and personnel that will enable him to set up a program to carry on his life's work after he becomes unable to work. Should he die at this time, the work probably will end. _____

*Hostages*                                                                                      *Your rank*

3.   Juan Garcia is 45. He has a history of heart trouble and might
     not survive the stress of a prolonged hostage situation. He is a
     wealthy businessman whose estate would easily provide for his
     wife and three young children, even if he should die in the
     hijacking. His business, however, which has employed and given
     dignity to many Hispanic people, probably would fold without
     his vision and drive, putting many people out of work who will
     not be able to find jobs.                                                                  _____

4.   Elijah Brown is 52. He did time in jail for armed robbery. Since
     his release two years ago, he has worked hard, gone to school
     part time, and supported his invalid wife and youngest child (the
     only one remaining at home). There would be no money to
     provide for his family in the event of his death.                                          _____

5.   Betsy Bates, 29, is a well-known and successful model. Married
     a little over a year to rock star Duke, she has just found out that
     she is pregnant, a discovery she views with mixed feelings.                                _____

6.   Congresswoman Jan Perkins is 47. Widowed young, when her
     husband died in Vietnam, she has devoted her life to politics.
     She has been an effective and eloquent worker for peace and
     for the rights of women and minorities. Her death would be a
     crushing emotional blow to her elderly parents, though she has
     provided for them financially in her will. Perkins is widely seen
     as the most likely candidate for the first woman President of the
     United States.                                                                             _____

7.   D. B. Calhoun is 43. Little is known about him, except that he
     is a very bigoted person with an unstable employment history.
     He reads *Soldier of Fortune* and similar magazines, and dreams
     about being a mercenary. It is quite possible that he will try
     some hostile action against the hijackers and ruin any chance of
     getting the remaining hostages out alive.                                                  _____

8.   Andrea Ohms, at 19, is already a distinguished pianist, having
     started performing professionally at age 8. Her performances
     give immense pleasure to thousands of people around the world.
     She is engaged to be married.                                                              _____

# "Hostages" Group Worksheet

*Instructions:*

Your task is to reach a consensus ranking of the four hostages to be released by the terrorists. This means that the ranking for each of the four should be agreed upon by each member of the group before it becomes part of the group decision. Here are some guidelines to use in reaching consensus.

1. Don't argue stubbornly for your own point of view just because it is yours. Listen to other members of the group and be willing to change your views on the basis of reason and logic.

2. On the other hand, don't change your mind simply to avoid disagreement. Seek differences of opinion and try to get every member involved in the decision-making process. The more information you have, the better chance you will have of making a sound decision.

3. Avoid such techniques as majority vote, averaging, flipping coins, and bargaining.

After your group has reached consensus on how to rank the hostages, fill in the "group rank" column below. You have 20 minutes to complete this phase of the exercise.

| Hostage | Group Rank |
|---|---|
| 1. Brenda Jones | _____ |
| 2. Fr. John O'Brien | _____ |
| 3. Juan Garcia | _____ |
| 4. Elijah Brown | _____ |
| 5. Betsy Bates | _____ |
| 6. Jan Perkins | _____ |
| 7. D.B. Calhoun | _____ |
| 8. Andrea Ohms | _____ |

**Discussion:** *Like "Lost on the Moon," this is an excellent exercise to acquaint students with the processes of small-group discussion. But whereas "Lost on the Moon" deals with scientific and technical matters on which there are right and wrong answers, "Hostages" revolves around subjective personal values that cannot be incontestably established as right or wrong. As a result, you should be prepared for some fairly intense discussions in the individual groups. You should also be prepared for that intensity to spill over into the general class discussion afterward. You may need to work to keep that discussion focused on the process of small-group communication rather than allowing it to turn into an extended debate on the specific decisions of each group regarding which hostages to save.*

3.  Assign students the "Twelve Angry Men" group consultation project, as follows\*.

    First, divide the class into groups of 5-6 members. The task of each group is to view the classic film "Twelve Angry Men," which revolves around the efforts of eleven members of a jury in a murder trial to convince one member to change his "not guilty" vote to "guilty." The film dramatizes many of the aspects of small-group discussion covered in the textbook, including the kinds and functions of leadership, interpersonal conflict, hidden agendas, and the creation of consensus. Because the film is 96 minutes long, each group will have to arrange a time to view it out of class.

    Second, give each group the following instructions: For this assignment, your group is to act as a consultant to the jury in the movie "Twelve Angry Men." The purpose of this assignment is for you to demonstrate your knowledge of group processes by evaluating a group's decision making. There is no single correct answer to this assignment. Your task as a group is to demonstrate that you understand and can apply the concepts of small-group discussion presented in the textbook and in class.

    Third, have each group consider the following questions in its analysis:

    a.  What are the strengths of the group portrayed in "Twelve Angry Men"?

    b.  What are the weaknesses of the group?

    c.  What kinds of leadership does the group demonstrate?

---

\*Adapted from Bruce C. McKinney, "The Group Process and 'Twelve Angry Men,'" *Speech Communication Teacher* (Winter 1990), 1-2. This article is also reprinted in Stephen E. Lucas (ed.), *Selections from the Speech Communication Teacher, 1986-1991*, which is part of the instructional supplement that accompanies *The Art of Public Speaking*.

d.   What role do hidden agendas play in the deliberations of the group?

e.   If you were the leader of the group, what would you do to eliminate some of its interpersonal conflict?

f.   Who are the most effective communicators in the group? The least effective? Why?

g.   How could the group improve its decision making and problem solving?

Fourth, conduct a general class discussion in which each group reports a summary of its deliberations and recommendations. Use the discussion to illustrate points about speaking in problem-solving small groups.

> **Discussion:**  *This assignment is particularly valuable in helping students understand the dynamics of the group process. It can also be used as an alternative to the major problem-solving group discussion explained on page 40 of this manual. If so, however, it should probably be supplemented with a requirement that each student prepare either a written report or a journal of her or his group's activities—as explained in Additional Activities 5 and 6 below.*

4.   Divide the class into groups of 5-6 students each. The task of each group is to review the previous round of classroom speeches and provide constructive suggestions to help improve the next round. In its deliberations, each group should consider the following questions. Have each group present its thinking in a panel discussion.*

a.   How well did the class as a whole perform in narrowing their topics and adapting their speeches to this audience?

   • Were specific purposes sharply defined? Were they too broad? Too narrow? Too technical? Too trivial?

   • Which speeches were especially well adapted to the background, knowledge, and interests of the audience? What methods of audience adaptation were used in these speeches?

   • What advice would you give to the class about audience analysis and adaptation for the next round of speeches?

---

*Adapted from material supplied by Professor Douglas Pedersen, Department of Speech Communication, Penn State University. Used with permission.

b.   How well did the class as a whole perform in the area of speech organization?

- Which introductions worked especially well? Why?

- Which conclusions were particularly effective? Why?

- Did speeches follow a clear method of organization? Which speeches were especially strong in this respect?

- Did speakers make effective use of connectives to help listeners follow their ideas? Which speeches stood out in this regard?

- What advice would you give to the class about organization for the next round of speeches?

c.   How well did the class as a whole use supporting materials in this round of speeches?

- Which speakers made especially good use of examples? What made their use of examples so effective?

- Which speakers made especially good use of statistics? What made their use of statistics so effective?

- Which speakers made especially good use of testimony? What made their use of testimony so effective?

- What advice would you give to the class about the use of supporting materials in the next round of speeches?

d.   How well did the class as a whole deliver this round of speeches?

- Did speakers sound fluid, confident, and conversational?

- Did speakers manage their notes effectively and establish strong eye contact with listeners?

- Did speakers avoid distracting mannerisms? Did they use gestures to help communicate their ideas?

- Did speakers use visual aids effectively? Which speeches were especially noteworthy in this respect?

- What advice would you give to the class about delivery in the next round of speeches?

**Discussion:** *This assignment can be a helpful way to integrate group discussion into a public speaking class. Groups should be assigned before the start of the round of speeches they are to analyze. Be sure to tell the groups that this assignment will require them to meet outside of class and to reach consensus on their judgments about their classmates' speeches.*

*This assignment can also be used as an alternative to the major problem-solving group discussion described on page 40 of this manual. If so, however, it should probably be supplemented with a requirement that each student prepare either a written report or a journal of their group's activities—as explained in Additional Activities 5 and 6 below.*

5. If you assign students a major group project that requires work outside of class, have them prepare a 3-to-5-page written report on the deliberations of their group. In writing their reports, students should address the following:

a. *Leadership.* If your group has a designated leader, assess how well she or he performs. If your group does not have a designated leader, note what kind of leadership develops. Which members of the group assume leadership roles? Do you think your group would work better with a different kind of leadership?

b. *Responsibilities of group members.* Evaluate how well each member fulfills his or her five major responsibilities. Do members commit themselves to the goals of the group and cooperate to achieve them? Do they carry out their individual assignments? Do they avoid interpersonal conflict by keeping disagreements at the task level? Do they encourage participation by other people in the group? Do they work to keep the discussion on track?

c. *Use of reflective-thinking method.* Keep track of how your group deals with each stage in the reflective-thinking method. Does the group define the problem clearly and analyze it effectively? Does the group establish criteria for solutions and brainstorm to generate a number of possible solutions? Is the group able to reach consensus on the best solution or solutions? If not, how does the group reach its decision?

d. *Evaluation.* Are you satisfied with the work of the group and with your role in the group? If the group were to start its project over again, what changes would you recommend to help the group work more effectively?

**Discussion:** *This assignment requires students to look closely at the communication processes in their groups. To help with this assignment, each student should be encouraged to keep a journal of his or her group's deliberations. The journal should note what happens at each meeting of the group and what developments take place over time as the group works on its project.*

*Because this assignment requires a substantial investment of time, some teachers count it as a major part—25 percent or more—of the student's grade for the unit on group discussion. For an alternative to this assignment, see the next Additional Exercise/ Activity.*

6.    As in the preceding assignment, encourage students to keep a journal of their group's deliberations. The journal should note what happens at each meeting and what developments take place over time as the group works on its project. When the project is completed, have each student turn in a Participant Evaluation Form (next page) assessing the work of each participant in the group other than himself or herself.

**Discussion:** *This is an alternative to the detailed evaluation called for in the preceding Additional Exercise/Activity. Because this evaluation focuses on individual group members, it usually gives a pretty clear picture of who met their responsibilities and who did not. As a result, it can be an excellent aid in assigning students individual grades for their group projects.*

# Group Discussion Participant Evaluation Form

Person being evaluated _____

Your name _____   Group _____

*For each item, circle the number that best reflects your evaluation of the participant's contribution to the group.*

| poor | fair | average | good | excellent | |
|---|---|---|---|---|---|
| P | F | A | G | E | Appeared committed to the goals of the group |
| P | F | A | G | E | Participated frequently in group deliberations |
| P | F | A | G | E | Comments were clear, relevant, and helpful |
| P | F | A | G | E | Carried out individual assignments promptly |
| P | F | A | G | E | Assisted with procedural leadership functions |
| P | F | A | G | E | Assisted with task leadership functions |
| P | F | A | G | E | Assisted with maintenance leadership functions |
| P | F | A | G | E | Avoided interpersonal conflict with group members |
| P | F | A | G | E | Encouraged participation by other group members |
| P | F | A | G | E | Helped keep discussion on track |
| P | F | A | G | E | Overall contribution in comparison to other group members |

*Comments:*   (this space must be filled in)

# Extra Teaching and Learning Resources

## General

Baker, Deborah C. "A Qualitative and Quantitative Analysis of Verbal Style and the Elimination of Potential Leaders in Small Groups." *Communication Quarterly*, 38 (1990), 13-26.

Barge, J. Kevin. "Leadership as Medium: A Leaderless Group Discussion Model." *Communication Quarterly*, 37 (1989), 237-247.

Barker, Larry L., Wahlers, Kathy J., Watson, Kittie W., and Kibler, Robert J. *Groups in Process: An Introduction to Small Group Communication*, 4th ed. Englewood Cliffs, N.J.: 1991.

Beatty, Michael J. "Group Members' Decision Rule Orientations and Consensus." *Human Communication Research* (1989), 279-296.

Bormann, Ernest G. *Small Group Discussion: Theory and Practice*, 3rd. ed. New York: Harper and Row, 1990.

Brilhart, John K., and Galanes, Gloria J. *Effective Group Discussion*, 7th ed. Dubuque, Iowa: W.C. Brown, 1992.

Cathcart, Robert S., and Samovar, Larry. *Small Group Communication: A Reader*, 6th ed. Dubuque, Iowa: W.C. Brown, 1992.

Cline, Rebecca J. Welch. "Detecting Groupthink: Methods for Observing the Illusion of Unanimity." *Communication Quarterly*, 38 (Spring 1990), 112-126.

Cragan, John F., and Wright, David W. *Communication in Small Group Discussions: An Integrated Approach*, 3rd ed. St. Paul, Minn.: West, 1991.

Cragan, John F., and Wright, David W. "Small Group Communication Research of the 1980s: A Synthesis and Critique." *Communication Studies*, 41 (1990), 212-236.

Diehl, Michael, and Stroebe, Wolfgang. "Productivity Loss in Brainstorming Groups: Toward the Solution of a Riddle." *Journal of Personality and Social Psychology*, 53 (1987), 497-509.

Ellis, Donald G., and Fisher, Aubrey. *Small Group Decision Making: Communication and the Group Process*, 4th ed. New York: McGraw-Hill, 1994.

Gouran, Dennis, Hirokawa, Randy Y., Julian, Kelly M., and Leatham, Geoff B. "The Evolution and Current Status of the Functional Perspective in Decision-Making and Problem-Solving Groups." In Stanley A. Deetz (ed.), *Communication Yearbook 16*. Newbury Park, Calif.: Sage, 1993, pp. 573-600.

Hirokawa, Randy Y., and Poole, Marshall Scott (eds.). *Communication and Group Decision-Making*. Beverly Hills, Calif.: Sage, 1986.

Jablin, Frederic M. "Cultivating Imagination: Factors That Enhance and Inhibit Creativity in Brainstorming Groups." *Human Communication Research*, 7 (1981), 245-258.

Jensen, Arthur D., and Chilberg, Joseph C. *Small Group Communication: Theory and Application*. Belmont, Calif.: Wadsworth, 1991.

Kayser, Thomas. *Mining Group Gold*. El Segundo, Calif.: Serif, 1990.

Meyers, Renee, and Seibold, David R. "Perspectives on Group Argument: A Critical Review of Persuasive Arguments Theory and an Alternative Structurational View." In James A. Anderson (ed.), *Communication Yearbook 13*. Newbury Park, Calif.: Sage, 1990, pp. 268-302.

Pavitt, Charles, and Curtis, Ellen. *Small Group Discussion: A Theoretical Approach*, 2nd ed. Scottsdale, Ariz.: Gorsuch Scarisbrick, 1994.

Tubbs, Stewart L. *A Systems Approach to Small Group Interaction*. 4th ed. New York: McGraw-Hill, 1992.

Williams, Wendy M., and Sternberg, Robert J. "Group Intelligence: Why Some Groups Are Better than Others." *Intelligence*, 12 (1988), 351-377.

Wood, Julia T., Phillips, Gerald M., and Pedersen, Douglas J. *Group Discussion: A Practical Guide to Participation and Leadership*. New York: Harper and Row, 1986.

## Classroom Activities and Assignments

Bahti, Cynthia L. "California Dreamin'." In Stephen E. Lucas (ed.), *Selections from the Speech Communication Teacher, 1986-1991*. New York: McGraw-Hill, 1992, p. 31.

Bourhis, John. "Video Groups." *Speech Communication Teacher* (Summer 1992), 12.

Dittus, James K. "Giving Students What They Want: A Role-Playing Exercise with True-to-Life Groups." *Speech Communication Teacher* (Summer 1993), 2-3.

Mayhew, Virginia B. "Pennies and Poems." In Stephen E. Lucas (ed.), *Selections from the Speech Communication Teacher, 1986-1991*. New York: McGraw-Hill, 1992, p. 31.

McKinney, Bruce C. "The Group Process and *12 Angry Men*." In Stephen E. Lucas (ed.), *Selections from the Speech Communication Teacher, 1986-1991*. New York: McGraw-Hill, 1992, pp. 31-32.

Mino, Mary. "Making the Basic Public Speaking Course Relevant: A Group Project." In Stephen E. Lucas (ed.), *Selections from the Speech Communication Teacher, 1986-1991*. New York: McGraw-Hill, 1992, p. 33.

Neumann, David. "Building and Destroying Groups." *Speech Communication Teacher* (Spring 1992), 13-14.

Neumann David S. "Small Group Membership Contract." In Stephen E. Lucas (ed.), *Selections from the Speech Communication Teacher, 1986-1991*. New York: McGraw-Hill, 1992, pp. 33-34.

Ortiz, Joe. "Group Interaction: Processes, Problems, and Consensus." In Stephen E. Lucas (ed.), *Selections from the Speech Communication Teacher, 1986-1991*. New York: McGraw-Hill, 1992, pp. 34-35.

Renz, Mary Ann. "Job Specific Interviews." *Speech Communication Teacher* (Winter 1992), 4-5.

Smith, Robert E. "The Outstanding Senior Award: A Realistic Small Group Decision-Making Exercise." *Speech Communication Teacher*, (Winter 1994), 7-8.


## Films and Videos

"Abilene Paradox." CRM Films (1984). 28 minutes.

"Group Productivity." CRM Films (1984). 21 minutes.

"Groupthink," revised version. CRM Films (1991). 22 minutes.

"Interpersonal and Small-Group Communication." Insight Media (1989). 27 minutes.

"Leadership and the New Science." CRM Films (1993). 23 minutes.

"Meeting Robbers." CRM Films (1985). 20 minutes.

"Meeting the Meeting Challenge." CRM Films (1987). 35 minutes.

"Mining Group Gold." CRM Films (1992). 22 minutes.

"The Leadership Challenge." CRM Films (1989). 26 minutes.

"Workteams and the Wizard of Oz." CRM Films (1993). 13 minutes.

"You Know What I Mean?" CRM Films (1990). 21 minutes.

# Part V

# SPEECHES FOR ANALYSIS

# AND DISCUSSION

# Nothing to Sneeze At

Jeffrey Moran

---

*1*     You feel it welling up inside you, this delicate tingling, as if your every nerve were firing at once. You want to grope for the newspaper, your homework—anything—but you no longer control your body.

*2*     These seconds of helpless anticipation seem like an eternity, but then the spell is broken. You crash forward, your muscles contracting like a fist, and you can't even see that people are running away from you because something has forced your eyes shut.

*3*     And then it's over. You relax. Your head is clear, your body under control.

*4*     I'm talking, of course, about sneezing. I come from a long line of sneezers. My father sneezed, and his father and his father's father before him were all men for whom a blast from the nose was every bit as bracing as a plunge into the snow following a sauna.

*5*     This involuntary reflex known as the sneeze is not one of the burning mysteries of our time, but I'd like to tell you about some superstitions that have sprung up around sneezing and also let you know what's actually happening when you sneeze. Finally, in the interests of social harmony, I'll tell you how to sneeze safely and politely.

*6*     Sneezing is old. Citizens of the Roman Empire sneezed, but they were only following the tradition of the ancient Greeks, among them Aristotle, who considered the sneeze a favorable omen.

*7*     A sneeze worked wonders for Xenophon, the Greek historian and general. According to the *Concise Dictionary of Ancient History*, in 400 B.C. Xenophon, while still a mere foot-soldier, marched with the Greek army deep into hostile Persia, where the enemy slew all the Greek leaders and threatened to do the same to the confused troops when nightfall postponed the slaughter.

*8*     The desperate Greeks spent the night debating who should lead them in battle the next day. Xenophon rose to give a dramatic oration exhorting the men to follow him to liberty or to death. He spoke for an hour in the flickering firelight until a soldier to his right seconded his conclusion with a sneeze. Thinking this sneeze a favorable sign from the gods, the Greeks made Xenophon general, and when the sun rose the next morning, they marched to safety 10,000 strong behind their new leader.

*9*    Sneezing is seldom this dramatic, but many cultures echo the Greeks in their praise of the nose's most conspicuous function. Indeed, the *Encyclopedia of Occult Sciences, Superstitions, and Folklore* devotes eleven tightly spaced, oversized pages to the subject. For example, a Zulu who has just sneezed proclaims, "I am now blessed; the ancestral spirit is with me. It has come to me. Let me salute it, for it is he who causes me to sneeze."

*10*    Sneezing in India provokes a shorter, but no less salutary, response. If you were walking down the dusty streets of Karim Nagar, for instance, and you sneezed, bystanders would shout, "Live!" and you, as a polite tourist, must reply, "Live with you!" Most Indians consider sneezing healthy, if not supernatural; it is the inability to sneeze that is cause for alarm. *Science* magazine reports Indian scientists have labeled this malady "asneezia" and are currently researching ways to artificially induce the healthy sneeze.

*11*    In the West, despite the cheerful, almost compulsive blessing we give anyone experiencing spontaneous nasal expulsion, the sneeze has long been regarded with suspicion. Some people, my grandmother among them, believe we say "Bless you" because the heart skips a beat when you sneeze. It's true your eyes must close when you sneeze, but the heartbeat remains steady. I used to think we say "Bless you" because of the superstition that when you sneeze the soul exits through your nostrils. If no one blesses you, evil beings with a penchant for nasal drip will snatch your spiritual essence. Natives of Motlan and Mota in the South Pacific believe this, but our European blessing has a grimmer origin.

*12*    The Black Death of 590 A.D. left one half of Europe's population dead. The bubonic plague responsible for this holocaust didn't kill its victims without warning. Instead, it signified its presence by rosy rashes, swelling, and, as any medical student can tell you, telltale fits of sneezing. Since death so frequently followed sneezing, people began to say "Bless you"—a final blessing.

*13*    However differently a sneeze is reacted to throughout the world, its cause is generally the same: nasal irritation. Pollens from grass, trees, house dust, and a dozen other sources are basically harmless, but when they irritate the nose your body responds as if they were rampaging predators. In a case of mistaken identity and overkill, you inhale sharply and exhale with explosive force—up to 104 miles per hour.

*14* Pollen is not the only culprit, though. The nose mistakes strong odors, sudden chills, and even bright lights for more dangerous parasites, and it tries to defend itself by banishing the intruders with a sneeze.

*15* In addition to its physical causes, the *New York Times* reports a sneeze can also be brought on by psychological and emotional factors. If a man lunged at you with a knife, fear might make you sneeze. Once he left, your anguish and frustration over losing your valuables could cause you to sneeze again. If you decide to chase the criminal, bring along some tissues—the excitement could give you another sneezing fit.

*16* In each of these cases, sneezing is assisting the nose in reaching equilibrium. Strong emotions can cause your nasal membranes to shrink or expand, and a sneeze brings you back to normal quickly and forcefully.

*17* Occasionally, someone is blessed with an overly active equilibriating mechanism. In 1966 June Clark had a fit in which she sneezed every twelve seconds for 174 days. Before she finally stopped, doctors had tried tranquilizers, narcotics, x-rays, muscle relaxants, shock treatment, and even hypnosis, which almost worked until she sneezed and broke the trance.

*18* Sneezing will probably never give you the trouble it gave June Clark, but the odds are that sooner or later you'll have to sneeze in a social setting. This can be especially uncomfortable given that no one carries a handkerchief any more—at least not in my social circle. Nevertheless, when you're in a crowded room, don't try to stifle or abort your sneeze in the interests of social propriety—you don't want to stop a force going over 100 miles per hour. With the air pressure that builds up from a stifled sneeze, people have been known to get nosebleeds, pop blood vessels, or even go blind.

*19* Instead, open your mouth while you sneeze so your nose doesn't take all your force. Most important, cover your nose. Jane Brody writes in the *New York Times* that "An unimpeded sneeze sends two to five thousand bacteria-filled droplets into the air." With a single sneeze, any one of us could raise this room's bacterial count for the next forty-five minutes. Understandably, every etiquette theorist from Lord Chesterfield and Amy Vanderbilt to Eleanor Roosevelt and Miss Manners advocates being a quick draw with a handkerchief. Failing this, hold the hankie over your nose after the sneeze—it shows good faith.

*20* Whatever the cause and whichever country you're sneezing in, with practice and luck you'll be able to cover your sneeze quickly and effectively. Then you can sit back and relax, waiting for someone to bless you, wish you *gesundheit*, or, if you're in the right place at the right time, appoint you to high military command.

# Nothing to Sneeze At  *by Jeffrey Moran*

## Commentary

*"Nothing To Sneeze At" is a top-notch informative speech. It is interesting, clearly organized, fits well with the guidelines discussed in Chapter 14, and is short enough to be discussed in a single class session. It is also available as part of the videotape supplement to* The Art of Public Speaking. *Here is a synopsis of the speech.*

*Specific Purpose: To inform my audience about the superstitions associated with sneezing, the causes of sneezing, and the proper way to sneeze.*

*Central Idea: Sneezing has long been the subject of superstition, has a number of causes from pollen to strong emotions, and should be done safely and politely.*

*Method of Organization: Topical*

*Introduction: The introduction consists of paragraphs 1-5. After cleverly arousing curiosity and relating the topic to the audience in paragraphs 1-3, the speaker reveals his topic in paragraph 4 and previews the body of the speech in paragraph 5. His tongue-in-cheek approach to establishing credibility in paragraph 4 is consistent with the overall tone of the speech, but some listeners felt it should have been supplemented by a brief reference to the speaker's research.*

*Body: The body is arranged topically and contains three main points, the first of which deals with superstitions that have sprung up around sneezing (paragraphs 6-12). This point is particularly effective because it casts new and interesting light on what would appear to be a mundane subject. The story about Xenophon (paragraphs 7-8) is a model of clear explanation. Rather than assuming the audience knew about Xenophon before the speech, the speaker provides all the necessary details. Yet he does so in a way that does not oversimplify the story for someone already familiar with it.*

*The statement in paragraph 9 that "the Encyclopedia of Occult Sciences, Superstitions, and Folklore devotes eleven tightly-spaced, oversized pages to the subject" of sneezing not only identifies the speaker's source, but reinforces the importance of the subject. The final example of this section—about sneezing and the bubonic plague (paragraph 12)—is highly effective. Notice especially the dramatic impact of the final sentence: "Since death so frequently followed sneezing, people began to say, 'Bless you'—a final blessing."*

*The second main point in the body deals with the causes of sneezing (paragraphs 13-17). While the information about pollen is fairly ordinary, the speaker brings it alive through his use of colorful language. He follows this with the interesting observation that sneezing can also be caused by psychological and emotional factors. Rather than getting overly technical, however, he explains with a hypothetical example that personalizes the subject for his listeners (paragraph 15). The story of June Clark (paragraph 17) ends this section on a strong note.*

*It should also be noted how well the speaker uses connectives here (and throughout the speech) to help listeners keep track of his ideas. At the beginning of paragraph 13 he introduces the second main point with an excellent transition ("However differently a sneeze is reacted to throughout the world, its cause is generally the same: nasal irritation"). He then has a signpost ("Pollen is not the only culprit, though") at the start of paragraph 14. Another transition at the start of paragraph 15 leads listeners from the physical causes of sneezing to its psychological and emotional causes.*

*The third main point explains how to sneeze politely and safely in a social setting (paragraphs 18-19). Its first observation—that stifling a sneeze can cause nosebleeds, popped blood vessels, even blindness (paragraph 18)—is an important bit of information that was new to most members of the audience. Indeed, it was so new that some thought the speaker should have presented a source here. Although the second observation—that a person should cover his or her nose when sneezing (paragraph 19)—is commonplace, it could not have been left out of the speech. Fortunately, rather than just saying, "You should cover your nose when you sneeze," the speaker provides a wealth of colorful information that keeps the audience's attention.*

*Conclusion: The conclusion consists of only two sentences (paragraph 20). The first sentence subtly reminds the audience of the main points discussed in the body. A good question for discussion is whether the speaker should have provided a more detailed summary here. One point of view holds that he did not need such a summary because the body of the speech was sufficiently clear and nontechnical. Another point of view holds that a summary is always helpful in the conclusion of an informative speech because it helps the audience remember what the speaker has said. Whatever one's position on this question, there can be no doubt that the final sentence of the speech brings everything together and concludes on a spirited, upbeat note that gives the speech a sense of psychological unity.*

*It is also important to note that the conclusion—like so much of the speech—is related directly to the audience. One of the strongest features of this speech is that the speaker consistently personalizes his ideas. Rather than talking in abstract terms, he gets the audience involved by employing the terms "you" and "your." Particularly effective examples of this occur in paragraphs 1-3, 10-11, 15, and 18-20. Indeed, by my count, the words "you" or "your" occur sixty times in the full speech. In addition, there are a number of references to "us," "we," and "our"—all of which reinforce the personal tone of the speech.*

# The Heimlich Maneuver

Kelly Marti

---

*1*   Imagine this scene. You are sitting with a friend at dinner. You tell a joke and your friend bursts out laughing. Then, suddenly, he isn't laughing any more, or making any sound at all. His eyes seem about to pop out of his head; his face turns pale and then blue. Finally, he collapses over his plate. You rush to his side, trying to figure out what is wrong. Could it be a heart attack? Then you realize what has happened. Your friend has choked on a piece of food that "went down the wrong way." You start to pound him on the back, try to help in any way you can. But it is too late. Five minutes have passed, and your friend is dead.

*2*   This story is imaginary, but it could be real. Incidents like this one happen every day—in restaurants, in the home, in dormitory cafeterias. According to a report from the National Safety Council, choking causes 3,900 deaths per year, which makes choking the sixth leading cause of accidental death in the United States. This statistic is even more tragic because 95 percent of these deaths could be prevented—more than 3,700 lives could be saved each year—if someone near the choking victim knew of a simple technique called the Heimlich maneuver.

*3*   The Heimlich maneuver was developed by Dr. Henry Heimlich, a professor of clinical sciences at Xavier University in Cincinnati, and it is so easy to learn that even a child can perform it. I learned the maneuver from my mother, who is a nurse, and I have read several articles about it. Today I would like to teach it to you.

*4*   The effectiveness of the Heimlich maneuver depends on two factors—knowing the symptoms of a choking victim, and knowing how to perform the maneuver to save the victim. First I will explain the symptoms. Then I will demonstrate the maneuver.

*5*   If you are to use the Heimlich maneuver, you must be able to recognize when a person has a piece of food or some other object caught in the windpipe. You may be surprised to know that until Dr. Heimlich offered a clear list of symptoms, not even doctors were sure how to diagnose a choking victim. There is a famous story of a medical convention in Washington, D.C., at which a large group of doctors had gathered for a dinner meeting. All at once a member of the group began to choke on a piece of food. A hundred doctors sat by helplessly while the man choked to death, because the doctors didn't know what was wrong and didn't know what to do.

6     Fortunately, Dr. Heimlich has since provided a reliable list of symptoms. First, the choking victim is unable to breathe or to speak. Then, because not enough oxygen is reaching the brain, the victim becomes pale, turns blue, and falls unconscious. Of these symptoms, the most important is the victim's inability to speak. There are other conditions that might cause someone to have difficulty breathing and to pass out—a heart attack, for example. But when a conscious person cannot speak—or make any utterance whatever—it is usually because something is lodged in the air passage. In most cases, blockage of the airway is so complete that the choking victim is not able to make any sound at all.

7     It is important that you, as an observer, learn to recognize these symptoms and to act quickly. There is no time to waste. Within about four minutes the victim will suffer permanent brain damage. Within about five minutes the victim will be dead. Four to five minutes—that is just a minute or so longer than the amount of time that has passed since I began this speech.

8     Now that you know how to recognize when a person has something caught in the air passage, you are ready to apply the Heimlich maneuver. When applied properly, it is the most effective way to save the life of a choking victim. The principle behind the maneuver is quite simple. Even when a foreign object is lodged in the windpipe, there is still enough air left in the lungs to dislodge the object if the air is forced upward suddenly. The purpose of the Heimlich maneuver is to create a strong enough burst of air from the lungs to free whatever is stuck in the windpipe.

9     You can apply the maneuver in any of three positions—while a victim is standing, sitting, or lying on the floor. Let me demonstrate with each position.

10     If possible, hold the victim up in a standing position to perform the Heimlich maneuver. This is the most effective way to dislodge whatever is caught in the air passage. Stand behind the victim and put both your arms around his waist. Let his head, arms, and upper torso hang forward. Make a fist with one hand and place it thumb side in against the victim's abdomen—slightly above the navel but below the rib cage. Then cover the first with your other hand and press into the abdomen with a quick upward thrust, bending your arms at the elbows. [Here the speaker gently demonstrated the procedure on a volunteer.] Repeat this action as many times as necessary until the food pops out.

11     If the victim is sitting down and you cannot get him up, kneel behind him, put your arms around both him and the chair, and perform the maneuver in the

same way. [Demonstration by the speaker.] Again, continue the upward thrusts until the food pops out.

12    If the victim is already prostrate and you cannot get him up, you may have to perform the Heimlich maneuver with the victim lying down. In this event, lay the person flat on his back, with his face turned upward (not to the side). Kneel straddling the victim. Do not try to perform the maneuver from the side, because you could rupture the victim's liver or spleen. Place the heel of one hand against the choking victim's abdomen, above the navel but below the ribs. Put your other hand on top of the first one and press into the victim's abdomen with a quick upward thrust. [Demonstration by the speaker.]

13    As you can see, the Heimlich maneuver is easy to learn and easy to perform. Thousands of people, from children to senior citizens, have saved lives by using it. So if you are ever in a situation like the one I described at the start of this speech, remember what you have heard today: If your dinner companion suddenly can neither breathe nor speak, he or she has a foreign object stuck in the air passage. By applying the Heimlich maneuver, you can expel the object and save your companion's life.

## The Heimlich Maneuver  *by Kelly Marti*

## Commentary

Presented in a beginning speech class at the University of Wisconsin-Madison, "The Heimlich Maneuver" illustrates many of the principles of informative speaking discussed in Chapter 14. Students should pay special attention to how crisply the speech is organized, how the speaker adapts the topic directly to her audience, how she clarifies her ideas with concrete language and vivid description, and how she uses examples to personalize the speech and give it dramatic impact. Here is a synopsis of the speech.

*Specific Purpose:*  To inform my audience how to perform the Heimlich maneuver.

*Central Idea:*  The effectiveness of the Heimlich maneuver depends on two factors—knowing the symptoms of a choking victim and knowing how to perform the maneuver to save the victim.

*Method of Organization:*  Topical

*Introduction:*  The introduction is superb and consists of paragraphs 1-4. Vivid, dramatic, and realistic in its details, the hypothetical example in paragraph 1 relates the topic directly to the audience and gets them involved in the speech. In paragraph 2 the speaker uses statistics to show that the example is not far-fetched and that thousands of lives can be saved each year if people know how to perform the Heimlich maneuver. Paragraph 3 establishes the speaker's credibility, while paragraph 4 states the central idea and previews the main points to be discussed in the body.

*Body:*  The body of the speech develops two main points, the first of which begins in paragraph 5 and explains the symptoms of a choking victim. The story of the medical convention in paragraph 5 dramatically illustrates the importance of being able to recognize when a person has a piece of food or some other object caught in the windpipe. Here, as elsewhere, the speaker is adept at working human interest factors into her speech. Paragraph 6 explains the key symptom of a choking victim—the inability to produce sound—while paragraph 7 emphasizes the importance of acting quickly to remove the obstruction. The speaker does an excellent job in paragraph 7 of relating "four or five minutes"—the amount of time it takes a choking victim to suffer permanent brain damage—to the immediate experience of her audience.

A transition at the beginning of paragraph 8 moves the speaker into her second main point, in which she explains how to apply the Heimlich *maneuver. After stating the principle behind the maneuver (paragraph 8), the speaker provides an excellent internal preview of the three positions in which the maneuver can be performed (paragraph 9). She then explains how to perform the maneuver when the victim is in a standing position (paragraph 10), when the victim is sitting (paragraph 11), and when the victim in lying down (paragraph 12). In each case the speaker demonstrates the steps of the Heimlich maneuver on a volunteer from the class. She had arranged for the volunteer well ahead of time, and the volunteer participated in the speaker's final practice session. As a result, the volunteer knew exactly what to expect, and the speaker could get the timing of her demonstration just right.*

*Two other aspects of paragraphs 10-12 deserve mention. First, even though the speaker demonstrates the Heimlich maneuver, she also provides a clear step-by-step verbal explanation of it. This is important because a visual aid is usually no more effective than the quality of the explanation that accompanies it. Second, the speaker adopts a very personal tone throughout her demonstration of the Heimlich maneuver. Rather than talking about how an abstract "someone" might perform the maneuver, she talks in terms of "you." This strengthens the speaker's rapport with her listeners and helps keep them interested.*

*Conclusion:  The conclusion, which consists of paragraph 13, is short and to the point. By referring to the introduction, the speaker again relates the topic directly to her audience, cues listeners that the speech is nearing an end, and enhances the unity of the entire speech. The final sentences reinforce the central idea and summarize the main points of the speech.*

# Seatbelts: A Habit That Could Save Your Life

Andrew Kinney

*1*     As you may have noticed, I was on crutches for two months this semester. I had already been on crutches for three months before that, and last year I was on them for seven months. You see, I've had hip surgery three times in the last year and a half.

*2*     It all started when I experienced my first serious car accident. I swerved off the road to avoid a head-on collision with another car. My car rolled over and struck a large tree. I was not wearing a seatbelt. In the process of being thrown back and forth across the car, I chipped a tooth, cut the back of my head, broke my hip, and cracked three ribs, which resulted in a punctured lung and massive internal bleeding. When they got me to the hospital, my blood pressure was down from a normal 120-over-70 to 50-over-30 as a result of all the internal and external bleeding and as a result of shock. The doctors waited more than twenty-four hours to do surgery to repair my hip because they didn't think I was going to survive all of my other injuries.

*3*     Somehow I survived, and now a year and a half later I am finally walking normally, though I will be walking around for the rest of my life with a piece of metal this long in my hip, and I'm not allowed to do any athletic activities that require running.

*4*     All that pain and suffering could have been avoided if only I had been in the habit of wearing a seatbelt. But I wasn't in that habit, and I know from my class survey that 40 percent of you do not usually wear a seatbelt, and 75 percent of you do not always wear one. Yet the National Highway Traffic Safety Administration tells us that each person stands a one-in-three chance of being in a serious car accident at some time in his or her life. So we can possibly predict that one-third of you will be in a serious accident at some point. And it may sound corny, but I mean it, so I'm going to say it—I don't want what happened to me to happen to any of you.

*5*     So I want to talk to you about wearing seatbelts. First I'm going to tell you to what extent you will be protected by wearing a seatbelt. Then I'm going to look at some of the reasons why people don't wear seatbelts and point out the problems with those reasons. And after I've given you the evidence, I am going to ask you all to make a habit of wearing seatbelts.

6    So first, to what extent will you be protected by wearing a seatbelt? Well, the Wisconsin Department of Transportation says if you are in an accident and are not wearing a seatbelt, you are four times more likely to be killed than if you are wearing one. Furthermore, consider this—there are 35,000 deaths each year in the United States as a result of traffic accidents. The National Highway Traffic Safety Administration, the National Child Passenger Safety Association, and the Wisconsin Department of Transportation all estimate that traffic deaths would decrease from 35,000 to around 17,000 annually if everyone wore seatbelts.

7    So our most knowledgeable and reliable sources of information on seatbelts have all come to the same conclusion—that we would cut traffic deaths in half if everyone wore seatbelts, and that we would save 18,000 lives each year. Now let me put that number into perspective—18,000 people, or the equivalent of more than half the undergraduates on this campus, are needlessly killed every year because they do not wear seatbelts.

8    But why is this true? What does a seatbelt do to protect you? Well, in a head-on collision, which is usually the worst type, your body will be thrown forward into the steering wheel, into the dashboard, or through the windshield with incredible force. Imagine falling headfirst from the top of a three-story building. The force with which you would land on the ground is equal to the force with which you would be thrown forward in only a 30 mile-per-hour collision. But a seatbelt will absorb that force and prevent you from slamming into the interior of the car.

9    In my own experience there is little doubt that a seatbelt would have minimized my injuries. I looked at pictures of the car after my accident. The car was totaled, and it was an ugly mess, but the two front seats and the entire driving compartment were completely intact. I have to believe that if I had been strapped into that seat, I would have walked away from my accident with minor bruises. But remember I used the word "if"—if I had worn a safety belt.

10    So the evidence is strongly in favor of wearing seatbelts. That brings me to the next question—why don't people wear seatbelts?

11    People often say that in an accident they would rather be thrown free of the car, or at least be able to get out of the car in case of fire or submersion in water. Well, according to the Wisconsin Department of Transportation, accidents involving fire and submersion make up less than one out of every 200 auto accidents. Furthermore, you are actually more likely to be able to get out of the car if you are wearing a seatbelt, because you are more likely to be conscious and not seriously injured. And with regard to being thrown free of the car, the Wisconsin Department of Transportation says you are 25 times more likely to be killed if you are thrown

out of the car, because you can be thrown onto hard pavement, thrown into stationary objects, or struck by other cars. Clearly you are safer being strapped in than being thrown around.

*12* The other major reason why people don't wear seatbelts is that seatbelts are uncomfortable and restrict movement. Now, if this is your reason for not wearing a seatbelt, let me ask you to do something right now. Imagine in your mind a two-sided scale. On one side of the scale, put the value that you place on being completely comfortable while driving. And on the other side of the scale, put the value that you place on your life and your health. Which side is heavier? If your life and your health mean more to you than a little bit of extra comfort while driving, then it only makes sense to wear a seatbelt.

*13* So I'm here today to ask all of you to make a habit of wearing seatbelts. The statistics are simple—chances are that about one-third of you will be in a serious auto accident at some time in your life. It could happen fifty years from now, and it could happen tomorrow. And if you are in an accident, you are four times more likely to be killed if you are not wearing a seatbelt than if you are wearing one.

*14* So if you think you are safer not wearing a seatbelt, you're betting against heavy odds. And if you still won't wear a seatbelt, because a seatbelt is uncomfortable and inconvenient, then you're placing your momentary comfort ahead of your life and your health. So tell yourself that you are going to make a habit of wearing seatbelts. Then do it.

*15* There is nothing I can do about my accident now, and I don't plan to go around for the rest of my life kicking myself because I didn't wear a seatbelt that day. What's important is that I learned something from the experience. I've made a habit of wearing seatbelts when I ride in a car, and I'm hoping that each of you will do the same if you haven't already.

*16* I will never be able to play basketball or go downhill skiing again, but at least I'm here and at least I can walk. I was a lot luckier than 35,000 other Americans that year.

# Seatbelts: A Habit That Could Save Your Life   *by Andrew Kinney*

## Commentary

*Presented in an introductory public speaking class at the University of Wisconsin-Madison, "Seatbelts: A Habit That Could Save Your Life" is an outstanding persuasive speech on a question of policy. Because this speech is also available on the videotape supplement to* The Art of Public Speaking, *it works very well for class discussion. As students view the speech, have them pay special attention to how the speaker enhances his credibility and good will by drawing on his personal experience. Also have them keep an eye out for how the speaker repeatedly relates the topic to his listeners and draws them into the speech. Finally, direct your students' attention to how clearly the speech is organized and to how the speaker uses connectives to help his audience keep track of his ideas. Here is a synopsis of the speech.*

*Specific Purpose: To persuade my audience to use seatbelts every time they drive or ride in an automobile.*

*Central Idea: Because seatbelts are proven lifesavers and there are no good reasons not to wear seatbelts, everyone should get in the habit of wearing seatbelts whenever they drive or ride in an automobile.*

*Method of Organization:  Topical*

*Introduction:  The introduction consists of paragraphs 1-5 and does a superb job of fulfilling the functions of a speech introduction. Paragraphs 1-3 gain attention with a dramatic story based on the speaker's personal experience. The story is especially effective because of its specific details about the speaker's injuries and how close he came to dying. In contrast, imagine if the speaker had merely said, "A year and a half ago I was in a serious automobile accident." This would not have had nearly the same impact. Nor would it have done as much to establish the speaker's credibility and good will.*

*In paragraph 4 the speaker moves from his opening story to reveal the topic of his speech and to relate it directly to his audience. The final sentence of this paragraph—in which the speaker says, "I don't want what happened to me to happen to any of you"—had a strong emotional impact when delivered in class. In paragraph 5 the speaker ends his introduction by previewing the main points to be discussed in the body. Although it is longer than usual, the introduction of this speech is extremely effective in preparing the audience for the persuasive appeals that follow.*

*Body:* The body of the speech runs from paragraph 6 through paragraph 14 and has three main points. The first main point, developed in paragraphs 6-9, is that seatbelts are a proven way to reduce the chances of injury and death in an automobile accident. In paragraph 6 the speaker presents statistics to show that traffic deaths in the U.S. would be reduced from 35,000 per year to 17,000 per year if everyone wore seatbelts. In paragraph 7 he adroitly translates those statistics into terms that relate directly to his audience.

The speaker continues with his first main point in paragraph 8 by explaining why seatbelts are so valuable in helping to prevent injuries. He compares the force of a 30-mile-per-hour collision to falling headfirst from a three-story building. In paragraph 9 he draws on his own experience to reinforce his point about the value of wearing a seatbelt. The final sentence of this paragraph is especially effective.

After a transition in paragraph 10, the speaker moves into his second main point, which consists of paragraphs 11-12. These paragraphs are extremely important, for they answer the audience's two major objections to wearing seatbelts. Had the speaker ignored these objections, his speech would have been much less effective. In paragraph 11 he supports his position with statistics from the Wisconsin Department of Transportation. While this would not have been the best source of statistics for a speaker in another state, it was an excellent source for this speech, which was presented to a class at the University of Wisconsin.

In paragraph 12 the speaker deals with the fact that many people find seatbelts uncomfortable by asking his audience to imagine a two-sided scale on which they weigh the value of personal comfort versus their lives and health. Which do you value more, he asks, your life and health or "a little bit of extra comfort"? If you value your life and health more, he notes, it only makes sense to wear a seatbelt.

Paragraphs 13-14 develop the speaker's third main point, in which he calls for the audience to make a habit of wearing seatbelts. He begins the point in paragraph 13 by reiterating key statistics from earlier in the speech. This is an excellent technique. Rather than overwhelming listeners with a barrage of figures, the speaker uses a few well-chosen statistics to drive home his message. In paragraph 14 the speaker makes a direct call for action. Here, as elsewhere, his appeal is enhanced by his clear, forceful language.

It is also important to note that the speaker's appeal throughout the body of the speech is strengthened by his use of the words "you" and "your" to relate the topic directly to his listeners. In addition to increasing audience involvement, this gives the speech a strong conversational quality. As you will observe if you view the speech on videotape, the *speaker comes across as talking with the audience, not at them. This comes both from his personal tone and from his use of pauses, vocal variety, and eye contact to communicate directly with his listeners.*

*Conclusion: The speaker begins his conclusion in paragraph 15 by referring to the accident he had discussed in the introduction and by reiterating his call for action. Paragraph 16 ends the speech on a strong emotional note. The speaker's sincerity here and throughout the speech did much to strengthen his credibility and persuasiveness.*

# Drinking and Boating: A Deadly Combination

Sheila Mir

*1*     The proud owner of a splashy new sixteen-foot speedboat cruised up to a waterfront nightclub on Lake Pontchartrain in Louisiana for a drink, where he met a couple and invited them for a spin around the lake. The passengers will never forget the ride; the driver will never remember. He died when his boat smashed into the seawall. Investigators of the accident concluded that alcohol was the cause.

*2*     Drinking and boating is a deadly combination—a deadly combination that may affect you. Last summer I spent many afternoons on the lakes and beaches here in Madison, and I couldn't believe the number of drunk boat drivers I saw. As I researched this speech, I became more and more convinced that it is inconsistent for our society to be so obsessed with drinking and driving in automobiles and yet so willing to view boating and drinking as "recreational."

*3*     Today I would like to discuss this issue with you. First, I will show you that drinking and boating is a serious problem. Second, I'll explore the causes of this problem. And third, I will propose a solution. Let's start with the problem.

*4*     Recreational boating and alcohol-related accidents is a larger and more serious problem than we realize. The kind of tragedy I told you about in my introduction is repeated time and again each year in every part of the country. Just last summer, five people were killed in a collision between two speedboats on Fox Lake in Illinois. Alcohol was the cause. In another state, two men and a woman were heading home at 9 P.M. after consuming a considerable amount of beer. They didn't have the lights of their small boat turned on, and they collided with a much larger, lighted boat. The two men were killed instantly and the woman's body was found floating in the water the next day. Alcohol, again, was the cause.

*5*     Statistics show that these are not atypical examples. The National Safety Council reports that over 1,200 Americans died while pleasure boating last year. According to the United States Department of Transportation, that ranks boating second only to car crashes among transportation fatalities. Here in Wisconsin, a study by the State Center for Health Statistics found that there were 813 boating accidents between 1981 and 1985. These accidents killed 133 people, or an average of 27 per year. The United States Coast Guard estimates that half of the boating accidents in the U.S. are alcohol-related, while the National Transportation Safety Board concludes that alcohol may be a factor in 80 percent of boating fatalities.

6    Why is this such a problem? Why do we have so many alcohol-related boating accidents? The two main causes are a lack of education and inconsistency in the laws.

7    By a lack of education I refer to the fact that people don't understand that alcohol affects their bodies faster when they drink on water than when they drink at home or in a bar. The reason for this is a phenomenon known as "boater's hypnosis." According to a report by the National Transportation Safety Board, boater's hypnosis develops after four hours or more, when you are exposed to sun, wind, glare, noise, and vibration while on the water. It significantly slows your reactions—much as alcohol does. When you add alcohol, it greatly intensifies the effect of boater's hypnosis.

8    According to William Gossard, a national safety board official in Washington, D.C., car drivers are considered legally drunk with a blood-alcohol concentration of .10 percent or greater. But because of boater's hypnosis, on water a level as low as .035 percent can affect a person's ability to operate a boat. In other words, if you feel yourself losing control after drinking three cans of beer on land, you will feel yourself losing control after drinking one can of beer on water.

9    In addition to a lack of education about boater's hypnosis, the problem of drinking and boating is caused by two glaring legal inconsistencies. The first has to do with the blood-alcohol concentration level. In Wisconsin, as in most states, you are not supposed to operate a motorboat with a blood-alcohol concentration of .10 percent or more. This is the same blood-alcohol concentration used to determine drunkenness while driving a car. So the laws says, in essence, that you are capable of driving a boat safely until you have reached a blood-alcohol concentration of .10 percent. Yet as I stated earlier, due to boater's hypnosis, your ability to operate a boat can be impaired at a level as low as .035 percent. In reality, a boater may be drunk long before the police can pronounce him or her as legally drunk.

10    The second inconsistency in the laws is that it is legal to drink while driving a boat. We all know it is illegal to drink while driving a car. Why should it be legal to drink while driving a boat—especially since alcohol affects the body faster on water than on land? Just because lakes and rivers don't contain stop signs, speed limits, and center lines, it should not be legal to drink and drive on the water. After all, as *Newsweek* explains, some power boats have top speeds of up to 90 miles per hour and, unlike cars, no boat has brakes.

11    As you can see, the combination of booze and boats is a serious problem—serious because there is a lack of education about boater's hypnosis and

because there are inconsistencies in our laws about drinking and boating. So what can we do? How can we solve the problem?

*12* First, there should be mandatory boat safety education. In Wisconsin, children between the ages of ten and twelve are required to take a boat safety class if they want to operate a boat. If someone is convicted of driving drunk on the water, they too must take a boat safety class. But according to former state conservation warden Robert Arends, these are the only people who have to take a boat safety class. In Arends' view, however, all boaters should have to take a safety class. And I agree. It would make boaters aware of safety procedures and hazards, and it would give special attention to such topics as boater's hypnosis and the dangers of drinking while on the water.

*13* Second, we need some changes in our laws. To begin with, since alcohol affects the body faster on water than on land, the blood-alcohol concentration allowed for boaters should be lowered. No one should be allowed to operate a motorboat with a blood-alcohol concentration of greater than .035 percent. In addition, it should be illegal to drink while driving a boat just as it is illegal to drink while driving a car. According to Captain Frank Wood of the Maryland Department of Water Safety, this would go a long way toward reducing the problem of drunken boat drivers.

*14* Educating everyone and changing the laws will help solve this serious problem. But one factor is missing from our solution. That factor is you! You can make a difference in safer boating here in Wisconsin. You can write to either State Senator Fred Risser or State Assemblyman Spencer Black at the State Capitol, as I have. Let them know you want the laws changed so we can have safer waters here in Wisconsin. Then go one step further. If you are involved in any type of water sports, take a boat safety class. If you drive a motorboat, please don't drink—for your safety as well as for the safety of others.

*15* According to State Senator Lynn Adelman, the drunken boater is the "single biggest problem in boating safety today. Even when he does not kill or maim, the drunken boater detracts from everyone else's enjoyment of public waters." As I've tried to show you today, drinking and boating is a deadly combination from Louisiana to Wisconsin and everywhere in between.

*16* You are now aware of this problem, of its causes, and of a solution. Show that you are concerned, not only by writing to the state capitol but also in your actions. And this summer, when the sun is just a little too hot and you feel like cooling off in the lake for a while, remember to be careful. Because just when you thought it was safe to go back in the water, it may not be!

# Drinking and Boating: A Deadly Combination   *by Sheila Mir*

## Commentary

*"Drinking and Boating: A Deadly Combination" is an outstanding persuasive speech on a question of policy. Thoroughly researched and superbly organized, it illustrates many of the methods of persuasion discussed in Chapter 15 and provides an instructive model for students who are preparing their own persuasive speeches. Here is a synopsis of the speech.*

*Specific Purpose:  To persuade my audience that mandatory boat education and tougher laws curbing drinking and boating should be enacted to help reduce the problem of boating accidents.*

*Central Idea:  Drinking and boating is a deadly combination whose causes can best be dealt with by mandatory boat education and tougher laws to combat drunken boaters.*

*Method of Organization:   Problem-cause-solution*

*Introduction:  The introduction consists of paragraphs 1-3. In paragraph 1 the speaker uses a dramatic example to gain attention. In paragraph 2 she states the topic, relates it to the audience, and establishes her credibility. In paragraph 3 she provides an extremely clear preview of the body of the speech. All in all, this is an excellent introduction.*

*Body:  The body of the speech has three main points, the first of which deals with the issue of need by demonstrating that drinking and boating is a serious national problem (paragraphs 4-5). The speaker begins with two extended examples of alcohol-related boating deaths. Although the examples are clear, vivid, and directly relevant to the speaker's point, the second example would have been more effective if the speaker had identified exactly where it took place rather than just stating it happened "in another state."*

*In paragraph 5 the speaker presents evidence to show that the examples in paragraph 4 are not atypical. She provides a wealth of statistics from highly credible sources showing that over 1,200 Americans died in boating accidents last year, that such accidents are the second leading cause of transportation fatalities in the United States, that one half of the boating accidents in the U.S. are caused by alcohol, and that alcohol may be a factor in up to 80 percent of boating fatalities. Because the speech was delivered at the University of Wisconsin, the speaker also included statistics about the problem of drinking and boating in that state. This helped relate the subject directly to her audience.*

*Paragraph 6 provides an excellent preview of the second main point, which is developed in paragraphs 7-10. In this main point the speaker argues that the problem of drinking and boating has two major causes. The first is that people do not realize that alcohol affects their judgment and reactions more quickly on the water than on land (paragraphs 7-8). Although the discussion of boater's hypnosis could easily have gotten too technical, the speaker explains it clearly and, in the last sentence of paragraph 8, does a nice job of translating her statistics about blood-alcohol percentages into terms that relate directly to her audience.*

*It is also worth noting that when the speech was delivered in class, the speaker used a simple visual aid throughout paragraphs 8 and 9 so her listeners could see the figures .10 and .035. Even though the figures are not complicated, the phrases "point one zero" and "point zero three five," which is how the statistics sound when they are spoken, do not register sharply upon the mind. By printing the figures on a visual aid, the speaker made them much easier to grasp.*

*In paragraphs 9-10 the speaker deals with the second cause of the problem—a lack of consistency between the laws governing drinking and driving and those controlling drinking and boating. The speaker points to two such inconsistencies, the first of which is using the same blood-alcohol level to measure drunkenness in boaters as in drivers (paragraph 9). Drawing upon her explanation of boater's hypnosis in paragraph 8, she points out that this means boaters may be drunk long before the authorities can do anything about it. The second inconsistency in the laws is that it is legal to drink while operating a speed boat (paragraph 10). Reasoning from analogy, the speaker argues that boating and driving are similar enough that it does not make sense to allow boaters to drink while prohibiting drivers from drinking. The citation from Newsweek at the end of paragraph 10 is particularly effective.*

*An excellent internal summary and transition in paragraph 11 moves from the causes of the problem to the solution. The speaker's plan is two-fold. First, she calls for mandatory boat safety education classes for everyone who wants to get a boating license (paragraph 12). Second, she advocates laws that would make it illegal to drink while operating a motorboat and that would prohibit people from operating a boat when their blood-alcohol concentration exceeds .035 percent (paragraph 13). As should be the case in a problem-cause-solution speech, the plan deals directly with what the speaker had earlier identified as the causes of the problem.*

*As the speaker presents each part of her plan, she uses testimony to demonstrate its practicality. In paragraph 12 she cites Robert Arends, a former state conservation warden, on the value of boat safety classes. In paragraph 13 she cites Captain Frank Wood of the Maryland*

Department of Water Safety on the benefits of reducing the permissible blood-alcohol concentration for boaters.

The speaker ends her solution by calling for action from the audience (paragraph 14). Although a call for action is often reserved for the conclusion, it works very well here. Notice especially the statement: "Educating everyone and changing the laws will help solve this serious problem. But one factor is missing from our solution. That factor is you! You can make a difference in safer boating here in Wisconsin." By creating curiosity about the missing factor and then by relating directly to her audience, the speaker keeps attention at a high level. She also does a good job of specifying exactly what steps she wants her listeners to take.

Conclusion:  The conclusion consists of paragraphs 15-16. After a quotation that reinforces the seriousness of drinking and boating, the speaker summarizes her main point and repeats her call for action. The closing sentence relates the topic once again to the audience and ends the speech on a strong note.

# Warning: Household Chemicals

Susan Zaeske

---

*1*      In Portland, Maine, Halloween pranksters splattered eggs on the windows of a 68-year-old woman's house. In the morning, she decided to clean the windows using a combination of household ammonia and chlorine bleach. And the combination worked well. When she took the pail inside, however, she was overcome by toxic fumes. The woman's niece tried to revive her, but she, too, was overcome. Both women died.

*2*      This tragic incident, far from hypothetical, illustrates a threat that we face intimately every day—household chemicals. According to Lance Wallace, from the Harvard School of Public Health, "Your home may be more of a toxic waste hazard than Love Canal or a chemical company nearby."

*3*      I found this statement very surprising because I thought, like many of you, that the government regulates household chemicals. That's not true. The truth is that there is no law requiring the testing of a household product before it hits the market. The Food and Drug Administration merely requires that manufacturers clearly label their products and that they designate chemicals which have been called harmful. The result, as one scientist stated in *The Household Pollutants Guide*, is that "The consumer becomes a test animal in the laboratory of the home."

*4*      Let's take a cleaning tour through your house or apartment and discover some of the chemicals that may harm you in your home. Before we start, we'll stop at the supply cabinet to get the products we need. Then we'll clean the bathroom and the kitchen, where we will encounter caustic chemicals. Then we'll move into the living room, where we will encounter solvents. And finally we'll clean the bedroom, where we will get a dose of aerosols. When we're finished with the dirty work, I'll share with you some solutions to make your cleaning routine safer and cheaper.

*5*      The first stop in our cleaning tour is to get supplies. According to James Woods, senior scientist at Honeywell Corporation, if you're like most Americans, your home contains forty-five aerosol cans, each with fifteen different chemical compounds. Add to this two dozen nonaerosol containers, a few insect killers, paint thinners, and ink. In all, Woods says, there are more than 50,000 chemicals in the average home.

6     Now that you have the products you need, we'll start with our cleaning tour. Like it or not, most of us have had to clean the bathroom. Not only is this task unpleasant, it may also be dangerous because the majority of chemicals that you use to clean your bathroom are caustic.

7     Well, the drain is clogged, but don't despair—you're armed with Crystal Drano. Hopefully, you won't be harmed like the more than 10,000 people who are harmed in this country every year using drain cleaners or toilet cleaners. According to *Consumer Reports* magazine, when they tested products in May of last year, one individual who was doing the testing suffered lingering throat irritation when he inhaled Drano and other products like it, even though he followed the manufacturers' instructions exactly. Another product that was tested, Instant Plumber, which is simply diluted sulfuric acid, ate through its container and destroyed its instructions. *Consumer Reports* warns that when chemicals fail, consumers are often tempted to clean the drain by using a plunger. But this is dangerous because the caustic chemicals can splash in your face and burn your skin or blind you.

8     You have finished with the bathroom, and now you head for the kitchen to do the worst task imaginable—cleaning the oven. I had to do the same after a dinner party I had on New Year's Eve. And although I was extremely careful—using protective gloves and glasses, and opting for brush-on Eazy-Off rather than the aerosol spray—some of the substance managed to splash on my face, close to my eye, painfully burning my skin. And I am not alone, because the Center for Science in the Public Interest warns that 3,000 people are harmed every year using oven cleaners. Aerosol oven cleaners are even worse because they disperse droplets of the caustic chemical which may land on your skin or be inhaled into your lungs. Lung tissue doesn't regenerate like skin tissue, so you could suffer long-term harm.

9     Now that we know the dangers of household caustics, let's move to the living room, where we will encounter solvents. Since advertising tells us that homes must be dust-free, you grab the Endust and begin dustbusting. Well, this product is a solvent. Solvents put oils and waxes into solution so that after application they evaporate, leaving a protective coating on your furniture. Solvents such as Endust contain petroleum distillates, which can cause skin irritation; naptha, which can induce cardiac arrest; and oil of cedarwood, a nervous stimulant. In fact, the Center for Science in the Public Interest reports that in high concentrations oil of cedarwood has been used to induce abortions.

10     Your final task is to clean the bedroom. You walk to your roommate's side of the room and a pungent odor emanates from the hamper. You grab the Lysol to disinfect a pile of mildewy socks. Well, if you've ever used Lysol, you may guess that it is dangerous. Lysol contains creosol, which has been found to be the tumor-promoting agent in tobacco smoke. As long ago as 1975, the Mitre Corporation reported that absorbing enough creosol through the skin has been

found to cause digestive disturbances, nervous disorders with faintness, mental changes, and skin eruptions.

*11* Now, you may be saying to yourself, the danger of household chemicals is exaggerated. If I eat five pounds of almonds every day, I'll get arsenic poisoning. After all, none of us sniffs Lysol or sprays it on our skin, or actually drinks Drano. But the point is that *Consumer Reports, The Household Pollutants Guide*, and *Science News* have all shown that these products can be dangerous even when you follow the manufacturers' instructions.

*12* Well, the house is clean, so you're ready to go. You step outside onto the street, away from your house or apartment, which has now become a toxic waste dump, and glance at a chemical company nearby. Ironically, according to Lance Wallace, the Harvard scientist I quoted earlier, the air outside is probably safer than that in your house.

*13* It doesn't have to be this way, though. There are solutions you can take to make household chemicals—and your cleaning routine—much safer. Of course, you could get a self-cleaning oven and a maid. But for us more practical folks, Albert Fritsch from the Center for Science in the Public Interest states, "Only an alert and informed citizenry can bring about the proper sharing of responsibility for the safe use of chemicals."

*14* As we saw earlier, the government does not test household products, so you must take the initiative to make your house safe. Ask yourself, do I really need specialized cleaners, or will a few simple chemicals do? I think you'll agree that many household special cleaners are unnecessary. I can suggest a few alternatives you can use instead of household cleaners, and after my speech I will give you a fact sheet that outlines how you can make some of these alternatives.

*15* For example, never again will I use Eazy-Off to clean the oven. Instead, I will place one-fourth cup of household ammonia in the oven overnight to loosen the debris. Then in the morning, I will scrub the oven with baking soda. Baking soda can also be used instead of abrasive scouring powders like Ajax. It's less dangerous for your eyes and your skin, it works just as well, and it feels better on the wallet, too. Look at the fact sheet, and you'll find ways to make glass cleaners, furniture polish, air fresheners, and more.

*16* But if you don't want to use these alternatives, at least use common sense. The Food and Drug Administration has published several pamphlets which will tell you how to use chemicals more safely in your home. Some of their recommendations are that you should have proper ventilation when you're using chemicals; always read the label; wear protective gloves, glasses, and sometimes face masks; keep dangerous products away from children; and don't pour chemicals down the drain. Avoid wearing soft contact lenses while you're cleaning because they can absorb

376 Speeches for Analysis and Discussion

chemical fumes and hold them close to your eyes until the contacts are removed. Also be especially careful in combining chemicals. In fact, avoid it completely because such chemicals as bleach and ammonia can emit toxic gases when they are combined.

*17* We've seen, then, that although household products are not tested by the government, they are dangerous. The threat is not an outside force, something abstract, but the "friendly" products you invite into your home. I urge you to use simple, inexpensive alternative products, and to use common sense. Careless use of household chemicals is one case in which cleanliness may put you next to godliness before your time.

*18* The woman in Portland, Maine, was no doubt frightened by the spooks that lurked in the night, but ironically it was not the spooks that killed her, but the supposedly friendly chemicals she invited into her home.

# Warning: Household Chemicals *by Susan Zaeske*

## Commentary

*"Warning: Household Chemicals" was presented in a public speaking class by Susan Zaeske, a student at the University of Wisconsin-Madison. A persuasive speech on a question of policy, it is particularly interesting for both the effectiveness of, and the occasional flaws in, its use of supporting materials. Below is a synopsis of the speech, including special discussion of its use of examples, statistics, and testimony.*

*Specific Purpose:   To persuade my audience to take action to protect themselves against the possible dangers of household chemicals.*

*Central Idea:   Because many household products can be dangerous even when used according to manufacturers' directions, consumers should look for alternatives to potentially dangerous products and should exercise common sense whenever using household chemicals.*

*Method of Organization:   Problem-Solution*

*Introduction:   The introduction consists of paragraphs 1-4. After gaining attention with a dramatic story, the speaker states her topic and uses a quotation to indicate its significance. In paragraph 3 she corrects a common misconception by explaining that the Food and Drug Administration does not test household products before they hit the market. A clear preview statement in paragraph 4 tells the audience what to listen for and provides an effective lead-in to the body of the speech.*

*Body:   The body contains two main points, the first of which deals with the problem of household chemicals. This point is organized around a hypothetical cleaning tour that begins with a stop for supplies (paragraph 5) and then proceeds through the bathroom (paragraphs 6-7), the kitchen (paragraph 8), the living room (paragraph 9), and the bedroom (paragraph 10). In each room the speaker demonstrates the potential dangers of a common household cleaning product. This is a very effective way to bring the topic alive and is much more interesting than a dry recitation of facts about the products. The speaker is also adept at personalizing the problem by putting the audience into the speech. Notice that she takes a cleaning tour of "your house or apartment" and repeatedly refers to "you" throughout the speech.*

*After completing her "cleaning tour," the speaker answers a potential objection to her position (paragraph 11) and reemphasizes the seriousness of the problem by suggesting that the polluted air outside our homes is probably safer than the air inside our homes (paragraph*

12). Although paragraph 12 may be somewhat beside the point, paragraph 11 is extremely important. As we shall see in Chapter 15, listeners often argue mentally with a speaker—asking questions, raising objections, and creating counterarguments. The success of a persuasive speaker often depends upon how well he or she anticipates these internal responses and answers them in the speech.

The second main point, in which the speaker presents her solution, begins with an internal preview in paragraph 13. The first part of the solution calls for listeners to experiment with alternatives to standard household cleaners (paragraphs 14-15). By handing out a fact sheet about these alternatives after the speech, the speaker compensated for the fact that time limitations prevented her from discussing all of them in detail. The second part of the solution calls for listeners to use common sense whenever using household chemicals (paragraph 16). Recognizing that some listeners might not want to experiment with alternative cleaners, the speaker offers a number of sensible steps all people can take to use existing household products safely.

Conclusion:   The conclusion consists of paragraphs 17-18. In addition to summarizing the main points and referring back to the introduction, it uses vivid, clever phrasing to reinforce the central idea. Particularly effective in this regard is the statement, "Careless use of household chemicals is one case in which cleanliness may put you next to godliness before your time." The closing sentence is also highly effective and ends the speech on a strong, dramatic note.

Supporting Materials:  The speaker uses examples in paragraphs 1, 7, 8, and 18. Those in paragraphs 1 and 8 are extended examples. The first is an excellent attention-getter for the introduction. The second, based on the speaker's personal experience, illustrates the potential dangers of oven cleaners. In both cases the speaker follows the example with additional supporting materials to show that the example is not atypical. In paragraph 2 she quotes a Harvard scientist to demonstrate that the story of the woman in Portland, Maine, is "far from hypothetical." In paragraph 8 she cites statistics from the Center for Science in the Public Interest showing that the speaker is not alone in being harmed by oven cleaners.

Paragraph 7 contains two brief examples about the dangers of products such as Drano and Instant Plumber. The source of both examples is Consumer Reports, a highly respected independent magazine. Bringing up the example of the woman in Portland, Maine, again in the conclusion (paragraph 18) ties in with the introduction, reinforces the central idea, and gives the speech a strong sense of unity.

In addition to these specific examples, all of the "cleaning tour" section (paragraphs 5-10) can be seen as an extended hypothetical example. As *we noted earlier, this section is highly effective in dramatizing and personalizing the speaker's discussion of the problem.*

*The speaker uses statistics in paragraphs 5, 7, and 8. Those in paragraph 5 quantify the number of chemicals found in the average home. Those in paragraph 7 show that some 10,000 people in the United States are harmed each year by drain cleaners or toilet cleaners, while those in paragraph 8 indicate that 3,000 people are harmed by oven cleaners. The figures in paragraphs 5 and 8 are from highly credible, clearly identified sources—James Woods, senior scientist at the Honeywell Corporation, and the Center for Science in the Public Interest, a well-regarded independent public interest group. Although the statistic in paragraph 7 about the 10,000 people harmed each year by drain cleaners and toilet cleaners also comes from a strong authority—Consumer Reports magazine—the speaker did not clearly identify the source in her speech.*

*The speaker uses testimony more than any other form of support—in paragraphs 2-3, 7, 9-13, and 16. Not being an expert on the subject herself, she cites a number of credible authorities that lend persuasive weight to her position. Two of those authorities appear in the introduction. The first is Lance Wallace, an environmental scientist at the Harvard School of Public Health (paragraph 2). As we saw earlier, his vivid quotation helps establish the point that the opening example about the woman in Portland, Maine, is not far-fetched. The second quotation in the introduction—stating that "The consumer becomes a test animal in the laboratory of the home" (paragraph 3)—is also brief and dramatic, but it would have been more effective if the speaker had identified the scientist in addition to stating the publication in which his or her statement appeared.*

*Unlike the testimony in the introduction, which is presented as direct quotations, that in paragraphs 7 and 9-12 is paraphrased. The warning from Consumer Reports at the end of paragraph 7, on the dangers of using a plunger to clear drains when drain cleaners have failed, gains added force coming immediately after the two brief examples about the dangers of drain cleaners. The statement about oil of cedarwood from the Center for Science in the Public Interest at the end of the paragraph 9 is especially arresting—as is that about the absorption of creosol through the skin from the Mitre Corporation in paragraph 10.*

*It is possible, of course, to object that no household product contains enough oil of cedarwood or creosol to be highly dangerous. Recognizing that many listeners will raise this objection mentally, the speaker uses additional testimony in paragraph 11 to support her point that some household products can be dangerous even when they are used in strict accordance with the manufacturers' instructions. By citing* Consumer Reports, *the* Household Pollutants Guide, *and* Science News *all together, the speaker gains more persuasive power than if she had mentioned just one source.*

*The testimony from Lance Wallace in paragraph 12 is interesting, but it does not deal directly with household chemicals. Indeed, some listeners thought the speaker could have done without paragraph 12 entirely. The quotation in paragraph 13 from Albert Fritsch of the Center for Science in the Public Interest helps to introduce the speaker's solution by stressing the need for citizens to be alert and informed about the proper use of household chemicals.*

*Finally, the speaker cites the Food and Drug Administration in paragraph 16 on a number of ways consumers can use household chemicals more safely. Coming from the FDA, a highly credible government source, this material also helps to reemphasize the speaker's point about the potential dangers of household chemicals.*

# David—And a Lot of Other Neat People

Kathy Weisensel

---

*1* There is a problem which is shared by millions of people in the United States. It knows no barrier to age, sex, or social class. Yet, it is a problem that for years was hidden in society's darkest closet. Only recently has the closet door begun to open. That problem is mental retardation.

*2* One out of 33 persons is born mentally retarded. It is the most widespread, permanent handicap among children. It is among the least understood handicaps of adults. In Wisconsin alone, there are 120,000 retarded people.

*3* My involvement with mental retardation has been lifelong and deeply personal. For, you see, David, my older brother, is mentally retarded.

*4* As our family adjusted to David's problem, we became aware of a number of misconceptions which cloud the public's vision. Among these misconceptions are that mentally retarded people are mentally ill and therefore dangerous; that mentally retarded people are ineducable; and that mentally retarded people are incapable of leading happy and productive lives. Since these misconceptions are socially harmful and painful to the retarded and their families, it is important that they be corrected.

*5* How do you correct the notion that retarded people are somewhat crazy and therefore not really to be trusted? It may be helpful to start with a definition. According to Dr. E. Milo Pritchett, "Mental retardation is a condition of impaired, incomplete, or inadequate mental development. Mental retardation is NOT mental illness. Mental illness is a breakdown of mental functions which were once normal. Specialized care and treatment may restore the person to normalcy. Retardation is a condition for which there is no cure."

*6* But let's extend that definition with a series of contrasts. Mental retardation is always permanent; mental illness is usually temporary. Mental retardation is subnormal intelligence; mental illness is distorted intelligence. Mental retardation involves deficient cognitive abilities; mental illness involves emotional impairment of cognitive abilities. Mental retardation is manifested early; mental illness may occur anytime in life. The mentally retarded person is behaviorally stable; it is the mentally ill person who is given to erratic behavior. The extremely mentally retarded person is submissive and mute; the extremely mentally ill person may be violent and criminally dangerous.

7    Thus retarded people are retarded, and no more. We need no longer place them in pens with the criminally insane, as was the custom in medieval societies.

8    OK, the skeptic says, so what if they aren't mentally ill—they're still ineducable. Those who favor this misconception have, in the words of Dorly D. Wang, formerly of Woods School in Pennsylvania, "one-dimensional views of the retarded." They fail to "distinguish degrees of retardation" and tend to perceive "all the retarded with one image"—and that image is of the intellectual vegetable, more appropriately planted in a cell or ward than in the school classroom.

9    But retarded people are not all alike. Most psychologists identify three subgroups of mentally retarded people: the educable, the trainable, and the custodial.

10    The educable mentally retarded have IQs ranging from 75 to 50. In the nation's schools, they are placed in a curriculum with a special classroom base, but are encouraged to enter the curricular mainstream whenever it is possible. Most of these students share with normal students instruction in home economics, physical education, shop, and music.

11    The trainable mentally retarded's I.Q. is usually 50 to 30. In the schools, these students are not found in any normal class. Rather, they work exclusively in special classrooms under the direction of teachers who understand their needs. In these classes they learn self-care, and they train for social and economic usefulness. Three percent of the present school population is made up of the educable and trainable mentally retarded.

12    The custodial mentally retarded have IQs below 30. They are usually confined to institutions such as Central Colony, just across Lake Mendota from this university. These people experience little mental development. Few exceed the intellectual acuity of a normal three-year-old.

13    Thus the mentally retarded are not a faceless, hopeless mass. While not all of them may profit from schooling, many will. Careful and loving teachers will eventually be rewarded by what one teacher of the retarded has called "the smile of recognition."

14    But to say that the mentally retarded person is not mentally ill and is not ineducable is not enough. It does not destroy the myth that one must be of average mentality to be socially productive and happy. In a society characterized by speed, change, competition, and progress, it is difficult for us so-called "normals" to

understand that retarded people can live happily and productively in a life pattern alien to our own.

15    Bernard Posner, Deputy Executive Secretary of the President's Committee on Employment of the Handicapped, has captured society's dilemma in coming to grips with the mentally handicapped. He commented:

> Ours are norms in which change is a way of life. In the United States, we change jobs every five years and homes every seven years. We say that to stand still is to regress. Where do the retarded fit in, those without the capacity for constant change?

> Ours are norms of competition. We compete in school, at play, at love, at work. Where do the retarded fit in, those who can go to school, can play, can love, can work, but who cannot always come out on top in competition?

> Ours are norms of discontent. Life becomes a series of stepping-stones leading who knows where? Each of life's situations is not to be enjoyed for itself, but is to be tolerated because it leads elsewhere. Where do the retarded fit in, those who can be happy with a stay-put existence?

16    But retarded people do fit in and do lead useful and rewarding lives. A few years ago, I worked with a girl who is educably mentally retarded. Mary went to my high school and attended two normal classes—home economics and physical education. She had a driving desire to become a waitress. Her determination was evident as I tutored her in addition, subtraction, making change, and figuring sales tax. She is working today in a small restaurant—happy and self-supporting.

17    My brother David is another example. Under Wisconsin law he was entitled to school until age 21, and he spent all those years in a separate special class. There he learned the basic skills of reading, writing, and mathematics. After graduation he was employed by the Madison Opportunity Center, a sheltered workshop for the retarded. He leaves home each morning on a special bus and returns each evening after eight hours of simple assembly-line work. While he is by no means self-supporting and independent, he loves his work, and he is a happy man and a neat person with whom to share a family.

18    As a final example, I give you Jeff, age 14. He is custodially mentally retarded at Central Colony. In the three years that I have worked with him, I have found him to be incredibly happy and content in his "permanent childhood." He enjoys toys, writing letters of the alphabet, and watching "Sesame Street." This last summer he was especially proud to be selected as a jumper in the Special Olympics. To tell you the truth, he was chosen because he was one of the few kids in the ward

who could get both feet off the floor at the same time. But Jeff doesn't know that the competition wasn't keen, and he's proud and happy.

19   While misconceptions are slow to pass away, they must surely die. Our nation's retarded are not mentally ill, totally ineducable, or incapable of happy and productive lives.

20   I know, in a deeply personal way, the pain that these misconceptions inspire. But I also know that the world is changing. I have a deep faith that you and others of our generation will reject the senseless and destructive stereotypes of the past. As Bernard Posner has said:

> The young people of the world seem to be forging a new set of values. It appears to be a value system of recognizing the intrinsic worth of all humans, retarded or not, . . . a value system of acceptance: of accepting life as it is, and people as they are.

21   Thank you for your acceptance.

# David—And a Lot of Other Neat People  *by Kathy Weisensel*

## Commentary

"David—And a Lot of Other Neat People" was presented by Kathy Weisensel, a student at the University of Wisconsin-Madison. The text is taken from Wil A. Linkugel, R. R. Allen, and Richard L. Johannesen (eds.), Contemporary American Speeches, 5th ed. (Dubuque, Iowa: Kendall/Hunt, 1982). It is reprinted here with permission from Kathy Weisensel.

A persuasive speech on a question of fact, "David—And a Lot of Other Neat People" is especially interesting for its sharp, clear organization and its effective use of supporting materials. Below is a synopsis of the speech.

*Specific Purpose:* To persuade my audience that many popular beliefs about mental retardation are in fact misconceptions.

*Central Idea:* Mentally retarded people are not mentally ill, are not ineducable, and are capable of living happy and productive lives.

*Method of Organization:* Topical

*Introduction:* The introduction consists of paragraphs 1-4 and is a model of how to begin a speech. The speaker begins by arousing curiosity about a problem that is shared by millions of people and that "for years was hidden in society's darkest closet." She then reveals that the "problem" is mental retardation. After providing statistics to show how many people are affected by mental retardation, the speaker explains that she is deeply involved in the topic because her older brother, David, is mentally retarded. In addition to enhancing the speaker's credibility, this gives the speech deeper emotional resonance than it would otherwise have. Finally, the speaker previews the body of her speech by noting that she will seek to correct four misconceptions that cloud the public's view of mental retardation.

*Body:* The body of this speech contains three main points, the first of which distinguishes mental retardation from mental illness. It is introduced at the start of paragraph 5 with the question, "How do you correct the notion that retarded people are somewhat crazy and therefore not really to be trusted?" The speaker then uses a quotation from Dr. E. Milo Pritchett to define the differences between mental illness and mental retardation. The quotation makes the speaker's point quite well, but it would have been more effective if the speaker had identified Dr. Pritchett's qualifications as an expert on mental retardation.

*After the quotation from Dr. Pritchett, the speaker extends her point with a series of contrasts between mental retardation and mental illness. She then pulls all of these ideas together and concludes her first main point in paragraph 7 by saying: "Thus retarded people are retarded, and no more. We need no longer place them in pens with the criminally insane, as was the custom in medieval societies."*

*The second main point is introduced in paragraph 8 with the transitional statement: "OK, the skeptic says, so what if they aren't mentally ill—they're still ineducable." The speaker refutes this misconception by showing that all mentally retarded people are not alike. She identifies three subgroups of mentally retarded people—the educable, the trainable, and the custodial—and shows that each has their own unique characteristics. After the speaker's clear explanation of these subgroups, the audience is prepared to accept her statement in paragraph 13 that "the mentally retarded are not a faceless, hopeless mass. While not all of them may profit from schooling, some will."*

*The third main point is introduced at the start of paragraph 14 by a transitional statement: "But to say that the mentally retarded person is not mentally ill and is not ineducable is not enough. It does not destroy the myth that one must be of average mentality to be socially productive and happy." The speaker then develops two subpoints. The first is that society's norms of speed, change, competition, and progress are not applicable to the mentally retarded (paragraphs 14-15). The speaker supports this subpoint with a lengthy quotation from Bernard Posner, whom she identifies as Deputy Executive Secretary of the President's Committee on Employment of the Handicapped. The second subpoint is that retarded people do fit in and do lead useful and rewarding lives (paragraphs 16-18). This subpoint is supported with three poignant examples, one of which deals with the speaker's brother. As in other parts of the speech, the speaker's credibility and sincerity reinforce the impact of her ideas.*

*Conclusion:  The conclusion consists of paragraphs 19-21. After summarizing her main points, the speaker refers again to the personal pain she has felt because of society's misconceptions about mental retardation. She then appeals to her audience to reject "the senseless and destructive stereotypes of the past" and to develop a value system that accepts people as they are. The closing line—"Thank you for your acceptance"— is very effective and ends the speech on a strong note.*

# Ghosts

## Ken Lonnquist

*1*    There are ghosts in this room. We cannot see them, but they are here. They have come to us from a far off place—some billowing up out of the pages of history books, others returning to us after only a short absence. Some are large; some are old; some are very young; and some are very, very small. Some are the ghosts of men and women who more than a century ago trod upon the same ground which we are treading today. Some are spirits which look to us for justice—tiny spirits that look to us for retribution for an act of wrong that was committed against them. And then there are the other ghosts—ourselves, the ghosts which we, ourselves, have become—puppets in a judgment play which is being dusted off and reenacted by history after centuries.

*2*    I first became aware of these ghosts when I announced to you the nature of my discourse for today. Those who were hostile in their reaction to my subject—those who said to me, "Our minds cannot be changed," those who said in effect, "We will not listen"—made me think: "What kind of a people are we? What kind of a people have we become when we will no longer listen to one another?"

*3*    In that moment, I was haunted by visions of a bygone era—a time in which abolitionists were afforded much the same treatment as I had just been. For, you see, they too were involved in a titanic, moral struggle—a grave moral crisis. They were speaking out against a notion that was deeply imbedded in the minds of nineteenth-century men and women—the notion that black men and black women were not human. They were speaking out against slavery—that wicked by-product of prejudice. At times they were ignored by indifferent masses. At times they were tarred and feathered and run out of town. At times they were murdered. Never were they listened to, because the men and the women of the nineteenth century who favored human bondage had decided that their minds could not be changed on the matter. They had decided that they would not listen.

*4*    Now I have come here today, as you all know, to speak for life—human life and human rights. And there is something—something about my subject which seems strangely reminiscent—reminiscent of, and haunted by, the days, the people, and the events of the nineteenth century. It is more than just a parallel between the treatment that was accorded abolitionist speakers and the treatment that is accorded antiabortionist speakers today. It is deeper than that. It rests in the very heart of the issue—in the very heart of each moral struggle.

5    You see, in the 1840s it was argued by proslavery forces that their rights as citizens of the United States were being subverted by abolitionists who were working to eradicate slavery. "The abolitionists," they argued, "are denying us our constitutional right to hold property." They could not see that their rights of property could not supersede the rights of black men and black women to life, liberty, and the pursuit of happiness. They could not see, because they did not regard black men or black women to be of human life. They were blinded by the prejudice of their age.

6    And today a similar logic has been evolved by the proponents of abortion. They argue that their rights of self-determination are being infringed upon by those who would take away the option of terminating a pregnancy. They do not recognize that they are determining the course of not one life, but two. They cannot see because they do not recognize a human life in its earliest stages to be human.

7    Now there are many kinds of life, and what we have to ask ourselves is, "What is life? What is human life? What are the values we attach to human life? What are the rights we grant to those whom we say possess human life?" These are the questions which I believe must be asked when dealing with the matter of abortion. These are the questions over which this whole controversy rages.

8    The concept of life is not so difficult to understand. We look at a stone and we say, "It does not live." We look at a flower and we say, "It lives." We may crush the flower, it dies. A biological process has been halted, and the mysterious thing that we call life has been taken away.

9    As I said before, there are many kinds of life. And each is distinct from all the rest. The kind of life that we possess is human life. We all recognize this to be true. But down through the course of the centuries there have been those who, for reasons of fulfilling their own ends, have attempted to qualify the definition of human life. For centuries slaveholders claimed that blacks were not human. For them, color was the key element in defining the humanity of an individual. Today there are many who claim that a human being in its earliest states is not a human being—and that the life it possesses as a biologically functioning entity is not a human life. In their mentality, age becomes the key element in determining the humanity of an individual.

10    Once there was a color line. Today there is an age line. But an age-line definition of humanity is no more just—is just as fallacious, and just as evil, as was the color line which existed in the past.

*11* Even in the textbook *The Essentials of Human Embryology*, it says, "The fertilized egg is the beginning of a new individual." It cannot be denied. The fertilized egg is, itself, a human being in its earliest stages. It is not a zebra; it is not a monkey. It is human. Whether or not it is a fully developed human is not the issue. The issue is humanity. And a fertilized egg is human life.

*12* Look around you at the other members of this class. Just look for a moment and ask yourselves, "Was there ever a time in the existence of any of us here in which we were nonhuman?" I do not believe so.

*13* Now we have laws. We do not have any laws which govern the lives of plants. We have but one law which governs the life of an animal. That animal is man. The law has been written and rewritten down through the course of the centuries—in stone, on leather, on parchment, on paper, in languages that have been lost and long forgotten. But the law has remained the same. No man, it states, may take the life of another man. Perhaps you would recognize it this way: "We hold these truths to be self-evident—that all men are created equal and are endowed by their Creator with certain unalienable rights—that among these rights are life." Or this way, quite simply stated, in another book: "Thou shalt not kill."

*14* Whatever their form, the laws are there. And there were no qualifications written into these laws on the basis of race, on the basis of color, on the basis of creed, on the basis of sex—nor were there any qualifications written into these laws on the basis of age. What the whole matter boils down to is this: A human life has been determined by us, for centuries, millennia, to be sacred, and we have determined that it cannot be taken away. And a fertilized egg is human life.

*15* Now for any violations of these laws to occur, especially on a grand scale as is happening today, a mentality has to have been developed through which those who are going to commit a wrong can justify their actions and can appease the guilt that they might feel—the guilt that they might feel if they had to admit that they were killing a living human entity. And this is what we have done. This is what we are doing. We have learned to call a flower a stone. Why? And how?

*16* You see, we are blinded. Just as Americans of another generation were blinded by prejudice, we are blinded by violence. We live in a violent society, in which the killing of a young human being means no more to us than the holding in bondage of black men and black women meant to another generation of Americans. Said E. Z. Freidenburg on this matter, "Not only do most people accept violence if it is perpetrated by legitimate authority—they also regard violence against certain kinds of people as inherently legitimate, no matter who commits it." An abolitionist once was speaking about this condition, and he said, "You might call it paralysis of the nerves about the heart, in a people constantly given over to selfish aims." We have become selfish. And in our selfishness, have become heartless.

*17*   We say that it is our right to control our bodies, and this is true. But there is a distinction that needs to be made, and that distinction is this: Preventing a pregnancy is controlling a body—controlling your body. But preventing the continuance of a human life that is not your own is murder. If you attempt to control the body of another in that fashion, you become as a slave master was—controlling the lives and the bodies of his slaves, chopping off their feet when they ran away, or murdering them if it pleased him. This was not his right; it is not our right.

*18*   Abortion is often argued for in terms of its beneficiality. It is better, some say, that these young human beings do not come into the world. It is better for them; it is better for the parents; it is better for society at large. And they may be right. It may be more beneficial.

*19*   But what we are arguing is not beneficiality. We are not arguing pragmatism. We are not arguing convenience. We are arguing right and wrong. It was more convenient for slaveholders to maintain a system of slavery, but it was wrong. A matter of principle cannot be compromised for a matter of convenience. It cannot be done.

*20*   Now I'd like to say something more about the whole matter. I'd like to say something particularly to the women in the room, who I think should understand more clearly what I have to say now than the men.

*21*   For thousands of years women have been deprived of their rights. They have been second-class citizens and have been, in the eyes of many, something less than human themselves. For thousands of years they have been controlled, physically and mentally, by men. They have been controlled through physical power and physical coercion. But in this age of enlightenment—in this age of feminism—it has rightly been determined that might does not make right. The fact that males might be able to physically dominate females did not make their doing so just, and it did not mean that females were not deserving of protection under the law so that they might pursue the course of their choice.

*22*   But today, after tens of thousands of years, the tables are turning. Today men and women (who more than any man should understand the shamefulness and the unjustness and the inhumanity involved in control through physical power) have been determining not the roles that another segment of humanity will have in life, but whether or not this segment of humanity will have life at all. Under the pretext of controlling their own bodies, they are setting out on a course of controlling the bodies of others. After tens of thousands of years, they are transferring the shackles in which they themselves have languished, and against which they have struggled, onto a new segment of humanity—only with a difference. The shackles have been transformed into a guillotine.

23    Why? It has happened because no one will do anything about it. No one will stop it. We are all like ghosts in the fire. We are all involved. Although we do not hold the knife in our hand, neither do we stay the hand that does hold the knife.

24    History is repeating itself. Abraham Lincoln once said that the eyes of history were upon us and that we would be remembered in spite of ourselves. He also said, "We are engaged in a cause, a struggle, not just for today, but for all the ensuing generations."

25    And so are we. Ghosts are crowding around us, and looking, and watching what we do. Frederick Douglass once said, in speaking of black bondage, "I hear the mournful wail of millions." Today there are the ghosts of the past, the ghosts of the present, and the ghosts of all the ensuing generations watching us, and watching the struggle that is being repeated—the struggle of human life. I, too, hear the mournful wail of millions.

## Ghosts   *by Ken Lonnquist*

## Commentary

*"Ghosts" is particularly interesting because it provides an example of a classroom speech delivered to an audience made up almost entirely of people opposed to the speaker's point of view. It is reprinted here with permission from Wil A. Linkugel, R. R. Allen, and Richard L. Johannesen (eds.), Contemporary American Speeches, 4th ed. (Dubuque, Iowa: Kendall/Hunt, 1978). Here is a synopsis.*

*Specific Purpose: To persuade the audience that abortion is morally wrong.*

*Central Idea: Abortion is morally wrong because it is the taking of a human life.*

*Method of Organization: Topical*

*Introduction: The introduction is long (paragraphs 1-7), complex, and in some ways quite artful. Its major function, in addition to the usual functions of an introduction, is to get the audience to listen to the speaker even though they disagree with him. The opening paragraph does an excellent job of gaining attention with its suspenseful images of "ghosts in this room." In paragraphs 2-4 the speaker chastises listeners who say their minds "cannot be changed" and tries to build his credibility by identifying his position with that of nineteenth-century abolitionists. Paragraphs 5-6 introduce the central idea of the speech by claiming that the stand of people who favor legalized abortion today is analogous to that of pro-slavery forces in the 1840s. Paragraph 7 completes the introduction by previewing some of the major questions to be pursued in the body.*

*When delivered in class, this introduction worked very effectively. Many students who read it, however, find it troublesome. The initial paragraph, they say, is confusing because it suggests that the speech is actually about ghosts or some other paranatural phenomenon. Moreover, they feel that the comparisons among proabortionists, antiabortionists, and slave-owners are dragged out much longer than necessary. Finally, they claim that the topic of the speech is never clearly announced in the introduction. When this speech is discussed in class, a keen debate usually develops among students over the merits of the introduction.*

*Body: The body of the speech can be divided into five main sections. The first section starts in paragraph 8 and develops the speaker's view that "a fertilized egg is human life"—just like other forms of human life. The* second section begins in paragraph 13 and claims that it is wrong to take any form of human life, regardless of its color, creed, age, or sex. The third section begins in paragraph 15 and argues that the violence of our time has blinded many people from seeing the wrongness of abortion. The fourth section begins in paragraph 17 and deals with the counterarguments that women have a right to control their own bodies and that abortion is socially beneficial. The fifth section begins in paragraph 20 and is addressed specifically to the women in the audience.

*Conclusion:* The conclusion consists of paragraphs 23-25. The speaker seeks to reinvigorate feelings of guilt and personal responsibility for abortion. He turns again to the ghost imagery used in the introduction, and he invokes once more the analogy between abortion and slavery. The final paragraph is particularly effective in bringing the speech full circle and reinforcing its emotional appeal.

*Reasoning:* This speech is dominated by reasoning from analogy. The speaker develops a series of analogies in which the undeveloped fetus is compared with black slaves before the Civil War, proabortionists with slave-owners, and antiabortionists with abolitionists. Just as the slaves had a right to freedom, the speaker claims, so the fetus has a right to life. Just as slave-owners were wrong in claiming that their rights of property superseded the rights of black men and women to freedom, so proabortionists are wrong in claiming that the right of women to control their own bodies supersedes the right of the fetus to life. And just as abolitionists were right in fighting to free the slaves, so antiabortionists are right in fighting to save the lives of unborn children. These analogies run throughout the speech and can be found, explicitly or implicitly, in paragraphs 1-6, 9-10, 16-17, 19, and 24-25.

There is another major analogy in paragraphs 21-22. Here the speaker claims that the powerless state of women historically is similar to the powerless state of the undeveloped fetus today. Just as it was wrong for men to use their power to deprive women of their rights, so it is wrong for women to use their power to deprive "another segment of humanity" of its right to life.

These analogies focus attention on the questions of value involved in the abortion controversy. Yet in many ways the persuasiveness of this speech to a hostile audience may depend more on a question of fact than on a question of value. In essence, the speech can be seen as advancing an argument from principle:

*General Principle:* The killing of human beings is wrong.

*Minor Premise:* The fertilized egg is a human being.

*Conclusion:   Therefore, the killing of fertilized eggs is wrong.*

*The first premise, a question of value, is supported in paragraphs 13-14. Most listeners, regardless of their views on abortion, are likely to accept this premise. The second premise, essentially a question of fact, is supported in paragraphs 11-12. This is the crucial premise for listeners who favor abortion. Yet the speaker backs it up with only one piece of evidence. He says, "Even in the textbook, which is called* The Essentials of Human Life, *it says 'the fertilized egg is the beginning of a new individual'" (paragraph 11). But this quotation does not explicitly support the speaker's view. Moreover, even if it did, one brief quotation from a textbook whose author is not identified would probably not be strong enough evidence to persuade a listener who opposes the speaker's position. Given the opposition of his listeners, the speaker should have done a more thorough job of supporting his second premise.*

———————————

# The Mahatma and Satyagraha

Walter F. Stromer

*1*    When in a brash moment last October I volunteered to do a speech on Gandhi, I had no idea that with a week's postponement this speech would be given on Republic Day in India. This day in 1950 was the birth of the constitution of modern India. It is appropriate that we talk about Gandhi since he was instrumental in helping India attain independence and in shaping her constitution.

*2*    First let me define the terms in the title. "Mahatma" means "great soul," and was a title bestowed on Gandhi by the poet Tagore. Gandhi did not really like the term. He said if you talk about a great soul, then you assume there are also little souls, and he did not think there could be little souls.

*3*    "Satyagraha" comes from two Sanskrit words. "Graha" means "power" or "force." "Sat" means "truth," "essence," "being," "faithfulness," "honesty," "goodness," "keeping vows," plus many more ideas. Add to this the fact that, for Gandhi, truth was tentative and relative, and you will understand why the term is not easy to define precisely. It is translated as "clinging to truth," or "soul force," or "truth force." We think of it as "nonviolent resistance." Gandhi would want us to be clear that the resistance was important because he had no intention of accepting passively whatever injustice came his way.

*4*    To make clear that nonviolent resistance was a difficult and complicated concept, let me give you just some of the rules Gandhi required of the true Satyagrahi: You must not harbor hatred in your heart toward your opponent. You must not insult, embarrass, take advantage of, or coerce your opponent (though it must be said that one person's friendly persuasion may be another's coercion). You must be religious—no atheist can be a true Satyagrahi. Any actions taken must seem just to all parties involved. Finally, you must obey the Satyagrahi leader.

*5*    This is only a partial list of requirements, and it will help explain why Gandhi was often disappointed because people did not follow all the rules. In more thoughtful moments he recognized that only a few people could become true Satyagrahis.

*6*    Having defined those two terms, I'd like to talk about Gandhi as a person, about his leadership, and then about his legacy.

7    He is sometimes referred to as frail. By comparison with a 290-point linebacker for Nebraska's Big Red, he does seem frail. Yet when he was 30, as a volunteer in the ambulance corps in the Boer War, he sometimes had to help carry a man on a stretcher for as many as 25 miles in one day. If you have ever helped carry a man on a stretcher for even one mile, you know that such work requires considerable endurance.

8    When Gandhi was 60, he led 79 followers on the Salt March, to protest the government's tax on salt. They walked an average of 12 miles a day. After each day's march, Gandhi would spin cotton for an hour, write in his diary, hold a prayer meeting, and talk to the people who gathered to see him. Yet when he walked, some people had to run to keep up with him.

9    "Meek" is also a term sometimes applied to Gandhi. If that connotes a kind of spineless, milk-toast character, that is inaccurate. Gandhi was very determined, even stubborn. A friend who has seen the movie *Gandhi* tells me he got the impression from it that Gandhi was completely unbending in character. That, too, is not totally accurate. Gandhi often made compromises and frequently annoyed his followers by the compromises he made.

10   Evidence of his determined nature can be demonstrated from an incident in London when he was 19 and studying law. A friend who was trying to get him to give up being a vegetarian took him to an elegant restaurant one evening and ordered a meal for the two of them. When the soup came, Gandhi called the waiter back to make sure there was no meat in the soup. The friend was so outraged he told Gandhi to leave and meet him outside in an hour. Gandhi left.

11   Gandhi was deeply religious, though not in any strict, narrow, orthodox sense. He drew his religious views from the Sanskrit poem Bhagavad-Gita, from the Sermon on the Mount in the Bible, and from the Koran. For many years, his favorite hymn at prayer time was "Lead Kindly Light" by John Cardinal Newman. The line in that hymn which most typified Gandhi's thinking was, "I do not ask to see the distant scene, one step enough for me." Aside from the independence of India, Gandhi did not pursue any grand design or grandiose schemes. He tended to take life one day at a time, as the fates brought it to him.

12   A degree of anti-intellectualism was another of Gandhi's traits. He said, "Literary education does not add one inch to a man's character." When his oldest son wanted to become a lawyer, Gandhi decided that practical education was more important and would not help him with legal training. His son became bitter, became a law breaker, then a Moslem, then a heavy drinker, and ultimately gave less than a good account of himself.

*13*   Gandhi's humor was of the gentle, self-deprecating sort. A woman came to him one day and said, "Yesterday, I saw the ugliest man in the world." Gandhi frowned. She corrected herself. "I mean, the second ugliest." Gandhi smiled.

*14*   When asked if he was not embarrassed to visit the king of England dressed in a loin cloth, he replied, "Oh, no, the king had on quite enough for both of us."

*15*   Finally, Gandhi was more self-aware, more self-consistent, more honest than most men. Once he had decided that the simple life was desirable, he began to practice it by starching his own shirt collars, though he overdid it and the excess starch flaked off. He cut his own hair with a scissors and made a mess of the back. When the lawyers at court laughed, he said there were two good things about it—they got a good laugh and he saved money.

*16*   From John Ruskin's book *Unto This Last*, Gandhi got the idea that all work was equal, and equally dignified. It followed then that it was no disgrace for him to pick up a broom and help clean the latrines, even though that work was assigned to the untouchables.

*17*   He declared the untouchables, the outcasts, to be "harijans," or "children of God." When a father and mother and daughter asked for permission to live at the ashram (Gandhi's commune) at Ahmedabad, he readily agreed, even though he knew that accepting untouchables might cut off donations from others, which it did. At the last minute, the ashram was saved from bankruptcy when a man drove up in a car and gave Gandhi 15,000 rupees.

*18*   Gandhi said he tried to apply the eternal principles to daily life, and he seems to have done well at it.

*19*   So much for Gandhi the person. What about his leadership?

*20*   Most people would probably agree that he was a charismatic leader. What did he do to enhance his charisma? He won battles—not with tanks and guns but with bodies and with the force of truth. He stood up to the British Empire and made it back down. That impressed millions.

*21*   While living in South Africa before World War I, he showed courage by buying a first-class train ticket to Pretoria, even though he had been put off the first-class train on his first trip. The colored people were not allowed in first-class compartments.

*22*   His fasts—17 major ones—must have taken courage, as did his willingness to go to jail for breaking the law.

23   Charismatic leaders should know the value of symbols, and Gandhi did. In South Africa, he gathered 2,000 or 3,000 Indians in front of the mosque in Johannesburg and had them burn their registration cards to protest the Indian Registration Act. In India, he conducted a ceremonial burning of imported British cloth to show that India could get along without imported luxuries.

24   The spinning wheel became a symbol of village renewal and independence. With it the natives could spin their own thread and then weave their own cloth. Some people saw the spinning wheel as a symbol for regression, a nostalgic yearning for the past. But it was important enough in the development of the nation that it has won a place in the flag of India.

25   Gandhi's most famous and successful symbol was the loin cloth, which he adopted as his form of everyday dress in 1921, six years after he came back to India from Africa. It was the garment of the poorest peasant and it clearly identified Gandhi with the poor. It also emphasized his theme of simple living. Finally, it advertised khadi, the cloth made from native cotton.

26   Not only did Gandhi use symbols which identified him with the masses, but he had the capacity to empathize with them. Often it seemed that his inner voice was the voice of the masses of India. Ironically, as sometimes happens, this great man who was attuned to the voices of the family of man was not well attuned to the voices of his own family. He has been described as a difficult husband, a negligent father, and a moral tyrant over his followers. To the millions of the poor, though, he was their voice, their "bapu," or father.

27   He did have great difficulty understanding those who were very different in point of view or philosophy. He thought Hitler was a good, decent man who could be appealed to with love. He greatly underestimated the implacable nature of Jinnah, the Moslem leader. He could not have imagined the mind of a Tamerlane, the fourteenth-century Mongol invader who killed 100,000 Hindu prisoners in one day.

28   The successful leader must accept the adulation of his followers, and Gandhi did. After he became famous, great crowds would gather at every train station to see him as he rode by. He insisted on keeping the light on in his train compartment at night so these thousands could get a glimpse of him. He understood that they believed this would give them darshan, or blessing, just to see him; he fulfilled their expectations and added to his own charisma.

29   Aside from charismatic qualities, he also possessed some of the more mundane requirements of leadership. He was very well organized in his personal life. He always wore a cheap pocket watch pinned to his loin cloth and was punctual about appointments and time schedules. His day was so well organized that he could

dictate 53 letters, write in his diary, talk to the people, attend prayer meetings, and tend to other details at his ashram.

*30*　He was meticulous in keeping track of funds he collected for the party, and he would not operate the political party on borrowed money.

*31*　Not only was he well organized, but he thrived on organizing others. Within a few weeks of arriving at Pretoria, he called a meeting of Indians to discuss their grievances. Shortly thereafter, he organized them and collected 10,000 signatures on a petition protesting the treatment of Indians by the government.

*32*　In 1910, he organized Tolstoy Farm, about 1,000 acres, near Johannesburg. It was a kind of commune for followers of his movement. It was named for Tolstoy because Gandhi had been inspired by Tolstoy's writings on peace and nonviolence. It was said that Gandhi was in his element at Tolstoy Farm because there he was the prime minister, the chief magistrate, the main teacher, chief sanitary inspector, chief baker, and chief marmalade maker.

*33*　When he went back to India, he established his ashram at Ahmedabad on the banks of the Saburmati River near Bombay. He organized "hartals," or days of work stoppage, and Satyagraha movements for various purposes.

*34*　What is there to show for this leadership? What is the legacy of Gandhi?

*35*　The *New York Times*, October 2, 1969, the 100th anniversary of Gandhi's birth, said India finds him "inspiring but irrelevant." The *Times* pointed out that the birthday of this apostle of nonviolence was celebrated with a huge military parade and a proposal that his statue be placed just in front of the war memorial in Delhi. And only a few years later, India moved from the age of the spinning wheel to the age of the exploding atom. Many of Gandhi's ideas were swept aside as India rushed into the modern nuclear age.

*36*　His greatest contribution was to inspire the people of India to believe they could gain their freedom through nonviolent methods and to believe in their worth as a nation. In 1938 Tagore, the poet, wrote to the *Manchester Guardian*, "Now we can look down on Europe." Gandhi would probably have put it more modestly and said, "Now we can look at them as equals."

*37*　Gandhi inspired many individuals who carried on his ideas in various ways. Venoba Bhave, who was written up in *Time* magazine in 1952, walked the length and breadth of India asking the wealthy landowners to give up some land for the landless poor. In 14 years, he was given almost four million acres. That is not significant in changing the pattern of land ownership, but it is a significant tribute to the inspiration of Gandhi.

*38*   Did Gandhi leave only inspiration? No, there were also tangible gains. As a result of the Salt March in 1930, the salt tax was repealed on this day in 1931. The Indian constitution of 1950 and the General Act of 1955 reflected Gandhi's concern for the equality of all, regardless of caste. The intercaste marriage law legalized marriage across caste lines, but of course custom was much slower to change than was the law. Gandhi, who was married at age 13, worked strenuously for a reform in this area, and finally the minimum age for girls to marry was raised to 14. While Gandhi did not always treat his wife, Kasturbai, with utmost consideration, he did work for greater respect for women and brought many into work for the Congress party. He also contributed to the vote for women and to their right to inherit property.

*39*   The Textile Labor Association of Ahmedabad, which he organized, still exists and provides better than average working conditions for its members.

*40*   Gandhi's influence has spread beyond India. In this country, the best known example is the life and work of Martin Luther King, Jr. E.F. Schumacher, author of *Small Is Beautiful*, drew some of his inspiration from Gandhi. Jonathan Schell mentions Gandhi frequently in his book *Fate of the Earth*, as he discusses our need to find nonviolent solutions to political problems.

*41*   I think Gandhi would be most pleased to know that in Sri Lanka today there is a program of village renewal which follows his general idea of village self-sufficiency. Almost 3,000 villages are using a small amount of money from the World Bank, adding to it their own labor and decision making to create progress in self-improvement. This program is described very favorably in the 1980 annual report of the World Bank.

*42*   So Gandhi has left a legacy of practical accomplishments as well as a legacy of inspiration to people around the world.

*43*   In conclusion, let me quote Prime Minister Nehru, who described his own relationship to Gandhi as that of Alcibiades, the ancient Greek leader, to the philosopher Socrates. Alcibiades said of Socrates: "He is the only man who can make me feel ashamed. I know I ought to do what he tells me, but when I'm out of his presence, I don't care what I do. And yet, I have been bitten by something more poisonous than a snake. I have been bitten in the heart and the mind."

*44*   Having spent much more time than I had expected on Gandhi, I can agree with Nehru that one can indeed be bitten in the heart and the mind by the Mahatma.

# The Mahatma and Satyagraha *by Walter F. Stromer*

## Commentary

*"The Mahatma and Satyagraha" was delivered by Walter F. Stromer, Chairman of the Department of Theatre and Speech at Cornell College, Mount Vernon, Iowa, on January 26, 1983. It is an outstanding informative speech—especially in its clear organization and use of interesting supporting materials.*

*Professor Stromer has spent several years teaching about Mohandas Gandhi in his classes on leadership. This speech was presented to an audience of some 150 students and faculty as part of a weekly convocation series at Cornell College. It lasted about 30 minutes and was followed by a brief question-and-answer period.*

*In his career at Cornell College, Professor Stromer has taught public speaking to over 3,000 students. When asked the most important piece of advice he would give beginning speakers, he replies, "Take advantage of every opportunity you have to give speeches. You will not always succeed, but you will develop your skills and your confidence." He also urges aspiring speakers to read widely, and not just magazines like* Time *and* Newsweek. *"Read history, poetry, literature, speeches," he says, "anything that will stir your imagination and open your mind to ideas, for ideas are the soul of any speech."*

*The text of this speech is reprinted with permission from* Vital Speeches of the Day, *49 (March 1, 1983). It has been edited slightly to clarify references that were known to Professor Stromer's audience but that might be unfamiliar to readers. Here is a brief synopsis of the speech.*

*Specific Purpose:  To inform my audience about Gandhi as a person, about his leadership, and about his legacy.*

*Central Idea:  Gandhi was a complex man and a charismatic leader who left India and the world a legacy of inspiration and practical achievement.*

*Method of Organization:  Topical*

*Introduction:  The introduction, which runs through paragraph 6, does an excellent job of revealing the topic, defining terms, and previewing the body of the speech. It does not include an explicit credibility statement; but because Professor Stromer was already well known to his listeners* and was introduced by another speaker, he did not need to remind the audience of his qualifications.

Body:   The body contains three main points. The first deals with Gandhi as a person (paragraphs 7-18), the second with Gandhi as a leader (paragraphs 19-33), and the third with Gandhi's legacy (paragraphs 34-42). Each point is explained in concrete, nontechnical language and is developed with abundant examples that help bring Gandhi to life and get listeners involved in the speech. The speaker also uses a wealth of transitions and other connectives to help listeners keep track of his ideas. (See, for example, paragraphs 6, 19, 29, 31, 34 38, and 42.) All in all, this speech is a model of clear, concise organization.

Conclusion:   In keeping with his use of signposts throughout the speech, Professor Stromer signals that he is coming to the end of his talk by saying, "In conclusion . . ." The conclusion, which consists of paragraphs 43-44, does not contain a formal summary; but it probably does not need one given the clear organization of the speech and the internal summary in paragraph 42. The final paragraph is somewhat unusual, but effective. Although it ends the speech by talking explicitly about Professor Stromer's reaction to Gandhi, it also suggests implicitly that the audience, too, should now be "bitten in the heart and the mind by the Mahatma."

———————————————————

# My Grandfather

Kim Lacina

1    Every day people are born and people die. Human beings come into this world and leave it—most without their names being immortalized in any history books. Millions of people have lived and worked and loved and died without making any great claims to fame or fortune.

2    But they aren't forgotten—not by their friends, not by their families. And some of these people, some very special people, are not forgotten even by those who hardly knew them. My grandfather was one of these very special people.

3    What made him so special? Why is he remembered not only by friends and family but even by casual acquaintances? Very simply, because he was the essence of love. More than that, he was the essence of what I think of as "active" love. Just as his heart was not empty, his words were not empty.

4    He didn't just speak of compassion. During the Great Depression he took homeless people off the street into his home when they needed a place to sleep. He gave them food when they needed something to eat. And though he wasn't a rich man by any means, he gave them money when they had none. Those people off the street will remember the man who had enough love in his heart to share with them all that he had.

5    He didn't just speak of tolerance. During the 1960s, when his peers were condemning those "long-haired hippies," I can remember riding in the car with my grandfather, picking up dozens and dozens of those "long-haired hippies" who were hitchhiking, and going miles out of our way to give them a ride somewhere. Those men and women will remember the man who had enough love in his heart to bridge the gap between his world and theirs and to practice the spirit of brotherhood.

6    And he didn't just speak of courage. He proved his courage time and time again. He proved it to a little girl who was trapped in the basement of a burning building. He pulled her out of the flames and gave her back her life. And that little girl, now a grown woman, will remember the man who had enough love in his heart to risk his life for a person he didn't even know.

7     He also proved his courage, in a more personal way, to his family. In 1966 he was told he had leukemia and only a year to live. He immediately started chemotherapy treatment, and I don't know which is worse—the effects of the disease or the effects of those treatments. In the ensuing year we saw his hair fall out, we saw his skin turn a pasty shade of gray, and we saw him lose so much weight that he seemed to shrivel up into half the size he had been. We didn't want to see him go out that way.

8     And we didn't. He fought that disease with all his strength and all his courage. And despite the pain he endured, he never complained. I think about him when I catch myself complaining about my "tons of homework" or a "terrible headache," and suddenly that homework or that headache doesn't seem so terrible after all.

9     He lived through that first year, and he lived through eight more. And that disease never stopped him from working, and it never stopped him from caring. All through those years of suffering, he continued to show compassion and tolerance and courage.

10    He died in 1975. And though he left this world without ever making the pages of a history book, he still left the world a great deal. He left to the people who knew him a spirit to exemplify life—a spirit of unconditional, selfless, and truly inspiring love.

# My Grandfather  *by Kim Lacina*

## Commentary

*"My Grandfather" is a commemorative speech. Reprinted here with permission from Kim Lacina, it was presented in a public speaking class at the University of Wisconsin-Madison.*

*This speech illustrates how a commemorative speech should focus on the essence of its subject. Rather than presenting a biography that simply recounts the facts of her grandfather's life, the speaker deals with what she believes to be his most praiseworthy qualities. The speech also shows how students can use clear, simple language to convey meaning and to arouse emotion. Here is a synopsis of the speech:*

*Introduction:  The introduction consists of paragraphs 1-3. Because many previous speakers had dealt with famous people, paragraphs 1-2 were especially effective in capturing the attention of the audience. At the end of paragraph 2 the speaker announces the exact topic of the speech, and in paragraph 3 she presents the central idea—that her grandfather was the essence of "active love." The last sentence of paragraph 3 helps to clarify what the speaker means by "active love" and provides a smooth bridge to the body of the speech.*

*Body:  The body of the speech begins in paragraph 4 and runs through the next-to-last paragraph. Three main points are developed: "He didn't just speak of compassion" (paragraph 4); "He didn't just speak of tolerance" (paragraph 5); "He didn't just speak of courage" (paragraphs 6-9). The parallel wording of each main point reinforces the speaker's ideas and gives coherence to the body. So, too, does the repetition and parallelism in the last sentences of paragraphs 4-6. Throughout, the speaker gives her ideas life with specific examples that illustrate her grandfather's "active love." The language of the speech is clear, familiar, and concrete. Most of the words consist of one or two syllables, and there are few wasted words. The speech moves crisply from idea to idea. When delivered in class, it also picked up considerable emotional power as it proceeded.*

*Conclusion:  The conclusion consists of the last paragraph of the speech. By stating that her grandfather "left this world without ever making the pages of a history book," the speaker relates back to her introduction. This gives the speech a sense of unity and signals that the speaker is about to conclude. The final sentence ties the entire speech together by rephrasing the central idea clearly and vividly.*

# Hail to the Heroes

James Davis

*1*     There are many great sporting events in the world and there are many great athletes, but no sporting event nor athlete better exemplifies the definition of courage, determination, and stamina than the Tour de France bicycle race and its magnificent racers.

*2*     Over a 2,400-mile course through the French countryside they race. Across endless flatlands and over demoralizing mountains they endure—nay, they conquer. To win the race outright is no more than a pipe dream for all but a select few. The real victory is to finish the race. It becomes not a competition against the other racers, but a competition against one's self. The capacity to transcend relentless pain is an earmark of any great athlete, but the racers of the Tour de France deserve special credit.

*3*     Courage—the quality of being brave. They show me this. Prim and trim, dressed in racing tights that reflect a kaleidoscope of colors, they gather at the starting line. But the flash and glimmer of the starting line is fleeting. At the sound of the gun, the battle begins, and as in all battles, there will be casualties. I remember one racer who suffered a broken nose and still continued. I've heard of many a racer who had dinner-plate sized patches of flesh torn away by sixty-mile-per-hour crashes and still continued. I recall another racer who suffered a broken arm and had a team doctor set it on the spot so he could continue. For courage like that, I say hail to the heroes.

*4*     Determination—a firm intention. They show me this. Only by failing to finish the race, say the bikers, is one truly defeated. So with this in mind, they grit their teeth and pedal on. Through blinding downpours, they wipe their glasses dry and pedal on. Suffering from freezing cold on mountain tops and sweltering heat in valleys, they pedal on. Enduring the voice within that cries for rest and relief, they pedal on. Suffering from agonizing backaches and a never-ending barrage of leg cramps, they pedal on. For determination like that, I say hail to the heroes.

*5*     Stamina—staunch resistance to fatigue. They show me this. For twenty-two days they race. Each day brings a new level of exhaustion that must be endured and overcome. When watching the bikers go by, one can almost read their facial expressions: "I want to stop, but I can't. Push, push, push." "My chest is exploding,

I can hardly breathe, but I can't stop. Push, push, push." "One more climb. I can't make it. Yes, I can. Push, push, push." For this special brand of stamina, I say hail to the heroes.

6    In the morning light I often climb aboard my own bike. I push myself up hills and race down the other side. But not like they do. I pace myself on flatlands and straightaways. But not like they do. I have courage, determination, and stamina. But not like they do. So during the Tour de France, I climb off my bike and become one in a throng and watch them as they pedal by and silently say to myself, hail to the heroes.

## Hail to the Heroes   *by James Davis*

## Commentary

"Hail to the Heroes" is a splendid commemorative speech. Rather than reciting a history of the Tour de France, the speaker focuses on what he regards as the most praiseworthy aspects of the racers who participate in it. The speech also illustrates how students can use the resources of language discussed in Chapter 11 to express their ideas vividly, even eloquently. Here is a synopsis of the speech.

*Introduction:*  The introduction consists of paragraphs 1 and 2. In paragraph 1 the speaker announces his central idea—that "no sporting event nor athlete better exemplifies the definition of courage, determination, and stamina than the Tour de France bicycle race and its magnificent racers." In paragraph 2 he gives background information on the Tour de France for listeners who may not be familiar with it. The last sentence of paragraph 2 focuses attention back on the racers and provides a smooth lead-in to the body of the speech.

*Body:*  The body of the speech consists of paragraphs 3-5, in which the speaker develops three main points. The first deals with the courage of the Tour de France racers (paragraph 3), the second with their determination (paragraph 4), and the third with their stamina (paragraph 5). The parallel wording at the start of each main point clarifies the structure of the speech and reinforces the speaker's ideas. So, too, does the parallel structure and the repetition of "hail to the heroes" at the end of each main point.

Throughout the body of the speech, the speaker brings his ideas to life with a variety of stylistic devices. In paragraph 3 he uses vivid, colorful language in combination with a series of brief examples to illustrate the courage of bikers who race on despite their injuries. In paragraph 4 he employs sharp imagery that captures the torturous physical conditions the bikers must endure. He also repeats "they pedal on" at the end of five successive sentences to reinforce the racers' determination in the face of those conditions. In paragraph 5 the speaker uses imaginary dialogue to give voice to the bikers' internal feelings as they endure fatigue and exhaustion. The impact of the dialogue is strengthened by its parallel structure and by the restatement of "Push, push, push" at the end of each sentence.

*Conclusion:*  The conclusion consists of the final paragraph. By bringing himself into the speech at this point, the speaker not only reinforces the praiseworthy traits of the racers, but relates those traits to ordinary bikers such as himself. Once again he uses repetition and parallel structure to reinforce his ideas and to give them artistic unity. The final sentence provides a perfect ending for the speech—especially the repetition of "hail to the heroes" as the closing words.

# - NOTES -

# - NOTES -

# - NOTES -

- NOTES -